TREATY-MAKING POWER

AUSTRALIA

The Law Book Co. of Australasia Pty. Ltd.
Sydney : Melbourne : Brisbane

GREAT BRITAIN

Stevens & Sons Ltd.
London

INDIA

N. M. Tripathi Private Ltd.
Bombay

NEW ZEALAND

Sweet and Maxwell (N. Z.) Ltd.
Wellington

PAKISTAN

Pakistan Law House
Karachi

U.S.A. AND CANADA

Frederick A. Praeger, Inc.,
New York

TREATY-MAKING POWER

by

HANS BLIX, Ph.D., LL.D.

LONDON · STEVENS & SONS LIMITED

NEW YORK · FREDERICK A. PRAEGER, *Publishers*

1960

Published by
Stevens & Sons Limited
of 11 New Fetter Lane in
the City of London and
Frederick A. Praeger, Inc.
Publishers, 64 University
Place, New York, 3, New York

Printed in Sweden
by Almqvist & Wiksells
Boktryckeri Aktiebolag
Uppsala

Library of Congress catalog card number
60–7514

Almqvist & Wiksells
BOKTRYCKERI AKTIEBOLAG
UPPSALA 1959

TABLE OF CONTENTS

PART TWO

COMPETENCE TO CONCLUDE TREATIES ON BEHALF OF STATES

Section A

RULES APPLICABLE WHERE THE MUNICIPAL REGULATION OF THE MATTER IS LIKELY TO BE INEXISTENT OR INOPERATIVE

Section B

THE RULE WHERE THE TREATY-MAKING COMPETENCE IS
REGULATED BY MUNICIPAL LAW

PREFACE

It is, no doubt, a truism that, in the relations of states, treaties are matters of importance and frequent occurrence. The law of treaties, therefore, rightly occupies a central position in international law. Within this branch of the law, three broad categories of rules may easily be distinguished relating, respectively, to the conclusion, the interpretation, and the termination of treaties. It is with some aspects of the first of these categories that the present study is concerned.

In order that a treaty may be validly concluded on behalf of a state, two requirements of fundamental importance must be met. The first is that expressions of consent have occurred; the second, that these expressions shall emanate from persons who are competent to give them.

The original plan of the present study envisaged a full treatment of the rules of international law governing these two requirements. As the work proceeded, however, it became clear that no more than one of the topics could be treated within the framework of a thesis. Accordingly, the writer decided not to discuss the rules of international law relating to what constitutes an expression of consent to a treaty. The result of the writer's inquiry into the question whether, in cases of doubt, the signature of a treaty constitutes an irrevocable expression of consent, or whether ratification is required, is found in an article entitled "The Requirement of Ratification", published in volume 30 (1953) of the *British Yearbook of International Law*.

Consequently, the present study is restricted to a systematic examination of those rules of international law which relate to the identification of the authorities in the state who are competent to express the final consent of the state to a treaty. The question of the representation in contractual and treaty matters of subjects other than states, though occasionally discussed, is not systematically treated.

The present work deals with two distinct but interrelated problems. The first is that of the conditions under which the expressions of consent of an authority or person to a treaty are imputed to the state on whose behalf the authority or person purports to act. This is the question of identifying the competent treaty-making organ. The other problem is that of the conditions under which the expression of consent given to a treaty may be imputed to the treaty-making organ whose agent the individual purports to be. Both problems are of considerable difficulty. In the case of the second problem, that of the competence of agents, the difficulties are caused, chiefly, by the scant attention which the question has attracted. Material relevant to it has not been easily accessible, and the doctrinal discussion of the matter has hitherto been so limited that the present study perhaps may claim to be the first full treatment of the topic.

By way of contrast, many of the difficulties relating to the problem of the competence of treaty-making organs have been caused by the prolific treatment which it has been accorded at the hands of publicists. In an endeavour, therefore, to make some fresh contribution to this subject, the emphasis of this study has been placed on the investigation and discussion of the practice of states and the decisions of tribunals, both municipal and international. One consequence of this approach is to expose to criticism many of the views hitherto expressed on this subject, and it has, therefore, become necessary to attempt the formulation of a theory that is more consonant with the practice of states than, in the writer's view, most existing theories seem to be.

The study falls into two parts. Part I contains an examination of the problem of the competence of agents of treaty-making organs. Part II takes up the question of the competence of treaty-making organs. In Section A of Part II, this question is examined with particular reference to some situations where a municipal regulation of the treaty-making competence is likely to be nonexistent or inoperative. In Section B of Part II, the same problem is considered with reference to the most common case, namely, that where the law of a state provides an effective municipal regulation of treaty-making competence.

In preparing this study, the writer has benefited from the advice and help of several persons, and the generous assistance of several institutions.

The writer acquired his basic legal training at the University of Uppsala, and he wishes to express his thanks to Professor Halvar G. F. Sundberg of that University, who made the writer's, as so many other students', first contact with public international law an exciting experience.

He was equally fortunate in beginning his research in international law at the University of Cambridge. He is greatly indebted to Judge Sir Hersch Lauterpacht, who suggested the topic which is treated in the present study, and without whose continued encouragement and personal help it would hardly have been written. The author's thanks go further to his supervisor at Cambridge University, Professor R. Y. Jennings, for his patient and continued advice and support, and to Professor Torsten Gihl, whose great experience and erudition made his advice the more valuable.

For two academic years the writer had the privilege of working in the stimulating atmosphere of Columbia University and New York City, and of using the excellent facilities for research in the Law School of Columbia University. His gratitude goes particularly to Professor Philip C. Jessup, whose imaginative and yet exact approach to problems of international law was, and remains, a source of inspiration, and whose guidance and kind personal help were of the greatest value. He is equally thankful to Professor Oliver J. Lissitzyn for his superb instruction, his advice, encouragement and friendship.

The writer is greatly indebted as well to Professor Hilding Eek of Stockholm University for having read the whole manuscript in its various stages of development and offered unfailing support, advice and friendly criticism.

Thanks are further due for advice and assistance rendered by officers of the Legal Division of the Secretariat of the United Nations, and for similar aid by officers of the Swedish Ministry for Foreign Affairs, in particular by the Librarian of that Ministry, Dr. Ivar Beskow, whose long experience and thorough understanding of treaty-making practice made his help of the greatest importance.

The task of correcting the errors of someone whose native tongue is not English is necessarily tedious. The author is particularly grateful to his friend Professor Stephen M. Schwebel of Harvard University, who has performed this task despite a heavy burden of work of his own. He is further indebted to his friend Mr. Stig Strömholm, who has read the whole manuscript and offered many valuable suggestions, and to Miss Ellen Anders who has assisted in reading the proof.

The writer could never have completed this time-consuming study but for the economic assistance of various institutions. His thanks are due for scholarships given to him by the Trustees of the Humanitarian Trust Fund, by the Faculty of Law of the University of Stockholm, by the United States Government, and last, but not least, by the Swedish

State Council for Research in the Social and Legal Sciences. He also acknowledges his gratitude to the Trustees of the International Law Fund for economic assistance which enabled the writer to undertake some special research in England, to the Fund's Secretary, Mr. Elihu Lauterpacht, whose support has been more than financial, and to Professor Philip C. Jessup for assistance in the form of a most liberal employment.

HANS BLIX

Uppsala, August 1959

LIST OF ABBREVIATIONS

Articles and books which are frequently referred to will be cited generally only by the name of the author. The full titles will be found in the bibliography. Where more than one work of a writer is included in the bibliography, such abbreviated references have regard to the first work which is listed. If the writer is listed in more than one section of the bibliography, the reference is to the work found in the section on the law of treaties.

In addition, the following abbreviations will be used:

A.J.I.L.	The American Journal of International Law.
Annual Digest	Annual Digest and Reports of Public International Law Cases.
Bilag	Denmark (official publication), Bilag til Beretning til Folketinget afgivet af den af Tinget under 8. Januar 1948 nedsatte Kommission i Henhold til Grundlovens § 45; Part V: Udenrigsministeriet under Besaettelsen, Aktstykker Stenografiske Referater (Copenhagen, 1948).
B.F.S.P.	British and Foreign State Papers.
B.Y.I.L.	The British Yearbook of International Law.
Ceylon, *Hansard*	Ceylon, Parliamentary Debates, House of Representatives.
Cmd.	British Command Papers.
Cz. Y.	Czechoslovak Yearbook of International Law.
For. Rel. U.S.	Papers Relating to the Foreign Relations of the United States.
Hackworth's *Digest*	Hackworth, G., Digest of International Law (Washington, 1942).
Harvard Research	Harvard Law School, Research in International Law, Draft Convention on the Law of Treaties in *A.J.I.L.*, vol. 29 (1935), Supp.
I.C.L.Q.	The International and Comparative Law Quarterly.
I.L.R.	International Law Reports.
J.O.F.C.	Journal Officiel de la France Combattante.
J.O.F.L.	Journal Officiel de la France Libre.
Lauterpacht's *First Report*	Lauterpacht, H., Report on the Law of Treaties (U.N. Doc. A/CN. 4/63, 24 March 1953).
Lauterpacht's *Second Report*	Lauterpacht, H., Second Report on the Law of Treaties (U.N. Doc. A/CN. 4/87, 8 July 1954).
L.N.T.S.	League of Nations Treaty Series.
De Martens, *N.R.G.*	Nouveau Recueil Général des Traités.
Moore's *Digest*	Moore, J. B., A Digest of International Law (Washington, 1906).

N.C.H.	North China Herald.
P.C.I.J.	Permanent Court of International Justice, Publications.
Recueil des Cours	Académie de droit international de la Haye, Recueil des Cours.
R.G.D.I.P.	Revue Générale de Droit International Public.
Rives	Report by Mr. G. L. Rives to President Cleveland, published in *For. Rel. U.S.*, 1888, vol. 1, pp. 456 ff.
Rivista	Rivista di Diritto Internazionale, vol. 7 (1913).
S.Ö.F.	Sveriges Överenskommelser med Främmande Makter.
T.I.A.S.	United States, Treaties and other International Agreements Series.
U.N., *Compilation*	United Nations, Laws and Practices concerning the Conclusion of Treaties (United Nations Legislative Series, New York, 1953).
U.N. *Doc.*	United Nations, Document.
U.N.T.S.	United Nations Treaty Series.
United States, *Treaty Practice*	The Law of Treaties as Applied by the Government of the United States (mimeographed material ed. by the Department of State, Washington D.C., 31 March 1950).

PART ONE

THE COMPETENCE OF
AGENTS TO BIND TREATY-MAKING
ORGANS

CHAPTER I

INTRODUCTION

1. THE USE OF AGENTS AND THE LEGAL PROBLEM

The use of agents to enter into agreements is a universal practice. The need for it and its constant exercise have given rise to governing legal standards, which may vary with the character of the agency and the context in which it is carried out.

An agent always represents and acts in the place of another. The problem of ensuring that the acts of an agent approximate as closely as possible the hypothetical behaviour of his principal is universal, but the means used to solve that problem may vary: for example, the agent may be threatened with punishment for a breach of faith,[1] or the other party may be given clear indications of the outer limits of the agent's authority. The legal effect of acts which deviate from the desired hypothetical behaviour may also differ with the community and the sphere of action in question.

2. THE PROBLEM IN THE LIGHT OF HISTORY

Competence of agents of absolute monarchs

The use of agents to conclude treaties between the respective communities of their rulers and principals may be presumed to be almost as old as the very practice of making treaties.[2] Like the latter practice, the former must always have rested upon the existence of legal standards sanctioning the device. Yet, although the practice of states in the matter can be traced long before the 17th century, a developed theory concerning the legal position of agents in the conclusion of treaties cannot be found until that time.[3] This was the era of sovereign monarchs,

---

[1] The device has also been contemplated that he who received an unauthorized promise by the agent should be allowed to punish the agent. See Vattel, *The Law of Nations,* bk. 2, Ch. XIV, § 211, Classics ed. (1916), p. 182.

[2] On the antiquity of the practice of concluding treaties, see Nussbaum, *A Concise History of the Law of Nations* (Rev. ed., 1954), pp. 4 and 6.

[3] Ahnlund, N., *Den svenska utrikespolitikens historia,* vol. I: 1 (Stockholm, 1956),

of the kings *Dei gratiae,* and in the matter of conclusion of treaties the power of kings suffered no legal limitation.[4] The treaties they concluded, as indeed the state authorities they headed, were of a quasi-personal character.[5] Agents negotiating on their behalf were regarded as personal representatives, and the relation between the monarch and the agent was thought to be similar in some respects to that existing between principal and agent under private law.[6] One author quotes Vattel as saying that, at the end of the 18th century: "Full Powers are nothing else than an unlimited power of attorney."[7] Vattel was well aware, however, of the difference between the case of a private individual using an agent for the making of an agreement, and that of the sovereign of a state commissioning an agent to conclude a treaty. Were the agent of the private individual to be disavowed, the agent himself might be obligated to perform what he promised on behalf of his principal. With regard to the agent of the sovereign, such a rule would evidently be impractical. As Vattel put it, "matters are at stake which are infinitely beyond the power of the promisor to dispose of, things which he can not carry out himself or cause to be carried out, and for which he can offer neither an equivalent nor adequate compensation."[8]

p. 38, refers to the use of the procedure of ratification in Scandinavia from the 14th century. In this period, conditions were sometimes added in the process of ratification; and on occasion such conditions, being unacceptable to the other party, debarred the ultimate conclusion of a treaty.

[4] See Grotius, *De Jure Belli ac Pacis,* bk. 2, Ch. XV, Sec. 3, § 1, Classics ed., vol. 2, bk. 2 (1925), p. 392; Pallieri, pp. 470–471. The recent work on the history of Swedish foreign policy cited in the preceding note reveals, however, that King Gustav Vasa of Sweden (ruling 1523–1560) generally was eager to act with the support of the Council. The author of that work adds:

"During the first decades [of his rule] this was all the more necessary as the necessity for the consent and confirmation of the Royal Council was commonly taken for granted abroad, in conformity with older custom as regards settlements with Sweden." (Translation supplied by the present writer.)

It appears, furthermore, that the members of the Council appended their personal seals next to that of the King on treaties entered into, and that this custom continued even after the death of Gustav Vasa. Ahnlund, *op. cit.,* pp. 75–76.

[5] See Jones, pp. 12 and 16, as well as the following statement by an Austrian writer: "In den monarchischen, patrimonialen Einheitsstaaten erscheint der Vertragschliessende Fürst als Subjekt und nicht als Organ der Vertragschliessung." Bittner, p. 17.

[6] Jones, pp. 12 and 9.

[7] *Ibid.,* p. 12. For the full quotation, see below, p. 5, note 2.

[8] Vattel, *The Law of Nations,* bk. 2, Ch. XIV, § 211, Classics ed. (1916), p. 182.

It may be that the doctrine of the 17th century tried to apply the civil law theory of agency to the relationship between the negotiating diplomat and the sovereign. The realities of the two situations were very different, however, and there is indeed evidence, in the procedure that was used, that this difference was appreciated. In the full powers which the sovereign issued to his agent, the latter was granted wide authority to negotiate and the sovereign promised to ratify whatever the agent agreed to.[9] On the surface, it thus looked like a definite *ad hoc* delegation of part of the treaty-making power. Some protection against the dangers of misrepresentation was offered, however, not only by the threat of disciplinary action, but also by the procedure of ratification. The doctrine taught that the sovereign was under a strict obligation to ratify a treaty provided that his agent had remained within his "authority".[1] The precise extent of the "authority" of the agent accordingly became a question of the highest juridical moment. By keeping obscure the limits of his authority, the sovereign might well manage to retain a measure of discretion with regard to ratification.[2]

At one stage we find the authority of the agent indicated in some detail in his full powers. Although this method obviously offered some guarantees against misrepresentation, it had the disadvantage of narrowing the area of negotiation and bargaining, of constricting the room for maneuver. The practice was discontinued in the 18th century.[3]

During the period in which the authorities taught that ratification

---

[9] Jones, p. 3.

[1] *Ibid.*, pp. 6 ff., and see references in the following note.

[2] Note the following statement by Vattel:

"In these days, in order to avoid all risk and difficulty, princes reserve to themselves the right of ratifying agreements drawn up in their name by their agents. *Full powers* are nothing else than an unlimited power of attorney. Since these powers should be given their full effect, too much care can not be used in conferring them. But, as sovereigns can not be constrained, otherwise than by force of arms, to fulfill their engagements, it is usual not to consider their treaties final until approved and ratified by the sovereigns themselves. There is less danger, therefore, in giving full powers to a diplomatic agent if his acts are not valid until ratified by the sovereign. But cogent and substantial reasons are needed to justify a sovereign in refusing to ratify the act of his plenipotentiary, and in particular he must show that his minister has exceeded the instructions given." *The Law of Nations*, bk. 2, Ch. XII, § 156. Classics ed. (1916), p. 161.

See also Pufendorf, *De Jure Naturae et Gentium*, bk. 8, Ch. IX, art. 12. Classics ed. (1934), p. 1340; and Bynkershoek, *Quaestionum Juris Publici*, bk. 2, Ch. VII. Classics ed. (1930), pp. 174 ff. *Cf.* Harley, "The Obligation to Ratify Treaties", in *A.J.I.L.*, vol. 13 (1919), p. 389.

[3] Jones, pp. 10–11. It often occurred during the 18th century that full powers were reproduced in the texts of treaties. See Basdevant, p. 549. And *cf.* Jones, p. 4 note 3.

was a duty, sovereigns sometimes used the argument that their agents had exceeded their "authority" in order to justify a refusal to ratify.[4] It is understandable that, at a time when the means of communicating fresh instructions were poor, violations of instructions occurred with some frequency. Considering, however, that the precise extent of the authority of an agent could not be known to the opposite party, since the limits of the agent's authority were in fact drawn not only by his full powers but also by secret instructions, and considering the importance of the matters settled by agreements concluded by agents, it is not surprising that, in order to justify a refusal to ratify an unpalatable agreement, sovereigns sometimes argued in bad faith that an agent had exceeded his authority.

Competence of agents of early constitutional governments
Ratification as a safeguard

If it was only with difficulty that the absolute monarchs of the 17th century had granted real full powers—delegated authority—to agents acting on their behalf, and almost always retained as an ultimate safeguard the possibility of refusing to ratify, the age of constitutionalism made it completely impossible in many states to promise ratification at all. For a politically and constitutionally required legislative assent was often difficult to predict with any certainty. Although the process of change required a good deal of time, constitutionalism had a profound impact upon the legal rules regarding the position of agents. The outcome of the process was that ratification came to be recognized as legally discretionary. Justifications were no longer required for a refusal to ratify an agreement. With this development, the precise determination of the extent of an agent's authority, to negotiate and sign, and excesses of that authority became of less legal relevance.[5] If an agent actually misrepresented his principal, the latter

---

[4] See de Martens, *Traité de Droit International,* vol. I (1883), p. 521, and note the following statement by Jones: "At a time when the discretion to ratify was not yet established as a rule of law, the argument that an agent had exceeded his instructions was a convenient one." *Op. cit.,* p. 39. The reading of a recent detailed study on the foreign relations of Sweden in the 17th century gives the very definite impression, however, that the treaty-making authorities of the various states felt at complete liberty to refuse ratification, or to raise conditions for their ratification. See Landberg, G., *Den svenska utrikespolitikens historia,* vol. I: 3 (Stockholm, 1952), *passim.* But see Jones, p. 6.

[5] Jones, p. 39. Basdevant, admitting that it is often difficult to determine what an agent is empowered by his full power to do, remarks that the rule of necessity of ratification escapes this difficulty. *Op. cit.,* p. 575.

could now simply refrain from ratifying and yet unquestionably remain within the limits of his legal rights; it was not even necessary to disclose that the agent had violated his instructions. This option might have been found advantageous in cases where the admission of an error of a high officer would have caused embarrassment. On occasion it might of course still be politically desirable to justify a refusal to ratify. A number of instances will be cited below, in which ratification, although discretionary, was withheld with the express declaration that an agent had exceeded his authority.[6]

3. Instances of Excess of Authority by Agents concluding Treaties subject to Ratification

Incident of 1809 between the United States and Great Britain

On 18 April 1809 the United States Government entered into an agreement with the British Minister to Washington, Mr. Erskine, concerning the settlement of various matters. The British Government repudiated the agreement on the ground that Mr. Erskine had exceeded his instructions, and refused to ratify. Moreover, Mr. Erskine was recalled.

A correspondence concerning the agreement ensued between Mr. Erskine's successor, Mr. Jackson, and the Department of State. In a note of 11 October 1809, Mr. Jackson insinuated, in defense of the British repudiation, that the United States Government had been aware of the British Minister's exceeding his instructions. This insinuation was repeated in a subsequent note. In reply, the United States Secretary of State, Mr. Smith, denied categorically that his Government had had any knowledge of the violation of instructions, and declared that had his Government had such knowledge the arrangement would not have been entered into. He stated that the repeated insinuation of bad faith could not be tolerated and that, therefore, no further communication would be received from Mr. Jackson. The British Government reluctantly recalled a second minister.[7]

---

[6] It has been suggested that, at the present time, when plenipotentiaries usually submit the precise wording of a proposed treaty to their governments for approval before signature, a witholding of ratification is not easy to justify, except when ratification is dependent upon another organ of government than that which has negotiated the treaty. See *Satow's Guide to Diplomatic Practice* (4th ed. by Bland, 1957), p. 359.

[7] Moore's *Digest,* vol. 4, pp. 511–612, 515.

Incident from the 1820s, between Persia and Great Britain

The second case concerns a treaty figuring in the background of the British-Iranian dispute concerning sovereignty over the island of Bahrein.[8]

In 1822, a Captain William Bruce, who had been appointed a British agent at Bushire on the Persian Gulf, without any instructions or authorization negotiated and signed an agreement with a Persian minister, making it, however, expressly subject to the approval of the two Governments. The reaction of the British authorities has been described as follows:

"Having fundamental objections to the entire treaty, 'every article' of which was 'opposed to the views and intention of the Government', the Bombay Government expressed its surprise that Bruce should have entered into negotiations with Persia 'which were never contemplated' by Britain, and for which he had been 'neither furnished with instructions nor power.' The Government of Bombay 'in the most explicit terms' disavowed the treaty, which was considered inconsistent with the 'obligations of the public faith' and which would 'compromise the dignity of the British Government and overturn every part of the policy which it had adopted in relation to the powers of the Persian Gulf'."[9]

Bruce was removed from his post. The Persian Government was informed that Bruce had exceeded his powers in entering into negotiations, and that the treaty merely was his own act. It was accordingly repudiated and the desire was expressed that it should be considered exactly as if it had never been written. Captain Bruce's successor was instructed, furthermore, to express regret that no proof of Bruce's authority to conclude an agreement had been requested before he was allowed to enter into negotiations. In a later dispute between Persia and Great Britain regarding sovereignty over the island of Bahrein, the Persian Government attached importance to the treaty as an historical document, but apparently never asserted that it was valid.[1]

---

[8] The following account is taken from Adamyiat, *Bahrein Islands, A Legal and Diplomatic Study of the British Iranian Controversy* (1955), pp. 106 ff. The treaty referred to is reproduced at pp. 253–255.

[9] *Ibid.*, p. 109. The single quotation marks signify quotations from the original documents.

[1] See League of Nations, *Official Journal*, 9th year (1928), pp. 605–607, 1360–1362; *ibid.*, 10th year (1929), pp. 790–793; Smith, *Great Britain and the Law of Nations* (1935), vol. 2, pp. 62–76; and Adamyiat, pp. 212 ff.

Russo-Chinese incidents of 1858 and 1880

Two cases may also be cited from the foreign relations of China during the 19th century. One of these concerns the treaty of Aigun, concluded in 1858 between Russia and China. It appears that taking advantage of the weakness in which China found itself as a result of wars with Great Britain and France and the rebellion at Taiping, the Russian governor-general of Eastern Siberia, Count Muraview, induced the chief of the Chinese forces on the river Amur, Prince Yishan, to sign, on 16 May 1858, a treaty by which Muraview secured for the Czar a territory almost as large as France.[2] While for this service the Russian agent was granted the title of Count Amuriski by the Czar, the Chinese prince was not similarly rewarded. His Government was not disposed to ratify the treaty, and he was dismissed for his ineptitude and for overstepping his authority. A petition sent by the Prince to the throne following this event is characterized by one writer as one of the most humiliating documents in Chinese history.[3] Another writer states that the Emperor evidenced his displeasure at the treaty "by exposing the second in command in a wooden collar on the banks of the Amur for three days and nights."[4] Apparently the treaty remained unratified for some time. In the autumn of 1860, however, when French and English troops had occupied Peking, a Russian diplomat named Ignatiev promised the Chinese ruler, Prince Kung, that he would exert his influence on the occupiers to bring about the withdrawal of their troops —which, unknown to the Prince, was to take place anyway—if the Chinese recognized the treaty of Aigun. To this promise he added others and coupled them with threats in case of Chinese non-compliance. The allied troops were withdrawn, and by a treaty of 14 November 1860 with Russia, China confirmed the treaty of Aigun.[5]

The other Chinese case concerns the treaty of Livadia of 1879 and is still more extraordinary. In 1879 at Livadia, the residence of the Russian Czar, a Chinese Minister Plenipotentiary, Chung How, carried on negotiations concerning the return to China of the province of Ili.[6] As a result of these negotiations he signed a treaty on 2 October 1879.

---

[2] Wu, *China and the Soviet Union* (1950), pp. 66 ff. *Cf.* Weigh, *Russo-Chinese Diplomacy* (Shanghai, 1928), pp. 37 ff. and Morse, *Far Eastern International Relations* (1931), p. 182.

[3] Wu, p. 67.

[4] Weigh, p. 39, note 2.

[5] Wu, pp. 68–69; Weigh, p. 39.

[6] Wu, p. 105.

It appears to have been unfavourable to China, but contained a clause expressly making it subject to ratification.[7] The Chinese plenipotentiary thereupon returned to China without awaiting an authorizing Imperial edict. One writer suggests that Chung How suffered "not only from complete ignorance of the geography of Kashgaria, but from acute nostalgia; his one and only idea was to get back to China as quickly as possible."[8] Whether or not this statement is correct,[9] a council appointed after the diplomat's return to China charged with examining his acts in Russia unanimously found that he had disobeyed his instructions and exceeded his powers.[1] A Chinese scholar who submitted a memorial to the throne argued in favour of the ultimate penalty. He is reported to have written as follows:

"...According to international law, any disobedience shown to the orders of the Emperor is regarded as exceeding the powers conferred by his Majesty, and all the powers of such ministers are, point by point, made out by the government. Chung How's crime is the disregard he had for the secret instructions and for the imperial will. His case is similar to the one which brought Ki-ying to prison. The final decision is clear, and I therefore say, let Chung How be executed..."[2]

As to the validity of the treaty, this scholar submitted:

"Although the ambassador has signed the treaty, still he did not receive the imperial assent to it, and the treaty cannot therefore be considered as ratified. The case is precisely the same as described in old books, where no treaty concluded could come into force unless the blood of a sacrifice was sipped by the contracting parties..."[3]

On 3 March 1880 an Imperial edict condemned Chung How to "decapitation after incarceration". The Russian Government appears to have lodged a protest against this decision, requesting the release of Chung How and referring to "the international practice that no government has the right to punish an Envoy for the failure of negotiations."[4] The situation was tense, and it was even feared that war might break out if Chung How were to be beheaded. Appeals by Queen Victoria to

---

[7] Article 18. The treaty is reproduced in *For. Rel. U.S.*, 1880, p. 266.

[8] MacNair, *Modern Chinese History, Selected Readings* (Shanghai, 1933), p. 474.

[9] Chung How seems to have arrived in Petersburg as early as January 1879, some nine months before he signed the treaty. See Hoo, *Les bases conventionelles des relations modernes entre la Chine et la Russie* (1918), pp. 373–374.

[1] Wu, p. 106 and *For. Rel. U.S.*, 1880, p. 236.

[2] *Ibid.*, pp. 267–268.

[3] *Ibid.*, p. 269.

[4] Quotation from Wu, p. 106.

the Chinese Empress Dowager proved successful. A new Chinese negotiator was sent to Petersburg with the task of re-negotiating the treaty. His misgivings, expressed in a personal letter, are instructive with respect to the political, if not the legal, difficulties entailed in disavowing an agent and discarding the result of his negotiations. He wrote:

"A treaty entered into by the Minister Plenipotentiary of one country directly with the sovereign of another country is a solemn contract. Even a small and weak country will not submit to the complete revocation of such a treaty on the demand of another, to say nothing of a nation like Russia . . ."[5]

The fears he harboured were justified. The Russians first took the stand that no new negotiations were needed and that ratification was the only thing required. After some time, they agreed to modifications, however, and a new treaty was drawn up, signed, and eventually ratified.

It is of interest to see how this incident was reflected in the contemporary American diplomatic reports. In a dispatch of 12 January 1880, an older Chinese incident is cited in which one Ki Ying, having signed the "Cushing treaty" on behalf of China, was condemned to death for an offense similar to Chung How's. In the same dispatch, Chung How is described as one of the ablest members of the Chinese Foreign Office, and doubts are expressed that he really had acted without authorization. He is said to have been a very cautious man and to have been in constant communication with his own Foreign Office by telegraph. The conclusion is drawn that although it took this form, the disavowal was perhaps one that pertained to the whole Foreign Office, and issued from the ultra-conservative party.[6] A note addressed by the American representative in Peking to Prince Kung on the punishment of Chung How is of particular interest with respect to the position of negotiating agents. It casts light on the dangers of using harsh disciplinary measures against departures from instructions, or of relying upon allegations of acts *ultra vires* as subterfuges for political changes of course:

"This case is not without concern to foreign governments when viewed from the one or the other standpoint. They have invited you to establish missions abroad because they have desired to avert the recurrence of difficulties and to draw more closely the bonds of friendship. But what high officer will care hereafter to go abroad when the duty before him is so perilous? What

[5] *Ibid.*, p. 108.
[6] *For. Rel. U.S.*, 1880, pp. 206–210.

boldness or vigor can be expected of a minister who has to direct his steps to avert not only disaster from his state, but also disaster of the gravest sort for himself . . .?'[7]

United States incident of 1908

An incident in which an American diplomat signed treaties in violation of instructions is cited by Hackworth. In 1908, the United States Government declined to submit to the Senate two conventions signed by the American Minister to Roumania. In the case of one of these conventions, the Minister had had no authority whatsoever; in the case of the other, he had obtained full powers under representations to sign a wholly different document.[8]

Swedish incident of 1951

By way of contrast a recent case may be cited, in which a treaty, signed by a person without any authority whatsoever, was nevertheless confirmed by the government on whose behalf he purported to act. At a conference held at Stresa in 1951, a convention was drafted concerning the "appellations d'origine et dénominations de fromages". It was signed on 1 June and provided expressly for ratification. The list of signatures reveals that one Inge Mork signed on behalf of Sweden as well as Norway.[9] It appears certain that Mr. Mork was authorized to sign on behalf of Norway and it appears equally certain that he was not authorized to sign on behalf of Sweden. The Swedish Government did not, however, disavow his signature, but on the contrary subsequently expressed final consent to the convention.[1]

It is submitted that the foregoing cases tend to show that, while it may sometimes be politically difficult to disavow an agent who has signed a treaty in excess of his powers, the rule that ratification, when reserved, is discretionary, renders a signature in excess of authority of relatively little legal or practical importance.

4. PRESENT POSSIBILITIES OF EXCESS OF AUTHORITY BY AGENTS. DEFINITION OF THE PROBLEM

It might be thought that if all or most treaties were to enter into force by ratification, the problem of the legal bounds of the competence

---

[7] *Ibid.*, p. 222.
[8] Hackworth's *Digest*, vol. 4, p. 467.
[9] *Sveriges Överenskommelser med Främmande Makter*, 1954, p. 499 at p. 514.
[1] *Ibid.*, p. 499.

of agents would be eliminated. The problem of the effect of an excess
of authority on the part of an agent will remain, however, as long as ✓
the act that makes a treaty irrevocable under international law is not
undertaken by the treaty-making organ itself. There is general agreement that a treaty made to enter into force upon "ratification", becomes
irrevocable internationally by the exchange of the instruments of ratification.[2] While it is common that treaty-making organs themselves sign
the instruments of ratification, it happens rarely, if ever, that they carry
out the internationally relevant exchange of the documents. This task
again is performed by an agent, and the question of his competence
might arise if he were to exchange instruments of ratification without
being authorized to do so, or in spite of instructions to refrain from an
exchange for a certain time. It is clear, therefore, that the procedure
of ratification does not completely do away with the problem of excess
of authority by agents.

While the conclusion must be drawn that not even when treaties
are made by what has been termed "the complex procedure"[3]—*i.e.* comprising the trinity of full powers, signature and ratification—is it
possible completely to disregard the problem of the competence of
agents, it is obvious that this problem is of much greater importance
with regard to treaties (including exchanges of notes) entering into force
upon the signature of agents.[4] At the present time, this mode of bringing
treaties into force is predominant.[5] The question of the legal effect of
a signature appended to a treaty by an agent who lacks the requisite
authority or who acts in violation of instructions might therefore again
arise in acute form.[6]

[2] See Article 10 of the Harvard Draft Convention on the Law of Treaties, in
A.J.I.L., vol. 29 (1935), Suppl., p. 658; Oppenheim, vol. 1, p. 916; Hyde, vol. 2,
p. 1445.

[3] Bittner, pp. 5–6; Basdevant, p. 545; Blix, p. 375.

[4] To this group must be assimilated in this connexion treaties entering into force
upon the exchange of notes of approval or the deposit of instruments of acceptance
or the submission of any other document performing a function similar to that of a
ratification, but being signed by an agent rather than by the treaty-making organ
itself. See below, p. 54.

[5] Blix, pp. 362–363.

[6] Apparently not appreciating the dominating position of agreements in simplified
form, Fenwick could state, as late as 1951:

"... In the old days when plenipotentiaries signed in the name of a monarch,
it was of the greatest importance to determine whether the documentary evidence
of their authority was in good and due form. Today that question has ceased to be
of importance, and its place has been taken by the question whether the treaty has
been negotiated within the limitations of the national constitution..." "The Progress
of International Law in the Past Forty Years" in *Recueil des Cours*, 1951, vol. 2,
pp. 49–50.

It might perhaps have been expected—and it is expressly suggested by Basdevant[7]—that if treaties were to enter into force by the signature of agents, full powers indicating the competence of the agents would be of primary importance. Contrary to this expectation it appears, however, that the use of the traditional type of full power has continuously decreased during this century. What is even more surprising, full powers are more commonly used for the conclusion of treaties requiring ratification than for agreements which become binding upon the signature of agents. An explanation will be sought below for these seemingly paradoxical facts.[8]

The chief problem to be examined concerns the extent of authority possessed under international law by various agents signing agreements that enter into force upon signature, and the modes of establishing the existence of such authority. In other words, when is an agreement made in excess of the competence possessed by an agent under international law? What is the effect under international law of such an agreement?[9] Some subsidiary problems may be distinguished as well. It may be asked, for instance, whether the internal position of an agent is of any importance to his international competence to sign a treaty. Is there a difference in this respect between a foreign minister, an ambassador, and a chargé d'affaires?

The problems posed are similar to those concerning the effect under international law of a ratification made by the constitutionally indicated treaty-making authority in violation of constitutional limitations upon its power. There are important differences between the two questions, however, and accordingly they merit separate treatment. The limits upon the constitutional competence of the treaty-making power to ratify are embodied in the public order of the state. The limits upon the authority of an agent, if at all expressly indicated, are in the form of full powers which merely declare the topic of the treaty to be concluded and the name of the Power with which it is to be concluded, and from which the possible relevance of secret instructions do not appear.[1] In order to keep the two problems apart it may, unless the

---

[7] Basdevant, p. 549.

[8] Below, pp. 48 ff.

[9] While the question of the validity of the agreements will be discussed, no treatment is intended of the further question that may arise as to whether an agreement is void *ab initio* or voidable. On this problem, see Kelsen, *General Theory of Law and State* (Harvard University Press, 1949), pp. 159–161.

[1] McNair, p. 1; *cf. Satow's Guide to Diplomatic Practice* (4th ed. by Bland, 1957), p. 86.

contrary is indicated, be assumed throughout the following discussion of the competence of agents that all the treaties they sign as binding upon their signatures are such that fall within the exclusive constitutional competence of the executive branch of the government concerned, and that therefore the problem cannot be further complicated by a required constitutional assent.[2]

Despite the vast increase in the number of agreements which today are made to enter into force upon signature, incidents concerning the competence of agents who sign them have arisen relatively rarely. This may perhaps account for the scant attention paid to the problem by writers.[3] There may be several reasons for the apparent paucity of acute conflicts on this matter. One may be that, because of the facilities of modern communications, negotiating agents need not often act without express instructions from their principals. Another reason may be found in the practice of initialling an agreement at the end of negotiations and of submitting the final draft for the approval of the treaty-making power before signature is appended.[4] Reference may also be made to the practice of leaving multilateral instruments open for signature. This procedure enables states to scrutinize the instruments in question and to take a definite position before they authorize an agent to sign, when,

---

[2] Actually, agreements entering into force upon the mere signature of agents are not confined to matters that fall within the exclusive competence of the executive, as Chailley and others have suggested (see below, p. 19, and note therein). Although the majority of such agreements are undoubtedly of this kind, and although in some countries this might be an inflexible rule (see the Chilean memorandum in U.N., *Compilation*, p. 35), there would not seem to be any obstacle, at least in theory, to the submission to a legislature for its consent of a draft agreement, perhaps not even initialled. After the approval of the legislature, a diplomatic agent might be authorized to sign the agreement to become binding upon his signature. That such a procedure is in fact employed in practice can be seen from the French memorandum in the United Nations collection cited above (at p. 52). In Swedish practice, it has happened occasionally that an agreement approved by the legislature is made binding by signature. For an example, see the agreement between Sweden, Denmark and Norway concerning financial guarantees to certain airlines. It was approved by the Swedish Riksdag and later signed as binding at Oslo on 20 December 1951. For the text of the agreement, see *U.N.T.S.*, vol. 163 (1953), p. 309. A treaty may also be subject to executive ratification without there being any necessity for parliamentary ratification. See Hackworth's *Digest*, vol. 5, pp. 400 ff.

[3] Apparently only two writers deal extensively with the problem, Mervyn Jones, in his book *Full Powers and Ratification* (1946), and Fairman in "Competence to Bind the State to an International Engagement", *A.J.I.L.*, vol. 30 (1936), pp. 439–462.

[4] See below, pp. 70 ff.

as at times is the case, the instrument becomes binding upon signature.[5] While the circumstances mentioned may serve partially to explain the scarcity of cases, it may be surmised that in fact, the problem has arisen many times without causing public incidents. A government might find it embarrassing to disavow an agent,[6] and, regardless of the legal position, it may be thought politically difficult to do so. In this case, and perhaps others, the problem will not come to the surface.

[5] See below, pp. 70 ff.
[6] Ross, p. 206.

Chapter II

THE COMPETENCE OF THE AGENTS IN THE LIGHT OF THEORIES REGARDING AGREEMENTS IN SIMPLIFIED FORM

1. The Agreements in Question are not Envisaged by Constitutions

The public order of most states attributes to the head of state or some other supreme organ the function of making treaties on behalf of the state—the treaty-making power—normally with the proviso that certain categories of treaties require legislative approval. Few constitutions expressly authorize the treaty-making power to delegate any of its functions to other bodies or persons.[7] The circumstance that so many modern treaties become binding merely by being signed by persons not mentioned in the constitution accordingly may seem puzzling, and has caused doctrinal debate.[8]

It is beyond any doubt that, by a rule of international law, binding force may be accorded to such agreements, and it is equally certain that they may be valid under the municipal law of states. Indeed, the rule that may be deduced from international practice, and that practice itself, would never have come into existence, had the device been vitiated by constitutional invalidity at its inception. Against this background it might seem of little use to cite the views of some writers who attempt to explain the constitutional and the international validity of these agreements.[9] Yet, by finding out why, generally, these agreements —often termed agreements in simplified form—are valid, one may hope also to discover when they are invalid.

---

[7] See below, p. 21.

[8] Bittner, pp. 39 ff.; Chailley, pp. 207 ff.; Basdevant, pp. 617 ff.; Dehousse, pp. 97 ff.; Vitta, pp. 74 ff.

[9] See Pallieri (p. 492), who implies that municipal construction is irrelevant internationally.

2. Bittner's Theory: "Beurkundungsauftrag"

According to Bittner, the treaty-making power of states is expressed in their public legal order, and he found that, at the time of his writing, all constitutions made the head of state the treaty-making authority.[1] He concludes that under international law, the head of state, and he alone, is competent to make treaties on behalf of the state. The signing of agreements with binding effect by foreign ministers or diplomatic representatives, Bittner explains, does not in reality amount to an exercise of any part of the treaty-making power. He maintains that while by constitutional law—upon which the international norms rest in this respect—the forming of the "will" of the state is the function of the head of the state, there is no obstacle to this will being *declared* by somebody else.[2] This, he asserts, is the function fulfilled by the foreign ministers and diplomats. An examination of a large number of treaties revealed to him that in 95% of the compacts the persons signing purported to do so in virtue of an authorization, and he maintains that this "Beurkundungsauftrag"—an authorization and at the same time an instruction to sign[3]—gives to the agents no latitude of power. In signing and thereby expressing, but not forming, the "will" of the state, they merely act as proxies. According to Bittner, a competence to act as proxies, "Urkundspersonen mit voller Glaubwürdigkeit im völkerrechtlichen Verkehr",[4] is possessed only by the most senior officials of foreign offices, and of diplomatic representatives accredited abroad. It rests nationally upon customary administrative law; internationally it has acquired general recognition and become part of customary international law.

Bittner admits that a real delegation of treaty-making power takes place to governors of colonies and border areas, but he denies the treaty character of agreements between government departments.[5] He asserts that the subjects of these agreements are the departments and not states. He further maintains that formal full powers are issued for the negotiation and signing of treaties which are to be ratified, but not for agreements concluded in simplified form.[6] The authorizations, the "Beurkundungsaufträge", are internal acts, and no evidence of them

---

[1] Bittner, p. 16.

[2] *Ibid.*, p. 40.

[3] See Blix, p. 375.

[4] Bittner, pp. 48–49, 57.

[5] *Ibid.*, pp. 51, 54.

[6] *Ibid.*, p. 48.

is required in the intercourse between states, with the exception of the mentioning of them in the agreements.[7] The holding of the office of foreign minister or of an accredited diplomatic representative is deemed sufficient to allow another party to feel confident that a "Beurkundungs-auftrag" in fact has been given, when such an official purports to act upon one. The issuer of the final document is responsible, according to Bittner, under international law as well as under constitutional law, for assuring that all constitutional conditions are fulfilled for the declaration of will. Should this in fact not be the case, the issuer has committed an infraction of both constitutional and international law since he has abused his position as "glaubwürdige Urkundsperson". The state, however, must recognize the binding force of the agreement just as it is responsible for other infractions of international law committed by its organs.[8]

3. CHAILLEY'S THEORY: "TACIT DELEGATION"

Chailley, like Bittner, makes a distinction between treaties concluded with the formal intervention of the head of state and those in simplified form. In criticizing Bittner's theory on the validity of the latter category of agreements, he contends, however, that diplomats do not act merely as notaries of the treaty-making power, when they sign treaties, but possess by delegation some latitude of power. He finds support for this view in the circumstance that, in some treaties, the agents themselves purport to "have agreed".[9] He further maintains that Bittner's explanation does not cover agreements signed by technical officials, heads of public services and others, and suggests the concept of a *tacit delegation* from the treaty-making organ as a common explanation of the validity of all agreements in simplified form. Chailley seeks to adduce further support for this theory in the assertion that agreements in simplified form only regulate matters falling within the exclusive competence of the executive power of states. The absence of agreements in simplified form on other matters, he suggests, must be explained by the inability of the executive power to delegate power which it does not possess.[1] Chailley does not, as Bittner, consider it necessary to derive in each case the competence of the agents from an authorization by the head of

---

[7] *Ibid.,* p. 72.
[8] *Ibid.,* p. 100.
[9] Chailley, p. 209; *cf.* Basdevant, p. 620.
[1] Chailley, pp. 214 and 212. But see p. 15, note 2 above.

state as the only internationally competent treaty-making power. He contends that the delegation takes place on the basis, not of international law, but of the public law of the signatory states, and that this delegation is directly effective externally.[2] He reaches the view that the international validity of an agreement in simplified form depends directly upon its internal validity. The agreements are valid, Chailley maintains, because the agents have remained within the limits of the delegation.[3] Although Chailley himself does not make it explicit, the conclusion presumably may be drawn that an agreement concluded by an agent in excess of this "tacit delegation" would be an infraction of the municipal public law, and void or voidable internally as well as internationally. It does not appear, however, if the tacit delegation is thought to be dependent upon secret instructions.

4. Interdepartmental Agreements

It is not necessary at this stage to cite writers other than Bittner and Chailley, who represent two extreme viewpoints. But it may be convenient to narrow the discussion somewhat. As pointed out above, Chailley criticizes Bittner's theory of a "Beurkundungsauftrag" and proposes that of a "tacit delegation", for the reason, *inter alia,* that heads of public services of states among other officials, when concluding treaties have a broader authority than that of mere notaries. Chailley does not discuss Bittner's theory that agreements between postal administrations and the like are not treaties between states. Bittner found support for this view in the circumstance that the parties to this kind of agreements often style themselves not states or governments but departments.[4] Since the formal subjects of the agreements were departments there was—the reader is led to infer—no longer a need to establish a link with the treaty-making authority of the head of state. It is submitted that this theory cannot be sustained. If, for example, an international tribunal were to award damages on the basis of a postal agreement, it is presumably beyond dispute that the state as a juridical person would be responsible in the last resort for the payment of the damages. The conclusion would seem inevitable, therefore, that the obligations contained in the agreement, though undertaken by the postal authority, rest upon the state. Indeed, they may be presumed to rest

---

[2] *Ibid.*, p. 215.
[3] *Ibid.*, p. 212, note 319 bis.
[4] Bittner, pp. 54–55.

upon the state just as much as an agreement concluded by the government rests upon the state rather than upon the government.[5]

With respect to so-called interdepartmental agreements, the following
should also be noted. In modern states many internal functions have
become decentralized, *i.e.* distributed by the central government among
separate authorities, such as postal administrations. It merely amounts
to a completion of the decentralizing measures when these authorities
are attributed the competence to enter into international agreements
by which they promise conduct, the achievement of which lies within
their ordinary national functions. If this distribution of power should
occur in the form of constitutional provision or practice, there would
be no need or possibility to trace the treaty-making competence to the
central treaty-making organ. It appears, however, that such treaty-
making power is frequently delegated to services and administrations by
revocable government decrees,[6] sometimes expressly authorized and
contemplated by constitutional provisions.[7] Such delegation, like the
delegation of legislative power, may often be achieved only with difficulty under existing constitutions.[8]

5. GENERIC DELEGATION AND *ad hoc* LIMITED DELEGATION

Bittner admits that a delegation of treaty-making power occurs to
governors of border areas and colonies[9], and the above should be enough
to demonstrate that, as Chailley suggests, the same may be true also of
administrative services and similar authorities. They—and perhaps the
other contracting parties—find evidence of their treaty-making competence in laws, treaties, decrees, permanent full powers or practices
which enable them generally to conclude binding agreements whenever
they deem it opportune, and within the narrow spheres inside which
they are able to fulfil, themselves, what they undertake. Chailley does
not, however, distinguish these agreements which become binding upon
the signatures of the heads of the organs to which authority has been

[5] See Jones, pp. 58 ff. *Cf. ibid.*, p. 134.

[6] For Swedish practice in this regard, see Sundberg, *Lag och Traktat* (2nd ed.,
1942), pp. 22–23.

[7] See the provisions of the Austrian Constitution in U.N., *Compilation*, p. 9; and
the provisions of the Cambodian Constitution, *ibid.*, p. 23; see also Jones, p. 56.

[8] See Pallieri, p. 492; Ross, p. 213; see also Chailley, p. 212, note 319 bis; *contra*:
Vitta, p. 78. See also Jones, p. 59, and see below, p. 22, note 5.

[9] Above, p. 18. On this point, see also de Martens, *Traité de Droit International*,
vol. I (1883), p. 521.

delegated from agreements designed to come into force upon the signatures of diplomats or similar agents, but explains that the validity of the latter, too, is due to a "delegation" of power from the head of state.[1]

No doubt the word "delegation" may be defined in different ways. Criticising Bittner, Chailley contends that diplomatic agents signing treaties possess "au moins par délégation, le pouvoir de conclure" the same treaties.[2] If the word "delegation" is accepted for the conferral of power by a treaty-making organ upon a diplomatic agent, it is clear that this "delegation" differs substantially—in degree if not in kind—from the delegation by which administrative authorities are given slices of the treaty-making power.[3] These agents are never granted competence—like administrative authorities—to conclude agreements whenever they find it opportune, and they have no sphere of activity within which they are able to fulfil, themselves, what they undertake. No general full powers are given to them;[4] on the contrary, at least internally, they need specific authority for the signing of each treaty. They cannot in their turn "delegate" their power to sign to another agent as might perhaps be feasible for a postmaster general. The granting of authority to them does not often seem to encounter constitutional difficulties,[5] as do delegations of treaty-making power to administrative bodies. As Chailley himself admits, their competence is "limitée à la conclusion d'un accord déterminé portant sur un objet déterminé".[6] While the questions con-

---

[1] Chailley, pp. 209–210.

[2] *Ibid.*, p. 209.

[3] Ross (pp. 212–213), who distinguishes between treaties concluded directly between competent organs and those for which intermediaries are used, puts agreements between "ministers of the various state departments or military commanders" in the first category. There would seem to be good reasons for such classification.

[4] But see p. 43, note 7 below, on the power of some accredited diplomats to conclude treaties subject to ratification in case of an emergency.

[5] Bittner contended that no constitution in the world contemplated the activities of these agents (*op. cit.*, p. 39). Chailley's (*op. cit.*, p. 208, note 307 bis) and de Visschers' (*op. cit.*, pp. 128–129) references to the Austrian Constitution as evidence of the contrary do not seem pertinent. The Austrian Constitution—then and now—contemplated a delegation to ministers of departments and similar officers, not to diplomatic agents. (See U.N., *Compilation,* p. 9.) But see the very general provision contained in Article 46 of the Constitution of Cambodia (*ibid.,* p. 24), and see Article 53 of the Constitution of India (*ibid.,* p. 63). See, finally, Article 52 of the French Constitution of 4 October 1958 (*Journal du Droit International,* vol. 86 (1959), pp. 530–532).

[6] Chailley, p. 213.

cerning the derivation and the extent of the competence possessed by heads of various administrative bodies and similar officers to bind their states by agreements would seem to be easily distinguishable, and will not be treated here, the following discussion will deal with the problems of the competence of agents—appointed by central treaty-making organs or, indeed by treaty-making administrative officers[7]— who need specific municipal authority for each treaty they sign on behalf of their principals.

Even when the field of inquiry is thus limited, the views of the two authorities cited above differ widely. Bittner explains that the constitutional treaty-making authority, the head of state, has not abdicated any of its power: the agents merely express as notaries the will formed by the head of state. Chailley declares similarly that the head of state has not alienated any of his constitutional power, but maintains that, by delegation, the agents are granted competence to conclude a specific agreement on a specific subject, or at least to proceed to sign an agreement "de leur propre initiative et en toute liberté".[8] While Bittner suggests that, under customary international law, foreign ministers and senior officers of foreign offices and accredited diplomatic representatives have the competence to sign agreements which, with signature, become binding upon their states, Chailley believes that the competence of the agent is determined directly by domestic law and that under that law, the delegation described above takes place. When Bittner maintains that an agreement signed by an agent without "Beurkundungsauftrag" is binding nevertheless under international law, no conflict can arise, according to Chailley, between domestic and international validity since, in his opinion, only national rules on competence exist.

6. Is a Distinct Rule of International Law Governing the Issue Conceivable?

The first point that must be resolved is whether a difference is conceivable between the competence of an agent under municipal law and under international law. The answer would seem to be that there is no theoretical reason why a separate rule of international law should not have developed concerning the competence of agents.[9] Rules con-

[7] See Ross, p. 213, point 2.
[8] Chailley, p. 210.
[9] See also Pallieri, p. 475.

cerning agents affect not only the interests of the principals who are
represented but also those of the third parties with whom the agents
treat.[1] In any community, national or international, the accumulated
third-party interest will exert its influence upon the nascent rules, just
as the accumulated interest of the principals will exert its influence.[2]
No doubt, the fundamental interest of both the principal and the third
parties is that the agent should correctly represent the principal, for
only then may a genuine "meeting of the minds" be possible. In order
to satisfy this common interest, principals and third parties may each
for their part be found to have accustomed themselves to make a reasonable effort, e.g. to examine full powers or make sure that the person
purporting to be an agent is an accredited diplomat or has some other
official status, or threaten with sanctions agents who deviate from
secret instructions.

The relation between the principal and his agent—a matter falling
exclusively under municipal law and determinative of the internal
competence of the agent—is governed by full powers and instructions,
of which the latter may be largely secret. Agreements entered into by
an agent that deviate from full powers or instructions are municipally
ultra vires and presumably will not be municipally valid unless the
principal makes them his own, expressly, or implicitly. A third party
may not, however, be willing to negotiate with an agent if it must bear
the risk that the resultant agreement may be disavowed solely because
the agent has disobeyed secret instructions, which limit his competence
under national law. On the other hand, principals could adapt themselves to sustaining this risk,[3] which, were it to materialize, would force
them to accept as their own an agreement they do not desire, or to pay
damages for refusing to abide by it. Such an accommodation between
principal and third party, if in fact found to be an international
practice, might have matured into a rule of international law. Conversely, alleged principals may be presumed never to accommodate
themselves to running the risk that whoever purports, with a minimal
plausibility, to represent them, actually and faithfully does so; and
third parties may be forced to sustain the burden of establishing that
persons who purport to be agents actually have been commissioned, or

---

[1] See also Ross, p. 207.

[2] Of course, one and the same state represents the interest of a principal on one
occasion and that of the third party on another.

[3] And to guard themselves against it by disciplinary actions against deviations.
See below, p. 85.

at least have official status, or to run the corresponding risk of a repudiation of an agreement should they have neglected so to assure themselves. This alternative adjustment between the interests of the parties might equally in practice have translated itself into a rule of international law.

In summary, it would seem clear that the international competence of an agent need not necessarily equate with his domestic competence. As, it is submitted, the analysis of the relevant practice which follows demonstrates, the interests of principals as well as of third parties have asserted themselves vigorously, and governments have had no difficulty—theoretical or other—in concluding that a difference between external and internal competence is possible. A memorandum submitted by the Government of Luxemburg to the United Nations is in point:

"... les pouvoirs reconnus dans les relations internationales au Chef d'Etat et au Ministre des Affaires Etrangères pour représenter et pour engager l'Etat, sont bien plus étendus que ceux que le droit luxembourgeois reconnaît au Grand-Duc et au Gouvernement."[4]

The rules of positive international law which govern and reflect the process of accommodation between principals and third parties are to be found not in theory but in the practice of states. A first section of the following discussion of practice will be devoted to the competence of foreign ministers, who seem to occupy a special position; a second section will deal with the competence of diplomats, and a third will discuss the competence of other persons employed as agents.

[4] U.N., *Compilation*, p. 78. See also the holding of a United States Circuit Court of Appeal, quoted below, pp. 31–32.

CHAPTER III

THE COMPETENCE OF FOREIGN MINISTERS

1. THE GROWING INTERNAL COMPETENCE OF FOREIGN MINISTERS

Before evidence of the external competence of foreign ministers—*i.e.* their competence under international law—is discussed, it should be noted that their *internal* competence is always wider than that of the diplomatic representatives who are their subordinates. It appears that in several states the foreign minister has express and standing authority of a general kind to enter into agreements falling within the power of the executive branch of the government. Thus in Belgium, it seems that power to enter into certain agreements is permanently delegated from the Head of State to the Foreign Minister.[5] Similarly in England, the Secretary of State for Foreign Affairs and the Permanent Undersecretary of State for Foreign Affairs are respectively reported to hold a general full power from the Monarch, authorizing either of them to negotiate and conclude any treaty in respect of Great Britain and Northern Ireland.[6] In the United States, likewise, the Secretary of State seems to have wide powers in the negotiation and conclusion of executive agreements.[7] This internal authority which may possibly exist in other countries as well, is the result of a real delegation of part of

---

[5] See the following statement in an official Belgian memorandum submitted to the United Nations:

"Le Ministre qualifié pour contresigner les actes du Roi en matière de conclusion de conventions internationales est le Ministre des Affaires Etrangères. Il est admis, en outre, que *ce Ministre a une délégation permanente* du Chef de l'Etat pour agir en ce domaine dans les limites de sa compétence administrative. C'est à ce titre que le Ministre des Affaires Etrangères, de même que les chefs de poste diplomatique, engagent l'Etat envers d'autres Etats étrangers, sous forme de lettres, d'échange de notes et même de conventions qui ne portent que leur signature...": U.N., *Compilation*, p. 16 (emphasis supplied).

[6] *Satow's Guide to Diplomatic Practice* (4th ed. by Bland, 1957), p. 22. See also McNair, *The Law of Treaties* (1938), p. 61, and U.N., *Compilation*, p. 120.

[7] See Department of State, *Department Circular* No. 175, December 13, 1955, sec. 5.1 of which provides:

the treaty-making power, and enables the foreign minister to conclude certain treaties directly rather than as an agent.[8] Such internal competence is certainly not granted in all states,[9] and it cannot be said, therefore, that the municipal order of states universally holds out foreign ministers as competent to bind their states by agreements falling within the power of the executive branch of government. A number of circumstances may nevertheless have combined to bring into existence such a competence under international law.[1]

"Negotiations of new treaties, or new executive agreements on matters of substance, are not to be entered into until authorized in writing by the Secretary or the Under Secretary."

And sec. 5.5:

"...Except as otherwise specifically authorized by the Secretary or the Acting Secretary, a complete text of a treaty or other international agreement shall be delivered to the Secretary or the Acting Secretary, or other person authorized to approve the text, before any such text is agreed upon as final or any date is agreed upon for its signature." (The *Circular* is printed in *A.J.I.L.*, vol. 50 (1956), pp. 784–789.)

In a letter of March 25, 1944, to the Coordinator of Inter-American Affairs regarding procedure for signing supplemental health and sanitation agreements with certain Latin American Republics, the Department of State wrote as follows:

"As you are aware, international agreements can be concluded in the name of the United States Government only by persons who are duly authorized to do so. Such persons must have received full powers from the President in the case of treaties and conventions, or *specific authorization from the Secretary of State in the case of informal agreements such as exchange of notes...*": United States, *Treaty Practice*, pp. 37–38; emphasis supplied.

The memoirs of President Truman provide some instructive reading concerning the relation in practice between the Secretary of State and the President. According to the memoirs, Secretary of State Byrnes, attending the Moscow conference of the foreign ministers of the Great Powers at the end of December 1945, made important foreign policy decisions and signed a protocol without informing, much less consulting the President. Mr. Truman resented such behaviour. The gist of his views on the relation between himself and his Secretary of State would seem to have been that he, the President, remained at all times responsible for all acts of the Secretary, that he should take all basic decisions, and that he should be kept informed of all significant developments. See Truman, *Memoirs* (1955), vol. 1, pp. 545–551, *passim*, and see statement by Mr. Byrnes in the *New York Times,* 4 November 1955.

[8] See Parry, p. 150 and note 3 therein. And see *Report of the International Law Commission Covering its Eleventh Session, 20 April to 26 June 1959* (U.N. Doc. A/CN.4/122), p. 47.

[9] Under Swedish constitutional law and practice the foreign minister is not entitled to bind the state to an agreement without being so authorized by a decision of the King in Council. As to the competence of the Foreign Minister of Poland, under the Constitution of 1952, see Skubiszewski, "Poland's Constitution and the Conclusion of Treaties" in *Jahrbuch für Internationales Recht,* 7 Band, Heft 2/3 (1958), p. 216.

[1] See the quotation from the case of *State of Russia* v. *National City Bank of New York et al.,* below, p. 31. See also Oppenheim (vol. 1, p. 764), who states with

It may be expected, in the first place, that the awareness of such internal competence of the foreign ministers of some states (especially of influential states like Britain and the United States)—and of the possible possession of the same competence in many other states—may have contributed toward a general tendency to regard foreign ministers as competent under international law to bind irrevocably the executive governments of which they are members, and of identifying foreign ministers with the exercise of the treaty-making power of states to such a degree that often no clear border line is drawn in this respect between the formal treaty-making organ and the minister. This seems to be the import of a statement made in a recent official memorandum of the Government of Luxemburg:

"... les Etats étrangers et les organisations internationales attachent toujours foi à l'acte fait par le Chef d'Etat et le Ministre des Affaires Etrangères, sans contrôler si cet acte est régulier au regard du droit interne de l'Etat en cause."[2]

2. Foreign Ministers are not, Generally, Requested to Exhibit Full Powers

It seems to be a settled international practice, furthermore, that a foreign minister signing an agreement not subject to ratification,[3] in his own capital, is never requested to exhibit a full power or other

reference to the foreign minister that "his position at home is regulated by Municipal Law. But International Law defines his position regarding international intercourse with other States." But see Fairman citing Satow, who says that the foreign minister is "the regular intermediary between the state and foreign countries. His functions are regulated by domestic legislation and tradition." Fairman comments: "So he does not have a competence fixed directly by the *jus gentium*". *Op. cit.*, p. 457.

   [2] U.N., *Compilation*, p. 78. See also Guggenheim's opinion, quoted below, p. 34, note 8, and see the statement made in the International Law Commission on 22 June 1950 by Mr. François. U.N. *Doc.* A/CN.4/SR.52, p. 21.

   [3] Where the agreement is subject to ratification, a full power may or may not be issued for the foreign minister. In the practice of the United States, it seems a full power is always issued in these cases. See Hackworth's *Digest*, vol. 5, p. 39. For examples, see *Enabling Instruments of Members of the United Nations*, Part I: *The United States of America* (compiled by Zeydel and Chamberlain, Carnegie Endowment for International Peace, New York, 1951), pp. 114–115.

   A convention on poor relief between Sweden, Denmark, Finland, Iceland, and Norway was signed at Stockholm on 9 January 1951 (*S.Ö.F.* 1951, p. 67). It was in the form of a treaty between the heads of states and the persons signing described themselves as "plenipotentiaries". It was signed by the Swedish Foreign Minister on the part of Sweden. The file at the Foreign Office in Stockholm reveals that all the

evidence of authority given to him.[4] It is doubtful, on the other hand, if even comity precludes a party from making inquiries as to the competence of the minister.[5] The reason for waiving full powers for foreign ministers may perhaps have been that the risk has been thought negligible that a foreign minister should act without a required

agents except the Swedish Foreign Minister deposited formal instruments of full powers.

In order to sign at Copenhagen a convention of 18 November 1946 between Denmark and Sweden on the transfer of labour (*U.N.T.S.,* vol. 7 (1947), p. 251) the Danish Foreign Minister was supplied with a full power to sign (but not to negotiate), subject to ratification. The full power pledged such ratification with regard to all that the plenipotentiary agreed to in conformity with his instructions.

[4] See the Belgian memorandum submitted to the United Nations, stating that in Belgian practice a Full Power from the King is made out for the conclusion of treaties in solemn form—here referring to treaties in which the parties are described as heads of states—but which makes the following reservation: "Toutefois, il est de règle de ne pas exiger de plein pouvoir pour le Ministre des Affaires Etrangères." U.N., *Compilation,* p. 16.

Hackworth cites the instance of a treaty of establishment of 21 November 1936 between Greece and the United States, reciting that the United States Minister to Greece, and the Greek Under Secretary of State for Foreign Affairs had communicated their full powers, while, in fact, the Greek plenipotentiary had not presented any full power, and informed the American Minister that "he had full power by virtue of his position as Permanent Under Secretary and that no document was customary under the circumstances". Quotation from Hackworth's *Digest,* vol. 5, p. 40.

Jones states that "the practice of negotiating without Full Powers is also quite common where a Foreign Secretary, acting in his own capital (in London usually under a General Full Power), negotiates with a foreign envoy:" *Op. cit.,* p. 25.

Exceptions to the practice can no doubt be found. See, for instance, the full power issued for an under-secretary of state for foreign affairs cited below, p. 50, note 9. And see Meissner, *Vollmacht und Ratifikation bei völkerrechtlichen Verträgen nach deutschem Recht* (1934), p. 23.

[5] The only pertinent case found concerning the possibility of inquiring into the competence of a foreign minister gives a negative answer to the question. That case is related below, p. 261. It may nevertheless be convenient to quote in this context, as well, the relevant passage of Moore's account of a report, connected with the case, and given in 1892 by Mr. Foster, Secretary of State of the United States. Single quotation marks signify quotations from the original source:

"Into the authority of the Secretary of State either to give or to withdraw the notice, the British government was 'incompetent to inquire'; it 'could only accept and respect the withdrawal as a fact.' The question of competency, 'being a matter of domestic administration, affecting the internal relations of the executive and legislative powers,' in no wise concerned Great Britain. The raising by her of a question as to 'the authority of the executive power' in the matter, would have constituted 'an unprecedented and inadmissible step in the international relations of governments.'": Moore's *Digest,* vol. 5, p. 170, and *cf. ibid.,* p. 323.

See also Fairman (p. 444), who cites the incident and maintains that "certainly no [such] inquiry would be tolerated".

authorization in a place where he can presumably easily procure one, or exceed his authority where he is able to receive ample advice as to its extent. What the precise practice is regarding foreign ministers concluding agreements abroad is not so easy to ascertain. It seems probable, however, that also on these occasions full powers generally are not requested,[6] especially in view of the fact that it is common for foreign ministers to issue instruments of full powers and ratification.[7] There would, of course, be little point in requesting a foreign minister to issue a full power for himself.[8]

It may be presumed that as a rule evidence of authority is exhibited at the request of, and—it accordingly may be inferred—for the protection of the third parties, and that negligence in this respect must therefore be taken to occur at the risk of the third party. When such "negligence" assumes the character of a consistent practice, however, it can hardly be explained as a reliance *ad hominem*, as a demonstration of

---

[6] Jones demonstrates that, as early as the middle of the 19th century, foreign ministers were regarded as having diplomatic status, and therefore did not need letters of credence when on a mission to a foreign country, though they did require full powers for the conclusion of treaties. *Op. cit.*, p. 36.

From the Philippine case cited below (p. 33), it will appear that the Philippine Foreign Minister signing an agreement in Washington held a formal full power from the President, although the treaty was an informal one. See also below, p. 32, and see the full power for Ribbentrop quoted below, p. 83, note 4. But the Belgian memorandum cited above, p. 29, note 4, indicating that no full powers are used for a foreign minister, does not restrict this statement to refer to his acting in his own capital.

[7] See the letter from the State Department to the Coordinator of Inter-American Affairs quoted above, p. 27, note 7, and the passage on the American practice quoted at p. 51, below. On Soviet full powers signed by the Minister for Foreign Affairs, see below, p. 273, note 7. In Swedish practice, telegraphic full powers signed by the Foreign Minister are a perfectly normal form of evidence of authority to sign agreements which are not concluded solemnly (between heads of states and calling for the procedure of ratification). For the type of telegrams used, see below, p. 51, and see Blix, pp. 376–377 and notes therein.

Meissner (pp. 25 ff.) gives an interesting account of a controversy between the German 'Reichspräsident' and the German Foreign Office concerning the right of the Foreign Minister to issue full powers, a controversy which led to rather precise directives establishing the extent of the Minister's competence to issue full powers.

It is well known among writers that foreign ministers issue full powers. See, for instance, Bittner, p. 117 and Jones, pp. 53 ff.

[8] Hackworth states that it would be useless to request full powers where the President is to sign an agreement with a foreign head of state. *Digest of International Law*, vol. 5, p. 40. See also Jones commenting upon the curious practice at Geneva, where delegations sometimes issued "full powers" for themselves. *Op. cit.*, p. 25.

confidence in the particular foreign minister in question, but rather must rest upon the conviction that evidence of this kind is not needed to obtain the protection of the law.

3. JUDICIAL PRACTICE

Judicial practice confirms the impression gained from the practice of states that under international law a foreign minister by his very position possesses a certain competence to conclude treaties. Two municipal judgments, as well as one of the Permanent Court of International Justice, are of principal interest.

The Litvinoff assignment

In the case of the *State of Russia* v. *National City Bank of New York et al.,*[9] the defendant contended that the so-called Litvinoff assignment was invalid. This assignment, which was an incident of the United States recognition of the Soviet Government, was made in the form of a letter of 16 November 1933, signed by the Foreign Minister of the Soviet Union, Maxim Litvinoff, and addressed to the President of the United States. Litvinoff there declared that the Soviet Government assigned to the Government of the United States amounts found to be due or admitted to be due to the former as the successor of prior governments of Russia, or otherwise, from American nationals, and agreed not to object to the settlements made by the United States with respect to obligations of Russian governments.[1] It does not appear from the letter whether Mr. Litvinoff carried a full power or any other documentary evidence of having been authorized to write the letter on behalf of the Soviet Government. The letter was acknowledged by the President of the United States.[2] With respect to the authority of Litvinoff the United States Second Circuit Court of Appeal held:

" 'While specific powers and duties of a secretary or minister for foreign affairs of a nation are generally prescribed and regulated by the municipal law

[9] 69 F. (2 d) (C.C.A. 2 d 1934). The case is digested in the *Annual Digest,* 1933–1934, pp. 63–65. A comment on the case is to be found in *A.J.I.L.,* vol. 28 (1934), pp. 545–546.

[1] Part of the letter is reproduced in the report of the case in the *Annual Digest.* Original publication in *Establishment of Diplomatic Relations with the Union of Soviet Socialist Republics* (United States, Department of State, Eastern European Series, No. 1 (1933), p. 13).

[2] The assignment came to be recognized as an executive agreement in the United States. See the *Congressional Record,* vol. 78 (11 January 1934), p. 440 (as cited in the *Annual Digest, loc cit.*).

of that nation at home, international law defines his position regarding intercourse with other nations... The minister of foreign affairs in his public
character is the regular political intermediary between the state and foreign
government. He has plenary authority to represent his state at conference and
diplomatic negotiations... If the minister is commissioned to undertake special
negotiations of a public character which require his presence in a foreign
jurisdiction, he must and usually is furnished with powers to negotiate. The
powers may be embodied either in an ordinary letter of credence or in special
letters patent. These powers within reasonable limits define the authority for
his acts, which acts will be binding upon his government...'

" 'As to the authority of Foreign Commissar Litvinoff to make the assignment
on behalf of his government, there is a presumption of authority in his designation, recognition, and the President's acceptance of the assignment. It is a
matter of political action in foreign affairs, and the question of who represents
and acts for a sovereign or nation in its relation to the United States is determined, not by the Judicial Department, but exclusively by the political branch
of the government.' "[3]

Though the last sentence quoted seems to imply that anyone whose
authority might have been found satisfactory by the State Department
would also have been considered competent by the Court, and, that,
therefore, the discussion of the Court of the competence of a foreign
minister constitutes an *obiter dictum,* the views of this high tribunal
nevertheless are of course entitled to respect. The first point that
emerges is the opinion of the Court that a foreign minister negotiating
abroad needs special authorization for the purpose. Second, if his
authorization should be laid down in a document ("the powers *may* be
embodied"), the formulation of this instrument determines the competence under international law of the minister. The interesting
qualification "within reasonable limits" may perhaps refer to limits
resulting from an application of the principle of good faith. Third,
acts falling within his competence thus determined are binding upon
his state under international law. Finally, without citing any documentary evidence of the authority of the minister concerned—letter of
credence or special letters patent—the Court found that his designation,
his recognition, and the American acceptance of the assignment raised
a presumption of authority.

Philippine case

A similar tendency may be seen in the judgment of a Philippine
court in the case of *USAFFE* (United States Army Forces Far East)

[3] Quoted from the *Annual Digest, loc. cit.*

Veterans Association, Inc. v. *The Treasurer of the Philippines.*[4] The plaintiffs had contended that an agreement signed at Washington on 6 November 1950[5] by Carlos Romulo, Secretary of Foreign Affairs of the Philippines on behalf of the Philippines, and John Snyder, United States Secretary of the Treasury, on behalf of the United States, did not have the character of an executive agreement, among other reasons because Secretary Romulo had had no written authority from the President to sign the agreement. Rejecting this argument and holding the compact to be a valid and binding executive agreement, the court said *inter alia*:

"...the court knows of no law, international or municipal, which requires that the representatives of a State negotiating and signing an international agreement must have the written authority to negotiate and sign. There is even authority holding that an international agreement to be binding need not be written...

"If an international agreement to be binding need not be reduced to writing, with stronger reason the authority of the agent who negotiates or signs an international agreement need not be in writing to render that agreement binding."[6]

In the case before it, the court found that Secretary Romulo, although lacking written authority, had had sufficient powers. The court stated specifically that there was a presumption—which the plaintiffs had not even attempted to overcome—that Secretary Romulo had been authorized to sign. This presumption arose under Sec. 69 (1), Rule 123, Rules of Court, reading:

"*Disputable Presumptions.*—The following presumptions are satisfactory if uncontradicted, but may be contradicted and overcome by other evidence:

(a) ...

(1) That a person acting in a public office was regularly appointed or elected to it;

(m) That official duty has been regularly performed;"[7]

In addition, the court found it proved—by exhibits—that President Quirino of the Philippines had cabled Secretary Romulo full powers to sign the agreement.

[4] Philippines, Court of First Instance of Manila. Civil Case No. 24277. Judgment of 5 January 1956. Report in *A.J.I.L.*, vol. 50 (1956), pp. 686–689.

[5] See *United States Treaties and Other International Agreements*, vol. 1 (1950), p. 765 (*T.I.A.S.*, 2151).

[6] Report in *loc. cit.*, p. 688.

[7] Moran, *Comments on the Rules of Court*, vol. III (2nd rev. ed., Manila, 1949).

It should be noted, with respect to the presumptions referred to that in neither of the foregoing cases did a contracting state contest the authority of its representative. The disputes arose under the domestic laws of the United States and the Philippines, and in both cases the presumption probably was primarily conceived of as operating between private parties. In such cases, it is no doubt reasonable that the party asserting that an act by an official is *ultra vires* should bear the burden of proof in establishing that contention. It is not impossible that the presumption—at least in the State of Russia case—was equally designed to operate vis-à-vis foreign governments, more particularly between the parties to the agreements. To be meaningful in this connexion, however, and to afford protection against disavowals made in bad faith by the other party, the evidence permitted in rebuttal of the presumption must be limited to such circumstances as were perceptible to both parties at the time when the presumption arose. That is to say, unless special evidence reveals the lack of competence of a foreign minister, who purports to be authorized to bind his state, the representatives of other states may feel confident that international law accords binding force to an agreement signed by a foreign minister.[8]

Eastern Greenland case

The third, and most important, case is that of *Eastern Greenland*, decided by the Permanent Court of International Justice in 1933.[9] One of the issues before the Court in this famous case turned upon the legal effect of an oral declaration made by the Norwegian Foreign Minister, Mr. Ihlen. The circumstances were as follows: In 1919, the Danish Government was anxious that the sovereignty of Denmark over Greenland should be universally recognized. Several foreign governments accordingly were approached by Danish diplomatic agents.[1] Thus it was that on 14 July 1919 the Danish Minister to Oslo called on the Norwegian Foreign Minister, Mr. Ihlen, and assured him that at a

---

[8] This would seem to be the stand taken by Guggenheim, who states: "Eine widerlegbare Vermutung für die Kompetenz zum Abschluss völkerrechtlicher Verträge besteht zugunsten des Staatsoberhauptes und des Ministers des Äussern . . .: "*Lehrbuch des Völkerrechts,* vol. I, p. 61. See also Rousseau who explains the binding force of agreements in simplified form by "la présomption de légalité qui s'attache aux actes accomplis par un organe étatique—ici l'organe exécutif—dans les limites de sa compétence *fonctionelle*". (Emphasis supplied.) *Principes généraux du droit international public* (Paris, 1944), vol. I, p. 258.

[9] *P.C.I.J.,* Ser. A/B, No. 53, Judgment of 5 April 1933.

[1] *Ibid.,* pp. 56 ff. *Cf. Ibid.,* Ser. C, No. 62, pp. 40 ff.

forthcoming conference Denmark would raise no objections to the Norwegian claims to sovereignty over Spitzbergen. He equally expressed the hope that Norway would make no difficulty with regard to the Danish claim to Eastern Greenland. On this occasion Mr. Ihlen merely replied that the question would be considered.[2] Eight days later, on 22 July, after having informed his colleagues in the Norwegian Cabinet of his conversation, Mr. Ihlen told the Danish Minister that "the Norwegian Government would not make any difficulties in the settlement of this question", and this statement was recorded in minutes.[3]

The Norwegian Government contended before the court that, to conform with Norwegian constitutional law and standing instructions for the Government, the declaration—if binding—ought to have been deliberated by the King in Council.[4] Since this formality had not been observed, the declaration was one made in excess of the constitutional authority of the minister, and invalid internationally. The Danish Government maintained that Mr. Ihlen was invested with the necessary constitutional authority to give the said declaration of recognition, and that he, even if this had not been so, had the necessary powers in international law.[5] In an oft-quoted passage the Court said:

"The Court considers it beyond all dispute that a reply of this nature given by the Minister for Foreign Affairs on behalf of his government in response to a request by the diplomatic representative of a foreign Power, in regard to a question falling within his province, is binding upon the country to which the Minister belongs."[6]

A passage in the dissenting opinion of Judge Anzilotti is quoted almost as often:

"... it must be recognized that the constant and general practice of States has been to invest the Minister for Foreign Affairs—the direct agent of the

---

[2] *Ibid.*, Ser. A/B, No. 53, p. 57. *Cf. ibid.*, p. 70.

[3] *Ibid.*

It is stated, in a recent biography of Mr. Ihlen that his declaration was given not only with the prior unanimous consent of the cabinet, but also without opposition from any member of the foreign relations committee—Utenrikskomiteteen—of the Norwegian Parliament—the Storting. In this committee, where the political parties were represented by their foremost members, Mr. Ihlen is reported by his biographer to have said, indeed, that he wished to declare "openly and honestly that he had the same feeling as President Castberg [President of the Storting] that it was not altogether agreeable to give away Greenland. But we cannot make difficulties vis-à-vis Denmark." See Fasting, K., *Nils Claus Ihlen* (Oslo, 1955), p. 356.

[4] *P.C.I.J.*, Ser. C, No. 62, pp. 566–568 (Norwegian counter-memorial).

[5] *Ibid.*, Ser. C, No. 66, pp. 2761–2762 (Danish oral statement).

[6] *Ibid.*, Ser A/B, No. 53, p. 71.

chief of the State—with authority to make statements on current affairs to foreign diplomatic representatives, and in particular to inform them as to the attitude which the government, in whose name he speaks, will adopt in a given question. Declarations of this kind are binding upon the State."[7]

The Court thus declared that, in its view, the question was "beyond all dispute". If its view was advanced as a rendering of the law of the matter, it was an exaggerated one. Not even the decision of the Court, unfortunately, put the matter beyond dispute. In fact, widely differing interpretations have been given to this holding of the Court.[8] On the one hand, it has been used as authority for the view that a foreign minister has unlimited authority to bind his state.[9] On the other, its formulation has been thought to be so qualified that the value of the case has been seen not in the decision, but in Denmark's accepting the contention that constitutional requirements are relevant internationally.[1]

The first question to determine is whether the decision is at all relevant in the law of treaties. Since the majority spoke of "a reply of this nature", and Anzilotti referred to "declarations of this kind", it may be possible to suggest—as Mervyn Jones does[2]—that the answer to this question is in the negative. In view of the circumstances, however, such an interpretation seems unnecessarily restrained. The parties had devoted lengthy arguments to the matter, and though neither of them admitted the declaration to be a treaty, both of them seem to have assumed that the law of treaties was relevant to it. It seems likely that the Court intended to settle the question by its decision.[3] The borderline between "a reply of this nature"—so formal as to be embodied in minutes and given with the knowledge that a *quid pro quo* would follow—and some treaties in simplified form, like exchanges of notes, or agreed minutes, if at all existent, is very difficult to establish, and

---

[7] *Ibid.,* p. 91.

[8] See Hambro, "Gjensyn med Ihlen Erklaeringen" in *Nordisk Tidskrift for International Ret,* vol. 26 (1956), pp. 36–47. An English translation of the article entitled "The Ihlen Declaration revisited" is found in *Fundamental Problems of International Law,* Festschrift für Jean Spiropoulos (ed. by Constantopoulos, Eustathiades and Fragistas, 1957), pp. 227–236.

[9] Schwarzenberger, *A Manual of International Law* (3rd ed., 1952), p. 39; and the same, *International Law,* vol. 1 (3rd ed., 1957), p. 158.

[1] Jones, p. 148. This view has been critized by Cheng, *General Principles of Law* (London, 1953), p. 199, note 24.

[2] Jones, p. 148.

[3] *Cf.* Hambro, p. 44.

rules applying to one category may with good reason apply to the other. Finally, it would be strange if international law enabled a foreign minister to do by "a reply of this nature" what he could not do by an informal agreement such as an exchange of notes.[4] For these reasons, it is not far-fetched to assume that the pronouncements of the majority of the Court and of Judge Anzilotti are relevant to the law concerning treaties in simplified form.

It is not believed, on the other hand, that the Court took any position in the doctrinal controversy over the possible need under international law of a constitutionally required parliamentary assent. That controversy was simply not at issue in the case.[5] It was not contended on behalf of Norway that the consent of the Norwegian "Storting" would have been required, and it was indeed expressly recognized by Denmark that such constitutional provisions as require the assent of a legislature for the conclusion of a treaty are relevant under international law.[6] It may be concluded, therefore, that the decision does not provide any authority on this question. The error which Norway submitted had been made under Norwegian law—if the declaration had been designed to be binding—merely concerned a formality. Mr. Ihlen had "informed" his colleagues in the Cabinet of the matter, but he had not submitted the question to the formal decision of the King in Council. Though Denmark attempted to prove that that procedure had not been required even under the internal Norwegian regulations, it asserted emphatically that such a formality was irrelevant internationally.[7] The decision of the Court would seem to have sustained the Danish argument.

Though it is true, as Fairman remarks,[8] that the Court did not indicate what it meant by "a question falling within his province", it has been demonstrated that it could hardly have been just any matter concerning foreign affairs, for such matters as were subjected to the

---

[4] See also Schwarzenberger, *International Law,* vol. 1 (3rd ed., 1957), p. 429.

[5] *P.C.I.J.,* Ser. C, No. 63, p. 877.

[6] *Ibid.,* p. 880.

[7] *Ibid.,* pp. 878–889. At p. 880, the following statement is found:

"Il n'y a aucun doute que, d'après la conception du droit international existante, le ministre des Affaires étrangères d'un pays est légitimé pour exprimer d'une manière obligatoire la volonté de son gouvernement à l'égard d'autres pays et attester avec force obligatoire qu'une déclaration de volonté valable a été donnée par son gouvernement. L'autre Partie contractante ne saurait être tenue à rechercher si certaines pratiques de pure forme d'une espèce ou d'une autre, mais appartenant au droit interne, ont été observées ou non."

[8] Fairman, p. 458.

assent of the "Storting" were not at issue. On the other hand, however, the Court could not very well have referred only to matters which under Norwegian law and standing instructions the Foreign Minister was entitled to settle without a formal decision by the King in Council. In the proceedings before the court, the parties discussed in great detail, and disagreed, on the interpretation of various internal provisions regulating Mr. Ihlen's competence. It seems inconceivable that by the expression "within his province" the court could have intended to settle the arguments of the parties on this point, whereas the interpretation is perfectly plausible that the court sought to avoid taking any position on an extremely subtle question of municipal law, and decided that, whether or not Mr. Ihlen had been acting in conformity with the Norwegian provisions, he was at any rate acting within his competence under international law.[9]

It is submitted that the court supplied an excellent description of the most important channel for the informal settlement of matters arising between states, and that the court wanted to protect the reliability of that channel. In accordance with the above discussion, it is further submitted that the decision is authority for the proposition that by his position a foreign minister is competent under international law to bind his state by agreements concerning matters "generally settled by arrangement between foreign secretary and diplomatic agent",[1] but that the court took no position in the controversy over the international relevance of constitutional provisions requiring legislative assent, or countersignature or forbidding the conclusion of certain types of treaties.

[9] But see the following statement made in the comment to Article 21 of the Harvard Draft on the Law of Treaties: "Apparently, if the Court had been convinced that the Norwegian Minister for Foreign Affairs had not been competent to make the declaration of July 22, it would not have held the declaration to be binding on Norway:" *A.J.I.L.*, vol. 29 (1935), *Suppl.*, p. 1007. The statement is cited by Hyde, vol. 2, p. 1385, note 5. Hambro, as well, does not exclude the possibility of this interpretation. *Op. cit.*, p. 46.

[1] See Fairman's conclusion on the competence of foreign ministers quoted below, p. 39. Though the first impression gained from Hambro's article cited above (p. 36, note 8) is that he criticizes the court, a more careful reading reveals that his criticism is directed primarily to various interpretations which he finds unwarranted. Professor Hambro himself reaches the conclusion that presumably the import of the declaration is that a state may be bound by oral agreements, provided that there is no obstacle to this in the constitution of the state. That interpretation leaves open the question concerning the relevance under international law of standing instructions, regulations etc.

4. OPINIONS OF WRITERS

Few writers have dealt specifically with the question of the competence of foreign ministers to conclude treaties on behalf of the governments to which they belong. Referring to non-ratified "inter-governmental agreements", by which he means agreements whose formal parties are not heads of states,[2] Mervyn Jones states, however, that "the validity of such agreements depends entirely on the authority of the person by whom they were signed. If they are signed by the Minister of Foreign Affairs their validity is indisputable."[3] In another context, the same writer maintains that foreign secretaries "must certainly be regarded as having the necessary authority *ipso jure* to bind their governments by international agreements."[4] Since Mervyn Jones does not believe that agreements entered into by a head of state in violation of a constitution are valid under international law,[5] it may be assumed that his statements are not intended to suggest that a foreign minister has the power to bind his state in violation of the constitution.

Guggenheim maintains that there exists a rebuttable presumption in favour of the competence of the head of state and the foreign minister to conclude treaties, and that, therefore, other parties need not closely scrutinize their authority.[6] Though Guggenheim has in mind constitutional competence, his statement must apply with even greater force to the competence of the foreign minister in relation to the treaty-making organ of the state.

After a careful study of the problem, Fairman reached the following cautious conclusion:

"The position, [then], with regard to agreements made by foreign ministers and diplomatic agents seems to be as follows: In principle, international law leaves it to each state to fix the competence of these representatives. An undertaking given in disregard of limitations disclosed or otherwise known does not bind. Limitations found to have been notorious might be deemed to have been known. In practice, certain matters are so generally settled by arrangement between foreign secretary and diplomatic agent that for a state to constitute such officers would seem to amount to a representation (in the absence of notice to the contrary) that they are authorized to dispose of matters customarily settled by that channel."[7]

[2] Jones, p. 53.
[3] *Ibid.*, p. 157.
[4] *Ibid.*, p. 65.
[5] *Ibid.*, p. 135.
[6] Guggenheim, vol. 1, p. 61. See also p. 34, note 8, above.
[7] Fairman, p. 459.

Reference may also be made to Cohn, who held that an agreement concluded by a foreign minister without authorization or in excess of an authorization binds his state, provided that his act does not amount to an infraction of the constitution, especially provisions regarding the competence of the head of state.[8] Sir Gerald Fitzmaurice, finally, has recently suggested that the Head of State, the Prime Minister, and the Minister of Foreign Affairs possess inherent capacity to bind the State by virtue of their offices, and the International Law Commission has tentatively accepted that position.[9]

5. Conclusion

It is fortunate, of course, that not more diplomatic incidents or court cases have arisen over the matter under discussion, but the paucity of accessible material bearing on the question makes it somewhat difficult to deduce an authoritative rule. The practice and cases compiled and analyzed above nevertheless seem to reflect a definite tendency, a tendency which has been translated into an outline of a rule by the writers discussed. This tendency and its present effects seem to be the following: With respect to the conclusion of treaties, the internal competence of the foreign minister is increasingly identified with that of the head of state (as the presumed constitutional executive treaty-making organ). This development cannot be said, however, to have led to the creation of a rule of international law to the effect that binding force is accorded to any agreement entered into by a foreign minister, provided only that it would have been binding if concluded by the head of state (or other treaty-making organ). The rule seems to have emerged in practice, however, and to have received the support of some writers, that at present, by his very position, in which no full power is required, a foreign minister is competent under international law—unless there is evidence in the particular case to the effect that municipally he is *not* competent, or this is known to the other party—to bind his state by an agreement falling within the treaty-making power of the executive branch of the government, and especially thus to bind his state by an

[8] Cohn, "La théorie de la responsabilité internationale", *Recueil des Cours*, 1939, vol. 2, pp. 286–287.

[9] Fitzmaurice, *Report on the Law of Treaties* (U.N. Doc. A/CN.4/ 106, 14 March 1956), p. 27; *Report of the International Law Commission Covering the Work of its Eleventh Session, 20 April to 26 June 1959* (U.N. Doc. A/CN.4/122), pp. 46–47.

agreement reached in his own capital with the accredited representative of a foreign state on a matter customarily settled through diplomatic channel. It seems justified, finally, to suggest that the scope of this rule extends to acting foreign ministers and assistant foreign ministers as well.[1]

[1] See above, p. 27, note 7, and p. 29, note 4.

CHAPTER IV

THE COMPETENCE OF DIPLOMATS: PRELIMINARY REMARKS

While the increasing domestic competence of foreign ministers in the conclusion of treaties has been found above to have contributed to giving them a relatively wide treaty-making competence under international law by their very position, the same circumstance does not influence the international competence of diplomatic agents. It has been shown that there is disagreement among writers as to the latitude of the municipal competence of diplomatic envoys who sign treaties which become binding upon their signature. While Bittner contended that they merely act as notaries, as proxies for the treaty-making organ, and sign instruments which have already been approved in each and every detail by their principals, Chailley maintained that they possessed by delegation some latitude of power.[2] It suffices to say that it seems probable that, with respect to the negotiation of the draft of an agreement, the instructions of diplomats generally afford some latitude of power: the negotiators are informed of the aim of the negotiations, and perhaps of a minimum result which might be acceptable.[3] Authority to negotiate, however, is not the same as authority to express the binding consent of the state.[4] It may be presumed that normally authoriza-

---

[2] See above, p. 23.

[3] Stewart (p. 231) reports that the amount of discretion entrusted to a United Kingdom plenipotentiary may vary in each case.

[4] A memorandum of 10 October 1947 by the Assistant for Treaty Affairs in the United States State Department, Mr. Barron, reads in part:

"Authority to negotiate an agreement is not *per se* authority to sign the agreement which is negotiated. Thus, the agreement on petroleum with the United Kingdom was signed for the United States on August 8, 1944 by Mr. Edward R. Stettinius, Acting Secretary of State, rather than by the Secretary of the Interior, Acting Chairman of the Cabinet committee appointed by the President to negotiate the agreement:" United States, *Treaty Practice*, pp. 37–38.

See also a memorandum submitted to the United Nations by the Government of Luxemburg and stating, *inter alia*, that "le simple mandat de négocier (qui ne comporte pas le pouvoir de signer) est délivré dans une forme quelconque...": U.N., *Compilation*, p. 80.

tion to sign or otherwise to express final consent contains much less leeway, if any, than authorization to negotiate. However that may be—and the matter will be discussed later in this section[5]—it is certain that under the municipal law of all states, diplomats need express authorization from their governments in order to give the final consent of the state to an international agreement.[6] There does not seem to be any disagreement on this point, though Bittner chooses to speak of a "Beurkundungsauftrag" and Chailley, somewhat loosely, refers to a delegation.

It is true that in the past some diplomats have been supplied with very wide powers for the conclusion of treaties in various contingencies, and some diplomats have had the power under general instructions issued in their country to conclude treaties in emergencies,[7] but in both of these cases the powers were conferred subject to ratification. To the extent that real delegation of a general and standing character, to conclude binding agreements within some specific area, as distinguished from *ad hoc* delegation in a particular case, has taken or takes place the matter should be treated in connexion with a discussion of interdepartmental agreements.[8] The latitude of power that agreement subject to approval may entail is not under discussion here, but a possible latitude of power, e.g. that of giving an authoritative interpretation of some clause or of consenting to an additional protocol, in connexion with an authorization to express the final consent of a state by exchanging instruments of ratification or notes of approval, is germane to the topic under discussion.

As it is certain that, but for exceptional circumstances, a diplomat needs a special authorization in the case of each agreement to be mu-

---

[5] See below, pp. 67 ff.

[6] On this requirement in American practice, see p. 27, note 7, above. As to the practice of the United Kingdom:

"His Majesty's representatives abroad receive a separate full power for each treaty to be signed in respect of the United Kingdom except where a subsidiary instrument on the same subject is to be signed at or about the same time, in which case the one full power suffices for the signature of both instruments." Stewart, pp. 230–231.

[7] Crandall quotes Sec. 243 of the standing instructions of 1897 to diplomatic officers of the United States. It reads:

"In case of urgent need a written international compact between a diplomatic representative of the United States and a foreign government may be made in the absence of specific instructions or powers. In such cases it is preferable to give the instrument the form of a simple protocol, and it should be expressly stated in the instrument that it is signed subject to the approval of the signer's Government." *Treaties, Their Making and Enforcement* (2nd ed., Washington, 1916), p. 93. *Cf.* Moore's *Digest,* vol. 5, p. 179.

[8] Such discussion is outside the scope of the present inquiry. For some remarks on the subject, see above, p 20.

nicipally competent to express the consent of his state, it may well be asked whether such authorization—or rather evidence of it—is required also to make him competent under international law. It will be considered first if under international law the very existence of such authorization is relevant, and, then, if the precise extent of the authorization is relevant.[9] To put it differently, the first part of the inquiry will concern the question what is the effect, if any, under international law of an agreement concluded by a diplomat who has no internal authorization to sign any agreement whatever, or, only to sign an agreement with a different party or on another topic than that which he has chosen. Should it be found that such agreement would be invalid, a second part of the inquiry will deal with the effect, if any, under international law, of an agreement—or part of an agreement— concluded by a diplomat who has been municipally authorized to express consent to an agreement of the type in question, but who has acted in violation of instructions in some consequential respect.

[9] This distinction is made, with respect to constitutional competence, by Ross, p. 204. See also *Harvard Research*, p. 992.

Chapter V

THE COMPETENCE OF DIPLOMATS: RELEVANCE OF THE EXISTENCE OF MUNICIPAL AUTHORIZATION

1. References in Agreements to Municipal Authorization

While it is rare that agreements binding upon signature make any express reference to full powers having been exchanged, most agreements in simplified form refer to the agents signing as "duly authorized" or "duly empowered"; and exchanges of notes often refer to the issuer as acting upon instructions. Undoubtedly this practice demonstrates at least what has already been stated above, namely, that those who sign need municipal authorization from their principals. It may be asked, however, why these expressions are included in the texts of treaties, and, more particularly, if their inclusion is evidence of any need under international law of the authorizations referred to. There does not seem to be any simple answer to these questions. On the one hand, the recording in an agreement that the person signing has authority to do so must indicate at least that the parties have shown some concern for the question. If the authorizations were a matter exclusively of domestic interest to either party it would be difficult to understand why such expressions appear. On the other hand, they do not—as does the phrase "the plenipotentiaries having exchanged their full powers", often used in treaties subject to ratification—demonstrate that the parties have been so concerned that they have confirmed the evidence of the other's authority. The expressions used do indicate, of course, just like the signatures of the agents, that the agents have purported to be authorized. It is logically inconceivable, however, that the agents should become internationally competent by the insertion of these words, if they did not possess the same competence without the inclusion of the phrase.[1] If, as Bittner maintains,[2] their international

---

[1] But Genet considers absence of a reference to the authority by which the agents have been acting as a 'véritable vice de forme', curable only by ratification. See *Traité de Diplomatie et de Droit Diplomatique* (Paris, 1932), vol. 3, p. 413.

[2] Bittner, p. 72.

competence is independent of any documentary evidence, it must flow, as he consistently concludes, from their position as accredited representatives. It does not seem safe, on the other hand, to conclude—as does Basdevant[3]—that the absence in a few agreements of any reference to authorization or full powers indicates that the persons signing have possessed the power by their position to sign.[4] Even if these phrases were lacking in all these agreements, the above conclusion would not follow, were the parties *in fact* to exchange or exhibit evidence of authorization.

2. Consistent Use of Evidence of Municipal Authorization would point to its International Relevance

While it must be admitted that the phraseology of agreements in simplified form gives no sure indication of the international competence of the agents, it may be expected that an inquiry into the use of evidence of authorization for these agreements would prove more conclusive. If it could be shown, indeed, that before or when the final consent of a state to an agreement is expressed by an accredited diplomat, the other party always or almost invariably requests the foreign envoy to prove that he has been authorized by his government, this would be a strong indication that a party neglecting to demand evidence of municipal authorization would do so in response to considerations of politics or personality rather than law. If an envoy whose powers have not been examined should be disavowed, the agreement would not be binding. Could it be demonstrated, on the other hand, that accredited diplomats are hardly ever required to give evidence of their having been municipally authorized to consent to an agreement, this would tend to support the conclusion that—like foreign ministers—their position, as Bittner holds,[5] is enough to enable the other party to assume that the agreement is valid under international law, whatever was the competence of the agent under his domestic law.

An extensive and authoritative inquiry which would establish whether or not it is a practice to demand evidence of special authority, such

---

[3] Basdevant, pp. 618–620.

[4] Vitta, p. 79. Exceptionally the practice of inserting a reference to an authorization may be constitutionally required. To this effect, see the memorandum submitted by Thailand to the United Nations, in U.N., *Compilation,* pp. 102–103.

[5] Bittner, p. 72.

as full powers or letters of authorization,[6] for the conclusion of agreements in simplified form, is very difficult to make and it will, for our purposes, be necessary to limit examination to evidence given by writers and various other sources as to what is the practice of states in this regard.

To start with, there is the contention made by Bittner that it is even a customary rule that diplomats are not required to give evidence of their "Beurkundungsauftrag":

> "Die Vollmachten werden dem Vertragsgegner stets vollinhaltlich mitgeteilt und ihre Prüfung und Austausch in den Unterhändlerurkunden eigens festgestellt. Beim Beurkundungsauftrag findet etwas derartiges nicht statt. Er wird als rein interner Akt behandelt, von dem der Vertragsgegner entweder gar nicht oder eben nur durch eine Erwähnung in der Urkunde des Ministers Kenntnis in beglaubigter Form erhält."[7]

In another context, the same writer states:

> "Es ist gewohnheitsrechtlich festgestellt, dass die Vertragsparteien bei derartigen Vertragsschliessungen voneinander keinen Nachweis über den Beurkundungsauftrag verlangen, wie etwa bei der Führung von Vertragsverhandlungen durch bevollmächtigte Unterhändler die Vorlage der Vollmachten verlangt wird."[8]

It appears certain that if the above statements were apt at the time they were made, which is doubtful, the practice of states no longer justifies such categorical conclusions. A rigid distinction between full powers which are issued and exhibited or exchanged at the conclusion of treaties which are to be ratified, and, "authorizations" which constitute national instructions to sign, is simply not upheld in practice. While Bittner maintained that special documents embodying full powers were always or practically always issued for treaties requiring ratification, other writers have cited a sufficient number of instances in which full powers have been dispensed with to permit the conclusion

---

[6] Bittner would object to the use of the term full power in connexion with agreemens binding upon signature. 'Letters of authorization' might be a suitable English expression for the evidence issued of what Bittner terms a 'Beurkundungsauftrag'. While it might be possible as a matter of form to distinguish between the two types of instruments, they appear to be used interchangeably in the conclusion of treaties subject to ratification and agreements which enter into force upon signature. See Jones, p. 54; Basdevant, p. 618; and see below, p. 51. See also Blix, pp. 376–377.

[7] Bittner, p. 48.

[8] *Ibid.*, p. 72.

that the practice of states is not consistent on this point. Thus, both
Dunn and Satow refer to multilateral conventions, drafted and signed
at conferences, at which the diplomats participating and accredited at
the place of the conference were not requested to exhibit full powers.[9]
It is no doubt still frequently true, on the other hand, that treaties
providing for ratification have also been signed by representatives
who have exchanged or exhibited full powers.[1] For treaties concluded
under the auspices of the United Nations, the Secretariat of the Organization seems to assure the maintenance of this practice.[2]

It is tempting in the case of many treaties to explain the use of the
procedure of ratification, and of formal full powers as well, by reference
to a desire for solemnity.[3] When formal full powers are dispensed with
at the conclusion of a treaty requiring ratification, the reason may
simply be that the parties did not trouble to include this element of
solemnity. It should be noted, however, that while the large volume of
international transactions has given rise to a general tendency toward
simplification of procedure, treaties which are still concluded in solemn
form are often, though by no means always, such that the parties attach
great importance to them. Solemnity may in these cases be considered
as another aspect of elaborate and cautious procedure. Formal full
powers issued for the signature of a treaty which is to be ratified need
not, therefore, be purely ceremonial, although it is difficult to see how
they could be of any profound importance.

[9] Dunn, *The Practice and Procedure of International Conferences* (1929), pp. 90,
105, 205–206, Satow, *A Guide to Diplomatic Practice* (2nd ed., 1922), vol. 2, pp. 149,
153, 163.

[1] Apparently this is a consistent practice in the United States: "It is the invariable
practice, in the case of an international agreement of the United States deemed to be
a treaty in the constitutional sense, to issue a Full Power authorizing the United
States Plenipotentiary to sign." Memorandum approved by the State Department and
included in U.N., *Compilation,* p. 126. To the same effect, see Hackworth's *Digest,*
vol. 5, p. 39.

[2] With respect to the practice of the United Nations, see Leriche, "L'évolution récente de la société internationale et les traités multilatéraux" in *Revue de droit
international, de sciences diplomatiques et politiques,* vol. 29 (1951), p. 35. And see
*Notes on the practice of the United Nations Secretariat in relation to certain ques-
tions raised in connection with the articles of the Law of Treaties* (U.N. *Doc.*
A/CN.4/121, 23 June 1959). See also below, p. 71, note 5.

[3] In the case of many other treaties, ratification is admittedly not only a question
of confirmation, but a matter subjected to comprehensive consideration, notably when
politically important treaties are submitted to legislatures, or a convention signed
by technical experts is submitted for approval of political authorities. See Dunn,
op. cit., p. 172.

For the conclusion of agreements not subject to ratification, there is no reason why full powers should be used to augment the element of solemnity, but here caution could be expected to induce states to use and request full powers or letters of authorization unless they feel absolutely confident that they are not needed to obtain the protection of the law. Bittner, who possessed an impressive knowledge of the practice of states, maintained firmly that full powers were never used in these cases. Though it is possible that a good many of these agreements become binding by the acts of agents exhibiting no evidence of their authorization, it is impossible to subscribe to the contention that the practice of states is consistent in this matter. On the basis of a careful study of the practice of states, especially that of the United Kingdom, Mervyn Jones states, with reference to inter-governmental agreements, by which he means agreements the formal subjects of which are governments rather than heads of states, and which may be subject to ratification but frequently enter into force by signature:

"The practice relating to inter-governmental agreements is certainly less formal than that adopted with regard to agreements taking the form of the traditional treaty between heads of States. They may recite the issue of 'Full Powers', they may refer to 'due authorization', or they may be merely made 'in the name of the respective governments', and 'as a temporary arrangement' without any reference to authorization. But, as a rule, evidence of authority is required in accordance with the traditional standards, though the form of such evidence may differ from that customarily used in the negotiation of the traditional type of treaty."[4]

Judge Read who gained the impression from Canadian practice that, when agreements were concluded in the form of exchanges of notes, full powers were usually dispensed with, reached a conclusion similar to that of Mervyn Jones with regard to other inter-governmental agreements:

"When an international agreement has been negotiated, in point of form, between governments, the Full Power is a much simpler matter. The only formal requirement is a written authority, signed by the Secretary of State for External Affairs. It may, but need not necessarily, include his seal or the seal of the department."[5]

In a recent work on diplomatic practice, it is similarly reported that a diplomatic agent to whom a negotiation is entrusted for the conclusion of a treaty "requires as a general rule a special authorisation, called a

---

[4] Jones, p. 54.
[5] Read, "International Agreements" in *Canadian Bar Review,* vol. 26 (1948), p. 524.

full power". Agreements made in the form of exchanges of notes, however, are reported to constitute an exception to this rule, and to be
normally concluded without any prior exhibit of full powers.[6]

A member of the legal department of the United Nations significantly
has reported that the importance of full powers is appreciated at the
United Nations in connexion with the conclusion of treaties to which
states may become parties by signature without reserving subsequent
"acceptance". With reference to this procedure, he states:

> "Elle signifie tout d'abord que le plénipotentiaire muni de pouvoirs à cet
> effet va pouvoir lier définitivement son gouvernement en signant l'accord sans
> réserve d'acceptation ultérieur. Cela permet de mesurer l'importance des pleins
> pouvoirs en une telle hyphotèse. Ils deviennent un élément juridique de la
> validité du traité. C'est un retour apparent à la pratique du pouvoir mandat."[7]

Further on Mr. Leriche reports on the practical consequences:

> "Lors de la cérémonie de la signature, le Secrétaire général vérifie si les
> pleins pouvoirs des plénipotentiaires sont en bonne et due forme, notamment
> s'ils émanent d'une autorité compétente, s'ils se réfèrent à l'Accord intéressé,
> s'ils contiennent une clause prévoyant une ratification ultérieure, etc. Ce
> dernier point est d'autant plus important aujourd'hui que nous avons vu que
> certains Accords permettent aux Gouvernements de se lier définitivement par
> la signature et que certains autres n'admettent même pas une signature ad re-
> ferendum."[8]

An examination undertaken of a number of agreements concluded
by the Swedish Government with various other governments, and entering into force upon signature by agents, revealed instances where formal
instruments described as "full powers" had been used.[9] It also appeared

[6] *Satow's Guide to Diplomatic Practice* (4th ed. by Bland, 1957), pp. 82 and 341.
[7] Leriche, p. 26.
[8] *Ibid.*, p. 35.
[9] An air transport agreement between the Swedish Government and the Provisional
Government of France was signed at Paris on 2 August 1946 (*U.N.T.S.*, vol. 27 (1949),
p. 251). It stipulated expressly that it was to enter into force upon signature, and
the agents signing referred to themselves as being "duly authorized". A formal French
full power was issued on 26 July 1946 by the President of the Provisional French
Government, Georges Bidault, to an under-secretary of state for foreign affairs to
"négocier, conclure et signer avec le ou les Plénipotentiaires également munis de
pleins pouvoirs de la part de leur Gouvernement, tels convention, déclaration, ou
acte quelquonque qui seront jugés nécessaires dans l'intérêt des deux Pays." (From
the file in the Swedish Foreign Office.)

Another air transport agreement was concluded between the Governments of
Sweden and Portugal and signed at Lisbon on 6 March 1947. (*U.N.T.S.*, vol. 35
(1949), p. 245.) It contained an express clause making it enter into force by signature,

that the Swedish Government made extensive use of telegraphic full powers, or authorizations (it not being possible to distinguish between the two). In contrast with ordinary internal instructions, which were addressed to "svensk", written in Swedish, and signed "cabinet", these cables—never sent without a prior approval of the complete draft text of the agreement by the King in Council—were addressed personally to the emissary empowered to sign, written in a foreign language and signed with the name of the Swedish Foreign Minister.[1] There can be no doubt that these cables were intended to serve as internal authorizations, and, equally, as documents to be exhibited to the other party at its request. There were no traces in the files of the Swedish Government of similar cables sent to agents of other governments, a circumstance which need not be taken to mean that the practice is an isolated Swedish phenomenon. It rather would seem to indicate that such cables are not exchanged but merely exhibited upon request. There is no doubt, indeed, that similar cables are sent in the practice of other states. Thus, in the United States:

"Informal authorization from the Department of State is regarded as sufficient authority for the head of a delegation to an international conference or an Ambassador to sign an international agreement for which a full power is not to be issued. Thus, the authority of the United States representatives to sign the agreement for the prosecution and punishment of the major war criminals of the European Axis was contained in a telegram to London on June 30, 1945, signed by the Acting Secretary of State, which states that:
Justice Jackson is authorized to sign agreement regarding prosecution European Axis leaders and associates which conforms with general principles already enunciated by him."[2]

and the agents signing referred to themselves as being "duly authorized". The Portuguese agent was provided with a formal full power signed by the Portuguese President on 5 March 1947. (From the file in the Swedish Foreign Office.)

As a third instance may be mentioned a protocol between the Swedish and Soviet Governments concerning the exchange of goods, signed on 20 April 1951 (*S.Ö.F.*, 1951, p. 237). Without any express clause to this effect, it entered into force by the signatures of the agents who expressly referred to their possession of full powers from their governments. The Soviet full power was signed on 31 March 1951 by Stalin, as the chairman of the Council of Ministers of the U.S.S.R., and countersigned by V. Zorin, Vice-Minister for External Affairs. The Swedish full power was signed by the King of Sweden on 23 February 1951. (From the file in the Swedish Foreign Office.)

[1] See also Blix, p. 376, note 3.

[2] United States, *Treaty Practice*, p. 33. *Cf.* Memorandum approved by the State Department in U.N., *Compilation*, p. 126.

The agreement in question was signed in London on 8 August 1945 and contained an express clause providing that it would enter into force upon signature.[3] Other states as well, perhaps most states, send informal authorizations in the same or in a similar manner.[4]

Evidence in the form of cables of authority to sign treaties has a considerable tradition.[5] No difficulties appear to have sprung from this method, though it might be thought less impeccable than a formal instrument signed by the head of state or other treaty-making organ.[6] In fact, practice would seem to have established that a party, having requested a diplomatic agent to exhibit evidence of authority to sign, and having examined a cable of the type described above, may rest assured that under international law its position is the same as if he had requested and inspected a formal full power.

The foregoing account may perhaps suffice for the conclusion that, in the practice of states, diplomatic agents signing agreements binding upon their signatures are sometimes, but not consistently, requested to exhibit evidence of their being authorized to sign; or, at least, that envoys are expected to be equipped with such evidence in case a request should be made. This being so, it is logically impossible to deduce from this practice alone any rule of international law. Either the full powers are requested *ex abundanti cautela* or, when evidence of authority is not

---

[3] *U.N.T.S.*, vol. 82 (1951), p. 279.

[4] The Philippine case cited above (p. 33) reveals that a telegraphic full power had been sent from the President to the Foreign Minister who was negotiating at Washington. Meissner states that in German practice full powers were issued—usually by the Foreign Minister—for agreements in simplified form. He adds that these full powers often reserved not ratification, but an informal approval by the government. *Op. cit.*, p. 19–20.

[5] Bittner, p. 120; Jones, p. 33; Basdevant, p. 609; Moore's *Digest*, vol. 5, p. 207; Meissner, p. 33.

[6] It may here be noted that, at its eleventh session, held in 1959, the International Law Commission tentatively adopted the view that persons other than the head of a state or of a government, or a foreign minister, require full powers to sign an agreement, and that, although a telegraphic full power is admissible as evidence of authority to sign, a signature appended in such circumstances will be ineffective if a formal full power does not subsequently arrive. See U.N. *Doc.* A/CN.4/122, 2 July 1959, pp. 46 and 48. For a number of instances of treaties subject to ratification, for the signing of which the United States State Department sent telegraphic full powers to be used until the arrival of a formal full power, see Hackworth's *Digest*, vol. 5, p. 39. This writer was told by a diplomat accredited in London that the British Foreign Office declined to accept evidence of authorization in the form of a teletype message, presumably because that method was not regarded as offering sufficient security.

required, there is a reliance upon the integrity and ability of the foreign envoy and upon the particular surrounding circumstances rather than upon the law of the matter.

3. Full Powers no longer Required for the Exchange of Ratifications

It should be noted in this connexion, however, that there is one situation in which diplomats convey the final and binding expression of the consent of states without normally being requested to exhibit any evidence of authority. This is when they exchange or deposit instruments of ratification or accession issued by the head of state, the foreign minister or prime minister. While in earlier practice full powers were issued for these occasions,[7] such documents appear largely to have disappeared in modern practice. The possession of the instrument of ratification by a foreign minister or an accredited diplomatic representative is regarded as sufficient evidence of authority to exchange or deposit it.[8] It may be inferred from this practice that, should the diplomat concerned in fact not have been authorized to proceed to exchange the instruments, this circumstance is irrelevant to the binding effect under international law of the exchange or the deposit. The question of the competence under international law of a diplomat effecting the exchange of the instruments of ratification to express the consent of his government to supplementary agreements or agreed inter-

---

[7] Crandall, *Treaties, Their Making, and Enforcement,* p. 93; Jones, pp. 61–62 and references therein.

[8] Without a doubt this is now a settled practice. See Jones, pp. 61–62, 33; Meissner, p. 30; Bittner, p. 268; Polents, *Ratifikatsiia mezhdunarodnykh dogovorov,* p. 18. *Satow's Guide to Diplomatic Practice* (4th ed. by Bland, 1957), p. 358. That the Government of the United States conforms to this practice is seen from an instruction of 10 December 1944 from the Department of State to the American Ambassador to France, reading as follows:

"Ordinarily the Department considers that it is not necessary to furnish a Full Power for the purpose of effecting an exchange of ratification. Possession of the instrument of ratification is regarded as sufficient evidence of authority in this respect. This is understood to be the general international practice . . ." U.N., *Compilation,* pp. 126–127.

For earlier American practice along the same line, see Hackworth's *Digest,* vol. 5, pp. 69–70. It is reported, however, that in modern Polish practice, full powers are issued on these occasions. See Skubiszewski, "Poland's Constitution and the Conclusion of Treaties" in *Jahrbuch für Internationales Recht,* 7 Band, Heft 2/3 (1958), p. 219.

pretations by virtue of his competence to effect the exchange is a matter touching the extent of the authority of a diplomat, and will be discussed in the following chapter.[9]

4. Competence to Exchange or Deposit Notes of Approval

Some attention must be paid also to the procedure, not uncommon in the modern practice of states, by which an agreement, signed or initialled, is brought into force by an exchange of notes or a deposit of notes of approval.[1] This method, though being less solemn than the exchange of instruments of ratification, fulfills largely the same function as that procedure. There is, however, this difference: while an instrument of ratification is customarily signed by the head of state or some other high dignitary, and gives, therefore, assurance that internally, the ratification has been effected, notes of approval frequently emanate from the accredited diplomatic representative, there being no evidence of approval by a government.[2] Accordingly, there would seem to exist as good reason to expect the use of full powers in these situations as when agreements are signed to become binding upon signature, if indeed, full powers are necessary or helpful in the latter situation. The practice of exchanging or depositing notes expressing consent is too new to have caused much doctrinal comment,[3] and there is no way of knowing whether or not evidence of authority is custom-

[9] See below, pp. 76 ff.

[1] See Blix, pp. 363–364.

[2] The procedure established for the bringing into force of the Versailles treaty was not dissimilar: by an express clause of the treaty (Article 438) the ambassadors to Paris of certain powers signing were allowed to issue instruments of ratification upon the receipt of telegraphic authorizations from their government. In this case, however, the procedure was only designed to achieve a provisional entry into force of the treaty, pending the arrival of formal instruments of ratification. In modern practice, on the other hand, there is nothing provisional about the entry into force achieved through the deposit of notes of acceptance, signed by diplomats. An instance from the practice of the United States illustrates this point. When the Government of Brazil, having previously deposited with the United States a diplomatic note constituting an instrument of acceptance, proceeded to deposit a formal instrument of ratification, the United States Government stated that this action would not effect the date of entry into force of the agreement with respect to Brazil. Presumably the Brazilian action constitutes an exception. See United States, *Treaty Practice*, p. 134. *Cf.* Pallieri, p. 509.

[3] But see a thought-provoking discussion of some aspects of the procedure by Pallieri, pp. 509–512, and see the article by Leriche, cited above, p. 48, n. 2, and Blix, pp. 363–364.

arily or even often requested from diplomatic agents who sign and deliver notes.[4] Some conventions concluded under the auspices of the United Nations have permitted states to become parties by "instruments of acceptance", which appear to be of the same character as notes of approval. Distinguishing between instruments of ratification and accession on the one hand and instruments of acceptance on the other, Leriche states:

> "La différence pratique consiste en ce que le Secrétaire général des Nations Unies a considéré en tant que dépositaire que l'acceptation pouvait avoir lieu par un instrument moins formel que ceux généralement requis pour les instruments de ratification et d'adhésion. C'est ainsi qu'*une lettre émanant du représentant permanent, accompagnée de pouvoirs à cet effet,* a été reçue comme instrument d'acceptation." (Emphasis supplied.)[5]

While this statement is of great interest, the absence of broader knowledge of diplomatic practice in this regard, of incidents and cases, makes it difficult to draw any inference as to the possible need for full powers for protection in this procedure.

5. United States Memorandum on the Competence of Accredited diplomats

From the practice of states in the matter of the competence under international law of diplomatic agents, there must further be noted a highly interesting memorandum in which the legal adviser of the United States Department of State unequivocally declared that the position of his Government was to consider a head of diplomatic mission competent under international law by his very position not only to sign an agreement, but also to certify the authority of other agents:

> "... any agreement signed on behalf of a foreign government by a person whom that government officially designates as authorized to sign such an agreement is fully binding on such government. This Department accepts the advice of the duly recognized chiefs of the diplomatic missions of foreign governments in the United States as to who is authorized to bind their governments and as to the extent of such authority. A chief of mission who signs an agreement is assumed to be acting within his authority. Even if, under the

---

[4] One instance in which a Swedish Ambassador was authorized to issue a note of approval and was supplied with a telegraphic full power is cited in Blix, p. 377, note 1.

[5] Leriche, p. 26.

domestic law of his country, he, or a person whom he has certified as qualified
to act, may have exceeded his authority, his government would not be excused
from performing under the agreement."[6]

6. THE KAUFFMANN INCIDENT

While apparently there are no court cases bearing on the question of
the effect under international law of an agreement signed by a diplomatic agent who has neither exhibited evidence of internal authorization, nor received such authorization, an incident must be cited concerning an agreement signed in 1941 by the Danish Minister at Washington, Mr. Henrik Kauffmann.

Immediately after the German occupation of Denmark on 9 April
1940, Mr. Kauffmann informed the Department of State and the
American press that he had come to the United States in order to
represent his King and an independent people, that he was still there
for this purpose, and that he would work for the reestablishment of a
free and independent Denmark. He reported these statements to the
Danish Foreign Office.[7] In a dispatch of 4 September 1940, he stated
furthermore that to safeguard Greenland, it was absolutely necessary
that matters concerning Greenland, whether handled by the authorities
in Greenland or by himself, should be decided without reference to the
Government in Copenhagen.[8] He further reported that, with his approval, the United States had sent coastguard cutters to patrol the coast
of Greenland, and both the United States and Canada had established
consulates in Greenland. As might indeed be expected, the German
occupation authorities in Denmark were far from pleased with the
activities and attitudes of Mr. Kauffmann,[9] but as no formal recall had
yet been effected, and his acts had not been even disavowed, the inference must be drawn that the Government in occupied Copenhagen
allowed Mr. Kauffmann a remarkable latitude of power.

---

[6] The Legal Advisor of the Department of State (Fisher) to the Administrator of
General Services (Larson), 24 January 1950. Quoted from United States, *Treaty
Practice.*

[7] See *Bilag til Beretning til Folketinget afgivet af den af Tinget under 8. Januar
1948 nedsatte Kommission i Henhold till Grundlovens § 45,* Part V: Udenrigsministeriet under Besaettelsen, Aktstykker Stenografiske Referater (J. H. Schultz A/S, Copenhagen 1948), p. 195. This volume will be cited as "Bilag" below. See also Briggs,
"The Validity of the Greenland Agreement" in *A.J.I.L.,* vol. 35 (1941), p. 508, and
notes therein. Some of the relevant documents are printed in *N.T.I.R.,* vol. 12 (1941).

[8] *Bilag,* pp. 196–208, at p. 204.

[9] *Ibid.,* p. 11.

Such was the background when, on 7 April 1941, the United States Secretary of State, Mr. Cordell Hull, addressed a note to Mr. Kauffmann. Referring to previous informal conversations, he appended a draft of an agreement relating to the defense of Greenland. He adduced five reasons for the conclusion of the agreement, only the fourth of which is relevant here: the situation in Greenland was unusual, for the United States recognized Danish sovereignty over the island, but considered the Government in Copenhagen unable to exercise that sovereignty during the occupation. In a note of 9 April 1941, Mr. Kauffmann replied that in his opinion the proposed agreement was "under the singularly unusual circumstances, the best measure to assure both Greenland's present safety and the future of the island under Danish sovereignty".[1] The preamble of the agreement itself[2] ended with the following phrase:

"The undersigned, to wit: Cordell Hull, Secretary of State of the United States of America, acting on behalf of the Government of the United States of America, and Henrik de Kauffmann, Envoy Extraordinary and Minister Plenipotentiary of His Majesty the King of Denmark at Washington, acting on behalf of his Majesty the King of Denmark in his capacity as sovereign of Greenland, whose authorities in Greenland have concurred herein, have agreed as follows:"

By Article 1 of the agreement, the United States reiterated its recognition of the Danish sovereignty over Greenland and accepted "the responsibility of assisting Greenland in the maintenance of its present status". Articles 2 to 9 laid down the right of the United States to make defense installations in Greenland, and regulated to some extent the mode of their establishment and operation. Article 10, finally, provided that the agreement should remain in force "until it is agreed that the present dangers to the peace and security of the American Continent have passed", and prescribed modes for the modification and termination of the agreement.

It appears that Mr. Kauffmann had agreed with Mr. Hull not to inform the Government in Denmark of the agreement until it was to be published, at noon on 10 April 1941.[3] On that day, Mr. Kauffmann cabled Copenhagen informing it of the conclusion of the agreement.[4]

---

[1] *Ibid.,* pp. 227 and 229.

[2] For the text of the agreement, see the United States, *Executive Agreement Series,* No. 204. The text is also found in *A.J.I.L.,* vol. 35 (1941), Suppl., pp. 129 ff. and in *Zeitschrift für ausländisches öffentliches Recht und Völkerrecht,* vol. 11 (1942), pp. 107–112.

[3] See cable of 14 April from Mr. Kauffmann to Copenhagen, *Bilag,* p. 212.

[4] The cable—in Danish—is found in *Bilag,* p. 209.

He stated that the German interest in Greenland had increased since the summer of 1940, and a German occupation was regarded as imminent. In order to forestall this, to protect Greenland and the rest of the American continent, and to safeguard Danish sovereignty over Greenland, the United States, Mr. Kauffmann reported, offered to assume the responsibility for the defense of the island. Although the United States continued to recognize Danish sovereignty over Greenland, it maintained, on the basis of the Monroe doctrine, that under present conditions, Danish sovereignty could not be exercised from Copenhagen, and when, in addition, for military reasons, the United States requested that the proposed agreement should not be entered into at Copenhagen, the only solution was that he, Mr. Kauffmann, the free representative of Danish sovereignty, as "Negotiorum Gestor" for the Danish Government, which could not itself act, should sign the agreement with the assent of the two governors in Greenland. This he had accordingly done.

Following demands by the German authorities in Copenhagen,[5] the Danish Government cabled Mr. Kauffmann on 12 April that it strongly disapproved of his concluding the agreement without any authorization from Copenhagen, and in violation of the constitution, that, by a royal resolution of 12 April, he had been recalled from his post, and that he was requested to come to Copenhagen immediately.[6] A note of protest that was sent to the United States Chargé d'Affaires at Copenhagen read in part as follows:

"The Royal Danish Government hereby begs to enter a definite protest against the Government of the United States of America . . . initiating negotiations and concluding an agreement with the Danish Minister at Washington without his being warranted to act on behalf of the Danish Government *either ex officio or pursuant to special authorization from his Government* . . . [Emphasis supplied.]

"As the said agreement . . . is signed by Mr. Kauffmann without his being authorized to do so, it goes without saying that it will not be binding on Denmark in point of intern[ation]al law.

"As Mr. Kauffmann thus has decidedly exceeded his powers and as his behaviour most emphatically must be disapproved of, His Majesty the King has to-day decided to recall him from his post as Danish Minister at Washington . . ."[7]

[5] *Ibid.*, pp. 210–211.

[6] *Ibid.*, p. 211.

[7] *Ibid.*, p. 230. The contents of this note were given in a message to the press; see *ibid.*, p. 221. At p. 230, the *Bilag* actually speaks of "internal" law, but it is clear from the Danish translation at p. 231 and from the message to the press at p. 221, that this is merely a misprint, and that "international" law is meant.

On 14 April, Mr. Kauffmann cabled the Danish Foreign Office that he believed the action taken in Copenhagen for his recall, as well as that concerning the agreement, to have been taken under duress, and that he considered it "invalid both from the point of view of Danish and of generally recognized common law". He stated further that he thought it his duty to carry on his work as Minister, and that the Secretary of State had concurred in these views.[8] Upon the receipt in Copenhagen of this cable, Mr. Kauffmann was dismissed from the Foreign Service, and a criminal action was brought against him by the Government.[9] Mr. Kauffmann remained in the United States, however, and continued to be recognized by the United States Government, and to purport to act on behalf of Denmark. Numerous notes concerning the authority of Mr. Kauffmann were exchanged between the two Governments during 1941,[1] but no modification in the legal positions which the parties had staked out for themselves took place.

Later during the war, Mr. Kauffmann took steps toward the conclusion of treaties on behalf of Denmark, but he never went as far as to purport to bind Denmark definitely.[2]

[8] *Ibid.,* pp. 212 ff.   [9] *Ibid.,* p. 222.

[1] See *ibid.,* pp. 233 ff.

[2] See *Proceedings of the International Civil Aviation Conference,* Chicago, Illinois, November 1 – December 7, 1944 (U.S. Government Printing Office, 1948. Publ. 2820), esp. p. 119. And see the United States, *Executive Agreement Series,* No. 430 for an exchange of notes effected at Washington on 16 December 1944, concerning air transport services stipulating that they should enter into force provisionally on 1 January 1945 and "definitely upon confirmation by a Free Danish Government when such a Government shall have been established following the liberation of Denmark." It should be noted that in his note of reply, Mr. Kauffmann nowhere pretended to act as an agent of any organ in Denmark. The notes are found also in *U.N.T.S.,* vol. 10 (1947), p. 213.

It appears, nevertheless, that the Greenland agreement was not the only treaty concluded by Mr. Kauffmann in 1941. It is thus reported that an "oral understanding" for the taking of Danish vessels was made in 1941 by representatives of the United States Department of State and the Danish Minister to Washington, and, indeed, that the Minister concurred "despite the contrary instructions of the Government of occupied Denmark". See the *Department of State Bulletin,* vol. 39 (1958), pp. 474–475.

For interesting comments upon the difference in the status accorded during the war to Mr. Kauffmann and that accorded to representatives of the Norwegian Government in exile, and for the reasons underlying this difference, see Lie, *Hjemover* (1958), pp. 104–110. For the reasons advanced by Mr. Kauffmann and others against the establishment of a Danish Government in exile, see Hæstrup, J., *Hemmelig Alliance, Hovedtræk af den Danske Modstandsorganisations Udvikling 1943–1945,* vol. I (Copenhagen, 1959), pp. 191 ff.

At the first session of the Danish "Rigsdag" after the liberation, in
May 1945, the Prime Minister, in his opening speech, stated that the
forced dismissals of the Danish envoys to London and Washington
were rescinded, and that the Government adhered to the Danish-Ameri-
can agreement on the defense of Greenland.[3] The agreement was, in
fact, submitted to the "Rigsdag", and the Foreign Minister, introducing
it for the approval of the chamber, stated *inter alia* "I think that I
may now be allowed to state that our colleague [Mr. Kauffmann now
being a Cabinet minister] on that occasion acted quite correctly and
looked after the Danish interests in the best possible manner."[4] The
"Rigsdag" having given its assent, the agreement was approved by the
King by a Royal resolution of 23 May 1945. Presumably this action was
thought to have a retroactive effect, although the official Danish treaty
series does not contain any indication to this effect.[5]

Analysis of this extraordinary affair will be limited to the question
of the validity of the 1941 agreement as a treaty between Denmark and
the United States.[6] The absence of any pronouncement upon the episode
by impartial authority, and the fact that neither of the Governments
involved yielded in the position it had initially taken (except insofar as
the Danish actions of 1945 might be viewed as such) renders the incident
less instructive than it might otherwise have been. These features,

[3] *Rigsdagstidende. Forhandlinger i Folketinget.* 96th ordinary session (1945), p. xi.

[4] *Ibid.,* cols. 31 ff.

[5] *Lovtidende for Kongeriget Danmark for Aaret 1945,* Afdeling C, Danmarks
Traktater, Nr. 2 (1945).

[6] Conceivably, one might try to see it as an agreement between the Government
of the United States, and a *de facto* authority governing Greenland. Reference may
be made, in this connexion, to the agreement signed on 2 October 1939 on behalf
of the French Government by its Premier, M. Daladier, and, on behalf of "The
Provisional Government of the Czechoslovak Republic", by the Czechoslovak Minister
to Paris, Dr. Osuský. When the agreement was signed, Germany had occupied
Czechoslovakia, and no exile government had yet come into existence. One writer who
is well acquainted with all the legal aspects of this affair expresses the view that the
agreement could only become valid if the Provisional Government had been constituted and had approved the signing of the agreement. He further maintains that
the competence to conclude treaties generally belongs to the head of state or the
government, and that Dr. Osuský, "had not, and could not, at the time of the
signing of the Agreement, have the full powers which are usual and necessary when
such acts are signed". See Táborský, *The Czechoslovak Cause* (1944), p. 69. Some weeks
after the signing of the agreement, an exile body—the Czechoslovak National Committee—was established, and immediately made its own the agreement of 2 October
which until then must be deemed to have constituted only a personal act of the
Czechoslovak Minister. For a discussion of the agreement, see also below, p. 162.

among others, are worth noting. The legal contentions of the Government of occupied Denmark were clear.[7] Mr. Kauffmann, as accredited Danish Minister was not competent "ex officio", nor "pursuant to special authorization from his Government", and the agreement accordingly was not valid under international law. In the opinion of the Danish Government—or perhaps of the German occupation authorities —Mr. Kauffmann would have needed a full power, and to be binding, the agreement would further have required the assent of the Danish "Rigsdag". Mr. Kauffmann, on the other hand, took the position that he had acted as a "Negotiorum Gestor" for the Danish Government. It is notable, however, that neither in its reply to the Danish protest, nor in the ensuing correspondence, did the United States Government choose to advance any arguments on the point which had been the most vigorously pressed by the Danish Government, namely, that concerning the competence Mr. Kauffmann had possessed, not to represent Denmark generally, but to make the agreement. Perhaps this circumstance may be taken as an admission of the difficulty of advancing any contrary contention. The Government of the United States, indeed, contented itself with the argument that the Danish Government was unable to recall Mr. Kauffmann, and to denounce the agreement, because it could not exercise its sovereignty. The American attitude might possibly be interpreted to have meant that the agreement was voidable,[8] but that

[7] It is succinctly stated in a passage of a note of 26 April 1941 from the Danish Foreign Minister to the United States Secretary of State:

"In 1939 Mr. Henrik Kauffmann was accredited with the President of the United States of America as Envoy Extraordinary and Minister Plenipotentiary for Denmark, and it goes without saying that in this capacity he was only warranted to act on the basis of and in conformity with the general authorization or special instructions given him by the Danish Government. By signing on his own account against the will and knowledge of His Majesty the King, the Cabinet and the Danish Rigsdag an agreement of the 9th of April 1941 on the defence of Greenland, he has exceeded his authority as Accredited Minister and acted against the Constitution, as such an agreement according to Danish constitutional law can only be made with Royal full powers and with the consent of the Rigsdag. As Mr. Kauffmann refused to comply with the order of recall the Danish Government, therefore, to its great grief, had at once to dismiss him and to take extraordinary measures against him." *Bilag*, p. 235.

[8] A passage from a note of 5 May 1941 sent by Mr. Hull to the Danish Foreign Minister may perhaps support this interpretation:

"...my Government is confident that in their hearts the people of Denmark fully understand my Government's action... and that when they are once again free to express their true feelings they will give public approval of the measures which have been taken... for the protection of Danish sovereignty over Greenland", *Bilag*, pp. 240–241.

The conclusion, cited above, p. 59, note 2, of an agreement subject to the confirmation of a free Danish Government may possibly also be seen as supporting the interpretation suggested in the text.

there was, at that time, no authority able validly to denounce it. Even with this explanation it is somewhat difficult to understand, however, why, when supposedly the Danish Government was unable to exercise its sovereignty, Mr. Kauffmann nevertheless purported to bind it in law by the agreement.

The views of the free Danish Government upon the question of international law involved do not definitively emerge from a consideration of its actions of 1945. On the one hand, it is obvious that, since it submitted the agreement to the "Rigsdag" for its assent, and had it approved by a Royal resolution, it did not consider the agreement otherwise valid municipally. Moreover, it appears that this approval of the two branches of government was communicated by the regular diplomatic channel to the United States Government, from which it could be argued to follow that the Danish Government considered the agreement voidable, or possibly even void.[9]

Writers who have discussed the Kauffmann incident have been unanimous in considering that Mr. Kauffmann was incompetent to conclude the agreement. Grewe—writing in Germany in 1941[1]—expressed the view that a regular diplomatic representative is never by himself able to conclude an international agreement which binds the country he represents. When he is charged with the formal conclusion of a treaty, he needs a special full power which is usually examined before the signing. In the case of the Greenland agreement, Grewe points out, not only was this examination of full powers neglected, but the United States authorities knew in advance that the Danish envoy lacked a full power from his Government. Briggs—writing in the United States in 1941[2]—found the conclusion irresistible that unless the State Department had been aware of the Danish Government having secretly authorized Mr. Kauffmann, he had lacked competence to bind Denmark. Hyde,[3] noting the Danish repudiation of the agreement, states that it was not apparent how Mr. Kauffmann could have been deemed

---

[9] This writer is indebted to the Legal Adviser of the Danish Foreign Office, Professor Max Sørensen, for the information that the free Danish Government communicated to the United States Government the fact that the agreement had been approved by the "Rigsdag".

[1] Grewe, "Der Grönland-'Vertrag' von Washington" in *Monatshefte für auswärtige Politik,* Heft 5, Mai 1941, p. 431.

[2] Briggs, "The Validity of the Greenland Agreement" in *A.J.I.L.,* vol. 35 (1941), pp. 506–513; Ross (p. 204), likewise, comes to the conclusion that the agreement was invalid, because Mr. Kauffmann lacked competence.

[3] Hyde, vol. 2, p. 1386.

competent to bind Denmark, and suggests that the chief importance of
the agreement might have been that it registered some Danish approval
of the American activities in, and the United States' defense of, Greenland. Jones,[4] finally, submits that insofar as the "agreement" had any
effect, it could only have been as a unilateral declaration of the United
States. Though Mr. Kauffmann had been accredited to Washington,
and had not been recalled until after he had signed the agreement, the
existence of diplomatic status was not enough for the purpose of
negotiating and signing an agreement. A full power would have been
required, Mr. Kauffmann had not had one, and there was nothing to
show that the King had authorized him to act as he did.

It appears impossible, indeed, to defend the position that the agreement could have been valid as between the Danish and United States
Governments, for it is inconceivable that diplomatic status could raise
more than a presumption of competence to conclude agreements; and
the question is, whether such a presumption exists at all. Where it is
reasonably clear—from express declarations or otherwise—that no
municipal competence to conclude an agreement exists, a possible
presumption—if such should exist under international law—falls to the
ground. It is true that, in the instant case Mr. Kauffmann, without
being disavowed, had been able to take several important steps toward
making Greenland independent of the authorities in Copenhagen, but
it is submitted that, at the time, the political and strategic situation was
such as to nullify any arguable presumption as to competence on his
part to conclude the agreement.

7. Opinions of Writers

The opinion of some writers on the question of the authority of
diplomats have been recorded above, but it remains, finally, to report
the views of some other authorities, who have not discussed the Kauffmann incident. Satow writes:

"A diplomatic agent to whom a particular negotiation is entrusted for the
conclusion of a treaty or a convention, or an agent who is deputed to take
part in a congress or conference for a similar purpose, requires as a general
rule a special authorization, called a full power, from the head of the State
whom he represents; or, it may be, from his government, if the proposed treaty
arrangement is to be between governments."[5]

[4] Jones, p. 64.
[5] *Satow's Guide to Diplomatic Practice* (4th ed. by Bland, 1957), § 128, p. 82.

In a paragraph devoted to letters of credence of diplomats, Oppenheim similarly declares:

"Now a permanent diplomatic envoy needs no other empowering document if he is not entrusted with any task outside the limits of the ordinary business of a permanent legation. But in case he is entrusted with such a task as, for instance, the negotiation of a special treaty or convention, he requires a special empowering document—namely, so-called *Full Powers (pleins pouvoirs)*."[6]

While Meissner[7] takes precisely the same view as Oppenheim, Bittner's view to the contrary has already been quoted.[8]

The account given above of the practice of states, and of the opinions of a number of authorities, does not point with certainty to any particular rule. It may be said with confidence that there is a tendency—witnessed in practice by an often rather carefree attitude shown by states to full powers, and even more evidenced by the United States memorandum cited—to see in the position of accredited diplomats a presumption, which may be relied upon unless there is any evidence to the contrary at the time the treaty is concluded, of competence under international law to express irrevocable consent to treaties. On the other hand, it is well known that municipally all diplomats require authorization in order to be competent to express the consent of their governments, and the inclusion of references to these authorizations or instructions in most treaties as well as the apparent practice of not infrequently issuing and exhibiting full powers—formal or telegraphic— for the making of such agreements, seem to point to the conclusion that some evidence of the municipal authorization is believed to be required in the practice of states. This latter conclusion would have the support of the majority of writers, and it could not, moreover, be said to impose any great practical inconvenience.

8. Conclusion

The difficulty in choosing between these alternatives evidently lies in the rather heterogenous picture that is offered by the practice of states. Neither can be said to embody settled law. Under such circumstances, caution would advise a government to request evidence of the authority of an envoy with whom it proposes to conclude a treaty. Perhaps the telegraphic authorizations described above, addressed personally to

---

[6] Oppenheim, vol. 1, p. 780.
[7] Meissner, p. 23.
[8] See above, pp. 18–19.

the agent authorized, and signed with the name of the prime minister, foreign or acting foreign minister, or assistant foreign minister, offer a convenient mode of issuing an instrument serving both as an instruction and as evidence of authorization.

Should a party neglect to request a diplomat to exhibit evidence of his authorization, or fail to establish that there exists evidence of such authorization, a presumption as to the competence of the diplomat must nevertheless arise, of course, if his government, having acquired knowledge of the agreement he has purported to conclude on its behalf, and perhaps even acted upon it, does not denounce it and disavow the agent as having acted *ultra vires*. In this case it is not the position of the diplomat, however, that raises the presumption, but rather inaction over a period of time, which may bring into play the doctrines of acquiescence and estoppel.[9]

[9] On these principles, see MacGibbon, "Estoppel in International Law" in *I.C.L.Q.*, vol. 7 (1958), pp. 468–513, at p. 471.

CHAPTER VI

THE COMPETENCE OF DIPLOMATS: RELEVANCE OF THE EXTENT OF THE MUNICIPAL AUTHORIZATION

1. INTRODUCTION

Had it been possible to demonstrate above that there exists a presumption under international law to the effect that, by his status, an accredited diplomat proceeding to make an agreement, entering into force upon his signature, is authorized to do so, there would have followed another presumption, namely, that in concluding such an agreement, an accredited diplomat acts within the limits of his authorization. The second presumption would allow the other party to feel confident that each and every part of the agreement in question would be binding upon the government represented by the agent, even if, in agreeing to some particular provision the agent was in fact violating his instructions and, thereby, acting in excess of his municipal competence. This, of course, only would be true were there nothing to suggest that the agent was acting *ultra vires*.[10] It has been shown, however, that the existence of a presumption to the effect that an accredited diplomat has been municipally authorized cannot as a matter of law be proved, and accordingly no presumption that a diplomat is acting in accordance with his instructions follows. The question may then be put whether, when there is evidence, in the form of a full power or otherwise, or it is not disputed, that an accredited diplomat has been

---

[10] Rather than speak of a rebuttable presumption under international law, some may prefer the view that the competence of the agent is always the same under international law as under his municipal law, but that the effects of such a principle are tempered by the protection offered under international law by the principles of good faith. See Pallieri, p. 508. The determination of circumstances under which a party may reasonably have been in good faith does not seem to differ, however, from the determination of circumstances under which a presumption of authority may arise. *Cf.* p. 83, note 8, below.

authorized to conclude an agreement, there exists a presumption that he is acting within the limits of this authorization as it is determined by his instructions.

2. Procedures Employed Tend to Eliminate Risks of Transgressions

An important circumstance that must be noted initially is that the procedures normally adopted in the practice of states for the conclusion of agreements in simplified form tend to minimize, though not completely to eliminate, the significance of the distinction made here between the existence of authority and the extent of authority. To Bittner, of course, there appeared to be no distinction at all: practice, as he had found it, demonstrated that whenever diplomats signed agreements meant to be binding, the full texts of the agreements had already been approved by their governments, and they were merely acting as proxies.[1] Basdevant and Chailley, however, reacted against this reduction of accredited ministers to "notaires diplomatiques".[2] While one may dispute Chailley's contention that the diplomats proceed to sign "de leur propre initiative et en toute liberté",[3] it is no doubt true, as he contends, that the legally binding force of the agreement arises with the consent expressed by the diplomatic agents. This does not prove, however, that the power to sign agreements is something more than and different from the power of "notaires".

Authorizations to sign normally refer to complete drafts

In negotiating drafts, diplomatic agents possess some latitude of power, of course, however frequent instructions they may receive, but a final draft is not a binding agreement.[4] The question is whether the municipal authorizations of diplomats ever or often grant them any leeway in expressing final consent. As has been seen, writers have expressed varied opinions on this matter,[5] the answer to which could have

---

[1] See above, p. 18.
[2] Basdevant, pp. 619–620. Chailley, p. 210. *Cf.* Vitta, p. 79.
[3] Chailley, p. 210.
[4] See above, p. 42.
[5] The matter of delegation has already been discussed in a preliminary fashion above, p. 21. It has been shown that Basdevant—and to some extent Bittner, too—drew conclusions regarding the authority of agents from a verbal analysis of expressions used in treaties, which seems to offer a rather unreliable method.

Ross (p. 213) states that the difficulty in constitutional states of delegating treaty-

been authoritatively supplied by treaty divisions of foreign offices. It is submitted that *generally* the municipal authorizations received by diplomats to express final consent refer to complete drafts, which have been already approved by their governments, thus—as maintained by Bittner—leaving the agent no latitude of power, at any rate not under his domestic law. That such is the normal practice of the United States appears clearly from a circular already cited:

"... Except as otherwise specifically authorized by the Secretary or the Acting Secretary [of State], a complete text of a treaty or other international agreement shall be delivered to the Secretary or the Acting Secretary, or other person authorized to approve the text, before any such text is agreed upon as final or any date is agreed upon for its signature."[6]

A similar practice seems to prevail in the United Kingdom:

"... a United Kingdom plenipotentiary would not, under ordinary circumstances, proceed to the signature of any treaty until the text in final form had been approved by the Foreign Office. When the negotiations have been concluded, the points of agreement are embodied in a draft treaty which, after approval by the Foreign Office, is signed in duplicate ..."[7]

A memorandum submitted by the Austrian Government to the United Nations reveals that, with respect to some agreements at any

---

making power largely excludes a conclusion of treaties between authorized intermediaries. *Contra,* see Vitta, p. 78. And see Dehousse (p. 98): "... dans l'élaboration des accords passés en forme simplifiée, la fonction de l'organe n'est pas toujours réduite ... à une simple attestation du consentement du Gouvernement, mais ... pour divers accords, il s'agit bien de la stipulation d'obligations *par l'organe.*"

In affirming that agents sometimes exercise real treaty-making power, some authorities have expressed concern over this method. Thus, speaking in the International Law Commission, Mr. Scelle appears to have said that "it was quite inadmissible for the State to be committed by the mere will of plenipotentiaries and for such plenipotentiaries to declare that to expedite procedure they would sign the instrument there and then." (Summary Record of the 86th meeting, held 22 May 1951. U.N. *Doc.* A/CN.4/SR 86, p. 10.) In the same vein, see Cavaglieri, "Règles générales du droit de la paix", in *Recueil des Cours,* 1929, vol. 1, p. 519; Genet, "La clause tacite de ratification" in *R.G.D.I.P.,* vol. 38 (1931), p. 758. But see Pallieri, who, discussing the procedure of notes of approval finds it a great advantage that the notes emanate from a responsible officer able to make sure that each and every internal requirement is satisfied before he issues the note, rather than from "un organe très élevé, comme le chef de l'Etat, souvent irresponsable et vers lequel il n'y a pas de contrôle." *Op. cit.,* pp. 511–512.

[6] Sec. 5.5. of Department of State, *Department Circular* No. 175 issued 13 December 1955. Cited above, p. 27, note 7.

[7] Stewart, p. 231.

rate, the same procedure is followed by Austria. The memorandum reads in part:

"In the case of economic matters the representatives of the two parties usually conduct negotiations without written authorization and initial the results of their negotiations. The head of the Austrian delegation reports on the results of the treaty negotiations, whereupon the competent Federal Ministry submits a proposal to the Council of Ministers requesting the latter to approve the agreement, and to appoint a plenipotentiary to sign the treaty on behalf of the Federal Government."[8]

A modern authority on diplomatic practice is quite explicit on this point of procedure. The last edition of *Satow's Guide to Diplomatic Practice* (1957), contains the following passage:

"...In modern times, when all the capitals of the civilised world are in telegraphic communication, it is the usual practice for plenipotentiaries to submit the precise wording of the proposed treaty to their governments for approval before signature..."[9]

An examination undertaken by the present writer of some 80 treaties concluded by Sweden in 1951 has further revealed it to be the consistent practice of the Swedish Government not to issue an authorization to a diplomatic agent to express final consent to an agreement until it has received a full draft text of the agreement and subjected it to the approval of the King in Council.

It appears, in addition, that both in Swedish practice and in the practice of other states, signature of treaties which are to be subjected to a subsequent approval of some kind—ratification or acceptance or the like—is often, though not always, appended only after authorization given upon the approval of a full draft text of the treaty in question.[1]

---

[8] United Nations, *Compilation*, p. 12. A similar procedure is described in a memorandum from the Government of South Africa, *ibid.*, p. 106. See also statement by a former Chinese Foreign Minister, Dr. Koo, cited below, p. 74.

[9] 4th ed. by Bland (1957), p. 359.

[1] A memorandum submitted by the Finnish Government reads in part:

"The usual procedure is that the treaties and other international agreements are submitted to the approval of the Government, for which reason the signing takes place only after a preliminary approval has been obtained. After a treaty has been concluded it must be ratified by the President...": U.N., *Compilation*, p. 45.

See also the following passage from a memorandum by the Iranian Government:

"Une fois l'approbation du Conseil des Ministres obtenue, le Ministère des Affaires Etrangères priera sa Majesté Impériale de vouloir bien daigner d'accorder un Ferman autorisant la signature du traité ou de la convention par le Ministre des Affaires Etrangères ou par son remplaçant ou par un représentant dûment authorisé:" U.N., *Compilation*, p. 66.

It appeared that in Swedish practice authorization to negotiate and to sign subject

Late issuing of full powers. Treaties open for signature. Initialling

The limitation upon the power of diplomatic agents, both with respect to agreements entering into force upon signature and to those which become binding by a subsequent act, to sign only what has already been approved as drafts, can be deduced also from the common, probably even general, practice of issuing full powers to sign only after the end of the negotiations, and following governmental approval of draft texts.[2] The practice of leaving multilateral treaties open for signa-

---

to ratification—and a full power as evidence of that authority—was given before the beginning of negotiations only when this was considered indispensable, e.g. sometimes for a delegate to an international conference convoked to draw up a convention. To the same effect, see also the passage of the Austrian memorandum quoted below, p. 71, note 4, and the reference to British practice in the same note.

In Swedish practice signature was nevertheless consistently appended to one type of treaties without any previous approval by the government of a draft, namely to bilateral commercial agreements drafted by mixed commissions. The formulations used in these reveal clearly that the signatures have not been appended upon government approval of the drafts, and they are expressly made to become binding by a subsequent exchange of notes of approval. This exchange of notes is formally considered as the agreement between the two states and its date is the date of the agreement. For an example, see the agreement noted in *S.Ö.F.*, 1951, p. 212. The procedure is described in Statens Offentliga Utredningar 1950: 9, *Utredning angående de handelspolitiska arbetsformerna m. m.*, part II (Stockholm 1950), p. 11.

[2] See Jones (p. 29) who reports that the practice of states since 1815 shows that it tends to be the exception rather than the rule that full powers are issued at the beginning of negotiations. Referring to the practice of the United Kingdom, Stewart states:

"Although by the terms of the existing form of full power issued from the Foreign Office, the person therein named is authorized both to negotiate and conclude the treaty, in actual practice the treaty negotiations may be virtually completed, or in certain cases the treaty may, indeed, be in final form before the full power is issued:" *Op. cit.*, p. 231.

Bittner holds the same opinion:

"Sehr oft werden die Vollmachten erst ausgestellt, wenn bereits der letzte, zur Unterzeichnung fertige Entwurf der Unterhändlerurkunde vorliegt:" *Op. cit.*, p. 119, cf. *ibid.*, p. 137.

Having noted this circumstance, Bittner suggests logically, and with great foresight, that a further development along the same line might make the procedure of ratification redundant in many cases:

"Falls die eben angedeutete Entwicklung weiterschreitet, müsste sie zu einer wesentlichen Vereinfachung, zu einer fortschreitenden Verdrängung der zusammengesetzten Beurkundung führen. Denn in vielen Fällen, in denen die Vollmachten nach Abschluss der Verhandlungen ausgestellt werden, würde ein Beurkundungsauftrag zum unmittelbaren Vollzug genügen und die Ratifikation könnte entfallen." *Op. cit.*, pp. 138–139.

On the late issuing of full powers, see also Meissner, pp. 32–33 and Hackworth's *Digest*, vol. 5, p. 26. But McNair (p. 1) states the conventional view:

ture is a device which provides time in which the draft texts may be submitted to governments for their approval, and for the issuing of authorizations to sign.[3] Admittedly, it seems likely that full powers are more commonly issued at an early stage in the case of multilateral than in the case of bilateral treaties,[4] but often these early full powers only confer authority to negotiate, and a subsequent authorization is needed to permit signature.[5] Bilateral treaties and treaties among a small

"The first step taken upon the meeting of persons designated as representatives of States for the negotiation and conclusion of a treaty is the mutual verification of powers, for it would clearly be idle to embark upon negotiations with a person who was not properly accredited."

[3] See Basdevant, pp. 594–595; Hackworth's *Digest,* vol. 5, p. 47, citing *Report of the Committee for the Progressive Codification of International Law to the Council of the League of Nations, League of Nations Doc.* C. 357. M. 130. 1927. V (1927. V. 16), 24 March 1927.

[4] See, for instance, the following passage from the Austrian memorandum sent to the United Nations:

"In the case of negotiations with a State on other matters [than economic], and when representatives are to be sent to a diplomatic conference of States for the conclusion of a multilateral treaty, the competent Federal Minister, before the beginning of the treaty negotiations, submits a proposal to the Council of Ministers to the effect that it shall resolve to send representatives to attend the negotiations. At the same time, the Federal Minister applies for authorization from the person competent in the particular case to obtain full powers for the representatives to participate in the negotiations, and, if necessary, to sign the treaty:" United Nations, *Compilation,* pp. 12–13.

Stewart reports similarly:

"At conferences where the delegates are required to produce full powers before taking part in the discussions, the United Kingdom delegates are provided with full powers at the outset. Ordinarily, however, full powers are required only when the time comes for signature:" *Op. cit.,* p. 231.

[5] The result of an inquiry made by this writer into the 'credentials' carried for the negotiation of a convention on the recovery abroad of maintenance payments may here be noted. The drafting conference was held at the United Nations headquarters 29 May – 20 June 1956 and the convention was open for signature until 31 December 1956. All signatures were subject to ratification. The rules of procedure of the conference laid down that within 24 hours of the opening of the conference a delegate should deliver 'credentials' issued either by the head of his state, the foreign minister or the prime minister. (U.N. *Doc.* E./Conf. 21/2 of 2 May 1956.) The first meeting of the credentials committee was held by the middle of the conference. Of documents submitted, some were letters from permanent representatives to the United Nations. Upon the suggestion of the committee, the conference accepted these letters as evidence of authority to participate in the conference, and agreed further that cables containing evidence of authority to sign should be accepted. (U.N. *Doc.* E./Conf. 21/L 15; 13 June 1956.) At a second meeting the committee drew up a list of the representatives it considered as having produced credentials satisfactory for participation in the conference. No decision was taken, however, by the committee, nor by the conference as to whether the credentials were satisfactory for

number of parties, on the other hand, are commonly initialled[6] by the negotiators when the drafts are complete but before authorizations to sign have been issued. This practice is followed at the conclusion of treaties subject to subsequent approval as well as agreements in simplified form.[7] It appears certain that unless there is clear evidence to the contrary, the initialling of a treaty does not bind a state.[8] It merely

---

the purpose of signing the convention. Such examination is undertaken, with respect to the credentials of each delegate who proceeds to sign, by the Secretariat of the United Nations. On this point, see Leriche, p. 35. See also Dunn, *The Practice and Procedure of International Conferences* (1929), p. 206; U.N., *Compilation*, p. 47; Bittner, pp. 119–120; and Stewart, p. 231.

[6] It is submitted that the French term "parapher" and the English "initial" are equivalent. See, to this effect, Guggenheim, vol. I, p. 70, and Freymond, *La ratification des traités et le problème des rapports entre le droit international et le droit interne* (1947), p. 38. But see Mr. Barthélemy, pleading for the Hungarian petitioners in the case of *Emeric Kulin et al.* v. *the State of Roumania* before the Roumanian-Hungarian Mixed Arbitral Tribunal, Judgment of 10 January 1927 (Jurisdiction) in de Lapradelle, *Recueil de la Jurisprudence des Tribunaux Arbitraux Mixtes créés par les Traités de Paix*, vol. 4 (Compétence), pp. 414–415.

Signature *ad referendum* is sometimes used with the same purpose as initialling before the treaty-making authority has been enabled to approve of the draft. See, for instance, the instructions of 28 November 1905 issued to the American representatives at the conference of Algeciras, ending:

"If an international convention should be required to formulate the results, you will, unless otherwise instructed, subscribe *ad referendum* merely, reserving formal plenipotentiary signature until you shall be duly empowered:" *For. Rel. U.S.* 1905.

The expression *"ad referendum"* may also be used, however, to indicate merely that a signature is subjected to the procedure of ratification. See memorandum of the Government of Luxemburg in U.N., *Compilation*, p. 80. In addition, see an instruction by the United States Department of State concerning the validity of an agreement of 21 August 1909 with Venezuela, quoted in Hackworth's *Digest*, vol. 5, pp. 156–157. To sign *ad referendum*—meaning subject to ratification—a treaty which already expressly provides for ratification is meaningless, of course. See Hudson, *International Legislation*, vol. 1 (1931), p. xlvi. On initialling and signature *ad referendum*, see further the enlightening treatment in the *Report of the International Law Commission Covering the Work of its Eleventh Session 20 April to 26 June 1959* (U.N. Doc. A/CN.4/122, 2 July 1959), pp. 44–45.

[7] See the Austrian memorandum quoted above, p. 69, and see the Luxemburgian memorandum reading in part:

"Le simple mandat de négocier (qui ne comporte pas le pouvoir de signer) est délivré dans une forme quelconque, par le Ministre des Affaires Etrangères. En général, il est rédigé comme lettre patente. Le mandat de négocier doit être considéré comme comprenant le pouvoir de parapher; en effet, le paraphe sert à documenter simplement l'accord personnel des négociateurs sans engager la décision du Governement." U.N., *Compilation*, p. 80.

To the same effect, see the French memorandum and the Iranian memorandum in *ibid.*, pp. 47, 66.

constitutes evidence that the draft text has been drawn up and personally approved by those who have initialled it, and the authority to initial seems to be comprised in the power to negotiate.[9]

Wang-Karahan incident of 1924: non-binding effect of "preliminary" signature

In this connexion, a Russo-Chinese incident which occurred in 1924 is of interest. At the end of March 1923, Dr. C. T. Wang was appointed by the Chinese Government as chief of a mission to negotiate with Soviet representatives.[1] During the last months of 1923 and the first months of 1924, Dr. Wang negotiated with the Russian delegate, Mr. Karahan, and it appears that on 14 March 1924 the two delegates had reached agreement on the text of a final draft.[2] Whether or not Dr. Wang signed the draft, or merely initialled it,[3] the document was later described by both sides as a "preliminary text", and the two delegates seem to have agreed to affix formal signatures on a clean copy which was to be made out.[4] Meanwhile, the agreement was submitted to the Chinese Government, which refused to accept it without modifications.

[8] For a remarkable case in which the initialling was expressly given the most important binding effects, see the memorandum of understanding reached in London on 5 October 1954 between the Governments of Italy, the United Kingdom, the United States and Yugoslavia regarding the Free Territory of Trieste. (Reprinted in *The New York Times*, 6 October 1954.) It is possible that in this case the inconspicuous form of "practical arrangements" (Article 1 uses that expression), merely initialled, was used to cloud somewhat the impression that, by the arrangement, the parties to it really proceeded to modify the Italian Peace Treaty of 10 February 1947, without the consent of all the parties to that treaty. Agreements entering into force upon initialling are also cited by Brandon, "Analysis of the Terms 'Treaty' and 'International Agreement' for the Purposes of Registration under Article 102 of the United Nations Charter" in *A.J.I.L.*, vol. 47 (1953), p. 65, note 67. See also Parry, p. 173, and *Satow's Guide to Diplomatic Practice* (4th ed. by Bland, 1957), p. 329.

[9] See the Luxemburg statement quoted above, p. 72, note 7. See further Guggenheim, vol. 1, p. 70; Freymond, p. 38; Camara, *The Ratification of International Treaties* (Toronto, 1949), p. 57. But see the Roumanian-Hungarian incident reported below, p. 85.

[1] *China Yearbook,* 1924, p. 864.

[2] *Ibid.,* pp. 876 ff.

[3] Two Chinese writers, Ken Shen Weigh and A. K. Wu, cited below, have described Dr. Wang's act as one of initialling, but most documents refer to it as one of signature.

[4] Letter of 16 March from Mr. Karahan to Dr. Wang, reproduced in *China Yearbook,* 1924, p. 879. Note from the Chinese Government to Mr. Karahan, *ibid.,* p. 885.

This act of disavowal having come to the knowledge of the Russian representative, he sent an ultimatum to Dr. Wang on 16 March declaring himself willing to wait for three days for confirmation of the agreement by the Chinese Government.[5] Mr. Karahan dispatched a note of similar tenor to the Chinese Foreign Office. He referred expressly to a note of 28 March 1923 by which the Foreign Office was said to have informed the Soviet Government that Dr. Wang had been appointed official delegate for the negotiations with the Soviet Union. He stated further that his Government considered the negotiations with the official delegate of the Chinese Government as concluded, and refused to reopen the discussion. Replying to Mr. Karahan,[6] Dr. Koo, the Chinese Foreign Minister, who assumed charge of the matter upon Dr. Wang's resignation,[7] is reported to have stated that on 2 October 1923, Dr. Wang had been commissioned to discuss and to reach decisions, all decisions being subject to the approval of the Government. Mr. Karahan had admitted himself—according to Dr. Koo—that he had not seen the credentials of appointment of Dr. Wang. If he had, he would not have acted as he did, Dr. Koo suggested.[8] The controversy came to an end when, on 31 May 1924, Mr. Karahan and Dr. Koo signed an agreement and a declaration,[9] there emerging no express conclusion as to the competence of Dr. Wang.

It appears probable that, in fact, Dr. Wang had not received, much less given evidence of, any authorization to sign, and that when he signed—or initialled—the agreement, he thereby expressed only his personal approval of the text before submitting it to his Government.[1] Interviewed by a Chinese scholar in Paris in 1939, Dr. Koo is reported to have said that Dr. Wang had been "authorized only to negotiate, but not to sign any agreement before it passed through the Cabinet meeting and was approved by the President." Dr. Koo added significantly that "such is the international practice".[2] It is conceivable that the Soviet

---

[5] *Ibid.,* p. 879.

[6] *Ibid.* The note is also found in Degras, *Soviet Documents on Foreign Policy,* vol. 1 (1951), p. 435.

[7] Ken Shen Weigh, *Russo-Chinese Diplomacy* (Shanghai, 1928), p. 296.

[8] A. K. Wu, *China and the Soviet Union* (New York, 1950), p. 150.

[9] *Ibid.,* p. 155. And see *China Yearbook,* 1924, p. 886.

[1] Weigh (p. 296) states: "As experienced a diplomat as Dr. Wang naturally would not fix a final signature to a preliminary agreement until he was sure that it would be indorsed by his Government; hence his transmission of it to the Cabinet for action."

[2] Wu, p. 152.

representative, on the other hand, misunderstood Dr. Wang's signature. A circular cable of 25 March from the Chinese Government to various Chinese authorities stated in part:

"We are now surprised that the representatives of the two countries have signed the preliminary agreement without instructions from the Government being given to Dr. Wang as Director-General. This was done on the 14th instant and not until two days later was the Government advised by Dr. Wang that the signature was affixed only as a preliminary measure, which differed from a formal signature. The Russian representative, however, thought it a formal signing and thereupon gave a three-days' limit for a decision."[3]

Whether or not the above was an apt description of what had taken place, it is of interest to note that the Russian delegate, being unable to refer to any evidence of Dr. Wang having been authorized to bind his Government by a formal signature, could not insist that Dr. Wang's act of initialling—or signing—amounted to more than a provisional approval of the draft text. That provisional approval required the confirmation of the Chinese Government, and was not in itself binding, Mr. Karahan's only recourse being to declare himself not bound in the event of confirmation being refused.[4]

Conclusions emerging from the procedures employed

Considering the practice of states as described above, it may be concluded that when an envoy presents evidence of an authorization to sign an agreement, issued after the end of the negotiation of the agreement—which may or may not have been initialled—that authorization refers to the specific text which has been finally drafted, even though on the face of it the authorization will normally only vaguely identify the agreement. In this situation, a party satisfied as to the existence of an authorization may also feel confident that the agent has not exceeded the extent of his competence, unless, of course, the agent should have fraudulently submitted another text to his government than the one drafted, a contingency which may presumably be disregarded.

3. SITUATIONS IN WHICH THERE IS A RISK THAT MUNICIPAL AUTHORITY MAY BE EXCEEDED

Disputes as to the extent of authority of agents may arise in some situations, one being that, immediately before his proceeding to sign an

[3] *China Yearbook* 1924, pp. 882–883.
[4] *Ibid.*, p. 879.

agreement upon the basis of an authorization received after the end of negotiations, the agent agrees to something beyond the draft. The same problem arises if an agent proceeding to exchange or deposit instruments of ratification or notes of approval purports to consent to something beyond the signed text. Another possibility that must be envisaged is that the agent has received authorization to sign before his government has had opportunity to approve a complete draft, and that—whether he has exhibited evidence of this authorization to the other party, or the existence of it is not in dispute—he disregards instructions, and is disavowed on this ground.

4. Competence of an Agent where Authorization to Bind is Given Upon Approval of a Final Text

With respect to the first situation described above, it should be noted that in practice authorizations issued for the signing of a draft text do not always completely deprive the agents of discretionary power. Thus, the examination undertaken of the practice of the Swedish Government revealed that, when an authorization to sign an agreement was adopted by the King in Council, the power to make minor modifications was often granted concurrently. Sometimes this power was given to the agent authorized to sign, while on other occasions it was given to the Foreign Minister, to whom presumably the agent would then have to apply for permission to effect a modification. No case was found in which this narrow discretionary power was spelled out in a cable embodying authorization to sign. It seems likely that similar provisions are found in the authorizations granted by other countries as well. It may then be asked what is the competence under international law of an agent to agree to modifications when proceeding to sign, having been so authorized after the end of the negotiations. No case or incident has come to light which turns on this point. Three not very modern incidents are relevant, however, with respect to the parallel problem of the power to agree to modifications by virtue of an authorization to exchange instruments of ratification.

Controversy concerning the treaty of Erzerum

The first of the three incidents concerned a treaty between Persia and Turkey, signed at Erzerum on 31 May 1847.[5] Before the treaty was

---

[5] This incident is cited by Jones, pp. 39–40. For the text of the treaty, see League of Nations, *Official Journal*, 16th year (1935), pp. 225–226.

signed, on 26 April 1847, an explanatory note was addressed to the Ottoman Government by the agents of Great Britain and Russia, which were mediating Powers.[6] The note was accepted by the Ottoman Government before the treaty was signed, and, on 31 January 1848, it was acknowledged by the Persian envoy stating to the British agent:

"I hereby declare to Your Excellency that, in virtue of the mission with which I am entrusted by my Government for the exchange of ratifications of the Treaty of Erzerum, I concur entirely . . ."[7]

The exchange of ratifications took place on 21 March 1848.[8] In a dispute discussed in the Council of the League of Nations in 1935, Iraq—as the successor of Turkey—invoked the treaty of Erzerum.[9] The Persian Government objected that the treaty was void because the agent of Persia had exceeded his competence by accepting the explanatory note.[1] Although the delegate of Iraq argued not surprisingly that "the plea that a Government is not bound by the act of its duly accredited representative is always . . . a very weak one in law", he added:

"Whether or not the Persian envoy in fact exceeded his powers depends upon a number of considerations, including his instructions, which have not been produced . . ."[2]

The Council did not, however, pronounce itself upon the matter, which was subsequently left to the negotiation of the parties.

Incident of 1849 between the United States and Mexico.

The second incident arose over a protocol signed in connexion with the exchange of ratifications of the treaty of peace between the United States and Mexico, signed at Guadalupe Hidalgo on 2 February 1848.[3] The treaty having been signed, the United States Government submitted it for the advice and consent of the Senate, and though such was given, the Senate attached certain reservations. Subsequently, the Mexi-

---

[6] *Ibid.*, p. 217. Text of the note at pp. 199–200.

[7] *Ibid.*, p. 233.

[8] *Ibid.*, p. 114.

[9] *Ibid.*, p. 196.

[1] *Ibid.*, p. 217.

[2] *Ibid.*, p. 115.

[3] The diplomatic correspondence from which the facts above are taken is found in Manning, *Diplomatic Correspondence of the United States*, Inter-American Affairs 1831–1860, Vol. IX—Mexico (Washington, 1937), pp. 11–37; 306–343.

can legislature approved the treaty, including the United States reservations.

With a view to the exchange of ratifications, the United States Government appointed two commissioners, who proceeded to Mexico. In one of their notes to the Mexican Foreign Minister, the commissioners apparently mentioned that they were authorized to give "explanations" of the reservations made by the Senate.[4] As a result, such explanations were given verbally, and later, upon the request of the Mexican Foreign Minister, they were put in writing in the form of a protocol, signed by the Minister and the commissioners.

When, early in 1849, the American President referred to the protocol as "the substance of conversation held",[5] the Mexican Minister to Washington informed the United States Secretary of State that in his opinion, the protocol was a "real diplomatic convention, concluded between the Government of Mexico and that of the United States and equally binding on both."[6] He disapproved of the President's referring to the protocol as a "memorandum of conversations" and maintained that the instrument had "most properly been given the name of "Protocol" and that what had been held in Mexico were "conferences" and not "conversations." He also pointed to the protocol containing a declaration to the effect that the commissioners had acted in virtue of "full powers from their Government to make to the Mexican Republic suitable explanations in regard to the amendments" and that "the said explanations were given by the Plenipotentiaries in the name of their Government, and in fulfilment of the commission conferred upon them". The Mexican Government had treated with the commissioners in good faith and it could not assume that they had exceeded their powers and instructions. The Minister further asserted that if the protocol were annulled, the Mexican ratification of the treaty of Guadalupe could not subsist, for it was predicated upon the protocol, which, indeed, contained the following clause:

"And these explanations having been accepted by the Minister of Relations of the Mexican Republic, he declared in the name of his Government, that with the understanding conveyed by them, the same Government would proceed to ratify the Treaty of Guadalupe, as modified by the Senate of the United States."

[4] *Ibid.,* p. 319.

[5] *Ibid.,* p. 11.

[6] See *ibid.,* pp. 311–317 for this and the following quotations from the statements of the Mexican Minister.

The United States Secretary of State appears to have thought that the Commissioners had not, in fact, exceeded their powers; they had represented themselves as authorized to make "explanations" not "interpretations", and "a mere power to make explanations in regard to the amendments of the Senate would not have authorized them to give an interpretation or construction to these amendments changing their true meaning." Similarly, he pointed out, in a letter to the Mexican Foreign Minister, his predecessor as Secretary of State had made certain explanations with reference to the amendments made by the Senate, but "nothing could have been further from his intention than to suppose that the Mexican Government were to receive or that his own Government was to be bound by these explanations either as a substitute for or as a construction of the amendments."[7] Indeed, referring to the contention put forward by the Mexican Minister that the protocol was a diplomatic convention capable of modifying the treaty, his predecessor had stated that such device, if it were valid, would enable diplomatic agents to "usurp the powers of the American Senate and bind the Government of the United States in express violation of the Constitution". He had termed it a "monstrous proposition" that "the diplomatic agents of the two Governments, by an agreement in the form of a Protocol, possess the power to change, modify and annul the articles of this Treaty at pleasure."

The Secretary of State sought further support for his view that the protocol was not a diplomatic convention in the circumstance that no full powers had been exchanged for its conclusion, and stated:

"A treaty between two sovereign states is an act too solemn and momentous to be hastily or unadvisedly entered into. Whatever, therefore, may be the disposition of one party, he is bound to be sure that it is met by the other, and that their respective governments have conferred upon them like powers for accomplishing the object of their negotiation. The mere assurance of one to the other, whatever may be the confidence due to his integrity, ought not to be sufficient. He is liable to err in regard to both the nature and extent of his powers, and if the other party, instead of satisfying himself of their real character by ocular inspection, is content with assurances as to their import, he cannot justly complain of the consequences of his own neglect."

Pointing to the texts of the full powers carried by the American commissioners, the Secretary of State rightly concluded that if the Mexican Government had inspected them it would have been apprised

[7] See *ibid.,* pp. 17–24 for this and the following quotations from the statements of the Secretary of State.

of the fact that the commissioners had "no authority to add to or subtract from the amendments proposed by the Senate of the United States, or to propose any new stipulation . . ."

Though the Secretary of State had asserted that he was not aware of any instance in which a treaty had been concluded by the United States without the powers of the negotiators being exchanged, he was able to cite an instance where, in conjunction with the exchange of ratifications, and by means of a simple document drawn up without any full powers being exchanged, the United States and Mexico made an important modification in a treaty which was to be ratified. A boundary treaty between Mexico and the United States had been ratified in 1832. It had stipulated that commissioners were to meet within one year from the ratification to mark the boundary line. The Mexican Government having failed to appoint a commissioner within the time prescribed, an additional convention became necessary to prolong the period stipulated. On 3 April 1835, the United States Chargé d'Affaires in Mexico signed such a convention. In the autumn of that year it was discovered, however, that the new convention provided only for the "appointment" of commissioners instead of the "meeting" of commissioners. The Mexican Government then sent a special envoy to Washington to conclude yet another convention. Meanwhile, however, the incorrectly formulated convention had been submitted to, and indeed approved by, the Senate, and the Mexican proposal for a new convention was declined. The convention providing for the "appointment" of commissioners was ratified by the President, but the same day the instruments of ratification were exchanged, a paper was drawn up and signed by the Secretary of State and the Mexican envoy, stating that the convention which was to be ratified was not "clearly expressed", and that "the intention of the governments . . . was that it should have stipulated that their Commissioners and Surveyors were to meet within the time and at the place prescribed by the original Convention." This "instrument" was not submitted to the Senate, and the Secretary of State adds that when it was later communicated to Congress "it escaped the attention and animadversion of that body and the public which its illegal character deserved."[8] From his account of the incident it is thus clear that the Secretary of State thought the procedure practised impermissible even for the purpose of correcting a simple error.

[8] *Ibid.*, p. 37.

Incident between the United States and Turkey
regarding a treaty of 1874

The third incident in point concerned a convention on naturalization, signed at Constantinople on 11 August 1874 by representatives of the United States and Turkey.[9] The convention was subject to ratification, and while the United States Senate—to which it was submitted—gave its approval, it inserted two reservations. After new negotiations, the Sublime Porte accepted these amendments, but made it a condition that they were to be interpreted in a certain manner. Mr. Baker, the Minister of the United States at Constantinople, agreed to the interpretations, and ratifications were exchanged on 22 April 1875. As soon, however, as Mr. Baker's consent to the Turkish interpretation came to the knowledge of the State Department, it disavowed him, declaring that he had been mistaken, and indicating the authoritative American interpretation. After long negotiations, the Sublime Porte accepted Washington's interpretation. Referring to this incident in a letter of 15 October 1896, Mr. Olney, the Secretary of State, declared:

"Mr. Fish [then Secretary of State] treated the exchange of ratification at Constantinople as invalid, in view of the construction placed upon the amended text . . . by the Turkish memorandum, and declared that there had been in fact no real exchange of ratifications."[1]

Conclusions emerging from the incidents cited

All three incidents described above illustrate the difficulties which may arise when an agent charged only with the task of exchanging instruments of ratification proceeds to consent to something which has not received the express approval of his government. It may be concluded that the competence to exchange or deposit instruments of ratification or notes of approval does not create authority under international law to express consent to new interpretations or additional instruments of any kind. Nor does there seem to be any reason to suppose that an agent, having been authorized to sign a draft agreement approved by his government, should be competent under international law to agree to modifications or addenda or interpretations concerning the substance of the agreement. This conclusion seems inescapable where, as is common, the written or cabled authorization only speaks

---

[9] All the facts related are taken from *For. Rel. U.S.*, 1896, pp. 929 ff.
[1] *Ibid.*, p. 934. The case is noted by Hyde, vol. 2, p. 1445, n. 5.

of power to sign. But even where a formal full power is issued authorizing the agent to "negotiate and sign", the power to negotiate
must be assumed to refer to the negotiations which have already been
concluded. The inclusion of the word is no doubt a relic from the
practice of issuing full powers at the beginning of negotiations.

When it is established that an agent has exceeded his competence
by accepting additional provisions of some kind, the addenda are thus
thought to be voidable, but it may well be asked whether, as was
suggested in the Turkish-American incident, such addenda really make
the whole agreement voidable at the option of the party whose agent
exceeded his competence. It would seem more reasonable if, as was
suggested by the Iraqi delegate in the Council of the League of Nations,[2]
the main treaty was voidable only at the option of the party which has
been deprived of possible benefits under the addenda.

In spite of what has been said above, agents expressing the final
consent of states to treaties by exchanging or depositing instruments
of ratification, or notes of approval, or by signing, or otherwise, must
be deemed to possess—by the practice of states, if not under their
domestic authority—the competence to agree to modifications of form
and style, and to emendations not affecting the substance of the agreement.[3] Moreover, should there be evidence of an authorization issued
after the end of the negotiations and expressly conferring some latitude
of power upon the agent—e.g. empowering him to sign an instrument
along the lines of the draft—the other party may, of course, rely upon
actions taken by the agent on that basis.

5. Competence of an Agent where Authorization to Bind is Given before a Final Text Exists

The question remains whether a diplomatic agent who, before his
government has had opportunity to approve of a draft, has been
municipally authorized not only to negotiate, but also to sign, an agreement, may be legally disavowed under international law on the ground
that on some point he has exceeded his competence by violating his
instructions. Although this kind of authorization, or at least evidence of
it, is no doubt not frequently issued, it seems certain that it is given

---

[2] League of Nations, *Official Journal,* 16th year (1935), p. 115.

[3] Hackworth's *Digest,* vol. 5, pp. 93 ff. See also Ross, p. 215, and *cf.* p. 91, note 1,
below.

on occasion.[4] For example, on 30 June 1945, the Acting Secretary of State of the United States cabled:

"Justice Jackson is authorized to sign agreement regarding prosecution European Axis leaders and associates which conforms with general principles already enunciated by him."[5]

The agreement referred to was signed—and became binding—on 8 August 1945, and it seems likely that, when the authorization was issued, the State Department did not possess a complete and final draft of it.[6] An agreement signed on the authority of a cable such as this might conceivably be successfully disavowed on the basis of the qualification attached to it. If conformity with instructions should have been expressly prescribed in a full power,[7] there would presumably be little difficulty in a renunciation of an agreement reasonably alleged not to have been reached in conformity with such instructions. Where no such qualifications are made, however, it is submitted that, for the following reasons, a disavowal of signature appended on the basis of an authorization otherwise given in the same circumstances and terms would not be effective under international law, unless it had been known to the other party or was manifest that the agent exceeded his powers.[8]

[4] See, for instance, the following instrument issued by Hitler:

"Full Powers"

"To the Reich Foreign Minister, Herr Joachim von Ribbentrop, I hereby grant full power to negotiate, in the name of the German Reich, with authorized representatives of the Government of the Union of Soviet Socialist Republics, regarding a non-aggression treaty, as well as all related questions, and if occasion arises, to sign both the non-aggression treaty and other agreements resulting from the negotiations, with the proviso that this treaty and these agreements shall enter into force as soon as they are signed."

"Obersalzberg, August 22, 1939."

Adolf Hitler
Ribbentrop

Nazi-Soviet Relations 1939–1941 (ed. 1948 by Sontag and Beddie, Department of State Publication 3023), p. 69. See also Vitta, p. 76, note 1, and Ross, p. 213.

[5] United States, *Treaty Practice*, p. 33 (also cited above, p. 51).

[6] The text of the treaty is found in *U.N.T.S.*, vol. 82 (1951), p. 229.

[7] Jones (p. 38) states that full powers which do not give authority to negotiate and sign are open to objection, while it is no objection to full powers that they prescribe "conformity with instructions" as a condition of the binding effect of the agent's acts. Such full powers would keep the legal possibility of a disavowal open until some time after signature.

[8] It is then assumed that a full power only constitutes evidence of authority (*cf.* Jones, p. 33): it raises a presumption of the existence of authority. This presumption may be relied upon unless rebutted by other evidence. When it can be shown that the other party knew the presumption to be wrong, principles of good faith preclude him from relying upon it. When it is manifestly wrong, there is, by definition, evidence rebutting the presumption.

The reluctance of states, as demonstrated above, to exchange, at an early stage in negotiations, evidence of authority to sign may well be taken to mean that the governments often consider the early issuing of full powers as involving a risk, and seek to protect themselves against becoming bound through any inadvertent acts of their agent. A full power to negotiate and sign, given before the negotiations or early in the negotiations, may therefore probably be understood to confer a fairly wide latitude of discretion. To allow this latitude to be limited with international effect by secret instructions which may be given from time to time would enable a government to disavow its agent if the agreement signed were thought inconvenient. The other party would not be able to feel certain of the validity of a signed agreement until a reasonable period had passed after its signature. If the acts of the agent were not disavowed during this period, the assumption would arise that either the agent had in fact acted in accordance with his instructions, or else that his government had acquiesced in such deviations as he might have made. This, indeed, seems to be the position to which Mervyn Jones adheres. Referring to inter-governmental agreements, he states:

"... their validity depends on the authority given to the agent, either in his Full Powers or by express instructions. Of course, if he signs an agreement contrary to his Full Powers or instructions the agreement may be repudiated. If not repudiated within a reasonable time it is binding."[9]

It does not seem altogether clear whether in the words "express instructions", Mervyn Jones included instructions not communicated to the other party. Nor can it be stated with any certainty whether Sir Gerald Fitzmaurice, to whom Merwyn Jones refers, in suggesting that a state is entitled to repudiate the action of an agent as *ultra vires,* "provided the breach of authority can clearly be shown",[1] thought evidence of instructions not known to the other party permissible to demonstrate "clearly" a breach of authority. If these writers had in mind only such instructions as had been communicated or were otherwise known to the other party, principles of good faith would, no doubt, have precluded that party from relying upon action taken in violation of instructions. It seems more probable, however, that Mervyn Jones and Sir Gerald thought secret instructions to be internationally relevant. Assuming that this interpretation of their view is correct, and

---

[9] Jones, p. 157.

[1] Fitzmaurice, "Do Treaties Need Ratification?" in *B.Y.I.L.,* vol. 15 (1934), p. 137, note 1.

that their view is itself correct, the existing situation could be briefly described as the same as that which once led to the procedure of ratification becoming both necessary and discretionary.[2]

Though modern requirements of expeditiousness have led to a decreased use of ratification, it may not be argued that the requirement of reliability in modern relations between states should in any way have been lessened so as to tolerate the ambiguity and uncertainty that would result from conceding the international relevance of undisclosed instructions. It is perfectly permissible under international law for a negotiating party to inquire of the Foreign Office of the other party as to whether its agent has respected his instructions, and, though such inquiries must be rare, instances have been recorded.[3] A right to inquire is not of much value, however, to a party not suspecting the agent of the other party of violating his instructions. While the common interest of reaching genuine agreement seems to have led to the duty of every party to exercise reasonable and feasible caution—by checking evidence of authority to express final consent, and being on guard against evident violations of instructions—it cannot be expected to have had more far-reaching consequences. It is not unreasonable to assume that the risk of an agent departing from his instructions, in circumstances when the other party is unaware of such departure, is borne by the agent's principal. States may thus be obliged to seek to protect themselves against such deviations by stipulating penalties or disciplinary action against agents guilty of them. Such provisions are indeed found in municipal law.[4]

Practice of states: controversy between Hungary and Roumania

There is little in the modern practice of states that tends to resolve the problem. An incident brought before the Council of the League of

[2] See above, p. 5.

[3] It is reported that, when during the Washington conference of 1921–1922, a deadlock had been reached in the Sino-Japanese negotiations over the problem of the Shangtung railway, Mr. Obata, the Japanese Minister at Peking, called on Dr. Yen, the Chinese Foreign Minister, on 27 December 1921, three days after the appointment of a new Chinese Cabinet, inquiring whether the Chinese delegates might perhaps be acting in excess of their official authority, and receiving the reply that the stand taken by the delegates was fully in accord with the attitude of the Government. See Pollard, *China's Foreign Relations*, 1917–1931 (N.Y., 1933), p. 245, n. 132.

[4] The Swedish provision is found in Chapter 8, Article 2 of the Penal Code of 16 February 1864 as modified on 30 June 1948; the corresponding Norwegian stipulation is found in Chapter 8, Article 89 of the Penal Code of 22 May 1902.

Nations may be reported, however. Under the chairmanship of the Japanese delegate to the Council, Mr. Adatci, and at the express recommendation of the Council, negotiations were opened at Brussels on 26 May 1923 between representatives of Hungary and Roumania with a view to the settlement of a dispute regarding land owned by Hungarian nationals and expropriated by the Roumanian Government in the course of an agrarian reform.[5] The full powers carried by the Hungarian delegates were issued before the negotiations and read as follows:

"Budapest, 23rd May, 1923.

"I, the undersigned, Royal Hungarian Minister for Justice entrusted with the direction of the Ministry for Foreign Affairs, certify by the present note that the Royal Government of Hungary has charged His Excellency the Count Emeric de Csáky, former Minister for Foreign Affairs, as delegate, and Monsieur Ladislas Gajzágo, Councillor at the Ministry for Foreign Affairs, as assistant delegate, to represent the Kingdom of Hungary in the negotiations which are to take place on May 26th of the present year at Brussels, between the Kingdom of Hungary and the Kingdom of Roumania, on the question of the expropriation of the landed property of the Hungarian optants.

"The delegates above mentioned are provided with full powers to treat and to sign in the name of the Royal Government of Hungary the provisions of the agreement to be concluded.

(signed) Géza de Daruváry."[6]

Minutes of the conversations at Brussels were drafted by a League official, and though they were neither signed nor initialled by the Hungarian delegates, the latter do not seem to have raised any objection to the account given of their statements.[7] The minutes included *inter alia* a passage recording recognition by the Hungarian representatives that the Treaty of Trianon did not preclude the expropriation of the property of optants for reasons of public welfare, including the social requirements of agrarian reform.[8] In addition, a draft resolution to be submitted to the League Council was drawn up at Brussels, and its contents were submitted for the approval of the delegates. According to later Hungarian statements in the Council, the Hungarian representative had declared that he participated in the procedure in his

[5] League of Nations, *Official Journal*, 4th year (1923), pp. 611, 1011. Of the rather voluminous doctrinal treatment of the dispute, see Deák, *The Hungarian-Rumanian Land Dispute* (N. Y. 1928), and Petrasco, *La réforme agraire roumaine et les réclamations hongrois* (Paris, 1931).

[6] League of Nations, *Official Journal*, 4th year (1923), p. 899.

[7] *Ibid.*, pp. 901, 1009.

[8] *Ibid.*, p. 1012.

personal capacity only.[9] However that may have been, it is certain that, on the morning of 29 May 1923, Count Czáky initialled a portion of the text reading:

"The Council is convinced that the Hungarian Government, after the efforts made by both parties to avoid any misunderstanding on the question of optants, will do its best to reassure its nationals."[1]

A preamble of the text stated that the Council took note "of the various declarations contained in the minutes", thus including the passage reported above. A third paragraph of the resolution referred to the duties of the Roumanian Government, and was similarly initialled by the representative of Roumania.

On 12 June, Mr. Adatci received a letter from the Hungarian Foreign Minister, disavowing the acts of Count Czáky.[2] In a separate memorandum,[3] the Hungarian full power was cited, and it was stressed that the instructions given to the delegates had only had reference to an agreement with Roumania. It was admitted that Count Czáky had appended his initials in the name of his Government, but it was pointed out that the Hungarian full power only authorized direct negotiations with Roumania. The Hungarian Government, not having been aware that a report was to be drafted, had not been in a position to delegate powers for this purpose. The Hungarian Foreign Minister contended that the drafting of the report did not enter into the tasks of the negotiators, and that, moreover, the Hungarian representatives had stressed repeatedly that they did not have full powers or instructions as to the drafting of the report. The memorandum continued:

"Il est donc évident que ledit délégué du Gouvernement royal hongrois a franchi les limites de ses pleins pouvoirs et que le Gouvernement royal de Hongrie, à son grand regret, ne peut pas, malgré l'apposition du parafe d'un de ses représentants sous une partie du texte, adhérer au projet de résolution."

In a reply to the letter of disavowal, Mr. Adacti stated:

"Il est clair que l'activité du Conseil de la Société des Nations en vue de maintenir les bonnes relations entre les Membres qu'un différend sépare,

[9] *Ibid.*, p. 901.

[1] *Ibid.*, p. 1011.

[2] Deák, p. 39.

[3] The following account is from Deák, pp. 170–171. The original publication appears to have been in *Recueil des Actes et Documents relatifs à l'affaire de l'expropriation par le Royaume de Roumanie des biens immobiliers des Optants Hongrois* (published by the Hungarian Foreign Office, Budapest, 1924), pp. 62–63.

serait rendue impossible, si, contrairement à tout usage international, les délégués envoyés par les parties et dûment autorisés par elles pour négocier, sous les auspices d'un Membre du Conseil, pourraient ensuite être désavoués par leurs Gouvernements."[4]

Mr. Adacti added that he did not understand the Hungarian Government to have disavowed what its agents had done within the strict limits of their full powers, that in his view the discussions had led to certain agreed conclusions on several points, and that these had been recorded in the procès-verbal. In his opinion, these conclusions could not be challenged. He subsequently referred to them and relied upon them when the matter came before the Council of the League of Nations on 5 July 1923.[5] During the meeting the Roumanian delegate strenuously argued that an agreement had been reached at Brussels.[6] It is of interest to note that Lord Robert Cecil supported this contention. His statement, as recorded in the minutes of the Council, reads in part:

"He was quite aware that the Hungarian Government said that the agreement had only been obtained because its representative had exceeded his powers. He did not propose to examine the legal grounds for that contention; he desired simply to say that it did not seem to him that the powers of the Hungarian representative had been so restricted as to prevent his entering into such an agreement. In these circumstances, he thought that the Council could assume that an agreement had been entered into by the representative of Hungary, and it was extremely undesirable that that agreement should not be considered by the Council as having great weight."[7]

Mr. Branting, the Swedish delegate, concurred in the remarks of Lord Cecil, while the French representative, Mr. Hanotaux, considered that what had taken place at Brussels did not amount to an agreement, but only to the first step toward conciliation. To the gratification of the Roumanian delegate, who saw the "Brussels agreement" thereby confirmed, the Council approved the report of Mr. Adatci and adopted the draft resolution based upon it.

In a case which subsequently came before the mixed Roumanian-Hungarian tribunal, the State of Roumania, as defendant, sought to rely upon the "Brussels agreement".[8] In its judgment, the tribunal

---

[4] Deák, pp. 173–175.

[5] League of Nations, *Official Journal*, 4th year (1923), pp. 1009–1014.

[6] *Ibid.*, p. 896.

[7] *Ibid.*, pp. 904–905.

[8] See de Lapradelle, *Recueil de la Jurisprudence des Tribunaux Arbitraux Mixtes crées par les Traités de Paix*, vol. 4 (Compétence), (Paris, 1927), p. 135.

avoided entering into the question of the competence of Count Czáky, but rejected the view that a formal declaration—if such it had been—which had been made in the course of negotiations, and perhaps in the hope of winning a concession from the other party, could be isolated and interpreted as an agreement.[9] After the Roumanian Government had refused to recognize the jurisdiction of the tribunal,[1] the question of the "Brussels agreement" came again before the Council of the League, but no new light was shed upon it.[2]

Perhaps the most interesting aspect of the Hungarian optants incident is the various views expressed on the question of what constitutes an agreement. The incident also demonstrates the great difficulty of disavowing an agent once he has been supplied with evidence of authority to negotiate and express a government's final consent. The difficulty in this case is the more remarkable in view of the fact that the agent had only appended his initials. Evidently the Council attached some weight to the full power upon which Count Czáky had acted, but it does not appear that the lack of instructions of the agent on the point on which he was disavowed made any impression upon the Council.

Opinions of writers. Conclusions

The conclusion that, within the limits imposed by considerations of good faith, violations by agents of their secret instructions are irrelevant under international law has the support of several writers. Thus, Basdevant states that "on ne peut exiger d'un ministre qu'il communique ses instructions: sa lettre de créance ou ses pleins pouvoirs suffisent pour qu'on garde foi à sa parole."[3] Lord McNair writes similarly that a question as to the limitations contained in the secret instructions "could hardly arise in the case of a treaty of a kind not requiring ratification provided that the negotiators held full powers couched in the customary extensive language." He continues: "If it should arise, it would seem clear that secret instructions given by one party to its plenipotentiary

---

[9] Case of *Emeric Kulin et autres c. Etat Roumain*, judgment of 10 January 1927. See de Lapradelle, *loc. cit.*, pp. 428–430.

[1] Deák, pp. 75–77, 88.

[2] League of Nations, *Official Journal*, 8th year (1927), pp. 350–372.

[3] Basdevant, p. 602. But see the same writer's comment to the Politis incident which is found in *ibid.*, p. 617, note 2; and see *ibid.*, p. 575, where the same writer states that the question what a plenipotentiary is empowered to do by his full power is difficult.

cannot affect the other party who has no notice of them."[4] This conclusion, it is submitted, is a reasonable one, whose compelling character derives a certain support from the practice of states.

6. Authority Conferred by a Full Power Silent as to the Need for Ratification

A separate aspect of the problem of the extent of authority of an agent is found in the question sometimes discussed of whether full powers that do not expressly declare that the agreement to be concluded is subject to ratification confer authority to sign treaties binding upon signature.

It was perhaps understandable that, in a period in which the desire to safeguard constitutional procedures led many writers to the view that the procedure of ratification was discretionary where promised, and required where it had not been stipulated, the view should also have been current that a reservation as to ratification should be read into the full powers of agents where no express stipulation to that effect was to be found in them.[5] To-day such a view is utterly untenable; the majority of treaties do not enter into force upon ratification, and, though the issuing of instruments of full powers or authorizations may have been neglected in the case of many treaties entering into force otherwise than by ratification, those which have been issued have not reserved the right to ratify, nor can such a reservation be read into them. It does not follow, however, that every full power that is silent as to ratification raises a presumption of competence to bind by signature.

Though several states seem always to include a reservation as to ratification in full powers issued for the conclusion of treaties intended to enter into force by ratification,[6] and though such a practice may probably even be said to be general,[7] instances seem to occur where full powers not reserving the right to ratify are issued for the signature of treaties entering into force by ratification.[8] The absence in a full power of a reservation as to ratification cannot be said, therefore, to

---

[4] McNair, pp. 2–3.

[5] For some quotations, see Fitzmaurice, pp. 122–123. See also Jones, p. 30.

[6] Such seems to be the practice of the Soviet Union. See Polents, p. 52. See also Taracouzio, *The Soviet Union and International Law* (1935), pp. 240–241; Triska and Slusser, "Ratification of Treaties in Soviet Theory, Practice and Policy" in *B.Y.I.L.*, vol. 34 (1958), pp. 312 ff.

[7] Fitzmaurice, p. 121.

[8] See Blix, p. 376, esp. note 4.

imply with any certainty that the treaty is to enter into force upon signature.[9] Nor does it seem possible to contend that the absence of such reservation should *always* imply that the agent is empowered to affix a conclusively binding signature: where the full power—as is often the case—is issued only when a complete draft has already been drawn up, the draft will normally be found to contain an express provision prescribing that the treaty shall enter into force either by signature or by ratification, or possibly in some other manner. The full power must then be understood to refer to the complete draft. In case the full power should not expressly reserve the right to ratify, while an express clause in the draft does so, there would be no reason to suppose that the agent proceeding to sign was competent to agree to modifying this clause so as to make the treaty enter into force upon signature. This conclusion conforms with the general rule deduced above as to the lack of competence of agents holding full powers issued at the end of negotiations to agree to modifications when proceeding to sign.[1]

With the exception suggested in the preceding paragraph, it appears likely, however, that any full power to sign that does not reserve the right to ratify confers competence to bind by signature.[2] Thus, if a full power not reserving ratification rights has been issued before there is a complete draft—as seems to have been the case with the full power issued to Mr. Justice Jackson[3]—the state issuing the instrument cannot later renounce a treaty that, on the basis of the full power, was signed to come into force upon signature, with the argument that the instrument did not raise a presumption of authority to bind by signature, nor, indeed, that a reservation as to ratification should have been read into the full power. Similarly, a full power issued at the end of negotiations that does not reserve ratification rights, and that refers to a draft which is silent as to the mode of its entry into force, or which offers a choice of procedure on this point, must be understood to confer *competence* to conclude a treaty binding upon signature.

[9] See *ibid.*, p. 377, note 2.

[1] See above, p. 81. But see Ross, who suggests that agents may make minor additions, and gives the example of a separate protocol concerning the coming into operation of a treaty. *Op. cit.*, p. 215.

[2] From the existence of this competence alone, there does not, however, follow as a logical corollary any presumption that the treaty is made to enter into force upon signature: the agent might have stipulated or by some means implied that it should be ratified. *Cf.* Blix, p. 377, note 2. In case of doubt, it has been suggested that the treaty enters into force upon signature. See *ibid.*, p. 380.

[3] See above, p. 51.

This conclusion has been strongly advocated by Sir Gerald Fitz-maurice.[4] It would seem also to be suggested by the certainty that the modern relations of states require, and to derive some support from modern diplomatic practice as well. Thus, it is reported by Leriche[5] that, in the practice of the United Nations, with reference especially to the conclusion of treaties allowing governments to become bound by signature with or without reservation as to subsequent acceptance, the Secretary-General examines the full powers of the agents proceeding to sign, checking notably whether they contain any reservation as to ratification—the implication being that if no such reservation is found the Secretary-General considers the agent competent to sign without a reservation as to ratification.

A recent diplomatic incident is in point. A European conference of Ministers of Transport was held at Brussels from 13 to 17 October 1953, at which a protocol was drawn up.[6] It was open for signature from 17 October 1953 to 1 May 1954. In accordance with Article 14 (2) of the agreement, a government could become a contracting party either by signature without reservation, or by signature with a reservation as to ratification, followed by ratification. Paragraph 4 of the same Article stipulated that the protocol was to enter into force when six governments had finally approved it.

It appears that the protocol was signed on 17 October 1953 without any reservation as to ratification by the representatives of Germany, France, Italy, and Switzerland. In the case of France, the signature was appended by its Minister of Transport, M. Chartelein, by virtue of a telegraphic authorization that did not reserve the right of ratification.[7] A formal full power reserving ratification rights that was submitted somewhat later appears to have led the Belgian authorities to inquire as to the reason for the discrepancy between the two documents. The answer received seems to have explained that the written full power was incorrect and that the telegraphic authorization should prevail. A letter received later by the Belgian Foreign Office from French au-

---

[4] Fitzmaurice, pp. 121–125, 129. To the same effect, see Ross, p. 215.

[5] Leriche, pp. 26, 35. A verbatim quotation is found above, p. 50.

[6] See Statement of treaties and international agreements registered or filed and recorded with the Secretariat during January 1954. U.N. *Doc.* ST/LEG/SER A/83, p. 8.

[7] The facts presented in the text have been related by responsible sources to this writer personally. It has not been possible to obtain any official confirmation of them.

thorities stating that the French Minister had exceeded his full powers, and that his signature must be considered *"ad referendum"*, did not meet with Belgian approval. The protocol is found to be registered by Belgium with the United Nations, and France is there listed as having bound itself by signature without a reservation as to ratification.[8]

[8] See the statement cited above.

Chapter VII

THE COMPETENCE OF AGENTS OTHER THAN DIPLOMATS

If it had been possible to demonstrate that there exists a presumption under international law to the effect that diplomatic agents are competent to bind their principals by a treaty when they purport to be authorized to this effect, a question would have arisen as to whether the group of agents was limited to any category of diplomats, or as to whether the principle perhaps extended to apply to some other groups of individuals as well. Bittner, who affirmed the existence of the presumption, maintained that it applied to Foreign Ministers, leading officers of the Foreign Offices, and accredited diplomats, but no others.[9] The foregoing examination of the question has confirmed Bittner's view with respect to Foreign Ministers, but, though a tendency in the direction of the presumption has been found to be unmistakable with regard to accredited diplomats, no more than a tendency can be shown to apply to them. This being so, there is no reason to expect that the presumption could possibly apply to agents of lesser diplomatic standing, or others who might purport to act on behalf of a state.[1] Questions

---

[9] Bittner, pp. 48, 56–57. *Cf.* above, p. 18.

[1] No principle of international law limits a state in its choice of agent to sign a treaty. In the case of *The USAFFE Veterans Association Inc.* v. *The Treasurer of the Philippines et al.* (cited above, p. 32), the Court of First Instance of Manila stated without making any qualification:

"... Anyone, in fact, may be appointed agent of a State for the purpose of negotiating or signing an international agreement." *A.J.I.L.*, vol. 50 (1956), p. 688.

To the same effect, see Hyde, vol. 2, p. 1419, and Jones, p. 47. The choice of agents is not even limited to nationals of the state issuing the authorization:

"There is no rule of international law which requires that one State issue a full power to sign an international agreement only to its own officials and nationals. The President of Haiti issued his full power authorizing the American Ambassador at London to sign in the name of the Government of the Republic of Haiti the protocol to prolong after August 31, 1944, the International Agreement Regarding the Regulation of Production and Marketing of Sugar, signed at London on May 6, 1937, as

as to their competence must be assumed to be regulated by the same rules as have been shown above to apply to accredited diplomats. Accordingly, a special discussion of their situation does not seem to be called for.

enforced and prolonged by the protocol of July 22, 1942..." United States, *Treaty Practice,* p. 33.

It is clear, on the other hand, that states normally prefer to have diplomatic agents sign treaties, even in situations when persons who have not diplomatic status have negotiated the drafts. To this effect, see memoranda on the practice of the United Kingdom in U.N., *Compilation,* p. 121, and of the practice of Luxemburg in *ibid.,* p. 80, and of Austria in *ibid.,* p. 12. See also the quotation above, p. 42, note 4.

Part Two

COMPETENCE TO CONCLUDE TREATIES
ON BEHALF OF STATES

Chapter VIII

INTRODUCTION

The Existence of a Rule

Before a discussion may be undertaken of the content of the rule of international law that determines what authorities are competent to conclude treaties, an answer must first be sought to the preliminary question of whether any such rule may be expected to exist. It has been asserted by at least one writer that the answer is in the negative. On the basis of an examination of various constitutional texts, Dr. Chailley denies that there is a rule of international law and ascribes the determination of the competent treaty-making power exclusively to the constitutional laws of various countries. He concludes:

"... selon la conviction juridique des Etats, ce n'est pas au droit des gens, mais au droit constitutionnel en tant que tel qu'il appartient de déterminer les règles de compétence et de procédure, sans l'observation desquelles un traité ne pourra pas être considéré comme internationalement valide."[1]

This conclusion cannot be accepted. When desiring to treat with a foreign state, any government will try to deal with the authorities it believes competent to undertake obligations binding under international law. If there is found to be uniformity and consistency in the convictions of governments as to the criteria of competence, that very conviction, evidenced by practice, will constitute a rule of international law. Thus, if governments invariably look to the constitutional laws of other countries to find the authorities competent to make treaties, the conclusion would be inevitable that a principle of international law refers the determination of the competent treaty-making authorities to the various constitutional provisions.[2]

Chailley's statement quoted above is therefore a contradiction in terms. It amounts, indeed, to saying that, by international law, it is not to international law, but to constitutional law one must look for a determination of a competent treaty-making power. But this is actually

[1] Chailley, p. 180.
[2] See Anzilotti, *Cours de droit international* (French ed. by Gidel, 1929), p. 362.

to say that a principle of international law refers the determination of the competent treaty-making organ to constitutional law, a principle the very existence of which Chailley denies. Indeed, while there is much disagreement as to the content of the rule of international law indicating the treaty-making authorities, an overwhelming body of opinion assumes the existence of such a rule. The following examination of the question will record ample evidence in support of that assumption.

Most Important Theories

Evidence of the rule—or rules—of international law governing the competence to conclude treaties on behalf of a state must be sought in the practice of states and cases of courts. Before we embark upon an examination of such evidence, a brief indication of the chief lines along which doctrinal discussion has endeavoured to define the rule may be useful.

According to one school of thought, the head of each state possesses by international law a *jus repraesentationis omnimodae*.[3] The origin of this rule is obviously found in the circumstance that, at one time, a few hundred years ago, the political system prevailing in many states was that of absolute monarchy. The internal power possessed by the sovereign *Dei gratiae* was such as to justify another party relying upon his words alone.[4]

Though most absolute monarchies were later replaced by constitutional systems in which normally the power of the head of state was strongly curbed, so as to enable him to act only with the advice of ministers, and often only with the consent of an elected legislature, and though the theory of the *jus repraesentationis omnimodae* was thus deprived of its rationale, it continued to be asserted. It was now suggested by adherents of this theory that, in dealing with each other, states were not concerned with the question of what authorities had the actual power to carry out a particular undertaking, of—as it was expressed—"forming the will of the state". All they were interested in was to find the organ which was competent to declare that the state undertook the particular obligation, and this authority was almost universally the head of state.

Gradually the concept of constitutional government forced the discarding of the old theory, and most writers now hold that, as a matter

[3] For references and further discussion, see below, p. 388.
[4] See above, p. 4.

of international law, the constitution of states or the internal order of states determines the authority competent to make treaties.

It may be useful at this point to note that various municipal provisions may affect the treaty-making function of the state. Any distinctions between different kinds of provisions must necessarily be somewhat arbitrary. For the purpose of a discussion of the possible relevance in the international sphere of such provisions, or some of them, certain distinctions may nevertheless be convenient and even indispensable.

There are, first, the rules which identify the organ or organs whose assent is required for the conclusion of a treaty, or a certain type of treaty, e.g., the head of state or the legislature. These rules may be termed *limitations of competence in a narrow sense*. There are, further, the rules which prescribe the procedures that must be observed for the conclusion of various kinds of treaties. These provisions may be termed *procedural limitations*. It is the international relevance of these two categories of rules that is the most frequently asserted, and that will be of the greatest interest to this study. Unless otherwise expressly stated, it is to both these categories of rules, or to action in conformity with them or in violation of them, that reference is made in this inquiry when such expressions as "constitutional law", "municipal law", "formalities", "domestic regularity", etc., are used.

In addition to the municipal rules referred to above, there exist municipal provisions which may be termed *express limitations of substance*, by which the conclusion of treaties of special kinds are expressly prohibited, e.g., secret treaties or treaties by which territory is ceded. There are as well, of course, municipal provisions that prohibit all state organs from undertaking or authorizing action of specified kind, e.g., of a kind encroaching upon fundamental rights guaranteed to citizens. These provisions evidently do not directly debar the conclusion of treaties of any kind. Indirectly, they may nevertheless be understood to proscribe the conclusion of treaties which necessitate or make possible action of the defined character. These rules may be termed *implicit limitations of substance*.

Treaties entered into in derogation of implicit substantive limitations, or in breach of provisions that expressly forbid the conclusion of special kinds of treaties, have sometimes been alleged to be invalid under international law. The two categories of municipal rules thus asserted to be internationally relevant may together be referred to as *substantive limitations*. Unless it is expressly so indicated in the following inquiry, these municipal rules are not under discussion.

The theory that international law refers the question of competent treaty-making authority to constitutional law—hereafter termed the "constitutional theory"—is obviously much more flexible than the head of state theory, and, indeed, may even apply where the head of state still possesses the whole treaty-making power. While it takes into account the predominant factual situation of today in a fashion more satisfactory than does the old theory, it has given rise to much controversy regarding the international relevance of subtle constitutional interpretations, and the like.

Some who have felt concerned about safeguarding the observance of constitutional provisions have argued for their unqualified relevance under international law. Others, who have felt concerned about the need for reliability and predictability in international treaty relations, have maintained that there are certain limitations—flowing from principles of good faith or otherwise—upon the relevance of constitutions in the international sphere. Yet others, and perhaps those who have felt the most concerned at the far-reaching consequences of the theories held by the group of writers first mentioned, have persisted in their support of the head of state theory. To them, the traditional theory remains attractive because it seems simple to apply and incapable of being abused. At the same time, attaching binding effect, as this theory does, to the consent of an authority which is frequently devoid of all independent power under domestic law obviously makes possible the most severe conflict between domestic legal effect and effect under international law.

Opponents of the traditional rule, on the other hand, propound a rule which is complicated in application, permits of use as a subterfuge, but reduces to a minimum the risks of conflict between international law and domestic law. However, not even if this theory were found acceptable and accepted would the risk of conflict altogether disappear. For it would always be possible, of course, that, by the internal laws of some states, domestic legislation subsequent to and conflicting with a treaty would prevail over the treaty.

Proposed Method of Inquiry

Viewed against the earlier prevalence of the head of state theory, the broader modern adherence to the view that international law refers to constitutional law the determination of competent treaty-making authority marks a *rapprochement* between doctrine and the dominant reality—that of constitutional states—and, therefore, is a step forward. It is obvious, however, that this theory has emerged from an examination of, and aims at application to, precisely this large, but nevertheless limited category of international law subjects, namely, states which possess an effective constitutional regulation of the treaty-making power.

The international community contains several other categories of subjects of international law with which treaties are made. It is possible, of course, that special rules of international law may have developed, indicating the organs which are competent to represent such subjects. On the other hand, important and ever present practical considerations may conceivably have led governments to follow a uniform rule, whenever they conclude treaties. If so, the circumstance that writers have invariably focused their attention upon the competence of constitutional governments may have served to obscure a view of the rule which is capable of general application.

Whichever of the above alternatives may prove true, it seems that the international law rule—or rules—indicating competent treaty-making organs of states might, with advantage, be approached with a view to definition from several different directions, some of which have not been explored before. By an examination of the considerations which have guided governments and courts in this matter in a variety of situations, it may perhaps prove possible to deduce a paramount principle, should there be one, or the various principles followed, should there be several.

Accordingly, it is proposed to examine, in the first section of this part, a number of situations in which the municipal regulation of the treaty-making competence is likely to be non-existent or inoperative. Initially, the question will be taken up whether, under international law, states are, in fact, always deemed to possess competent treaty-making authority, and, if not, the conditions which are decisive in this regard; then, which conditions must be satisfied by revolutionary bodies to render them competent in the eyes of regular governments and courts to make treaties on behalf of the states they purport to represent; then, under what conditions are bodies in exile considered competent to assume treaty obligations on behalf of the states which they claim to represent; and last, which organs are deemed competent to conclude treaties on behalf of a state which has not yet developed, or redeveloped, a constitutional principle regulating the question in the municipal sphere.

In a second section of this part, the long-debated question of the rule of international law that indicates the competent treaty-making authority in a state, in whose municipal sphere the matter is effectively regulated will be examined. The conclusion or conclusions reached in the first section of this part will serve to give perspective to that problem, and to put it in its proper place, as an important case among others which are less frequent, but perhaps more likely to give rise to legal considerations.

Throughout the following inquiry the conditions in which treaties are deemed to be valid or invalid will be of the greatest interest, as these conditions may be expressive of the criteria of treaty-making competence under international law. It is not proposed to examine the further question, however, of whether treaties found to have been considered invalid as being made in excess of competence, are considered void *ab initio* or voidable.[5]

---

[5] On this problem, see Kelsen, *General Theory of Law and State* (1949), pp. 159–161.

RULES APPLICABLE WHERE THE MUNICIPAL REGULATION OF THE MATTER IS LIKELY TO BE INEXISTENT OR INOPERATIVE

CHAPTER IX

DO SUBJECTS OF INTERNATIONAL LAW INVARIABLY POSSESS COMPETENT TREATY-MAKING AUTHORITY?

It may be asked what is the position in international law, with regard to entities possessing no authority which appears able to secure the performance of treaty obligations, e.g., a state during a period of anarchy.[1] Does a rule of international law nevertheless point to the nominal head of state as the competent treaty-making power, or is it always true to suggest that

"in the absence of any special constitution containing provisions bestowing the exercise of the treaty-making power of the state on one or another agency of the government, international law would undoubtedly sustain the conclusion that the executive branch might act in that capacity and bind the state thereby"?[2]

While this problem does not seem to have attracted much attention, some writers have suggested that, though international law permits

---

[1] As it is generally admitted that the statehood of an entity may remain unaffected by belligerent occupation and by brief periods of anarchy, it may not be inappropriate to discuss the question raised above independently of the problem under what conditions an entity loses its quality of state, and, thereby, its capacity to be a party to treaties. See Oppenheim, vol. 1, pp. 118 and 133; Hall, p. 21; Verdross, p. 225; Sibert, *Traité de droit international public*, vol. I (1951), p. 99; see Baty, "Can an Anarchy Be a State?" in *A.J.I.L.*, vol. 28 (1934), pp. 444–455; and Raestad, "La cessation des états d'après le droit des gens" in *Revue de droit international et de législation comparée*, 3 ser., vol. 20 (1939), pp. 444 and 447.

[2] Potter, "Inhibitions upon the Treaty-making Power of the United States" in *A.J.I.L.*, vol. 28 (1934), p. 465. Jones asserts that where a revolution has destroyed the constitution of a state, it is permissible to rely upon "the traditional rule" to indicate the competent treaty-making power. In his opinion, it would be safe to make treaties with the head of state or the *de facto* government of the day. *Op. cit.*, p. 155. The position that, in the absence of constitutional regulation, the head of state is the competent treaty-making power was taken by the International Law Commission in 1951. See Art. 4 of *Law of Treaties, Text of Articles Tentatively Adopted by the Commission at its Third Session* (U.N. Doc. A/CN.4/L.28). Similarly Brierly, *Third Report on the Law of Treaties* (U.N. Doc. A/CN.4/54), p. 4.

states a wide latitude in the mode of their internal organization, certain minimum requirements are imposed in this respect. It is thus stated by Potter:

> "It must be admitted at once that international law does permit the national state to regulate to some degree the exercise of the treaty-making power on its behalf. The state might intrust the exercise of that power to some agency other than its chief executive officer, doubtless, provided that the agency selected were suitable or adequate to the purpose, although it is difficult to conceive of legislative or judicial agencies fulfilling this requirement."[3]

If the implication of the above statement is that international law imposes a duty upon states always to hold out authorities suitable to make treaties, it is difficult to accept. Though a state in which anarchy prevails for some time may presumably become liable for not respecting its international obligations,[4] it cannot be argued that it would incur international responsibility merely by not holding out any agency with which treaties may conveniently be made.

It must be concluded that states have no duty under international law to possess a treaty-making authority, just as they have no duty to conclude treaties. Admittedly, the conclusion is chiefly of theoretical interest. It is evident that, due to the need in most communities for international intercourse, and for the regulation of such intercourse, the authorities existing in the communities normally adapt themselves so as to offer convenient channels for treaty-making, and guarantees for the execution of treaties. If, however, for some period, a community

---

[3] Potter, p. 469. Scelle asserts in this connexion that "l'on peut constater que les nations ne peuvent se donner la constitution qui leur plaît que dans les limites où le Droit international le concède." See *Précis de droit des gens,* vol. II (1934), p. 439. Another writer expresses himself as follows:

"...on pourrait fort bien concevoir que le droit international ne reconnût pas telle ou telle règle constitutionnelle accordant compétence pour ratifier les traités à tel ou tel organe de l'Etat si cette règle se révélait dangereuse pour la sécurité des conventions internationales...": de Naurois, *Les traités internationaux devant les juridictions nationales* (1934), p. 164.

The following statement by de Visscher may also be noted:

"...on ne peut considérer comme satisfaisants les divers systèmes qui consacrent la primauté absolue de l'élément populaire en confiant directement aux assemblées le droit de conclure les traités ou en faisant même appel à la procédure du referendum. Ces systèmes constituent le triomphe d'une fausse idéologie démocratique et sont condamnables par cela même qu'ils sont incapables de garantir efficacement les intérêts de l'Etat:" *Op. cit., p. 122.*

[4] *Cf.* Article 4 of the Draft Convention on the *Responsibility of States for Damage Done in Their Territory to the Person or Property of Foreigners,* prepared under the auspices of the Harvard Law School, *A.J.I.L.,* vol. 23 (1929), Spec. Supp., pp. 146–147.

should completely lack governmental authority, the reaction of the international community might well be passive. Though such a community would continue to be regarded as a subject of international law, and as possessing the capacity to be a party to treaties, foreign governments might well simply abstain from attempting to make any treaty with it until it had established authority giving promise of ability to fulfil obligations. In practice, such cases arise in periods of civil war, or chaos following defeat in war. A few examples may be discussed to illustrate the point.

Sir Hersch Lauterpacht, who suggests that there is a presumption in favour of the international authority of a lawful government,[5] doubts nevertheless that "political or commercial treaties of a far-reaching character" may properly be made with such a government, even though it may remain in the national territory and assert authority, if it is seriously shaken by a revolutionary government that is gaining ground.[6] It may be inferred that in the opinion of Judge Lauterpacht, no treaty —of the kind mentioned—can be concluded in the situation envisaged.

In support of his view, Sir Hersch cites a dispatch of 1859 from the United States Minister to Mexico, which merits examination. In 1859, the United States recognized President Juarez' Constitutionalist Government at Vera Cruz in Mexico, and declined to recognize the revolutionary government of General Miramon which was then established in the capital. The American Minister to Mexico, Mr. McLane, even negotiated and eventually signed important treaties of alliance and transit with the Constitutionalist Government, but while negotiating with that Government he expressed doubts to the Secretary of State as to the prudence of acquiring territory from Mexico by a treaty of cession with a government as shaky as that to which he was accredited. In a dispatch of 25 June 1859, he wrote as follows:

"The cession of territory is the gravest and most important act of sovereignty that a government can perform; it is therefore questionable, whether it should be performed at a moment when it is in conflict with another government for the possession of the empire, even though it may be *de-jure* and *defacto* much more entitled to respect than that with which it is struggling in civil war, and this consideration is as important to the party purchasing as to the party ceding the territory."[7]

---

[5] The same presumption is advanced by Baty in his article "Can an Anarchy Be a State?" in *A.J.I.L.*, vol. 28 (1934), at p. 444.

[6] Lauterpacht, *Recognition in International Law* (1947), p. 93, note 3.

[7] Manning, *Diplomatic Correspondence of the United States, Inter-American Affairs*, 1831–1860, vol. IX (1937), Mexico, pp. 1093–1094.

These expressions of hesitation were not, however, typical of the attitude of the United States Government at the time. On the contrary, all the officers of that Government seem to have acted upon the assumption that a Mexican Government *de facto*, if only possessing a very limited degree of authority and stability was competent to bind the State—at least under international law. A passage of a report of 18 March 1858 from Mr. Forsyth—Minister of the United States to the revolutionary government residing in the capital of Mexico and recognized by the United States in the first half of 1858—to the Secretary of State is enlightening:

"I am still of the belief that the Govt. only lacks the moral courage to sell Territory. If it can be brought to that point—and nothing but stern financial necessity will do it—and the price is not an insurmountable barrier, the Treaty will be made. The favourable moment has just arrived, and I shall use every effort to take advantage of it. That moment is the period intervening between the flush of success, and the incipiency of new revolutionary movements."[8]

There is, further, no evidence that the United States Government was in any way deterred by a protest of 14 April 1859 in which the revolutionary government in the capital of Mexico warned that "any treaties, conventions, agreements, or contracts, which may have been or may hereafter be concluded between the Government of Washington and the so-called constitutionalist government, are null and of no force or effect . . ."[9]

The treaties which were eventually signed on 14 December 1859 did not include the provision on the cession of Lower California, not because of legal considerations, but because the Mexican Constitutionalist Government did not feel sufficiently powerful to take that step.[1]

Immediately after the signing of the treaties the revolutionary government in Mexico City voiced its protest. Contending that the actual authority exercised by the Constitutionalist Government was very limited, the Foreign Minister of the revolutionary government asserted that "no foreign government can enter into treaties like that which is proposed or has been adjusted at Vera Cruz." He added, in a sentence that merits consideration:

---

[8] *Ibid.*, p. 971.
[9] *Ibid.*, p. 1047.
[1] *Ibid.*, pp. 1093 and 1118; for the treaties, see *ibid.*, pp. 1137–1141.

"What would become of a country which would have to abide by what was done by a few men representing a faction or party under circumstances similar to those in which the Government at Vera Cruz is found? A short period of civil war might finish or put in the greatest danger its territory or its independence. The Government, therefore, of Veru Cruz, in approving of the treaty, has arrogated to itself titles and powers which it does not possess even by the charter which it invokes . . ."[2]

The validity of the treaties signed never came to be tested for the reason that, due to the failure of the United States Senate to approve them, they were never ratified.

While the above examples would seem only to show that even in this rather confused period, the United States Government was satisfied that there existed a government with which treaties—even those of the greatest consequence—might be made, it may nevertheless be assumed that some minimum requirements exist which must be satisfied by an authority in order that it may qualify as competent to assume treaty obligations on behalf of a state. The precise definition of these requirements will be discussed in the following chapter. It may here suffice merely to note some instances where the minimum standard was considered not to be attained and where, accordingly, a state was deemed to exist temporarily without any competent treaty-making authority.

It is recorded, in an American dispatch of 1926, a period in which China was torn by strife, that a British delegation to a conference negotiating a treaty with China found further negotiation purposeless because the Chinese delegation was unable to speak for the country as a whole.[3]

Even more to the point is the view expressed by a Czechoslovak diplomat regarding the situation of Czechoslovakia in the period im-

---

[2] *Ibid.*, p. 1148.

[3] See *For. Rel. U.S.*, 1926, vol. 1, p. 746. It is noted by one writer that after the French defeat at Sedan on 2 September 1870, Bismarck would not negotiate with the Provisional Government for the defense of the nation, until that Government had been upheld by a vote of the National Assembly. See Vitta, p. 65, note 1. See also the statement recorded below—at p. 121—of an American Minister to Chile. The following view of an authority may also be of interest in this connexion:

"... si l'on estime *a priori* qu'un État ne voudra ou ne pourra pas tenir ses obligations, il est inutile dans ce cas de traiter avec un gouvernement de fait, comme il serait inutile de traiter avec un gouvernement *de jure*. Pareillement, si on n'a point de confiance dans un gouvernement de fait, si l'on doute de sa continuité ou de sa capacité à exécuter ce qu'il a promis pour l'État, il vaut mieux attendre une consolidation ou un changement". Gemma, "Les gouvernements de fait" in *Recueil des Cours*, 1924, vol. 3, p. 355.

mediately preceding the establishment in 1940 of the Provisional Czechoslovak Government in exile:

"... the Czechoslovak Republic existed legally and was a responsible subject, capable of concluding treaties in accordance with international law. But there was no organ which, in the name of this subject, could duly bind itself and acquire rights."[4]

[4] Taborsky, *The Czechoslovak Cause* (1944), p. 69. See also the following statement by V. Benes: "... although the Czechoslovak State and its sovereignty continued to exist after March 15th [1939], there was no organ which would have been capable of exercising further the rights deriving from its continued legal existence": *Czechoslovak Yearbook of International Law* (1942), p. 212.

Chapter X

THE TREATY-MAKING COMPETENCE OF REVOLUTIONARY GOVERNMENTS

1. Preliminary Remarks

It has been shown above that where chaos or anarchy prevails, there is no organ competent under international law to make treaties. It may be asked what minimum conditions an authority must fulfil to qualify under international law to assume treaty obligations on behalf of a state. An examination of the treaty-making activities developed by revolutionary governments might provide an answer to that question, for such governments purport to act on behalf of states in conditions which frequently border upon anarchy.

It must be assumed that, in general, foreign governments will treat with a revolutionary government only if they are convinced that the treaties made by such government will be imputed to the state which it purports to represent—or, to put it differently, if they are convinced that under international law the revolutionary government is a competent treaty-making organ of the state. Accordingly, the mere fact that established governments conclude treaties with a certain revolutionary government which purports to act on behalf of a state must imply, in all likelihood, that they consider it satisfying the minimum conditions required of a treaty-making organ. Corroboration of their views may be sought in the attitude adopted by the governments succeeding the revolutionary authorities: their respect or disregard for treaties made by the predecessor will show, in all likelihood, whether they accept or reject the view that that regime possessed such qualities as to have constituted an organ of the state. For, by definition, a body that constitutes an organ of the state, is one—*inter alia*—whose acts will continue to be respected despite the disappearance of the particular person(s) who, at a given stage, constituted the organ.[1]

---

[1] The authorities ruling states have not always been looked upon as "organs" in the sense indicated above. In past centuries there has been no lack of application of the opposite principle, namely, that a treaty remained valid only so long as the

The ever present need in any modern community for governmental acts, and for continued respect for such acts—whether they be the issuing of marriage licenses or the conclusion of defense alliances—is so great that the character of "state organ" may—indeed must—be expected to be attributed to revolutionary governments, even if their mode of functioning only partially resembles that of a normal government. A revolutionary government cannot be considered in the light of a private law analogy as a thief trying to administer what he has stolen. "La chose publique n'appartient à personne",[2] and if it is not administered and so regarded, damage will follow. This argument applies as much to the conclusion of treaties as to the performance of domestic acts.[3] It is of interest to note in this connexion the practice of revolutionary governments to declare their intention of respecting treaties made by prior governments.[4] The inquiry here, however, will concern particularly the practice of governments that succeed revolutionary regimes in abiding by treaties made by the latter: what qualities must a

person concluding it remained alive. See Larnaude, p. 462; Gemma, p. 343; and Bittner, p. 17. It is obvious that very great disadvantages attached to this older doctrine, and it appears that as early a commentator as Grotius qualified it by distinguishing between "traités personnels" and "traités réels", the latter being binding upon the state rather than upon the prince. See Grotius, *De Jure Belli ac Pacis,* bk. 2, Ch. XVI, Sec. 16, Classics ed., vol. 2, bk. 2 (1925), p. 418; see also Pufendorf, *De Jure Naturae et Gentium,* bk. 8, Ch. IX, Classics ed. (1934), p. 1336.

Even in modern times feeble echoes of the old doctrine may be distinguished. Thus, the view is occasionally voiced that an American executive agreement should be binding only upon the Chief Executive concluding it. There is overwhelming authority, however, in favour of the view that an executive agreement binds successive administrations. See, for instance, *Harvard Research,* p. 667; and McDougal and Lans, "Treaties and Congressional-Executive or Presidential Agreements, Interchangeable Instruments of National Policy" in *Yale Law Journal,* vol. 54 (1945), at p. 318. See also the Finnish incident discussed below, p. 345.

[2] Larnaude, pp. 487, 472 and ff.

[3] It is possible, however, that the requirements which must be fulfilled by a revolutionary authority to endow it with the competence to conclude treaties on behalf of the state are stricter than those which the same authority must satisfy in order that continued validity be attributed to everyday administrative acts—even those of an international nature—performed by it, or by the administration subordinated to it. To this effect, see the judgment of 31 March 1926 of the United States Mexican Claims Commission in the case of *George W. Hopkins* v. *United Mexican States,* reported in United Nations, *Reports of International Arbitral Awards,* vol. IV (1952), at p. 43.

[4] For some examples, see Fauchille, *Traité de droit international public,* vol. I (1922), p. 340; and for a discussion of the apparent deviation from the principle by the Soviet Government, see Mirkine-Guetzévitch, p. 75 and Marek, p. 34.

revolutionary regime possess in order that subsequent governments will agree with foreign governments in attributing treaty-making competence to them?

2. Rules Theoretically Possible

In abstract theory there would be no objection to a rule of international law to the effect that only authorities certified by the General Assembly of the United Nations to be competent under international law to conclude treaties possess such competence. Nor would there be any logical objection to a rule prescribing that only such authorities would be competent to conclude treaties as were found organized in accordance with some hypothetical model constitution. Though it is obvious that no rule of either kind exists at the present time, governments have at times shown tendencies to enter into relations—including treaty relations—only with authorities deemed satisfactory in the light of some political ideology.

Ideas to the effect that only hereditary monarchs were "legitimate" rulers of European states were current in the first half of the 19th century.[5] It appears to have been during this period, indeed, that the term "de facto" governments was coined, in distinction to the "legitimate" governments, then thought to derive their authority from God.[6] The general opinion as to what constituted such a "legitimate" government changed radically in the 19th century, however.[7] The view that the "sovereignty" of a state was vested in the monarch receded before the ever stronger claim that "sovereignty" lay with the people.[8] The regime which supposedly had the approval of the people became "legitimate."

The existence of popular approval of a government has also sometimes been attributed definite international significance. Such was the case in the *Tobar doctrine,* a principle advanced in an annex to a General Treaty of Peace and Amity, signed by five Central American

---

[5] Marek, p. 51; Gemma, p. 320, n. 1. A clarifying discussion of the changes to which the concept of a "legitimate" government has been subjected is also found in Pinto, "The International Status of the German Democratic Republic" in *Journal du Droit International,* 86th year (1959), at pp. 353–361.

[6] See Larnaude, p. 465. That writer also quotes Chateaubriand who, speaking about the House of Bourbon, is said to have put the idea of monarchic legitimacy concisely as follows: "Tout deviendra légitime avec eux, tout est illégitime sans eux . . ." *Loc. cit.* See also Lauterpacht, *Recognition in International Law* (1947), p. 330.

[7] Marek, p. 53.

[8] Larnaude, p. 468.

states at Washington on 20 December 1907. The first article of this annex, apparently devised by Mr. Tobar, a former Foreign Minister of Ecuador, to discourage civil war in the Central American region[9] provided as follows:

"The Governments of the High Contracting Parties shall not recognize any other Government which may come into power in any of the five republics as a consequence of a *coup d'etat,* or of a revolution against the recognized Government, so long as the freely elected representatives of the people thereof, have not constitutionally reorganized the country."[1]

The "Wilsonian policy of recognition" was first enunciated on 11 March 1913 by the President in a statement prompted by the question whether or not the revolutionary Huerta regime in Mexico should be accorded recognition. He stated in part:

"... We hold, as I am sure all thoughtful leaders of republican government everywhere hold, that just government rests always upon the consent of the governed... We shall look to make these principles the basis of mutual intercourse, respect, and helpfulness between our sister republics and ourselves."[2]

Natural law was invoked in support of the claims of royal houses to rule states in Europe, and principles of conventional international law in favour of the need for popular approval of a government in Central America. The requirement of a particular form of government in a state must indeed be sought in norms superior to, and outside, the constitution of states, for while the legality of an amendment of a constitution may be gauged by a provision of the constitution for its revision— and such provision may therefore be regarded as superior to the rest of the constitution[3]—the legality of the constitution as a whole cannot be judged by any standards laid down in itself. Thus, unless its legality can be determined by reference to principles of natural law—which is not admitted—or by principles of international law—which is conceivable—the conclusion must be drawn that there exist no legal criteria

---

[9] See Gemma, p. 335; Marek, p. 54; Mirkine-Guetzévitch, p. 68.

[1] See Hackworth's *Digest,* vol. I, p. 186. It may be noted that a new General Treaty of Peace and Amity was signed by the same States at Washington on 7 February 1923, reiterating and strengthening the clause cited in the text. See *loc. cit.,* p. 188.

[2] See Hackworth's *Digest,* vol. I, p. 181.

[3] See Sander, "Das Faktum der Revolution und die Kontinuität der Rechtsordnung" in *Zeitschrift für öffentliches Recht,* vol. 1 (1919), p. 153; Marek, p. 25.

for its validity; only the maxim *ex factis jus oritur* will be applicable to it.[4]

In spite of a certain tendency favouring forms of government dependent upon popular approval, it cannot be said of course that international law prescribes any particular form of government or constitution.[5] It is not suggested that the international community should be completely indifferent to the kind of governments or constitutions existing in various states. On the contrary, it is certain that it is concerned, and that its concern is increasing, but this concern has not yet become so strong and productive of sanctions as to translate itself into law. Indeed, on the contrary, there has long existed a principle of international law prohibiting intervention.[6] It is paradoxical that, while the growing interdependence of states increases the mutual concern for the respective governmental systems, it makes indispensable state intercourse regardless of the governmental system practised. So strong is the need for commercial agreements, travel arrangements, trade relations etc., that states are apt to disregard considerations that are not strictly relevant to the fulfilment of these various needs.[7] The administration of President Hoover completely discarded the

---

[4] Marek, p. 563; Gemma, p. 316; Vitta, p. 66. This hypothesis must necessarily be true for international law itself. The validity of norms of international law is determined only by reference to what, as a matter of fact, functions as international law.

[5] Marek, p. 56; Gemma, p. 353. Both writers quote point 1 of the famous communiqué of 6 January 1922, adopted by the five allied powers:

"Les nations ne peuvent pas revendiquer le droit de se dicter mutuellement les principes suivant lesquels elles entendent organiser à l'intérieur, leur régime de propriété, leur économie et leur gouvernement. Il appartient à chaque pays de choisir pour lui-même le système qu'il préfère à cet égard." Cit. from Gemma.

[6] Marek, p. 55.

[7] See Vitta, p. 65. A passage from a dispatch sent from Mexico by Mr. R. McLane to the United States Secretary of State on 7 April 1859 is enlightening in this connexion. Mexico was then torn by civil war, and in spite of the circumstance that a revolutionary government ruled from Mexico City, Mr. McLane, on 6 April 1859, accorded his Government's recognition of the constitutionalist government residing at Vera Cruz. He stated in part:

"I have had to consider... only the question, whether any government existed in Mexico, that offered a sufficient and satisfactory prospect of stability, to justify me, under my instructions, in opening political relations with it. In any other country than Mexico, I should have had grave doubts in coming to the conclusion at which I have arrived, but in view of the very large interest, political and commercial, already involved... I felt it to be my duty to act promptly in opening political relations with some power, if such could be found..." Manning, *Diplomatic Correspondence of the United States, Inter-American Affairs, 1831–1860*, Mexico, vol. IX (1937), p. 1042. See also above, p. 109.

Wilsonian policy of non-recognition,[8] and by 1934 there were only three parties to the Central American Convention that had taken the place of the one cited above.[9] It may be concluded that although a particular form of government may be thought "legitimate" in the light of some political ideology, as yet no particular system of government can be said to be required under international law. The pertinence of the maxim *ex factis jus oritur* is, with respect to the system of government and the constitution that emerge, accordingly clear. This circumstance does not, however, preclude the expectation that international law must lay down the criteria by which it is determined whether a particular authority is competent to assume treaty obligations on behalf of a state.

3. TREATY-MAKING COMPETENCE AND RECOGNITION

The requirements which must be fulfilled in order to render an authority competent under international law to conclude treaties ought to be distinguished from those which may customarily be observed before recognition is accorded. It is true—as has been said by several writers—that a treaty cannot logically be negotiated with and entered into with a legally non-existent entity, or a legally non-existent authority. The conclusion of a treaty between two states must imply that the government of each party considers that there exists an organ competent under international law to act on behalf of the other party. It seems unnecessary, and perhaps even unfortunate, however, to term this consideration "recognition" of any kind.[2] If the term "recognition" were understood literally, its use in this connexion would be unobjectionable. The term is rarely understood merely literally, however, and it appears that in the practice of states "recognition" is mostly an act—a signal—to which various legal effects are attached in various legal systems.[3]

It is conceivable that objective criteria may be found, or may in the future be found, for the circumstances in which "recognition" should and should not be accorded to a state or a government. That problem will not be considered here. The following inquiry will only concern the

---

[8] See Hackworth's *Digest,* vol. I, p. 185; and Marek, pp. 54–55.

[9] Se *ibid.*

[1] Chailley, p. 217; Gemma, p. 370; Marek, p. 143.

[2] Some writers maintain that *de facto* recognition is accorded by the conclusion of a treaty. See, for instance, Vitta, p. 64, n. 6.

[3] See, generally, Oppenheim, vol. 1, p. 137.

question whether objective criteria may be found for the conditions under which an authority may validly assume treaty obligations under international law on behalf of a state. It is possible that such criteria, if found, would prove identical or similar to those which may—one day—be taken to indicate conditions in which the according of recognition is obligatory. It is certain, however, that in the present practice of states, treaties are sometimes concluded with entities not "recognized" as states, and authorities not "recognized" as governments.[4] This circumstance is not as illogical as has been contended.[5] It demonstrates simply that a government may be willing to have some relations under international law with another entity or authority, while holding other possible relations in abeyance, perhaps with a view to bargaining.[6] Conversely, it is possible that a government may have recognized a foreign government—and thereby placed itself in a certain relation to it—while declining to enter into any new treaty relations with it, because it considers it incompetent to assume such obligations on behalf of the state.[7]

Let us now turn to an examination of a number of diplomatic incidents and court cases in which the treaty-making competence of revolutionary governments was at issue.

4. Incidents and Cases

Salaverry incident 1835

In 1835 the validity of a treaty then concluded between Chile and Peru was the subject of several notes exchanged between the Government of Chile and the Minister accredited to that Government by the United States. On 3 April 1835, the American Minister reported to the Secretary of State that, not long before, a treaty which contained

---

[4] For instances, see Marek, p. 143; Gemma, p. 374; *China Yearbook* 1924, p. 866. A recent case in point is the payment agreement made by the Government of Finland with the Government of the German Democratic Republic on 19 July 1951, a date at which the latter State and Government was not recognized by the Finnish Government. On the legal status of the German Democratic Republic, and especially on treaties entered into by its Government, see Pinto, "The International Status of the German Democratic Republic" in *Journal du Droit International*, 86th year (1959), at pp. 375, 385 and ff.

[5] Gemma, p. 371.

[6] See also Lauterpacht, *Recognition in International Law* (1947), pp. 375 ff.

[7] See above, pp. 111–112, and statement by Gemma, quoted above, p. 111, note 3.

features detrimental to the interests of the United States had been signed between Chile and Peru; on behalf of the latter State by a representative of the constitutional government of General Obregon.[8] Subsequently a revolution led by General Salaverry broke out and gained ground in Peru. In the hope that this circumstance might lead the Chilean Government to reopen the question of the treaty, the American Minister tried to convince that Government that the treaty was unfavourable, but his efforts were unsuccessful.[9] In August 1835, the Minister learnt on the one hand that the government of General Salaverry had ratified the treaty, and, on the other hand, that forces of the constitutional government were marching towards the capital of Peru. In the combination of these circumstances he saw a possibility of challenging the validity of the treaty on the ground that it was ratified by an incompetent authority.[1] In the first place he argued that the treaty was null because, the Constitution of Peru not having been expressly revoked by Salaverry, and therefore, allegedly, being in force, the treaty required the assent of the legislature, and such had not been given. It is of greater interest in this connexion to note, however, that in the ensuing discussion both the Minister of the United States and the Chilean Foreign Minister recognized that treaties concluded by a revolutionary *"de facto* government" are binding internationally, and that the discussion focused upon the question whether the authority of Salaverry could be considered a *"de facto* government". It was thus argued by the United States Minister that the principle that a *de facto* government is one with which other nations may treat could not apply to the power of General Salaverry. In support of this contention, the Minister stated that, at the time of ratification, General Salaverry had had no control over four out of seven provinces of Peru, and the constitutional President of Peru was claiming his authority and preparing to vindicate it. Moreover, no member of the diplomatic corps at Lima had formally recognized the authority of Salaverry.[2] In the opinion of the American Minister, Peru had simply not possessed any authority competent to bind the State by a ratification:

[8] Manning, *Diplomatic Correspondence of the United States, Inter-American Affairs,* 1831–1860, vol. V (1935), Chile–Colombia, p. 45.

[9] *Ibid.,* pp. 51–64.

[1] *Ibid.,* pp. 78–80.

[2] *Ibid.,* pp. 80–81. But *cf. ibid.,* p. 63, where a dispatch of 12 May 1835 is recorded in which the Minister states that the United States Minister to Peru had officially recognized the Salaverry government.

"... there was an interregnum in the properly constituted Government of that country. General Salaverry having seized upon the Government cannot be considered as its organ until it is so determined by the people. Then it would seem that no act of his could be binding as the act of the nation."[3]

In reply to the contentions advanced by the American Minister, the Chilean Foreign Minister maintained that the constitutionality of a regime was irrelevant with respect to its authority to conclude treaties, provided that the regime was effective.[4] At the time when the treaty had been ratified, he argued, the authority of General Salaverry had been the *de facto* government of Peru:

"... nearly all Peru was subject to his authority, not by force of arms, but by a spontaneous act of nearly all the departments ... officials all vied with each other in proclaiming and recognizing him as the head of the nation ..."[5]

In addition to spontaneous support from citizens and recognition by officials, the Chilean Minister considered acquiescence of the rest of the nation evidence of *de facto* authority; and such authority was maintained to be enough to allow foreign states to treat with the government wielding it.[6]

Though in February 1836 the constitutional government of Peru defeated the forces of General Salaverry and executed him, and though it appears to have declared the treaty with Chile null and void,[7] the grounds advanced for these actions not being published, the chief interest of the incident lies in the clear adherence of the United States Minister and the Chilean Foreign Minister to the principle of the competence of a *de facto* government to conclude treaties, and to the not dissimilar criteria by which they determined the existence of a *de facto* government.

United States and Peru 1841

Another incident involving the United States and Peru had regard to the ratification of a Claims Convention signed between the two States at Lima on 17 March 1841.[8] Article 7 of the Convention laid down that

[3] *Ibid.*, p. 83.

[4] A quotation of his statement is found below, at p. 140.

[5] Manning, *loc. cit.*, p. 85.

[6] See below, p. 139.

[7] Manning, *loc. cit.*, pp. 96–97.

[8] Miller, *Treaties and other International Acts of the United States of America*, vol. 4 (1931), pp. 329–345.

ratifications should be exchanged within two years from the signing, and after approval by the United States Senate and the Congress of Peru. When, on 5 January 1843, the former body gave its consent, it was evident that the instruments of ratification could not be exchanged within the time prescribed, and the Senate therefore authorized the Government to effect that exchange before 20 December 1843. Executive ratification having been effected shortly after the Senate approval, an instrument was transmitted the same month by the Secretary of State to the United States Minister in Peru, with the instruction that, if he were to effect an exchange of ratifications after 17 March 1843—the deadline imposed by the Convention—he should see to it that the agent of the other party was duly empowered to do so. The Secretary of State continued:

> "A clause in the Convention requires for it the approval of the Congress of Peru previously to ratification by the Executive head of that Republic. If this sanction should not have been given and should in the existing state of things there still be deemed indispensable, you need not detain the bearer of this letter ... If, however, there should not have been a material change in the political affairs of that Country since the 8th of August last, it is supposed that the person exercising the functions of President of Peru will deem himself authorized to ratify the Convention without submitting it to the consideration of the Congress of that Republic. Under all the circumstances, it is not deemed necessary at present that any steps should be taken on our part with a view to a new Convention for the purpose of extending the time within which the exchange may take place."[9]

It appears that the United States Minister succeeded in persuading the administration of the "Supreme Director" General Vivanco to effect an exchange of ratifications, and such took place on 22 July 1843 without prior Peruvian legislative approval, there having been no session of the Peruvian Congress since 1840, and there being no prospect of one before April 1844.

Though the Peruvian instrument of ratification carried no date, it seems to have been signed before 17 March 1843 by the chief executive preceding General Vivanco. It contained that executive's approval of the Convention, but stipulated, at the same time, that the Convention and the ratification were to be submitted to the National Congress for final approbation, in accordance with Article 7 of the Convention. Two full powers, one similar to the other, issued by General Vivanco, authorized the exchange of ratifications, and laid down expressly that

---

[9] *Ibid.*, p. 337.

the exchange should take place without prejudice to the circumstances that the period prescribed in the Convention had lapsed, and, since Congress had been unable to meet "in opportune time" and, moreover, the Government was exercising the legislative powers "demanded by the needs of the state", without the approval of the National Congress. When transmitting the instrument of ratification and the full power to the State Department, the United States Minister expressed his opinion that, there having been no session of the Peruvian legislature, and the executive of that country exercising legislative power, the ratification was sufficient for any purpose, "absolute and unconditional."[1] Subsequently the Convention was proclaimed in the United States.

In October, 1843, General Vivanco was deposed, and the United States Minister to Lima reported to the State Department that the new government, which claimed to be constitutional, had decided that the ratification of the convention was insufficient, because effected by General Vivanco, whose government had been an usurpation, the acts of which were null, and because it had not been approved by the Peruvian Congress as was provided by its terms. The Minister added:

"All this affected reverence for constitutional forms, is but a subterfuge, the object being, I have no doubt, either to avoid the payment of the claims entirely or to postpone it indefinitely. There has been no Congress to approve the Convention, but being ratified by two executive chiefs ... the ratification could not have been more formal or more effectual."[2]

Two years later, in October 1845, the Peruvian Congress nevertheless approved the convention, though in doing so it added a further condition. That condition was subsequently submitted to the United States Senate as an "amendment" and approved, and new ratification of the Convention was authorized to take place within two years. The President of the United States thereupon issued a new instrument of ratification which made reference to the circumstance that Article 7 of the Convention had not been observed, and that the legislatures had given their approval. Instruments of ratification were exchanged on 31 October 1846.[3]

The fact that the United States issued a second instrument of ratification may be interpreted as acquiescence in the Peruvian claim that the

[1] Dispatch of 24 July 1843. See *ibid.,* p. 338.
[2] *Ibid.,* p. 340.
[3] *Ibid.,* p. 345.

first ratification had been void because effected without prior legislative approval, and because acts of General Vivanco were denied validity as being performed by an "usurper".[4] It must be noted in this case, however, that the constitutional Peruvian Government did not object to the contents of the Convention, but merely to the procedures employed. Had the Peruvian Government, as first feared by the United States Minister, repudiated the Convention altogether, on the ground that it was ratified by an incompetent authority, the United States Government might have endorsed the attitude taken by its Minister that "the ratification could not have been more formal or more effectual." The temptation must have been great to agree to a new process of ratification in order to attain Peruvian performance under the treaty, regardless of the view taken of the validity of the first ratification. It is worth noting, furthermore, that the United States Government appears, indeed, at least to have avoided conceding that the first Peruvian ratification was void as issuing from an incompetent authority. Both in the Senate resolution approving the treaty, and in the second instrument of ratification, the only ground expressly offered for the lack of validity of the first exchange of ratifications was that Article 7 of the Convention, requiring the exchange of ratifications within two years, had not been observed. Though, if the United States should have regarded General Vivanco as competent to authorize ratification, it may be difficult to understand why the full power issued by the General could not have been regarded as effecting a modification of Article 7 of the Convention, and though it is not known what degree of "effectiveness" the Vivanco government displayed, it is not unreasonable to suppose, on the basis of the foregoing, that the United States Government did not intend to acquiesce in the grounds advanced by the new Peruvian Government for the nullity of the first procedure of ratification, and that the attitude taken by the Secretary of State in his first instruction to the effect that legislative approval was irrelevant under the prevailing circumstances, was not belied by the subsequent agreement of that Government to a second process of ratification. It must be noted, finally, that since the Peruvian Government did not object to the contents of the treaty, its objection must have been prompted chiefly by reasons of principle. It is unfortunate that the documents do not reveal whether the Peruvian Government specified what it meant by an "usurper".

[4] See Jones, pp. 139–140.

United States and Peru 1847

A note of 22 April 1847 by the Peruvian Minister to Washington, and a reply of 9 June of the same year by the United States Secretary of State, Mr. Buchanan, provide some further material of interest to the topic under discussion.[5]

It seems not to have been disputed between the two Governments that by the end of 1835 General Santa Cruz, the President of Bolivia, invaded Peru, and that during 1835 he had subdued that country. He appears to have divided Peru into two states, North Peru and South Peru, and by a compact of April 1837 a confederation of Bolivia, South Peru and North Peru was decreed. Though this instrument is said to have been subject to the approval of the legislative bodies of the three states, such, apparently, was never given. By October 1837—according to the Peruvian note—South Peru was no longer under the control of Santa Cruz, in July 1838 the capital was said to have risen against him, and in 1839, finally, he was driven from the country.

In the early part of this unstable period, on 30 November 1836, plenipotentiaries of the President of the United States and of "the Supreme Protector of the North and South Peruvian States, President of the Republic of Bolivia, encharged with the direction of the Foreign Relations of the Peru–Bolivian Confederation" signed a treaty. Ratifications were exchanged much later, on 28 May 1838, and thus at a time when the General was losing ground. Though not long after his downfall a law was passed declaring that Peru did not acknowledge the treaty made with the United States, that law appears not to have been published until 1845. Notice of it was given to the United States only in 1847 by the Peruvian note cited above. This note is of considerable interest. Having referred to the circumstances related above, the Peruvian Minister denied that the Confederacy was sufficiently well established to possess the capacity to enter into treaties, and maintained that even if it had possessed such capacity, the treaty in question would have been entered into by an incompetent authority, because the Federal Compact prescribed that the consent of the Senate was required for the conclusion of treaties and that body was never assembled or even appointed.

Though the Minister readily admitted that "governments *de facto*" were competent to conclude treaties on behalf of the states they con-

[5] Miller, *Treaties and other International Acts of the United States of America,* vol. 4 (1931), pp. 102–106.

trolled, he denied that the authority of General Santa Cruz had constituted such a government. In his opinion, the General was only "a foreign chieftain who invaded the country without cause, ruled it by force of arms, and who was incessantly engaged in hostilities to maintain his power." He added:

> "None of the qualities which are thought indispensable to constitute a government de facto out of any authority—viz., the entire submission of the country, the undisturbed possession of the supreme power, strengthened and consolidated by time—constituted the powers of General Santa Cruz in Peru."[6]

The Minister also interestingly emphasized that nowhere would it be more fatal than in states exposed to the evils of political vissicitudes, if it were a principle that any authority, whatever its origin, the means employed by it to stay in power, however destitute of permanence implying the consent of the nation, would be considered competent to bind the state towards other nations. This, he avowed, was the reason why Peru denounced the treaty as "a sinister precedent" which might otherwise have been authorized by her silence.

The United States Government, in its reply not surprisingly stressed that seven years had passed between the Peruvian municipal law denouncing the treaty, and the Peruvian notification. In this period the Government of Peru had consistently respected the Convention. With regard to the authority of Santa Cruz, it was pointed out that he had achieved supreme power in the republic before the treaty was signed, and that his downfall had occurred only after the treaty was ratified.

As appears clearly from the above account, both sides in this controversy were agreed that a *"de facto* government" was competent to bind the state by a treaty. Their difference had regard only to the degree of respect an authority must enjoy, and the permanence it must evidence, to be considered a *de facto* government. The Peruvian Government maintained fairly strict requirements in this regard, and it may be presumed that the United States would have disputed them more severely, had it not thought the argument of Peruvian acquiescence conclusive.

Peru and Ecuador 1861

In the beginning of September, 1859, a revolution broke out in Ecuador. The constitutional president resigned his office and planned

[6] *Ibid.,* p. 104.

to withdraw to Chile. The capital and several cities and provinces fell into the hands of the revolutionary party, and at the end of November, the Provisional Government of that party appeared to have established its authority in all the provinces of the State, except that of Guyaquil, where a local government resisted, under the leadership of a general of the name of Franco.[7] This situation seems to have subsisted for some time. In March 1860 the United States Minister to Quito reported to the State Department that the Provisional Government had extended its authority over all the mountain country. The authority of General Franco at Guyaquil was confined to the lowlands west of the Andes. He further reported that General Franco's negotiating a treaty with Peru for the cession of a large region claimed by Ecuador East of the Andes had caused many local protests. The conclusion of the treaty had weakened the government of General Franco, and tended to strengthen the Provisional Government.[8] In September of the same year the army of General Franco seems to have been decisively defeated by the forces of the Provisional Government, and from then on that Government was the only authority acknowledged in the republic.

Such appears to have been the background of a note sent on 5 October 1861 by the Ecuadorian Government to the Peruvian Government. The note reveals that the Peruvian Government had demanded fulfilment of a treaty concluded at Guyaquil on 25 January 1860, in all probability the treaty referred to in the United States diplomatic correspondence cited above. In reply to this demand, the Ecuadorian Government declared:

"... les principes du droit international enseignent que la faculté de célébrer des traités publics appartient exclusivement au Souverain; que ces traités ne sont pas valides sans l'approbation du Pouvoir législatif dans les pays régis par des Constitutions qui le prescrivent de la sorte; et que l'échange des ratifications ne peut se faire qu'autant qu'il est précédé de l'approbation susmentionnée."

Though this declaration can perhaps only be interpreted as an endorsement of the theory that constitutional provisions requiring legislative approval of treaties are internationally relevant, the Ecua-

---

[7] The source from which description of this incident is drawn is Manning, *Diplomatic Correspondence of the United States, Inter-American Affairs, 1831–1860,* vol. VI (1935), Dominican Republic, Ecuador, France, pp. 427 ff. See also Jones, p. 140.

[8] Manning, *loc. cit.,* p. 431.

dorian Government did not, on the other hand, deny that apparent possession of power gives legal competence. It stated:

"... un traité de paix ne laisse pas que d'être obligatoire quoique ayant été célébré par une autorité incompétente, irrégulière et usurpatrice, *si cette autorité a la possession apparente du pouvoir qu'elle exerce.*"[9]

The Ecuadorian Government went on to declare that a local authority was not competent to exercise the treaty-making power which attached to the "sovereign". The treaty invoked by Peru was not valid because it had been made by a general who had exercised authority only over a small fraction of the state, while the authority of the Provisional Government had extended over the majority of the population. The alleged circumstance that neutral powers had not recognized the diplomatic agent accredited by the general to the Government of Peru proved, alone, that the authority which had signed the treaty had not represented the nation. In addition, the Ecuadorian Government protested, the treaty had been ratified by the general himself and had not been approved by Congress, which was indispensable.

Franco-Chilean arbitration 1901

An award rendered in 1901 by an arbitration tribunal in a dispute between France and Chile may also be examined in this connexion.[1] Although the award had regard to a contract made by an unconstitutional authority, the reasoning of the tribunal aimed primarily at the rules applicable to treaties concluded under similar circumstances, and is of considerable interest to this study.

A contract made in 1869 between the French enterprise Dreyfus Brothers and Co. and the Peruvian Government gave rise to a number of controversies between the parties. Complete settlement of these was attempted by means of a new compact entered into in November 1880 by the company and the government of the dictator Nicolas de Pierola, which purported to act on behalf of Peru.

Chile having succeeded to part of the debt of the State of Peru, a Franco-Chilean tribunal had occasion in 1901 to examine the competence of the Pierola government to represent Peru. Payment being claimed of a debt recognized in the compact made with the Pierola

[9] For the text of this note, see *Fontes Juris Gentium*, Ser. B, Sec. 1, Tomus 1, Pars 1, p. 725. (Emphasis supplied.)

[1] The text of the award is found in Descamps et Renault, *Recueil International des Traités du XXe siècle*, 1901, p. 393.

government, it was objected before the tribunal that the Government of Peru had contested the validity of the acts of the Pierola government. In support of that position it had invoked the Peruvian Constitution of 1860, Article 10 of which read as follows:

"Sont nuls les actes de ceux qui ont usurpé les fonctions publiques et les emplois confiés sous les conditions prescrites par la Constitution et les lois."

The tribunal found, however, that the constitutional provision invoked could have no effect unless it was in force at the time when the compact was made. Upon his seizing power in 1879 Pierola had promulgated "Provisional Statutes" which suspended the Constitution of 1860. The question whether that Constitution should prevail over the Statutes depended upon the validity of the dictatorial regime itself, and could not be determined by application of the Constitution. The Court said:

"...elle ne peut dès lors être résolue que par un principe supérieur à la loi positive, puisque les révolutions de l'organisme politique auxquelles les pouvoirs publics sont impuissants à résister échappent par leur force propre à l'application de cette loi, établie en vue d'un ordre de choses différent; ..."

This principle superior to positive—domestic—law, the tribunal sought in international law. It found that though in the interest of monarchies it had earlier been denied by European diplomacy, it was now universally admitted that the competence of a government to represent the state in international relations did not depend upon the "legitimacy" of its origin. The tribunal stated the principle as follows:

"...l'usurpateur qui détient en fait le pouvoir avec l'assentiment exprès ou tacite de la nation agit et conclut valablement au nom de l'Etat des traités, que le Gouvernement légitime restauré est tenu de respecter..."

The tribunal went on to say that this principle must be valid not only for treaties concluded under international law, but also for contracts made under public domestic law. The underlying rationale was the same in both situations, namely the circumstance that, apart from cases of pure anarchy, the continuous existence of the state necessarily calls for a power able to act in its name.[2] To satisfy this need, the application of the principle of competence and continuity must not, in the opinion of the tribunal, be restricted to authorities which had subsisted

---

[2] "...en dehors des cas d'anarchie pure, la permanence de l'existence de l'État suppose nécessairement la présence d'un pouvoir qui agit en son nom et qui le représente; ..." *Ibid.*, p. 395.

a prolonged period of time.[3] The tribunal found, indeed, that the conditions, the fulfilment of which were required by an authority in order that the principle of competence and continuity should apply to it, were identical with those required for its recognition, and the tribunal defined these as follows:

> "... les jurisconsultes modernes ... les plus considérables ... considèrent uniquement le point de savoir si ce régime [nouveau] présentait des caractères de stabilité et d'autorité tels qu'on pût envisager ses organes comme détenant en fait le pouvoir vacant par la chute du pouvoir antérieur; qu'ainsi il font dépendre la validité des actes d'un Gouvernement, même transitoire et usurpateur, de conditions identiques à celles auxquelles les Puissances étrangères subordonnent la reconnaissance d'un Chef d'Etat qui leur annonce son avènement."

Though the tribunal did not think this doctrine applicable to insurgents, it thought it must have regard to acts concluded by such intermediary or provisional governments as have proved their vitality and actually exercised power in an incontestable manner, and without finding themselves in conflict with a coexisting regular government. The tribunal attached some importance, furthermore, to the existence of popular approval of, or lack of popular opposition to, a regime:

> "... le Gouvernement qui dispose de tous les moyens d'action légale du souverain avec l'assentiment de la Nation manifesté expressément par un plébiscite ou tacitement par le fait qu'elle se soumet au pouvoir nouveau sans protester (Martens, § 81), s'impose à la reconnaissance de l'individu comme à celle des Gouvernements étrangers."

A number of instances having been cited in which the principle of competence and continuity had not been applied, the tribunal commented that these cases concerned insurrectionary governments still competing with regular governments, or governments which were in fact recognized neither by the nation nor by foreign states. Their acts and engagements would be denied validity also under the doctrine to which the tribunal had adhered. The tribunal concluded that the compact entered into by the Pierola government and the French company was binding upon Peru, because the government of Pierola had satisfied the conditions the fulfilment of which was thought required.[4]

---

[3] "... pendant un laps de temps prolongé ..." *Ibid.*

[4] The Court described as follows the factual situation which had existed in Peru. When, in 1879, the Chilean army had invaded Peru and the constitutional Peruvian President had fled from the capital, Pierola had seized the power. He had issued "Provisional Statutes" on the basis of which he had governed. From December 1879

Franco-Peruvian arbitration 1921

The reasoning adopted by the Franco-Chilean tribunal in the award related above was confirmed in an award rendered in 1921 by a Franco-Peruvian arbitration tribunal.[5] This case, too, concerned claims based upon the compact made between the Dreyfus Brothers and Co. and the Pierola government on behalf of Peru, and had regard to that part of the debt of Peru to which Chile had not succeeded. In reaching the conclusion that the compact was binding upon the State of Peru, the tribunal called attention to the circumstances that Pierola had been proclaimed chief of the republic by popular assemblies and been supported by numerous "plebiscitary adhesions", that he had exercised the executive, the legislative, and, in part, the judicial power, that his government had been recognized by a number of states, and that, finally, a British municipal court, a Belgian municipal court and the Franco-Chilean arbitration tribunal had deemed that Pierola's government had represented and bound the nation.

The Tinoco arbitration 1923

The conditions which must be fulfilled to render a revolutionary government competent under international law to bind the state it purports to represent was the subject of interesting treatment in an arbitration in 1923 between Great Britain and Costa Rica.[6] Though the obligations of the revolutionary government were undertaken towards private foreign subjects, the reasoning of the arbitrator would seem to apply with equal or even greater force to treaty obligations entered into under similar circumstances.

In January, 1917, Frederico Tinoco led a revolution against the

to July 1881, he had exercised the legislative, the executive, and, in part, the judicial power; he had imposed taxes, received revenues; he had been recognized as head of the State of Peru by foreign powers, notably by the Governments of France and Great Britain. If he had come to power by a military revolt, the resistance of the constitutional government did not seem to have lasted long. It seemed, furthermore, that he had ruled with the assent of the nation, if not recorded formally in a plebiscite, at least manifested either expressly by popular assemblies in all parts of the country, or implicitly by the fact that the rest of the population had submitted without opposition to the dictatorial government. *Ibid.,* p. 397.

[5] For the text of the award, see Scott, *Hague Court Reports* (2nd series, 1932), pp. 32 ff. The French text of the award is also found in United Nations, *Reports of International Arbitral Awards,* vol. I (1948), pp. 218 ff.

[6] For the text of the award, see *A.J.I.L.,* vol. 18 (1924), pp. 147 ff. The text is also found in Briggs, *The Law of Nations* (2nd ed., 1953), pp. 197 ff.

constitutional Government of Costa Rica and assumed power. Having called an election and established a new Constitution in June 1917, Tinoco governed the State until August 1919 when he retired and left the country. Shortly thereafter the old Constitution was restored, and new elections were held under it. In 1922 the constitutional legislature adopted a "Law of Nullities" invalidating all contracts made between the Tinoco government and private persons. Some British subjects having acquired substantial contractual rights of this kind, the British Government claimed that these had been wrongfully annulled through the Law of Nullities. The Costa Rican Government, on the other hand, disclaimed responsibility for the acts of Tinoco, and maintained that the Law of Nullities constituted lawful exercise of power.

The arbitrator found that the Tinoco regime had in fact been a sovereign government. For two years Tinoco had peaceably administered the State without any other government asserting power in the country, and the people had seemingly accepted the government with great good will. Though the arbitrator admitted that recognition of a government by foreign states constituted "an important evidential factor in establishing proof of the existence of a government in the society of nations", he did not think that *non-recognition,* when determined by inquiry not into the *de facto* sovereignty of the government but into its irregularity of origin, could outweigh other evidence as to the *de facto* character of a government "according to the standard set by international law".[7] The argument put forward by Costa Rica to the effect that to constitute a *de facto* government, the Tinoco regime ought to have been established in conformity with the Constitution of 1871 was considered a contradiction in terms by the arbitrator. He stated:

"... The issue is not whether the new government assumes power or conducts its administration under constitutional limitations established by the people during the incumbency of the government it has overthrown. The question is, has it really established itself in such a way that all within its influence recognize its control, and that there is no opposing force assuming to be a government in its place? Is it discharging its functions as a government usually does, respected within its own jurisdiction?"[8]

The circumstance, finally, that the plaintiff government had never itself recognized the revolutionary government did not, in the opinion of the arbitrator, estop it from advancing a claim. It was of no avail to show that the municipal courts of a state could not assume the

[7] Briggs, pp. 200, 201.
[8] *Ibid.,* p. 201.

de facto character of a government which was not recognized by the executive of that state. The executive branch of the government was free to change its position as to the *de facto* character of a regime which it had chosen previously not to recognize.

5. CRITERIA FOR COMPETENCE OF REVOLUTIONARY GOVERNMENTS

Much material bearing on the issues here under discussion could no doubt be gathered by an examination of circumstances in which states commonly begin to conclude treaties with governments emerging through revolutions and *coups d'état* without there arising any controversies regarding the validity of these treaties. An examination of that kind drawing on modern material would no doubt be of interest.[9] There are no reasons to believe, however, that it would add much to the conclusions which may be drawn from the cases and incidents cited above, which, unlike the more recent cases, are all found in easily accessible documents.

What, then, are the criteria emerging from the incidents and cases related above as determining whether or not a revolutionary authority is competent under international law to bind a state by a treaty?

General conclusion

The material examined above demonstrates that the rule which is sought must be expected to embody an adjustment of two functional needs ever present in the modern life of states. On the one hand, there is the need of every state community at all times to be represented by some body, and the need of the whole international community to be able to treat with a body representing the state. A gap in the representation of a state—a veritable interregnum—will inevitably cause damage in the state community as well as in the international community at large. This circumstance calls for acknowledgement of the competence of even rather ephemeral authorities.[1] On the other hand, a highly

[9] As an example of such material, the agreement on economic and technical co-operation between the Government of the Soviet Union and the revolutionary government of General Kassem, acting on behalf of Iraq, may be mentioned. At the time when the agreement was reported to have been signed, on 16 March 1959, the revolutionary government in Iraq experienced a great deal of difficulty in maintaining itself in control.

[1] See the statement by the American Minister to Mexico, quoted above, p. 117, note 7.

irresponsible authority might, not enjoying the confidence of any important force in the community, through some upset gain power for a brief period in a state before it is ousted. An authority of this kind might attempt to act on behalf of the state in a manner so contrary to the interests of the dominant forces of the state community that the acts may be expected not to be respected by a subsequent regime. This circumstance calls for the denial of international competence to an authority unless it appears to be the outcome of a reasonably permanent balance of social forces,[2] and to be speaking for that constellation. What adjustment has the practice of states produced between these two functional needs?

From all the cases and incidents cited above one requirement emerges clearly and convincingly, namely that which may be termed "effectiveness". This rather vague term calls for further definition. A number of elements are always taken into consideration as evidence of the "effectiveness" of an authority. Some of these have—erroneously, it is submitted—occasionally been claimed on the one hand as absolute requirements for international competence, and on the other, as conclusive evidence of such competence. These elements will now be considered one by one.

Permanence

According to one train of thought, an authority attains international competence as a *de facto* government only by subsisting a prolonged period of time.[3] This idea was adhered to in the note cited above in which a Peruvian Minister to Washington claimed that a *de facto* government would have to be "strengthened and consolidated by time".[4]

It is probably true in most cases that the initial period of a new government is critical,[5] and though this circumstance will no doubt most frequently make foreign governments reluctant to conclude treaties with a new government at its very inception, it would seem rash to conclude that subsistence for any period of time constitutes a *sine qua non* of international competence.

In the Franco-Chilean arbitration quoted above, the tribunal expressly rejected that idea, and there are doctrinal pronouncements to

---

[2] See the statement of the Peruvian Minister quoted above, p. 126; and that of the Foreign Minister of the government in Mexico City, quoted above, p. 111.

[3] See references given by Gemma, p. 310, note 1.

[4] Above, p. 126.

[5] Gemma, p. 310.

the contrary.[6] It is submitted to be rightly stressed by Dr. Gemma, on the other hand, that the subsistence of a government for a period of time may well raise a presumption as to its "vitality", or, to use the term chosen, its effectiveness.

Recognition

According to another school of thought, recognition of an authority conclusively proves its international competence to conclude treaties. It was thus maintained by the Government of Ecuador, in one of the incidents cited above, that the alleged circumstance that the representative in Peru of the general who had purported to conclude a treaty on behalf of Ecuador had not been recognized by the diplomatic agents in Peru of neutral powers, made it unnecessary to give other proof of the contention that the general did not represent Ecuador. The same idea is adhered to by Dr. Gemma who queries whether the Franco-Chilean tribunal could not, in the award cited above, simply have referred to the recognition accorded by foreign governments to the Pierola regime in order to prove conclusively that Pierola's government was competent to bind Peru.[7]

There are weighty arguments militating against this doctrine, and much authority that rebuts it. It may first be noted that the Ecuadorian Government, whose opinion was cited, was not content to rely upon the absence of recognition alone, but was careful to point out that the authority of the general who had concluded the treaty in question had extended only over a fraction of the State, while that of the government residing in the capital had extended over the majority of the population.

Similarly, though the Franco-Chilean tribunal did refer to the Pierola government's being recognized by foreign powers, it clearly considered this fact only as one among several others, which, taken together, led to the conclusion that the Pierola government was competent to represent Peru. It appears, indeed, that the tribunal considered recognition only indirect evidence of competence, for it invoked authority to the effect that the criteria for competence were *identical* with those by which states were said to determine whether or not to recognize an authority. The logical inference from this statement is obviously that recognition is not, in itself, an absolute condition for international

[6] *Ibid.*
[7] Gemma, p. 360.

competence, but is likely to indicate that those conditions which *are* required for such competence are satisfied.

In the Salaverry incident, similarly, the American Minister to Chile seems to have considered the non-recognition of Salaverry not as conclusively showing his lack of international competence, but only as indicating that the conditions required for competence were not fulfilled.

The clearest pronouncement on the relation between recognition and international competence is found in the Tinoco case. The judgment in that dispute gives strong support to the view that recognition constitutes only indirect evidence of competence. The arbitrator had no doubt that there was an international law standard by which the existence of an internationally competent government could be determined. This may be seen clearly from the fact that though he considered recognition of an authority important evidence of its competence, having found that in the case before him the non-recognition was caused by considerations extraneous to the legal standard he thought required, he refused to conclude from it that there was no internationally competent government. It followed as a logical consequence of this view that even a foreign government, having refused to recognize the authority in question, could later argue that that authority had been competent to bind the state it purported to represent.[8]

In the Tinoco case, it is important to note, further, the clear distinction drawn by the international arbitrator between his own power and that of a national court to decide on the international competence of a national authority. While he confessed that domestic courts could not without inconvenience be attributed such power,[9] and must, therefore, follow the conclusions reached in this matter by the executive branches of their governments, he did not admit that an international tribunal was in a similar position, but was clearly of the opinion that such a tribunal was entitled to reach its own conclusion concerning the international competence of a national authority.

It would, indeed, be peculiar if recognition accorded by a state to a revolutionary authority would at present automatically make that au-

---

[8] This conclusion would seem to refute the suggestion made by Gemma with regard to the Pierola case, to the effect that had France not recognized the Pierola government, the tribunal could not have substituted its own judgment of the competence of that government. See Gemma, p. 360.

[9] *Cf.* Gemma, p. 393; and see below, p. 367.

thority competent to bind the state it purported to represent. If such were the case, a foreign state might conceivably attempt to instigate a fake revolution and to recognize an ephemeral puppet authority in order immediately to conclude a desired agreement with it.[1]

Popular approval

In almost all the incidents and cases cited above the parties were careful to refer to the presence of popular approval or resistance to the revolutionary authorities concerned. In the Salaverry incident, for instance, the American Minister maintained that the general could not be regarded as an organ of the Peruvian Government until so determined by the people, while the Chilean Foreign Minister argued in support of his case that nearly all Peru had spontaneously subjected itself to the general, and that officials were eager to recognize him as head of the nation. In view of such expressions it might be asked if perhaps the popular approval of an authority constitutes a *sine qua non* for its international competence. The answer seems to be in the negative.

Though Dr. Gemma suggests confidently that a government cannot long maintain itself against the will of the people,[2] he cites, himself, the more moderate pronouncement by Cavour to the effect that the support of public opinion is the most secure means of preserving a government.[3] Evidently public support of an authority must be regarded as likely to strengthen it and to increase its stability. It is submitted that this circumstance, in addition to a certain tendency to international support for democratic forms of government, explains why the element of popular approval is generally taken into consideration by the international community. It would be erroneous, on the other hand, to see in such approval a *sine qua non* of effectiveness or competence. The tribunal adjudicating the Franco-Chilean controversy cited Martens to the effect that the assent of the nation is required either expressly in the form of a plebiscite or *tacitly* by its submission without protests to the new authority. It would seem that in the practice of states submission of the people without any active resistance is all that is required.

The means by which submission is brought about appear to be of only limited international significance. It is true that in the Salaverry

---

[1] See the statement by the Foreign Minister of the Mexican government residing in the capital in 1859, above, p. 111. See also below, p. 144.

[2] Gemma, pp. 316–317.

[3] *Ibid.*, p. 340.

case, the Chilean Minister emphasized in support of the competence of the government of Salaverry that the authority wielded by him was not founded upon the force of arms, and in the case of the government of General Santa Cruz, the subsequent regime in Peru was careful to stress, in arguing the lack of competence of that General, that he had ruled the country by force of arms. Against the background of such expressions it might perhaps be asked if the exercise of authority without the use of arms is an absolute requirement for international competence. The answer would seem to be that states are reluctant to treat with authorities still engaged in active hostilities. Provided, on the other hand, that the authorities have succeeded in subduing their enemies, and that their prospect of permanence appears reasonably good, foreign governments treat with them, even though they may be maintaining their authority by means of terror.[4] In this connexion the following statement found in a recent work may be cited:

"It must be regretfully conceded that it is of no relevance whatever whether the revolution expresses the will of the overwhelming majority of the nation or only of a fraction of terrorists. At the present time, 'man's right to government by consent' is still unprotected by positive international law, however obvious the connection between internal freedom and international peace."[5]

Command of respect

Step by step the above discussion has approached what seems to be the key requirement imposed upon a revolutionary authority in order to be considered effective: it must command general respect in the state it claims to represent.

The obvious explanation of the preoccupation and concentration of foreign governments upon this requirement must be seen in the circumstance that upon this respect depends the likelihood that the authority

[4] In 1957, however, the United Nations refused to accept the credentials of the Kadar government, established and maintained in power in Hungary in 1956 by the Soviet Union, and ruling by means of terror and with the aid of Soviet troops. This stand was followed, as late as 1958, by the International Labour Conference. See E. Lauterpacht, "The Contemporary Practice of the United Kingdom in the Field of International Law—Survey and Comment, VI, January 1 – June 30, 1958" in *I.C.L.Q.*, vol. 7 (1958), pp. 570–576.

[5] Marek, p. 59; *cf.* Charles de Visscher, *Théories et Réalités en Droit International Public* (2nd French ed., 1955), p. 291. The opinion of Spiropoulos may also be noted:

"The manner in which the *de facto* government maintains itself in power—whether it be through terror or by peaceful means—is irrelevant from the point of view of international law." Translation supplied in Marek, p. 59. The original passage— in German—is found in Spiropoulos, *Die de facto Regierung im Völkerrecht* (1926), p. 26.

will be able, in fact, to carry out the international obligations which it purports to undertake, as well as those which have been assumed in the past. The prognosis in this regard seems to be all that foreign states examine at present, pressed by the need to safeguard their interests and those of their citizens. A better illustration of the findings made above can hardly be found than the following opinion voiced in 1877 by Secretary of State Fish:

"The origin and organization of government are questions generally of internal discussion and decision. Foreign powers deal with the existing de facto government, when sufficiently established to give reasonable assurance of its permanence, and of the acquiescence of those who constitute the state in its ability to maintain itself, and to discharge its internal duties and its external obligations."[6]

The cases and incidents cited above also offer good illustrations of the same point. In the Salaverry incident the American Minister to Chile tried to demonstrate that the General commanded only limited obedience by alleging that he controlled only four out of seven provinces, and he described the prognosis as dark by the statement that the constitutional President of Peru was preparing to vindicate his authority. The Chilean Foreign Minister, on the other hand, supported his stand by claiming that nearly all Peru was subject to Salaverry's authority, and he tried to make the prospects of the General look good by emphasizing that the authority of the General rested on spontaneous support in nearly all departments and on acquiescence of the nation, but not upon the force of arms.

In the Ecuadorian case, the Government of Ecuador significantly admitted that a treaty would be binding although concluded by an internally incompetent, irregular and usurped authority on the condition only that it appeared to possess the power it purported to exercise. A general whose authority extended only over a fraction of the state could not appear to have such power; so much the less when there existed another government commanding the respect of the majority of the population.

In the Franco-Chilean arbitration, the tribunal similarly attached importance to the stability and "vitality" of an authority, to the question whether or not it was challenged by another authority, and to the acquiescence of the people. The tribunal adjudging the Franco-Peruvian case also stressed the popular approval of the Pierola regime,

[6] Moore's *Digest*, vol. I, p. 250.

and the circumstance that the dictator had in fact exercised all governmental authority there was to exercise.

The arbitrator in the Tinoco case emphasized that Tinoco's authority had not been challenged by anyone, and the people had submitted to him with "great good will", thus finding that there was, again, complete respect and prospects for continued respect.

Irrelevance of constitutions

If the material examined consistently points to effectiveness as the key condition for the international competence of an authority, it demonstrates, as the other side of the coin, that the violation of a constitution by a revolutionary regime is irrelevant for its international competence.

The American Minister to Chile having asserted that the treaty ratified by Salaverry was null because concluded in violation of a constitution which he had not expressly revoked, the Chilean Minister eloquently replied:

"If, in order to treat with a foreign government, its titles had to be examined and proved in the crucible of written constitutions, how many of the treaties which are to-day in force would there be? De facto possession is all that foreign nations verify in order to conclude commercial conventions among themselves."[7]

And further:

"... The acts of the supreme authority of the state openly recognized by an immense majority, must be presumed to be legitimate in the eyes of foreign nations, because they bear ... the sanction of that primitive authority which makes and unmakes constitutions at its will, and the expression of which is the first law."

It may be noted, further, that although the Peruvian Government succeeding General Santa Cruz and the Ecuadorian Government which had defeated General Franco both sought to support their contentions that the treaties made by these authorities were void by arguing that, under the respective Constitutions, legislative approval would have been required, neither of them denied that an "effective" *de facto* government was competent to make treaties.

In the case examined in the Franco-Chilean arbitration the Constitution which had been revoked by Pierola had contained a specific provision declaring null in advance acts of those who usurped the

---

[7] Manning, *Diplomatic Correspondence of the United States, Inter-American Affairs*, 1831–1860, vol. V, Chile–Colombia (1935), p. 85.

Constitution. The tribunal found, however, that this very provision could be valid only if the revolutionary order was found invalid, and that that question could not be resolved by reference to the old Constitution, but only by principles superior to domestic law, to wit, international law.

The arbitrator in the Tinoco case, likewise, expressed the opinion that it was irrelevant whether a revolutionary government respected constitutional limitations previously established, and that the real question was whether the control exercised by the new government was recognized and unopposed within its own jurisdiction.

6. Doctrine Confirming the Conclusions Reached

The conclusions reached above are confirmed by many writers, and it may suffice merely to quote some of them. Gemma maintains that the foundation of a *de facto* government lies in its aptitude to maintain order and to accomplish all the functions which attach to sovereignity. In his opinion, it is the ability and willingness of the government to fulfil its obligations that is decisive to enable it to be a party to a treaty.[8]

Anzilotti expresses himself as follows:

"... au point de vue du droit international, on ne distingue pas entre les gouvernements légitimes et les gouvernements illégitimes, les gouvernements *de iure* et les gouvernements *de facto*. Celui qui détient réellement le pouvoir de commander (*qui actu regit*) a, dans les rapports internationaux, la qualité d'organe de la personnalité internationale dont il s'agit; celui qui perd en fait ce pouvoir cesse de représenter internationalement l'État ..."[9]

Larnaude, in his study of *de facto* governments, pronounces the following opinion:

"Ce qu'il faut, mais ce qui suffit pour rendre aux yeux des puissances étrangères le gouvernement de fait capable d'être une personne du droit international avec qui elles peuvent traiter et qui représente valablement l'État, c'est la constatation que ce gouvernement est obéi en fait ..."

And further:

"Les États étrangers ont un critérium exclusivement réaliste pour distinguer les gouvernements avec lesquels ils sont appelés à avoir des rapports ...: c'est l'obéissance de fait... de la population régie par ces gouvernements. Il ne

---

[8] Gemma, p. 316, and see the statement quoted above, p. 111, note 3. See, however, the discussion in Spiropoulos, pp. 37 ff.

[9] Anzilotti, p. 179.

peut dépendre d'un État quelconque, et quelque respectable que soit le principe de souveraineté législative, d'exiger que les États étrangers renoncent à une règle qui, seule, leur permet de donner satisfaction aux intérêts dont ils ont la garde."[1]

The following statement by Marek may also be quoted:

"... As a rule, negotiations can only be conducted with a real and effective government; treaties can only be concluded with such a government which alone can give the guarantee of their implementation, and only a real and effective government can successfully be held responsible. In all those real transactions of international law fictitious or merely claimant governments can have no place."[2]

The views expressed by Chailley may finally be noted:

"... l'on peut dire qu'un État ne l'accorde [reconnaissance] à un gouvernement étranger que lorsqu'il a conscience ou se croit fondé à espérer que ce gouvernement fera preuve d'une vitalité telle que la conclusion d'un traité avec lui ne demeurera pas œuvre vaine. La reconnaissance et la conclusion du traité supposent que le gouvernement considéré présente des garanties de stabilité qui l'autorisent à représenter, dans les relations internationales, l'État au nom duquel il prétend parler: les principales de ces garanties sont l'effectivité de son pouvoir, l'obéissance qu'il reçoit ou sait obtenir de la généralité des gouvernés, la confiance qu'on lui accorde ou qu'il conquiert. En un mot, l'acceptation du gouvernement par les gouvernés est le fondement dernier de sa capacité internationale; ..."

And further:

"... lorsqu'un gouvernement a fini par se faire obéir d'une façon générale, sa compétence n'est plus contestée, en pratique, du point de vue juridique; *la conviction juridique est que ce gouvernement a un titre valable pour gouverner;* l'acceptation du gouvernement par les gouvernés est devenu le principe de sa compétence. C'est ce principe, et non l'idée d'une légitimité constitutionnelle, qui correspond à la conviction juridique des États et qui traduit le droit positif; c'est lui que fonde, en particulier, du point de vue interne, la validité des traités conclus par le gouvernement de fait."[3]

7. Criteria for Lack of Competence

If, as is hoped, the above discussion has made clear the criteria by which is determined the competence of a revolutionary government to conclude treaties, it should also have indicated, *e contrario,* when

---

[1] Larnaude, pp. 496 and 499.
[2] Marek, p. 59.
[3] Chailley, pp. 217 and 219.

such competence does not exist. In this connexion the following statement by Dr. Gemma may be quoted:

"... Ou bien le gouvernement insurrectionnel n'est pas arrivé à une consistance quelconque; c'est-à-dire il a menacé, mais il n'a pas bouleversé le droit public existant, et alors il était inutile de prévoir quoi que ce soit. Tous les actes d'un soi-disant dictateur, d'une soi-disant assemblée constituante etc., sont des actes contre la loi et leur nullité n'a point besoin d'une déclaration préalable. Ou bien la révolution, ou le coup d'état a réussi et le gouvernement de fait a trouvé sa légitimation ..."[4]

In some situations there will be no difficulty in establishing that a particular authority does not constitute a competent government. An interesting example is offered by the case of the Kuusinen government, which purported to represent Finland during the Russo-Finnish war of 1939–1940. At the beginning of the war, Otto Kuusinen formed a "Finnish People's Government" on a small fraction of Finnish territory, occupied by the Soviet Union. It claimed to be competent to represent Finland internationally, and attempted to brand the regular Finnish Government as the "Helsinki clique".[5] The Soviet Union immediately accorded recognition to the "revolutionary" government which—not surprisingly—had acceded to Soviet demands upon Finland, and even requested military aid from the Soviet Union. On the basis of these constructions, and in spite of the notorious existence of a shooting war, the Soviet Union contended that it was not at war with Finland. On 2 December 1939 it even purported to conclude a "Treaty of Mutual Assistance and Friendship" with the friendly Finnish government,[6] and,

---

[4] Gemma, p. 362.

[5] Dallin, *Soviet Russia's Foreign Policy*, pp. 126–128 (as cited by Marek, p. 66). See also Tanner, *The Winter War* (1957), pp. 101 ff.

[6] The preamble of this treaty reads as follows:

"The Presidium of the Supreme Soviet of the USSR on the one side, and the Government of the Democratic Republic on the other, being convinced that now, when the heroic struggle of the Finnish people and the efforts of the Red Army of the USSR are eliminating the extremely dangerous seat of war created on the frontier of the Soviet Union by the former plutocratic Government in Finland to please the imperialist Powers, and when the Finnish people has formed its democratic republic, based on the full support of the people, the time has come to establish lasting friendly relations between our countries and ensure by joint efforts the security and invincibility of our States; ... have appointed for this purpose as their plenipotentiaries:

The Presidium of the Supreme Soviet of the USSR: V. M. Molotov.

The People's Government of Finland: Otto Kuusinen, Chairman of the People's Government and Minister of Foreign Affairs of Finland,

who, having presented their credentials, which were found to be drawn up in due form and good order, agreed on the following ..." Degras, *Soviet Documents on Foreign Policy*, vol. 3, pp. 406 ff.

in a telegram of 5 December 1939 to the Council of the League of Nations, the Foreign Minister of the Soviet Union, Mr. Molotov, referred to the treaty as solving all the questions which the Soviet Government had "fruitlessly discussed with delegates [of the] former Finnish Government now divested of its power."[7] He declared that, accordingly, the League was not justified in convoking the Assembly. The League of Nations had no difficulty in concluding, however, that the Kuusinen "government" was incompetent to bind the State of Finland. It attached no value to the "treaty", but expelled the Soviet Union for its attack on Finland.[8] It is of interest to note also, that when the Soviet Government later concluded a peace treaty with Finland, it was compelled to sign it with the regular Finnish Government in Helsinki. The "revolutionary government" had then evaporated.[9]

Dr. Marek cites the Kuusinen case as an example of a "fake revolution"—a form of illegal intervention by a foreign state—and distinguishes this situation from that of a genuine revolution which, if successful, produces a government competent to speak for the state. In her opinion, the competence of a government emerging from a fake revolution, on the other hand, is doubtful, because the very statehood of a puppet "state" is in doubt.[1] This is not the place to enter into a full discussion of Dr. Marek's interesting analysis. It may be sufficient to point out that if the puppet government subsists for a prolonged period of time without being formally merged with that of the mother state, foreign states eventually tend to accept it and to treat with it. It seems probable that it is the instability attached to a puppet government that makes foreign states reluctant to attribute international competence to them. Even though complete order and obedience may have been established in a puppet state—as in an occupied territory—the prognosis is often uncertain. This appears to be the reason why competence is more reluctantly conceded to them than to other *de facto* governments. In the case of the Kuusinen government there was no problem at all, for it controlled only a fraction of Finnish territory, it was not accepted by the majority of the population, and its continued

---

[7] League of Nations, *Official Journal*, 20th year (1939), p. 512; and see Marek, p. 67.

[8] League of Nations, *Official Journal*, 20th year (1939), p. 540; and see Marek, p. 67.

[9] The text of the treaty is found in Tanner, V. *The Winter War* (Stanford University Press, 1957), pp. 263–265.

[1] Marek, pp. 70, 173 and ff.

existence was dependent upon the outcome of the war.[2] It was not even an effective puppet government, far less an effective *de facto* government.

8. BORDER REGION BETWEEN COMPETENCE AND NON-COMPETENCE

While the denial of competence to the Kuusinen "government" did not pose any problem for third parties, such questions must undoubtedly arise with some frequency in the practice of states. Indeed, any revolutionary government will—by definition—begin as an illegality, and it is only by augmenting its authority that it will eventually become competent under international law.[3]

In this connexion it should also be noted that when insurgents have established themselves relatively securely, although only in a limited area, foreign states sometimes treat with them in order to safeguard urgent interests. These are the so-called *"local de facto governments"*.[4] It is of interest to find that the competence of these governments, too, under international law, seems connected with their effectiveness and stability, *i.e.* elements which render it likely that they will be able in fact to fulfil the obligations they purport to undertake. It must be kept in mind, on the other hand, that these authorities are not, of course, regarded as organs of the state in whose territory they are active, but either as subjects binding themselves and no one else, or possibly as organs of the movements they claim to represent.

It must frequently be a delicate task to determine the precise moment when the authority of insurgents is sufficient to give them competence under international law to make treaties on behalf of the whole state, and when, correspondingly, the authority of the regularly constituted government is so undermined as to deprive it of the competence to act validly for the state.[5] It is conceivable, but difficult to verify, that in case

---

[2] Reference may also be made to the similar case of the Japanese puppet government established in Nanking in 1940 in the course of the Sino-Japanese war. In notes addressed to various governments on 30 March 1940, the regular Chinese Government declared *inter alia* that "tout acte d'une organisation illégale, telle que celle qui vient d'être établie à Nankin, ou de tout autre organ fantoche qui peut exister ailleurs en Chine, est nul et non avenu et ne sera jamais reconnu par le Gouvernement et par le peuple chinois." See *R.G.D.I.P.*, vol. 47 (1940), p. 217.

[3] Gemma, p. 316.

[4] See Larnaude, p. 474; Vitta, p. 65; Gemma, pp. 404–405; Spiropoulos, p. 73.

[5] Gemma, p. 318.

of doubt, a residuary rule of international law points to the older government as competent to represent the state. It may be, on the other hand, that in these situations states refrain altogether from making treaties with the state in strife, on the assumption that there is no government competent to make treaties on behalf of the state.[6]

The difficulties pointed to above are only problems arising in the application of a rule which was found to be established in the practice of states and accepted by writers. This rule, more than problems of detail, is of interest here, and it only remains to restate it as the conclusion of this section: A revolutionary government is competent under international law to conclude treaties on behalf of the state it purports to represent, regardless of the constitutional provisions traditionally respected, provided only that it appears to wield effective authority, so that there seems to be a high degree of likelihood that it will be able in fact to fulfil the obligations it is prepared to undertake, as well as those already assumed by the state. This conclusion is all the more important as disputes, generally, are perhaps more likely to arise as a result of the activity of an internally irregular government than that of a long-established constitutional government.

---

[6] See above, p. 111, and note therein. The position taken by many states vis-à-vis the Nationalist Chinese Government residing in Formosa might perhaps be considered as an extreme expression of the view that the older government is competent, until it is completely defeated, to represent the state in international relations. As it appears probable, however, that this position has been assumed chiefly on the basis of political considerations, the evidence of the example is slight. It may here be noted that the Nationalist Government not only remains recognized by a large number of states, but has also been accepted by these states as competent to bind the State of China by treaty. The Statute of the Atomic Energy Agency, opened for signature on 26 October 1956 was ratified by the Nationalist Government on 10 September 1957. Apparently only the Government of the United Kingdom objected. When, on 29 July 1957, the instrument of ratification of the United Kingdom was deposited with the Government of the United States, the British representative declared that as his Government recognized the Central People's Government as the Government of China, it reserved its position regarding the validity of the signature appended by the Nationalist Government. For the text of the Statute, see *T.I.A.S.* 3873. For the British reservation, see E. Lauterpacht, "The Contemporary Practice of the United Kingdom in the Field of International Law—Survey and Comment, VII" in *I.C.L.Q.*, vol. 8 (1959), p. 159. Generally on the question of the position of the Chinese Government, see Wright, "The Chinese Recognition Problem" in *A.J.I.L.*, vol. 49 (1955), pp. 320–338.

Chapter XI

THE TREATY-MAKING COMPETENCE OF GOVERNMENTS IN EXILE

1. Preliminary Remarks

During the second world war, as well as during earlier wars, there appeared in international relations groups of persons who claimed to be governmental authorities of various occupied states in which they did not reside. In many cases regular governments treated with these persons, who were deprived of the administrative control of the territories and peoples, the governments of which they purported to be. In other cases, although they were not held to be governments of states, they were considered at least as representing some kind of subject of international law. For convenience, the latter groups will here be termed "authorities in exile."

As will be shown, both governments and authorities in exile concluded numerous treaties between themselves, as well as with regular governments of allied states. It is no doubt advisable to be particularly cautious in regarding positions taken by governments in war as reflecting rules of customary international law. For, especially in war-time, immediate and pressing interests may sometimes induce governments to deviate from practices which are thought to satisfy the long-term interest, which alone is capable of producing customary rules. With this reservation, it is assumed that the regular governments which concluded treaties with governments and authorities in exile generally entered into these compacts in the conviction that the treaties were binding by virtue of international law, and that the exiled bodies—governments as well as authorities—with which they chose to treat, were competent under international law to assume the relevant treaty obligations on behalf of the international law subjects they purported to represent.

The positions taken by neutral states towards various governments in exile might perhaps have been expected to be of special interest, as likely to have been less influenced by war considerations than those of belligerent states. What little evidence of the attitudes of neutrals—in particular, that of Sweden—the writer succeeded in uncovering did not, however, confirm such expectation.[1]

The following inquiry aims primarily at defining the conditions in which competence under international law to make treaties on behalf of an occupied state is attributed to a government in exile. There may be some force in the objection that the criteria of treaty-making competence that may be thus deduced will rest upon a rather narrow basis, namely, that of the practice of allied states. In some instances it will be possible, however, to seek corroboration of this practice in attitudes taken after the war by other governments.

In a previous chapter, it has been concluded that the treaty-making competence under international law of revolutionary governments depended upon their "effectiveness", and that the fact that such governments lack constitutional title and do not function in conformity with a constitution was irrelevant from the point of view of international law. The position of the governments in exile differs in several respects from that of revolutionary governments. The exiled governments, which are deprived of the control of their proper territories, cannot compare in effectiveness with revolutionary governments. They may, furthermore, have made their initial appearance as regular, constitutional governments, while revolutionary governments have frequently acquired their title in violation of a constitution. On the other hand, governments in exile are similar to revolutionary governments in that they normally function—and conclude treaties—in disregard of certain constitutional provisions, e.g., those which involve parliamentary approval.

There appears to be no pertinent authority on the limited question

---

[1] It may here merely be noted that although the Swedish Government appears to have recognized the continued legal existence of all the occupied states, with the exception of Czechoslovakia, and to have permitted the diplomatic missions of these states to continue to function, and to represent governments in exile, it was not until 1943—in the case of Norway—and 1944—in the case of the Netherlands—that the Swedish Government accepted credentials issued by a government in exile for a new minister. See *Handlingar rörande Sveriges Politik under andra världskriget: Frågor i samband med Norska regeringens vistelse utanför Norge 1940–1943*. Aktstycken utgivna av Kungl. Utrikesdepartementet (Stockholm, 1948). See also La Ruche, *La neutralité de la Suède* (1953), p. 105 and Lie, T., *Hjemover* (Oslo, 1958), pp. 113 ff. and 138.

With the exception of two financial agreements made with the Norwegian Government in exile in 1944 (see Kungl. Utrikesdepartementet, *Kalender för 1946*, p. 301), there is no evidence of any treaties concluded by the Swedish Government with any government in exile.

of the basis in international law of the treaty-making competence of governments in exile. Available doctrinal and judicial authority on the broader question of the basis of the general competence under international law of governments in exile gives no uniform answer to the question of what elements give rise to governmental competence. There seems to be almost complete agreement, however, that governments in exile frequently act in disregard of the constitutions of their respective states, and that this circumstance does not affect their competence under international law. A brief survey will illustrate this.

2. Deficiencies in the Constitutional Functioning of Governments in Exile

While no court appears to have decided squarely on the issue of the international relevance of the constitutionality of a treaty made by a government or an authority in exile, at least one court has had occasion to pronounce upon the constitutionality of legislation promulgated by a government in exile, and upon the international relevance of constitutionality.

In *Re Amand* (No. 1), decided by a British court,[2] the validity of a decree issued by the Netherlands Government in exile was challenged on the ground of unconstitutionality. The judges of the King's Bench Division, admitting that, on the peculiar facts of the case, that contention was relevant in a British court, accepted the opinions of two experts to the effect that the decree was valid, because "legislation must continue in the interest of the life of the State", and the decree "could not be made in any other way." The experts stated further: "When a state of emergency exists... the Constitution does not apply first and foremost, but the vital interests of the State and People." The acceptance of these views seems to amount to an admission that, while the judges considered that the decree fulfilled a vital function for the State of the Netherlands, and accepted it as valid, they did not think the decree could be upheld on constitutional grounds.

---

[2] [1941] 2 K.B. 239 (Div. Court). The judgment is printed in full also in *Cz. Y.*, pp. 172–178; a digest is found in *Annual Digest*, 1941–1942, pp. 111–116; see also *B.Y.I.L.*, vol. 21 (1944), pp. 188 ff. Comments on the case are found in Táborský, *The Czechoslovak Cause* (1944), pp. 105–113; the same in *Cz. Y.*, pp. 192–193; Wolff, "The international position of dispossessed governments at present in England" in *Modern Law Review*, vol. 6 (1942–1943), p. 212; Lachs, in "Allied Governments in Exile" in *The Law Journal*, vol. 92 (1942), pp. 275–276.

The question of the constitutionality of the acts of governments in exile has been discussed by several writers. The following excerpt is from an article by Dr. Drucker:

"Although the Constitutions of the other Allied States [than Norway] all have various kinds of clauses dealing with authorization, it cannot be said that they cover the case which has now arisen, and if the various Constitutions were interpreted in a strictly literal manner important grounds could undoubtedly be put forward to show that the legislation of any one Allied State in the United Kingdom was not in accordance with the Constitution of the country in question."[3]

A British writer has expressed the following opinion:

"It is not surprising that there are no express provisions in the constitutions to remedy these difficulties [e.g. the absence of a parliament]. It would indeed be a strange idea for a constitution to stipulate what the government is authorized to do should it be ousted from the territory by enemy action. I do not know any example where a constitution provides for such an emergency."[4]

Dr. Marek, who distinguishes between governments in exile which before leaving their own states were properly constituted governments, and exiled authorities which have been constituted abroad, and who attributes the character of state organs only to the former category, submits that:

"It may perhaps be observed that the actual continuity of the exiled governments forms so strong an argument in favour of their continued character of State organs as to make up even for the often unavoidable flaws in their constitutional legality. The latter, whatever the initial basis and intention of the governments concerned, will rarely be fully achieved in exile."[5]

[3] Drucker, "The Legislation of the Allied Powers in the United Kingdom" in *Cz. Y.*, p. 46.

[4] Wolff, "The international position of dispossessed governments at present in England" in *Modern Law Review*, vol. 6 (1942–43), p. 213. See, however, on the Constitution of Luxemburg, Flory, p. 24. On the question of constitutionality, see also McNair, *Legal Effects of War* (3rd ed., 1948), p. 358. For the view that the authors of a constitution would, if they had anticipated the possibility of an occupation, have accorded legislative powers to the government in the course of an emergency, see Oppenheimer, "Governments and Authorities in Exile" in *A.J.I.L.*, vol. 36 (1942), p. 582. Oppenheimer's pronouncement is in accord with the following declaration which supplemented the ordinance of 27 October 1940, by which the French "Conseil de Défense de l'Empire" was set up: "Considérant ... Que les auteurs de la Constitution ne pouvaient prévoir, en effet, qu'un jour viendrait où des Français devraient procéder à la formation d'un pouvoir en dehors de la France continentale; ...": *Journal Officiel de la France Libre*, Première Année, No. 1, 20 janvier 1941, p. 4; also in de Gaulle, *Mémoires de Guerre*, vol. I (1954), p. 316.

[5] Marek, p. 97; for the view that the element of continuity is decisive, see also Mattern, *Die Exilregierung* (1953), p. 15.

The same writer even takes the position that an inquiry into the municipal legal standing of these governments would border upon "unlawful intervention".[6] In a thesis devoted wholly to the status of governments in exile, a French writer states:

"Sur le plan interne, aucun gouvernement peut prétendre, dans son exil, respecter entièrement la lettre de sa constitution; on pourra lui contester son départ, sa composition et l'ensemble de ses activités. Faudra-t-il alors, sous prétexte du respect de la constitution, lui enlever en droit la possibilité d'exister et le considérer comme un usurpateur?"[7]

In another monograph on the subject of exiled governments, the following statement is found:

"Die Frage, inwieweit eine Exilregierung für ihren Heimatstaat bindend Rechte oder Pflichten übernehmen kann, ist zwar nur im Einzelfalle zu entscheiden; grundsätzlich kann jedoch festgestellt werden, dass bei Verpflichtungen gegenüber dem Auslande auf die Erfordernisse der Verfassung des Mutterstaates abgestellt werden muss..."[8]

3. METHOD OF INQUIRY

Before a discussion can be undertaken of the conditions which may be required to be fulfilled in order that an authority may be considered a government in exile and attributed the competence to act on behalf of a state—in particular, to conclude treaties on behalf of a state—the practice of states must be examined. In that connexion, attention must be paid to the factual foundation, if any, of the view that flaws in the constitutional origin and functioning of exiled bodies are internationally irrelevant.

Within the framework of this study, it is obviously not possible to undertake a full-scale investigation of the treaty-making activities of all exiled governments that have existed, and the conditions upon which their competence in this regard appears to have been founded. For the present purpose, it has been thought convenient rather to select three cases and subject them to detailed study. Accordingly, the very dissimilar cases of the exiled bodies that claimed to represent Poland, Czechoslovakia and France during the second world war have been chosen. Of these three bodies, only the Polish had a regular constitutional origin,

---

[6] Marek, p. 97; *Cf.* Táborský, p. 113.

[7] Flory, *Le statut international des gouvernements refugiés et le cas de la France Libre* (1952), p. 11; see also *ibid.*, pp. 24 ff. and 112.

[8] Mattern, *Die Exilregierung* (1953), p. 64.

and continued to be considered a government until 1945; one, the Czechoslovak, arose abroad without any constitutional basis, but came to be considered a government; one, the French, arose similarly without any constitutional foundation, and its allies refused to consider it a government of France until it was, in fact, an effective territorial government. It does not seem unduly optimistic to expect that an examination of these three cases ought to uncover the criteria that are held to be decisive for the attribution to an exiled body of the competence to make treaties on behalf of a state.

4. THE CASE OF POLAND

Factual background

On 1 September 1939, Germany attacked Poland, and shortly thereafter a Franco-Polish agreement was concluded regarding the creation of a Polish armed unit in France.[9] On 17 September, the Soviet Union began to invade Poland, and on the same day President Mościcki returned briefly to Poland from Roumania. Under Article 24 of the Constitution which permitted the President of the State in time of war to designate his successor in case the post of the President should fall vacant before the restoration of peace, he designated W. Raczkiewicz his successor.[1] On 28 September, Germany and the Soviet Union concluded a boundary treaty by which they divided Poland between themselves. Two days later, Dr. Mościcki resigned his post as President. Raczkiewicz was sworn in as President at the Polish Embassy in Paris and, at his request, General Sikorski formed the first Cabinet in exile which, shortly thereafter, settled at Angers,[2] and, after the French collapse, in London.

The Polish Government in exile sought to rely for its competence on Article 79: 2 of the Polish Constitution, which had regard to exceptional circumstances created by war. It continued to be recognized by governments other than those of the Soviet Union and the Axis powers.[3] Polish Legations in Allied and neutral states carried on their activities as before the occupation, and foreign diplomats continued to be accredited to the Government in exile.

It is asserted by several writers that the transmission of power to

[9] Flory, pp. 250, 278; Marek, p. 504.
[1] Oppenheimer, p. 569; Flory, pp. 26, 250.
[2] See Flory, p. 250.
[3] Flory, p. 250; Marek, p. 438.

the Government in exile was effected in full conformity with the Polish Constitution, and that that Government continued to function largely in accordance with the Constitution.[4] It is of interest to note, however, that on 9 December 1939, in order to strengthen its representative character, the Government in exile established a National Council as a substitute for the regular Parliament, which was unable to meet.[5]

In its chief task, the pursuit of the war jointly with the Allies with a view to the liberation of Poland, the Polish Government in exile achieved a high degree of effectiveness. It controlled a Polish army, navy, and air force and directed a well-developed underground movement in the homeland.[6] Its claim to represent the resisting Polish State and the future liberated State was not disputed by Allied or neutral states until early in 1944. At that time, the Soviet Government, whose armies had successfully crossed into Poland, denied that the Polish Government in London had the capacity to speak and act for Poland. Diplomatic relations with the Soviet Union had been broken off by the London Government as early as April 1943, following the discovery of the mass graves of Polish officers in the Katyn wood.[7]

On 23 July 1944, a Soviet-fostered "Polish Committee of National Liberation"—later known as the "Lublin Committee"—announced its existence in Poland and declared the London Government to be "an illegal and self-styled authority". On 26 July 1944, the Committee signed the first of a series of agreements with the Soviet Government, and on 1 January 1945 it assumed the name of a "Provisional Government of Poland". At the same time, it declared that it would not recognize any financial obligations undertaken by the London Government, and a few days later it was recognized by the Soviet Union.[8] Other states nevertheless continued to recognize the London Government until, after the Yalta conference in February 1945 and negotiations following it in Moscow, a new Government—largely a diluted Lublin Committee —was recognized by France on 29 June, and by the United Kingdom and the United States on 5 July 1945.[9] These acts of recognition were followed by protests from the London Government in exile.[1]

[4] Marek, p. 439, note 3; Oppenheimer, p. 570; Flory, p. 250.
[5] Flory, p. 250.
[6] Marek, p. 440.
[7] Marek, pp. 452–453.
[8] Marek, pp. 454 ff.
[9] Churchill, *The Second World War*, vol. 6, p. 583; Truman, *Memoirs*, vol. I, p. 322; Flory, p. 279.
[1] Marek, pp. 503 ff.; Ciechanowski, *Defeat in Victory* (1947), p. 388.

*The internationally responsible character of the
Government in exile*

While the Polish Government in exile was recognized by the non-
Axis states, it concluded a large number of treaties.[2] Although some of
these agreements were concluded to satisfy the need of the moment,
and were not calculated to call for action by future Polish Governments, it is submitted that they were all considered to engage the
responsibility of the State of Poland. This suggestion is contrary to
the view advanced by Professor Guggenheim to the effect that the
Polish as well as other governments in exile were not organs of states,
but particular subjects of international law.[3] Dr. Marek, on the other

---

[2] The following list only offers a selection of agreements entered into by the
Polish Government in exile (as no collection of the relevant treaties appears to
exist, the sources are of various kinds): 18 November 1939: Anglo-Polish agreement
concerning the formation of a detachment of the Polish navy in Great Britain
(Marek, p. 440, note 1). 4 January 1940: Franco-Polish agreement on the re-establishment of the Polish army (Flory, p. 278). 5 August 1940: Anglo-Polish agreement
respecting Polish land and air forces (Marek, p. 440, note 1). 11 November 1940:
Polish-Czechoslovak declaration on collaboration and future economic co-operation
(text in *Cz. Y.*, p. 235; and comment on it in *ibid.*, p. 187). 3 December 1940: Anglo-
Polish protocol concerning the lending of British warships to the Polish navy (Marek,
p. 440, note 1). 30 July 1941: Polish-Soviet agreement declaring invalid changes in
Polish territories effected by the Soviet–German treaties of 1939 (text found in
Marek, p. 445; and in *Poland in the British Parliament* 1939–1945, vol. I (ed. by
Jędrzejewicz, 1946, p. 471)). 1 January 1942: United Nations Declaration (text in
Great Britain, *Treaty Series*, No. 5 (1942)). 25 January 1942: Polish-Czechoslovak agree-
ment on future confederation (Oppenheimer, p. 577). 1 July 1942: American-Polish
agreement on mutual aid (*A.J.I.L.*, vol. 36 (1942), Off. Doc., p. 222). 3 June 1943:
Signature of the Final Act of the Food and Agriculture Conference (text in *A.J.I.L.*,
vol. 37 (1943), Off. Doc., p. 159). 9 November 1943: Signature of the Agreement for
United Nations Relief and Rehabilitation Administration (Great Britain, *Treaty
Series*, No. 3 (1943)). 22 July 1944: Signature of the Final Act of the United Nations
Monetary and Financial Conference at Bretton Woods (Department of State Publication, Publ. 2187, *Conference Series* 55). 5 January 1945: Signature of amendment to the
International Sanitary Convention of 21 June 1926 (*Department of State Bulletin*,
vol. 12 (1945), p. 10). 5 January 1945: Signature of amendment to the Sanitary Convention for Air Navigation of 12 April 1933 (*Department of State Bulletin*, vol. 12
(1945), p. 10). 6 April 1945: Deposition with the Government of the United States of
instrument of acceptance of the International Air Services Transit Agreement signed
at Chicago on 7 December 1944 (*Department of State Bulletin*, vol. 12 (1945), p. 644).
6 April 1945: Deposition with the Government of the United States of instrument of
ratification of the Convention on International Civil Aviation signed at Chicago on
7 December 1944 (*U.N.T.S.*, vol. 15 (1948), pp. 295, 372).

[3] Guggenheim, vol. I, p. 199 and vol. II, p. 787, note 62.

hand, has convincingly argued the view adhered to above. Referring to Lend-Lease agreements, the Final Act of the Food and Agriculture Conference, the agreement establishing U.N.R.R.A., the Bretton Woods agreement and the Final Act of the International Civil Aviation Conference and the International Civil Aviation Convention, she states:

"It would hardly have occurred to anyone to conclude such agreements with mere 'governments', representing only themselves and having no link with their States which were thus to incur international responsibility and with whom alone such agreements could have been validly and reasonably concluded."[4]

Although, indeed, some of the agreements cited were adhered to by authorities which were definitely not considered governments of states, and although it may be questionable, furthermore, whether any substantial legal obligations were assumed under documents such as the Final Acts of the Food and Agriculture Conference and the International Civil Aviation Conference,[5] the conclusion that the governments who were parties to these agreements made the agreements with a Polish government which they considered an organ of the State of Poland, competent to bind that State, is permissible. Substantial legal obligations were assumed under some of the agreements, and where bodies not considered governments of states were admitted as parties, a clear formal distinction was drawn between such bodies and bodies held to be governments in exile.[6]

The internationally responsible character of the Polish Government in exile is further demonstrated by an incident occurring after the war. The Polish Government in exile signed the Convention on International Civil Aviation at Chicago on 7 December 1944. Ratification of the Convention was effected by the same Government on 6 April 1945[7] —at a time when the Soviet-sponsored Government in Warsaw, which claimed to be the only body competent to represent Poland, was recognized by the Soviet Union, but before other Allied states than Czechoslovakia had accorded recognition to it.

[4] Marek, pp. 93–94.

[5] The United States Department of State has expressed the following view: "...The proper purpose of a Final Act is to serve as an agreed record of the organization of an international conference. While there are some precedents to the contrary, a Final Act is not an appropriate instrument for recording international commitments between states..." United States, *Treaty Practice*, p. 29.

[6] Regarding the Final Act of the Food and Agriculture Conference, see below, p. 179.

[7] *U.N.T.S.*, vol. 15 (1948), p. 372.

It appears that the Warsaw Government later tried to adhere to the Convention, and that the Government of the United States, in its capacity of depositary, refused to accept the new instrument of adherence,[8] no doubt, it may be assumed, on the ground that the State of Poland was considered bound already by the adherence effected by the Government in exile. The stand thus taken must be understood to indicate a conviction on the part of the United States Government to the effect that the Government in exile continued to constitute an organ of the State of Poland as late as 6 April 1945, and to be competent at that time to bind that State by treaty.

There is evidence showing that the view taken by the United States was shared by a majority of the members of the I.C.A.O. On the ground that Poland had neglected to pay its membership fees from the beginning in 1945, the 6th Assembly of the I.C.A.O., held at Montreal in 1952, resolved to deprive that State of its right to vote in the Assembly,[9] thereby confirming an earlier similar resolution. The cumulation of membership dues, which continued until 1958, and the resolution must imply that, like the Government of the United States, the majority of the members of this international organization considered the State of Poland bound by the act of adherence performed by the Government in exile. The settlement of the affair is also not without interest.

In a note of 9 May 1957, the Polish Ambassador to Washington informed the State Department "that Poland has adhered without qualifications to the Convention on International Civil Aviation signed at Chicago on December 7, 1944, and has become a member of the International Civil Aviation Organization." Copies of this note were distributed by the State Department to the other members of the I.C.A.O. As the note did not specify the *date* of adherence, the conclusion is tempting that the Warsaw Government was eager to become an effective member without, however, conceding the validity of the adherence effected by the Government in exile. The correctness of this conclusion seems even more probable in the light of a letter of 13 March 1958, by which the Polish Government, through its Legation at Ottawa, submitted a proposal designed to allow the Polish People's Republic to resume full membership rights in the I.C.A.O.

As has been seen, the formulation of the note of 9 May 1957 had carefully avoided any mention of the date of adherence, thus allowing

[8] United States, *Treaty Practice*, section on adherence.
[9] See I.C.A.O. *Doc.* 7297. A 6 –P/2.

the interpretation—for those who preferred it—that the note referred to the adherence effected by the Government in exile in 1945, as well as the view—undoubtedly held by the Communist Polish Government— that the note, itself, effected the adherence. This "solution" of the legal problem was not, however, easily applied to the calculation of the arrears, for the latter inevitably had to be counted from some date. The letter of 13 March 1958, though perhaps not altogether successfully avoiding the inference that the Government admitted the validity of the adherence effected in 1945, nevertheless represents a remarkable effort in this direction. The proposal contained in the letter was as follows:

"a) Poland will pay current contributions starting from 1957 when she finally solved the legal problem concerning ratification of the I.A.C.O. convention.

b) Poland will resume her right to vote and full membership rights in the Organization.

c) The question of Poland's arrears will be considered in two years.

d) Poland's now difficult currency situation does not now allow her to take on any difficult additional obligations apart from payment of annual contributions."[1]

The vague formula quoted above did not, however, satisfy I.C.A.O. In the final settlement, which was approved by the 11th session of the I.C.A.O. Assembly, held at Montreal 20 May – 2 June 1958, the Polish Government was forced to consent to pay some 25 % of the arrears from 1945 and onward, payment to be effected in fifteen equal instalments commencing in 1961.[2] The conclusion must be drawn that the governments represented in the Assembly of the I.C.A.O. upheld in a remarkably firm manner the position taken by the United States to the effect that the Polish Government in exile was competent, in April 1945, to enter into a treaty on behalf of Poland. The conclusion is also inevitable that the Polish Communist Government in 1958 felt constrained eventually to allow the inference that it admitted and acted upon the legal position thus assumed by a large number of governments.

Basis of the treaty-making competence of the Polish Government in exile

Against the background of the above examination of certain facts relating to the Polish Government in exile, and of the agreements con-

[1] I.C.A.O. *Doc.* C–WP/2656, 25 March 1958, App. A.
[2] I.C.A.O. *Doc.* A11–WP/53–P/10, 3 June 1958, Resolution No. 15 at p. 22.

cluded by it, the basis in international law of the treaty-making competence of that Government may now be discussed.

Authorities were cited above to the effect that the transfer of power to the Polish Government in exile took place in full conformity with the Constitution of the State, and that, consequently, that Government possessed an original constitutional title. While it is conceivable that this circumstance was of importance in persuading other governments of the internationally responsible character of the exiled Government,[3] it does not seem arguable that a continued compliance by the Government with the requirements of the Constitution would have been necessary to render it competent under international law to conclude treaties on behalf of Poland.

Dr. Marek, whose views in the matter are entitled to great respect, based, as they appear to be, on extensive and penetrating research, does not seem to think that the Polish constitutional provisions regarding the conclusion of treaties were affected by the occupation and the Government going into exile. In discussing the claim which was directed to the Polish Government in exile by the Soviet Government in the beginning of 1942, and which had regard to the territories east of the so-called Molotov–Ribbentrop line, Dr. Marek maintains that the Polish Government was "in no case competent to effect the cession of half of Poland's territory, either on the basis of the existing Polish Constitution, or in view of the inherent limitations of a government in exile."[4] While the second reason invoked need not be discussed in this connexion, it should be noted that the constitutional obstacle referred to consisted in the impossibility of obtaining approving legislation by the Polish Parliament. The constitutional provision involved is quoted by Dr. Marek as reading:

"Art. 52.1. Agreements with other countries: commercial, customs tariff, permanently burdening the State Treasury, containing obligations to impose new burdens upon the citizens or evoking change in the frontiers of the State–require before ratification the agreement of the Legislative Chambers expressed in the form of a law."[5]

If it is correct, as thus suggested by Dr. Marek, that, without parliamentary approval, the Government in exile was not competent under the Constitution to agree to modifications of the frontiers of the State,

---

[3] For references to two authorities who hold this circumstance decisive for the competence of any exile government, see above, p. 150, note 5.

[4] Marek, p. 458.

[5] *Ibid.*, p. 458, note 1.

it ought to follow that the Government needed similar approval to be constitutionally competent to make treaties "permanently burdening the State Treasury". Yet, while it would appear that at least one of the treaties actually concluded by the exiled Government without parliamentary approval was of the latter kind, namely, the International Civil Aviation Convention, it seems that no doubts were voiced by other governments as to the competence of the Polish Government in exile to bind the State of Poland by this Convention.

Yet another occasion may be cited on which the Polish Government must be assumed to have been considered competent under international law to conclude a treaty on behalf of Poland, despite the fact that there appear to have existed reasons for doubts as to the constitutional competence of the Government. On 30 July 1941, Prime Minister Sikorski and the Russian Ambassador to London signed an agreement by which, *inter alia,* the Soviet–German treaties of 1939 concerning territorial changes in Poland were declared to have lost their validity. The agreement stipulated that it was to enter into force upon signature. Its conclusion was hailed by the British Government and greeted with satisfaction by members of the House of Commons. However, it seems doubtful whether General Sikorski was constitutionally competent to act as he did. It is reported that the Polish Deputy Prime Minister, General Sosnkowski, the Foreign Minister, Mr. Zaleski, and the Minister for Justice, Mr. Seyda, objected to the substance of the agreement and that, the Polish Prime Minister having rejected their criticism, these Ministers resigned on 25 July 1941. It is further reported that "notwithstanding their resignations and without the authorization of the President of Poland which is required by the Polish Constitution, Prime Minister Sikorski signed the Agreement on July 30, 1941."[6]

The two cases cited above may perhaps suffice to demonstrate that the governments which concluded treaties with Poland did not consider compliance with certain provisions of the Polish Constitution indispensable to render the Government in exile competent under international law to conclude treaties on behalf of Poland.

The above examination does not rule out the possibility that the governments which made treaties with the Polish Government in exile considered their own recognition of the Polish Government the basis of that Government's treaty-making competence under international

---

[6] See *Poland in the British Parliament 1939–1945* (ed. by Jędrzejewicz, 1946), pp. 471–472.

law. It seems more likely, however, that here, as in other instances, the element of effectiveness was held to be decisive for the treaty-making competence, as well as for the continued recognition of the Government. The Polish Government in exile wielded considerable authority. It possessed large armed forces which fought side by side with the Allies, the underground forces in Poland owed allegiance to it, and it was thought to have the support of the Polish people.[7] Most of the treaties concluded by the Government had regard to matters within its direct control. In cases in which the Government was enabled to commit the State of Poland for the future, its competence-creating effectiveness may have been seen in an expected future general public support for itself or its successor. When it became clear that the Government in exile would not, in fact, regain territorial control over Poland, and that future effectiveness would belong to another government, which had no constitutional origin, the exiled Government was denied opportunity to treat on behalf of Poland and recognition was withdrawn.

It is only natural that in a period when the effectiveness of one government seriously decreases, other governments may be somewhat tardy to react and to adapt their attitude to the new situation. It is natural, also, that unless they have some special reason for welcoming the effectiveness of a new authority, they may be inclined to continue to transact some business with the authority with which they are accustomed to deal, until they are convinced that it has definitely lost its power. This reasoning may well be applicable, at any rate, to the Polish Government in exile, for it would seem that on 6 April 1945, when the ratification of the International Civil Aviation Convention was received, the effectiveness of the Polish London Government was rapidly decreasing. At the Yalta Conference, 3–11 February 1945, the Anglo-Saxon powers themselves had indeed agreed with the Soviet Government that a new government should be set up in Poland. It does not appear, on the other hand, that the Western Powers were inconsistent in their attitude. It is true that, over its protests, the Polish Government in exile was not included among the governments which were invited by the United States to the San Francisco Conference, and that no Polish government took part in that Conference which opened on 25 April 1945. The reason, however, appears to have been that the invitations were issued by the United States *on behalf* of the great powers which

---

[7] See Churchill, *The Second World War*, vol. 6, pp. 128, 652; see also statement by General de Gaulle, quoted below, p. 161, note 8.

jointly sponsored the Conference, and that, in view of a Russian veto pronounced at the Yalta Conference, the United States did not feel free to issue an invitation to the Polish London Government.[8]

It may be concluded, in the case of Poland, that an original constitutional title plus a measure of current and expected future effectiveness seems to have sufficed to attribute treaty-making competence to, and continued recognition of, the Government in exile while the country was under belligerent occupation. Once that occupation was over, however, without the Government in exile succeeding in resuming power in the State, but the State in fact being ruled by a revolutionary government which purported to represent the State, the Government in exile was no longer attributed treaty-making competence, and recognition was withdrawn from it.[9]

It seems justified to conclude, finally, that non-compliance with the Polish constitutional requirements on the conclusion of treaties, or some of these requirements, did not, in the opinion of other governments, affect the treaty-making competence which they attributed under international law to the Government in exile.

---

[8] See "Chronicle of International Events" in *A.J.I.L.*, vol. 39 (1945), p. 573; Ciechanowski, *Defeat in Victory* (1947), pp. 364, 368. For the decision of the San Francisco conference in regard to Poland, see Kopelmanas, *L'Organisation des Nations Unies*, vol. I (1947), p. 32. Although it had nothing to do with the competence to conclude treaties, an episode, occurring, as early as March 1944, between the Soviet Union and the authority of General de Gaulle may be recorded in this connexion. It appears that, at that time, upon urgent requests from Mr. Mikolajczyk, the French Committee for National Liberation, headed by General de Gaulle, had decided to effect the transmission of a consignment of gold which had been placed by the Polish State Bank in the Bank of France in June 1940, and which was now under Free French control. The Russian Ambassador, Mr. Bogomolov, made remonstrances. In his memoirs, General de Gaulle reports that the Ambassador made a formal protest against the transfer of the Polish gold to the exiled Government on the ground that "celui-ci ne sera pas, demain, le Gouvernement de la Pologne." General de Gaulle quotes himself as replying, however, that the exiled Government was the Government of the day, that it was recognized by all the Allies, including the Soviet Union, that by its orders, Polish armed forces fought in Italy, and that he did not see what entitled the Soviet Government to intervene in a matter that concerned only France and Poland. See de Gaulle, vol. II, p. 208.

[9] It was not until early in 1959, however—Pope John XXIII having then succeeded Pope Pius XII—that the Holy See withdrew its recognition from the government in exile.

5. The Case of Czechoslovakia

Factual background

After the German invasion of Czechoslovakia in March 1939, and before the outbreak of the world war, there was no unified exile movement representing Czechoslovakia. The beginning of the Czechoslovak exile movement was somewhat unorthodox.

On 2 October 1939, the Czechoslovak Minister to Paris, Mr. Osuský, who purported to act on behalf of the "Provisional Government of the Czechoslovak Republic" concluded an agreement with the French Premier regarding the establishment in France of a Czechoslovak army.[1] As at that time there existed no Provisional Czechoslovak Government, the agreement could only, from a juridical point of view, have been considered a personal act of the Minister, not binding a government which might subsequently be set up.

Early in November 1939, a Czechoslovak National Committee was formed in Paris. In seeking permission to function on French territory, the Committee claimed competence to represent the "Czechoslovak people" and to carry out the agreement of 2 October.[2] By this step it may be said to have adopted the agreement which, until then, had been legally only a personal undertaking of Mr. Osuský. The French Government granted the permission that was requested and recognized the Committee as representing the Czechoslovak people.

The British Government and the governments of several British dominions granted similar recognition within six months after the French action.[3] This formula, which was also employed during the first world war,[4] did not signify that the Committee claimed to act on behalf of the State of Czechoslovakia. It is clear, on the other hand, that the Committee was attributed a certain competence under international law, including, indeed, the competence to be a party to a treaty.[5] The members of the Committee were persons who had not held office in

---

[1] The agreement is reprinted in *Cz. Y.*, pp. 232–234; see also Táborský, pp. 67 ff.; Beneš, *Memoirs of Dr. Eduard Beneš* (1954), p. 89; Marek, p. 311; Flory, p. 41, note 2.

[2] Táborský, pp. 70 ff.; Beneš, pp. 92 ff.; *Cz. Y.*, p. 229.

[3] For the British note of recognition of 20 December 1939, see *Cz. Y.*, p. 230.

[4] See Hackworth's *Digest*, vol. I, pp. 203 ff.

[5] To the same effect, see Táborský (pp. 76 and 84), who cites, in addition to the agreement of 2 October 1939, an agreement of June 1940 between the French Government and the Czechoslovak National Committee regarding the establishment and position of a Czechoslovak air force in France.

Czechoslovakia at the time when Germany engulfed that State.[6] The Committee later moved to London, submitted its activity to the Constitution of 1920, styled itself a "Provisional Government", and was recognized as such by the British Government by the end of July 1940.[7]

The competence under international law of the Provisional Government, whatever its extent, could not possibly have rested upon any title under the Constitution of 1920. The assertion must be correct that the Government was a "spontaneous creation of Czechoslovaks in exile; from the point of view of the Czechoslovak legal order it represented a revolutionary act."[8] What, in fact, was the extent of the international legal competence of this Government, and what was the basis on which that competence was attributed to it?

Extent of treaty-making competence and status of the Provisional Government in exile

The extent of competence attributed to the Provisional Government has been demonstrated to have been more limited than that of governments in exile which had been established as territorial governments before their going into exile.[9] Most convincing as evidence in this regard is, indeed, the form of the agreements concluded with the Provisional Government.[1] As it is a perfectly normal practice to make

---

[6] See Marek, p. 312; *cf.* Beneš, p. 92. The critical date is here taken to be March 1939. Various explanations have been advanced as to why Czechoslovakia should be considered as having continued to exist as a State under international law after March 1939. See Marek, pp. 328 ff. and 309; and Stone, *Legal Controls of International Conflict* (1954), p. 640. Whichever explanation is preferred in this regard, it seems somewhat far-fetched to claim that, in law, Dr. Beneš, who headed the exile movement, had remained the President of the Republic, on the ground that his resignation under pressure in 1938 was invalid. For that construction, see Táborský, *The Czechoslovak Cause*, p. 98; Táborský, *Czechoslovak Democracy* (1945), p. 148; and *The Opening of the Prague Parliament* (Message of President Dr. Eduard Beneš to the National Assembly of the Czechoslovak Republic, Prague 1946), p. 16. *Contra:* Marek, pp. 284 and 306.

[7] *Cz. Y.*, p. 231; Táborský, pp. 85 ff.; also Beneš, pp. 110 ff.

[8] Marek, p. 313; to the same effect, see Schwelb, "Legislation in Exile: Czechoslovakia" in *Journal of Comparative Legislation and International Law*, vol. 24, part II, p. 120; the same writer in *Cz. Y.*, p. 180; see also Beneš, p. 79; asserting a constitutional title for the Provisional Government, however, Kučera, "La continuité de l'Etat Tchécoslovaque" in *Bulletin de Droit Tchécoslovaque*, 5 Année (1947), No. 3–4, pp. 57–58.

[9] Marek, p. 315.

[1] The following agreements are cited in the *Cz. Y.* at p. 235:
Agreement of 25 October 1940 between the Government of the United Kingdom

treaties in inter-governmental rather than inter-state form, it may not in itself be very revealing that the Provisional Government did not enter into agreements in the name of the State of Czechoslovakia. That practice acquires a particular significance, however, when considered in the light of a note of 18 April 1941, in which Dr. Beneš asked the British Government to accord *de jure* recognition to his government. In that note, he also requested that "future agreements signed with the Czechoslovak Republic [will] be concluded, as before September 1938, in the name of the Czechoslovak Republic."[2] It must presumably be inferred that the British Government had refused to conclude agreements by which the Provisional Government purported to act on behalf of the State of Czechoslovakia.[3] To put it differently, the Provisional Czechoslovak Government had not been considered an organ of the State of Czechoslovakia competent to commit that State irrevocably.

It has been suggested that recognition as a provisional government "may be considered more or less as a recognition *de facto*", and that the only difference from a recognition *de jure* was that the former was revocable.[4] Whatever the merit of this theory generally, it does not seem to fit the present case. An authority recognized as a *de facto* government of a state will ordinarily be considered competent to undertake obligations definitely binding the state which it governs. The acts of the Czechoslovak authorities recognized as a "Provisional Government", on the other hand, were simply not imputed to the State of Czechoslovakia.

The circumstance that, while it was recognized as a provisional government, the Czechoslovak authority concluded only agreements relating to current problems not bearing on the future of Czechoslovakia,[5] fits well with the view adhered to above as to the international com-

---

and the Provisional Czechoslovak Government concerning the Czechoslovak armed forces; Financial agreement of 10 December 1940 between the Government of the United Kingdom and the Provisional Czechoslovak Government; Declaration of 11 November 1940 by the Polish Government and the Provisional Czechoslovak Government. See also Táborský, p. 93, note 115, and pp. 137–138.

[2] Marek, p. 317; Beneš, p. 125.

[3] But see Táborský (p. 93), who holds that through recognition (as a provisional government) "the Czechoslovak State acquired, of course, *the possibility of negotiating and concluding regular international treaties* with the States (Dominions) by which it has been recognized".

[4] See Táborský, pp. 89, 96; the same in *Cz. Y.*, p. 184; *cf. Four Fighting Years* (ed. by the Czechoslovak Ministry for Foreign Affairs, London, 1943), p. 181.

[5] See Marek, p. 316.

petence of that authority, although admittedly it does not necessitate that view. The Provisional Government itself appears indeed to have been clearly aware that it was not considered an organ of Czechoslovakia. In his quest for recognition *de jure,* Dr. Beneš stated:

> "The provisional character of the Czechoslovak Government will be understood in the future as being only an internal concern of Czechoslovak democracy. This means that the present Czechoslovak Government will, after the war, at once submit to a democratic Czechoslovak constitution. *From the international standpoint the provisional character of the Czechoslovak Government ceases to exist.*"[6]

The paragraph quoted above appears to suggest that the Government, although admittedly irregular from the point of view of Czechoslovak law, should nevertheless be *considered under international law as competent* to act on behalf of Czechoslovakia, and that its domestic irregularity would be regarded as irrelevant in the international sphere, and be left to that government to remedy after the war.

If the Provisional Czechoslovak Government was not an organ of the State of Czechoslovakia, what was it? Since the agreements concluded with that Government must be assumed to have been made under international law, it follows that the Government was thought competent to undertake *some* obligations and enjoy *some* rights under international law.

On the basis of a theory advanced by Professor Guggenheim, Dr. Marek suggests that the Provisional Czechoslovak Government, not being an organ of Czechoslovakia, was a subject of international law *sui generis.*[7] It would seem, however, that although the Provisional Government did not constitute an organ of the State of Czechoslovakia, it nevertheless constituted an *organ,* namely, of the whole Czechoslovak exile movement. While obligations undertaken by the Provisional Government would not be imputed to the State of Czechoslovakia, they would be imputed to the exile movement, whoever happened to be at the helm. The conclusion must be drawn, therefore, that the exile movement as a whole constituted a subject of international law *sui generis,* having capacity to conclude treaties, and that the Provisional Government was considered competent to exercise that authority.

---

[6] Quoted from Marek, p. 317 (italics added).

[7] Guggenheim, vol. I, p. 199 and vol. II, p. 787, note 62; see also above, p. 154; Marek, p. 316.

Basis of the treaty-making competence of the
Provisional Government in exile

It is not necessary here to discuss further the nature of the exile move-ment as a subject of international law. It must be assumed, however, that, as in the case of a territorial government, it was the effectiveness of the Provisional Government that prompted foreign governments to recognize it, and to ascribe some competence under international law to it. Just as the movement—like a new territorial state—would certainly not have been considered a subject of international law but for being organized and possessing a government at the summit, the Provisional Government would not have been thought competent, and have been recognized, had it not been able—to quote the words of one writer— "to rally round itself all, or the great majority of, its nationals abroad, to organize armed forces and other State organs, and to contribute to the war effort of its Allies".[8] The competence of the Provisional Gov-ernment could not, on the other hand, have flowed from the Constitu-tion of Czechoslovakia, for the establishment of the Provisional Govern-ment had no relation to that Constitution, nor could it have flowed from that Constitution *qua* charter of the movement, just as the com-petence of a revolutionary territorial government does not flow from the charter it may adopt, but from its effectiveness. Provided that here, as elsewhere, recognition be declarative of competence rather than constitutive, the competence could not, furthermore, have flowed from the acts of recognition that took place.

The internationally responsible character of the
Government in exile

Although the Czechoslovak authority in exile started out as represent-ing a movement and not a state, its status did not remain unchanged. On 18 July 1941, not long after the German attack upon the Soviet Union, a Soviet–Czechoslovak treaty was concluded which contained no implication as to limitations upon the competence of the Government in exile and, consequently, allowing the inference that that Government was considered an organ competent under international law to bind the State of Czechoslovakia by treaty.[9] On the very day of the conclusion of that treaty, the British Government expressly accorded full recognition

---

[8] Marek, p. 314.

[9] Text of the agreement reprinted in *Cz. Y.*, p. 236; comment to the agreement in *ibid.*, pp. 196 ff.; see also Marek, p. 317; Táborský, pp. 99–100.

to the Czechoslovak Government.[1] In a note transmitted on that occasion, the British Government declared itself in agreement with Dr. Beneš' memorandum of 18 April 1941, including the passage quoted above.[2] On the provisional nature of the regime, the British note explained:

"...the provisional character of the Czechoslovak Government would be understood in the future as being only an internal concern of Czechoslavak democracy."[3]

It has been rightly noted that treaties concluded by the Government in exile after its achieving full recognition were clearly made on behalf of the State of Czechoslovakia, and were not limited to current problems, but considered by the governments concerned to engage the responsibility of future governments of Czechoslovakia.[4] Such treaties were—to quote some examples from the list compiled by Dr. Marek—the United Nations Declaration of 1 January 1942, the Lend-Lease agreement of 11 July 1942 with the United States, the Final Act of the Food and Agriculture Conference of 3 June 1943, the Final Act of the International Civil Aviation Conference of 7 December 1944.[5] It must be concluded from the manner in which the Government in exile was designated in these instruments that it was considered an organ of the State of Czechoslovakia, competent under international law to conclude treaties on behalf of that State.

Basis of the treaty-making competence of the Government in exile

What was the basis of the treaty-making competence attributed to the Government? Since the latter lacked a constitutional origin then as much as ever, a title flowing from such origin could not possibly have been the basis of its competence. It seems, indeed, that the British agreement expressed with Dr. Beneš' view that the provisional character of the Government would be only an internal concern of Czechoslovak democracy indicated that the British Government continued to be aware of

[1] *Cz. Y.*, p. 231; Táborský, pp. 95 ff. The dates on which recognition was accorded by other governments are found in Masaryk, *Statement on the Foreign Policy of Czechoslovakia made before the Provisional National Assembly on March 6th, 1946* (Czechoslovak Sources and Documents, No. 27 (1946)), p. 11.

[2] Above, p. 164.

[3] Quoted from Marek, p. 318.

[4] Marek, p. 319.

[5] The texts are found in respectively *A.J.I.L.*, vol. 36 (1942), *Off. Doc.*, p. 191; *U.N.T.S.*, vol. 90 (1951), p. 258; *A.J.I.L.*, vol. 37 (1943), Off. Doc., p. 159; *A.J.I.L.*, vol. 39 (1945), Off. Doc., p. 111.

the absence of a constitutional title, and that it considered this circumstance not capable of depriving the Czechoslovak Government of the competence to bind the State of Czechoslovakia under international law.[6] If the position be maintained that recognition is declaratory of competence rather than constitutive, the only possible remaining source of competence of the Government in exile was its effectiveness.

The question may perhaps be raised whether there was any great difference in the effectiveness of the Czechoslovak Government in exile shortly before and at the time of its achieving full recognition. The answer may well be in the negative. Nevertheless, just as revolutionary territorial governments frequently start out as illegal authorities, and may first achieve recognition only as insurgents, in order to be accorded recognition as *de facto* governments when they have extended their authority, there is nothing extraordinary in the treatment accorded the Czechoslovak Government in exile. It started out as an unconstitutional, revolutionary body, and was not permitted to act on behalf of the State. In the course of time, it extended its authority and became, supposedly, ever more representative of the people of Czechoslovakia. On the assumption, presumably, that, after the liberation of Czechoslovakia, the Government in exile would be fully effective, and would be sustained in asserting that its acts were those of the State of Czechoslovakia, it was recognized and treated with as an organ competent to act on behalf of Czechoslovakia.

6. The Case of France

Factual background

After the French demand for an armistice with Germany, and General de Gaulle's appeal on 18 June 1940 for continued French resistance, the British Government sought to facilitate the formation of a representative French resistance movement outside metropolitan France. On 23 June 1940, it declared that it could not consider Pétain's government a government of an independent state, and that it would be ready to extend recognition to a Provisional French National Committee that would be fully representative of the French elements determined to

---

[6] Sir Hersch Lauterpacht, however, has expressed the view that the presence in England of the "last freely elected Head of State" of Czechoslovakia "and the government formed under him constituted the requisite link in legal continuity:" *Recognition in International Law* (1947), p. 92, note. *Contra:* Chen, *The International Law of Recognition* (1951), p. 297, note 39.

continue the fighting, and that it would treat with such a Committee in all matters concerning the pursuit of the war "as long as this Committee would continue to represent the French elements resolved to defeat the common enemy." Two days later, the British Government declared that it was ready to conclude the financial arrangements necessary to allow various parts of the French Colonial Empire to continue the war.[7]

In spite of this effort on the part of the British Government to inspire a general spirit of resistance among the French, and the arrival in Britain of prominent French politicians, no comprehensive French movement emerged. The lead taken by General de Gaulle nevertheless gained impressive adherence in French overseas territories not affected by the defeat in France, and, in a communiqué of 28 June 1940, the British Government declared that it recognized General de Gaulle as "leader of all Free Frenchmen, wherever they may be, who rally to him to defend the Allied cause."[8]

By a letter of 30 July 1940 to the British Prime Minister, General de Gaulle declared his intention to form a council for the defense of French overseas possessions. This body was to consist of civil and military leaders who exercised effective authority in French territory or over French forces, and who were united with him to continue the war. He wished the council to be recognized as competent to treat with the British Government in all matters concerning war efforts which were undertaken jointly by the British Empire and the parts of the French Empire which continued the war. Mr. Churchill replied favourably to this inquiry, but the actual establishment of the council only occurred some three months later.[9] Meanwhile, by an exchange of letters of 7 August 1940 between the British Prime Minister and General de Gaulle, an agreement was concluded regulating the establishment, with British assistance, of a French armed force.[1]

The creation of the Council for the Defense of the Empire was

---

[7] See de Gaulle, vol. I, pp. 80, 270–272 (translation supplied); Flory, p. 58.

[8] Flory, p. 60; de Gaulle, vol. I, p. 274 (translation supplied).

[9] For the text of the letters, see *R.G.D.I.P.* vol. 49 (1941–45), pp. 352–353; see also Flory, p. 62.

[1] For the text of the agreement, see *Documents on International Affairs, 1939–1946,* vol. II *Hitler's Europe* (ed. by Carlyle, 1954), p. 167; or *R.G.D.I.P.,* vol. 49 (1941–45), pp. 354–356. The agreement was modified by a new agreement signed by the British Foreign Secretary and General de Gaulle on 15 January 1941. See de Gaulle, vol. I, p. 126, and notice in *Journal Officiel de la France Libre,* Première Année, No. 3 (25 février 1941), p. 12.

announced by a decree issued at Brazzaville on 27 October 1940. Here, General de Gaulle declared that the Council was to treat with foreign nations in matters relating to French interests and to the defense of French possessions. The decisions of the Council were to be taken by the leader of the Free French, and the Council was to have a consultative function.[2] A new decree, of 24 September 1941, declared the establishment, in addition to the Council referred to, of a French National Committee—Le Comité National Français (C.N.F.). This body was to consist of national commissioners to be named by, headed by and responsible to the leader of the Free French. Article 4 of the decree prescribed that treaties, which, under the French Constitution of 1875, were subject to the approval of the Parliament, were to enter into force upon their ratification by means of an ordinance, considered in the Committee, signed by the leader of the Free French, and countersigned by at least one of the commissioners.[3]

In June 1942, the movement headed by General de Gaulle substituted the name "Fighting France" for the name "Free France", to mark the adherence and allegiance of the resistance groups in metropolitan France. Though this step marked the increased size of the movement, and of the greater actual authority of its governing body, it did not change the structure of the organization.[4] About a year later, after long negotiations, the French forces and administration in North Africa headed by General Giraud in Algiers and earlier under the authority of the Vichy Government, joined with the French National Committee to form the French Committee for National Liberation—Le Comité Français de la Libération Nationale (C.F.L.N.).[5] Article 3 of the ordinance instituting this Committee laid down, without further detail, that the Committee was to conclude treaties and agreements with foreign powers. No change occurred in this regard in connexion with the creation of a Consultative Assembly in September 1943.[6]

---

[2] The text of the decree is found in *J.O.F.L.*, Première Année, No. 1 (20 janvier 1941), p. 3; also in *R.G.D.I.P.*, vol. 49 (1941–45), p. 357; and in de Gaulle, vol. I, p. 303.

[3] The text of the decree is reproduced in *R.G.D.I.P.*, vol. 49 (1941–45), pp. 358–360; also in de Gaulle, vol. I, p. 616.

[4] The text of the relevant declaration is found in *R.G.D.I.P.*, vol. 49 (1941–45), p. 360; see also Flory, p. 66.

[5] The text of the ordinance is found in *R.G.D.I.P.*, vol. 49 (1941–45), p. 362; also in de Gaulle, vol. II, p. 489.

[6] The text of the relevant ordinance is reproduced in de Gaulle, vol. II, p. 539. The assembly met for the first time on 3 November 1943, *ibid.*, p. 153.

What was the international legal basis of the treaty-making competence attributed to the three successive committees, the Council for the Defense of the Empire, the French National Committee, and the French Committee for National Liberation? The answer to this question will be sought below after an examination of the constitutional character of the committees, of the status which they claimed, of the status which was expressly ascribed to them in formulae of recognition and, finally, of the treaty-making activity which they were enabled to exert. Thereafter, it will be described how the C.F.L.N., while still outside metropolitan France, proclaimed itself the Provisional Government of France, and the question will be discussed what was the status and basis of competence under international law of that body.

Status claimed by the French Committees

The first point to note in a discussion of the status of the Committees is their private—or revolutionary—origin. They did not pretend to represent any legal governmental continuity, and their non-constitutional character is easily discernible in their various official documents.[7]

The second matter of interest regarding the standing of the Committees is that none of them, until the spring of 1944, claimed to be a government of the State of France. It is clear from the memoirs of General de Gaulle that, in his opinion, the adherence he gained in the first month as the leader of the Free French was utterly insufficient to allow him to proclaim a government. He felt obliged even to postpone the establishment of the "simple national committee" which he had resolved to create in the place of a government, and limited himself in 1940 to proclaiming the Council for the Defense of the Empire.[8]

The ordinances instituting the Council for the Defense of the Empire only claimed for it the function, but not indeed the name, of a government for the parts of the French Empire which were free from enemy control, and the function of a "provisional central authority" for the defense of the overseas territories and the liberation of metropolitan France. They specified, furthermore, that the Council assumed these functions only provisionally and was to be responsible to the future free representatives of the nation.[9]

---

[7] See Article 1 of the ordinance of 27 October 1940, and the declaration of 27 October 1940; the documents are reproduced in de Gaulle, vol. I, pp. 303 and 314. See also discussion in Flory, pp. 74 ff.

[8] De Gaulle, vol. I, pp. 82–83, *cf.* p. 219.

[9] De Gaulle, vol. I, pp. 304, 316, 482.

The basic document establishing the French National Committee was issued on 24 September 1941, and like the documents of 1940 it did not proclaim a government.[1] The reason appears to have been that General de Gaulle felt the movement was not yet sufficiently extensive and representative. The following passage of his memoirs is relevant in this connexion:

"Pour la France Combattante, le Comité national serait l'organe de direction réuni autour de moi. ... le Comité serait le gouvernement. Il en aurait les attributions et la structure. Toutefois, il n'en porterait pas le titre, que je réservais pour le jour, si lointain qu'il dût être encore, où pourrait se former un pouvoir aux dimensions de l'unité française."[2]

Not even the French Committee for National Liberation pretended initially to be a government of the State of France, despite the fact that it had the support and allegiance of a much broader organization than that originally directed by the C.N.F. Though it claimed, on the one hand, to be "Pouvoir central français ", to exercise French sovereignty in all territories outside the control of the enemy, and to administer and defend all French interests in the world, it declared, on the other, in advance that it would transfer its powers to the Provisional Government which would be set up as soon as the liberation of the metropolitan French territory so permitted, and did not term itself a government.[3] General de Gaulle himself apparently still considered it premature to proclaim a fully fledged government. Before the establishment of the C.F.L.N., he stated to General Giraud that "La solution de bon sens consiste [donc] en ceci: Que de Gaulle forme, à Alger, un gouvernement de guerre qui deviendra, au moment voulu, celui de la République."[4] The subsequent transformation of the C.F.L.N. into a Provisional Government will be discussed in the last part of this section.

Status recognized to be possessed by the French Committees

None of the Committees, of course, was recognized as the government of the State of France.

The Council for the Defense of the Empire was recognized on 24

---

[1] *R.G.D.I.P.*, vol. 49 (1941–45), p. 358.

[2] De Gaulle, vol. I, pp. 219–220.

[3] See official communiqué of 3 June 1943 in *R.G.D.I.P.*, vol. 49 (1941–45), p. 361; or in de Gaulle, vol. II, p. 489.

[4] De Gaulle, vol. II, p. 82.

December 1940 by the British Government as an authority competent to treat matters regarding the collaboration with French overseas territories under the authority of the Council and respecting co-operation between the Free French forces and British forces.[5] The Soviet Government, similarly, by means of an exchange of letters effected on 26 September 1941, declared that it was ready to enter into relation with the Council in all matters relating to the collaboration with French overseas territories placed under the authority of the Council.[6]

Various formulae appear to have been used in the recognition of the French National Committee. The British Government is reported to have recognized the committee "as representing all Free Frenchmen wherever they may be, who rally to the Free French Movement . . .", and to have declared that it would "treat with the National Committee on all questions involving their collaboration with the Free French Movement and with the French Overseas territories which place themselves under their authority." This seemed to the British Government "to be the appropriate character in which to regard the executive organ of a movement which, under the fighting leadership of General de Gaulle, embodies the hope of Frenchmen of free mind, wherever they may be."[7] As it has been correctly remarked by one writer, the formula thus employed made it particularly clear that, in the opinion of the British Government, the Committee did not represent the whole of France.[8] Furthermore, although some other governments, in according recognition to the Committee, made use of various ambiguous formulae, none of them seems to have considered the Committee as an organ of the French State.[9] It is of particular interest to find that when, in August 1942, President Beneš had urged the Soviet Government to recognize the C.N.F. as the Government of France, General de Gaulle himself

---

[5] See de Gaulle, vol. I, pp. 142, 330.

[6] *Ibid.*, vol. I, pp. 194, 545.

[7] Statement by Mr. Eden on 26 November 1941. See *Parliamentary Debates*, House of Commons, vol. 376, col. 727; *cf.* Flory, p. 65; and see *Documents on International Affairs, 1939–1946*, vol. II *Hitler's Europe* (ed. by Carlyle, 1954), p. 179.

[8] Flory, p. 65. A heated discussion between Churchill and de Gaulle on 29 September 1942 may here be noted. In the latter's memoirs, Mr. Churchill is reported to have exclaimed: "Vous dites que vous êtes la France! Vous n'êtes pas la France! Je ne vous reconnais pas comme la France!" And General de Gaulle quotes his own reply as follows: "Si, à vos yeux, je ne suis pas le représentant de la France, pourquoi et de quel droit traitez-vous avec moi de ses intérêts mondiaux?" See de Gaulle, vol. II, p. 33.

[9] Flory, p. 65.

stated that although he would not object to such recognition, he never-theless considered that it would be premature.[1]

If the Soviet Government did not, in fact, recognize even the French Committee of National Liberation—the C.F.L.N.—as the Government of France, it was nevertheless the most generous in its appreciation of the competence of the committee. It regarded the committee "comme le représentant des intérêts de la République Française" and "comme le seul représentant autorisé de tous les patriotes français en lutte contre l'hitlérisme".[2] The protracted discussions which took place between the United Kingdom and the United States before any kind of re-cognition was accorded to this Committee have been described by Sir Winston Churchill in his war memoirs.[3] The expressions eventually used by Great Britain and the United States were more cautious than those employed by the Soviet Union, and it may safely be said that no government attributed to the Committee the competence to engage the future responsibility of the State of France. Indeed, the fear that any such inference would be drawn from recognition appears to have been the chief American objection to according recognition. In suggesting the term "acceptance" instead of "recognition", President Roosevelt wrote to Prime Minister Churchill:

"I do not think we should at any time use the word 'recognition', because this would be distorted to imply that we recognize the Committee as the Government of France as soon as we land on French soil."

It was Roosevelt's scepticism concerning the representativeness of General de Gaulle and of the Committee as a whole that evidently lay behind this reticence. The President wrote in the same letter:

"French political questions must be left to solution by the people of France when they have been freed from the present domination of the enemy . . ."[4]

Although it was necessary for the British Government to deal with the new Committee as a *de facto* authority, because the Committee

---

[1] See de Gaulle, vol. II, pp. 35, 348 and 352; the Russian formula eventually used was nevertheless interpreted in a French communiqué to mean that the Soviet Government recognized the Committee as the real Government of France. That inter-pretation, however, was hardly warranted. For the text and the communiqué, see *R.G.D.I.P.*, vol. 49 (1941–45), p. 360.

[2] For the text of this declaration, as well as others, see *R.G.D.I.P.*, vol. 49 (1941–45), p. 365; *cf.* Flory, p. 68.

[3] See Churchill, *The Second World War*, vol. 5, pp. 173 ff.

[4] Letter of 22 July 1943, quoted in *ibid.*, p. 181.

alone served the functions earlier fulfilled by the C.N.F., there was reluctance to "recognize it *de jure*"—whatever that expression meant in this connexion. The British Prime Minister wrote:

"We should avoid the use of the word 'recognition', and avoid also anything in the nature of a splash or a gesture, while at the same time working with them, for what they are worth, from day to day."[5]

It is of interest also to note that the effectiveness and the representativeness of the Committee was considered the decisive element for its recognition. Such seems to be the import of the following opinion of the British Prime Minister:

"... we should see how they conduct their business and themselves before deciding what degree of recognition we should give them as representing France."[6]

Even more characteristic of this attitude is a letter of 11 June 1943 from the Prime Minister to Mr. Macmillan:

"There can be no question of our giving recognition until we know what it is we have to recognize. See St. Matthew, chapter vii, verse 16: 'Ye shall know them by their fruits' ..."[7]

The Prime Minister looked upon the institution of recognition in the same commonsense manner. He wrote:

"What does recognition mean? One can recognize a man as an Emperor or as a grocer. Recognition is meaningless, without a defining formula."[8]

As noted above, the formulae eventually employed did not point to the committee as representing the State of France. The wording used by the United States Government was particularly explicit on this point:

"This statement does not constitute recognition of a government of France or of the French Empire by the Government of the United States. It constitutes recognition of the French Committee of National Liberation as functioning within specific limitations during the war. Later on, the people of France, in a free and untrammeled manner will proceed, in due course, to select their own government and their own officials to administer it."[9]

[5] *Ibid.*, p. 178.
[6] *Ibid.*, p. 174.
[7] *Ibid.*, p. 175.
[8] *Ibid.*, p. 179.
[9] *Department of State Bulletin*, vol. 9 (1943), p. 126. French text in *R.G.D.I.P.*, vol. 49 (1941–45), p. 364. See also Flory, p. 70.

Treaty-making activity of the French Committees

Let us now turn from the declarations of recognition, with their meticulous vagueness, to the actual treaty relations entertained by governments with the Committees.

A large number of agreements were concluded on behalf of the Council for the Defense of the Empire,[1] as well as for the French National Committee.[2] With one possible exception,[3] these agreements

---

[1] Reference may be made to the following:

Agreement of 21 January 1941 with the British Government regulating trade between the United Kingdom and the Cameroons under French mandate. (Text in *J.O.F.L.*, Première Année, No. 3 (25 février 1941), p. 12.)

Two agreements of 19 March 1941 with the British Government regarding credits, finance and foreign exchange. (Notice in *J.O.F.L.*, Première Année, No. 5 (29 avril 1941), p. 20. *Cf.* de Gaulle, vol. I, p. 127.)

Agreement of 20 May 1941 with the British Government to facilitate commerce between French Equatorial Africa and the United Kingdom. (Text in *J.O.F.L.*, Première Année, No. 7 (28 juin 1941), p. 28.)

In addition, it may be mentioned that a convention effecting a customs union was concluded on 28 January 1941 between the Governor of the French settlements in India with the approval of the Council for the Defense of the Empire given by General de Gaulle, and the Consul-General of Great Britain in the same settlements, acting in the name of the Governor-General of India (see notice in *J.O.F.L.*, Première Année, No. 7 (28 juin 1941), p. 28).

It may be mentioned, finally, that on 2 June 1941, the French Governor in New Caledonia was authorized to conclude an agreement on behalf of General de Gaulle and the Council for the Defense of the Empire with the Government of Australia, and that such an agreement was concluded (see de Gaulle, vol. I, pp. 138 and 363).

[2] Reference may be made to the following:

Agreement of 26 September 1942 with Great Britain regarding the recruiting of Free French forces (see notice in *Journal Officiel de la France Combattante*, Deuxième Année, No. 14 (30 décembre 1942), p. 75).

Agreement of 14 December 1942 with the British Government regarding the defense of Madagascar and Réunion (see notice in *J.O.F.C.*, Deuxième Année, No. 14 (30 décembre 1942), p. 76, and see de Gaulle, vol. II, pp. 56 and 426).

Declaration of 12 January 1942 regarding war crimes. Signed by governments in exile (text in Document issued by the Inter-Allied Information Committee, London, H. M. Stationery Office, 1942, according to reference from Lauterpacht in *B.Y.I.L.*, vol. 21 (1944), p. 60, note 1); for de Gaulle's comment to the effect that by concluding the agreement with him, the governments in exile evidenced their view of de Gaulle "comme le Français qualifié pour parler au nom de la France," see de Gaulle, vol. I, p. 213.

Exchange of notes constituting an agreement of 3 September 1942 with the United States regarding the principles governing the provision of reciprocal aid in the prosecution of the war (*U.N.T.S.*, vol. 24 (1949), p. 177).

Agreement on mutual aid of 9 July 1942 between the United States and Fighting France (see *A.J.I.L.*, vol. 36 (1942), Off. Doc., p. 213).

all had regard to the participation of the Free French movement in the pursuit of the war, and did not incur any future obligations for the State of France.

In this connexion, special mention should perhaps be made of a declaration made when, on 8 June 1941, British and French troops were about to liberate Lebanon and Syria from the control of Vichy. The declaration which was issued by General Catroux "au nom de la France libre, qui s'identifie avec la France traditionelle et authentique, et au nom de son chef, le Général de Gaulle", promised independence to Lebanon and Syria which were placed under French mandate. The very same day, the British Ambassador to Cairo declared that his Government supported and associated itself with that promise. On 26 and 27 September 1941, the declaration was followed by proclamations of independence for Lebanon and Syria. These acts, which also emanated from General Catroux, promised the assistance of Free France to secure recognition for the two States. They further laid down that only such restrictions upon the sovereignty of the States were to be retained as were necessitated by the war, and indicated that it was necessary definitely to regulate the relations with France by means of a treaty celebrating the independence of the States.[4]

While the British Government appears immediately to have recognized the independence of the two States, the United States delayed its act of recognition.[5] It is perhaps questionable whether Syria and Lebanon can be said to have acquired real independence by the proclamations. British and French troops were present in the two States, and the Free French Government considered the mandate as continuing in force, and, indeed, as irrevocable until after the war, when the authority which had conferred the mandate upon France—the League of Nations—would be able to relieve France of this task, and when treaties duly ratified by France could be entered into with the two States.[6] In view of these circumstances, much weight should perhaps not

[3] The possible exception being the declaration signed with governments in exile. See the preceding note.

[4] *R.G.D.I.P.*, vol. 49 (1941–45), pp. 325–331; *Documents on International Affairs, 1939–1946*, vol. II: *Hitler's Europe* (ed. by Carlyle, 1954), pp. 173 ff.

[5] See *Department of State Bulletin*, vol. 5 (1941), p. 440. See also Oppenheimer, p. 572.

[6] See de Gaulle, vol. I, pp. 159, 201; vol. II, p. 19; see also the communiqué of 5 November 1943 regarding the situation in Lebanon, *R.G.D.I.P.*, vol. 49 (1941–45), p. 332; and see Longrigg, *Syria and Lebanon under French Mandate* (1958), pp. 310, 321–323, 330, 350 and 362.

be given to the proclamations and the British declaration as possible evidence of the competence of the Free French Government to commit the State of France for the future.[7]

With regard to the French Committee for National Liberation—the C.F.L.N.—it is noteworthy that while recognition of any kind was still being withheld from the Committee, intercourse with it was nevertheless indispensable. Mr. Churchill stated in the British Parliament that the creation of the Committee had "superseded" the situation created by the exchange of letters between himself and de Gaulle in 1940, and brought to an end his official connexion with de Gaulle as the leader of the Fighting French. While it is not clear from the memoirs of Sir Winston Churchill whether the C.F.L.N. was regarded by the British Government as the legal successor of the C.N.F., and as continuing automatically in the rights and obligations of the latter, the memoirs reveal that Mr. Churchill "made haste to transfer to it [*i.e.,* to the C.F.L.N.] the engagements previously made with General de Gaulle." They further record that, at that time, the Prime Minister was of the following opinion: "This process must continue, as otherwise we should have no one to deal with about finance, propaganda, Syria and other French possessions, and the control of the French armed forces."[8]

The C.F.L.N. also entered into agreements in its own name. Two of these had regard to aid for the pursuit of the war, and two agreements concerned the handing over of all legislative and administrative powers in Lebanon and Syria.[9]

---

[7] But see Flory (p. 200), who claims that the Conseil de Défense here acted as a real Government, incontestably binding the State of France.

[8] Churchill, *The Second World War,* vol. 5, p. 178. It may here be noted that in the British formula of recognition, which was given on 27 August 1943, there was an express clause on the succession of rights and obligations. See *R.G.D.I.P.,* vol. 49 (1941–45), p. 364.

[9] Agreement of 25 September 1943 between the United States and the C.F.L.N. on Lend-Lease (see "Chronicle of International Events" in *A.J.I.L.,* vol. 38 (1944), p. 128, which gives as the source *The New York Times* of 26 September 1943, p. 41).

Agreements of 23 December 1943 between the C.F.L.N. and the Governments of Lebanon and Syria handing over all administrative and legislative functions. To be effective on 1 January 1944 (see "Chronicle of International Events" in *A.J.I.L.,* vol. 38 (1944), p. 300, giving as the source *The New York Times* of 25 December 1943, p. 4).

Agreement of 8 February 1944 between the C.F.L.N. and the Government of the United Kingdom on finance and mutual aid, the former being for the duration of

Basis of the treaty-making competence of the French Committees

In conclusion, it may be said that up to 3 June 1944—the events of and after that date will be discussed below—the three Committees were, on the whole, neither regarded by themselves as organs competent to bind the State of France, nor treated by other governments as possessing such competence. As pointing in this direction, the fact may be noted, in addition to those cited above, that the C.N.F. was not invited to sign the United Nations Declaration issued by the Allied governments on 1 January 1942. This omission is recorded with some bitterness in the memoirs of General de Gaulle.[1] Mention may also be made of the Final Act of the United Nations Conference on Food and Agriculture, which was adopted on 3 June 1943. While the preamble of this document referred to the governments of various states, it only spoke of "the French Representatives".[2]

The actual treaty relations with the three Committees, as described above, would seem to offer confirmation—with allowance perhaps for minor inconsistencies—of the view expressed in the various formulae of recognition that none of the committees was held competent to commit the State of France.[3] Put in these negative terms, the conclusions thus reached by the governments of various states have also been shown to have been shared by the Committees themselves.

While it is somewhat difficult to characterize and to define the status that actually was ascribed to the Committees, it seems clear that the decisive reason why they did not claim the status of a government, and why they were not accorded such status, lay in the opinion that the

---

the war (see "Chronicle of International Events" in the *A.J.I.L.*, vol. 38 (1944), p. 303, giving as the source *The New York Times* of 9 February 1944, p. 8).

[1] De Gaulle, vol. I, p. 184. While, as the depositary, the United States Government declared as early as 5 January 1942 that it would receive statements of adherence to the declaration "from appropriate authorities which are not governments", it was not until 1 January 1945 that French participation was effected. See *A.J.I.L.*, vol. 36 (1942), July, Off. Doc., p. 191, note; *cf.* Goodrich and Hambro, *The Charter of the United Nations* (2nd ed., 1949), p. 570, giving 26 December 1944 as the date when the French adherence was communicated.

[2] See *A.J.I.L.*, vol. 37 (1943), Off. Doc., p. 159.

[3] It may be appropriate to record in this connexion that, when according recognition to the C.F.L.N., the British and the United States Governments made clear that "les relations anglo-américaines avec le Comité pouvaient être modifiées à tout moment" and that "les questions particulières soulevées par elles devaient être résolues par des accords *ad hoc* à la lumière des circonstances du moment". See Flory, p. 69.

Committees were not fully representative of the French nation.[4] It is clear, furthermore, that the competence that actually was ascribed to the Committees was seen to flow from, and to be commensurate with, the degree of effectiveness that was displayed by them. There is, finally, no evidence suggesting that the lack of a constitutional origin of the Committees had any influence upon the status claimed or accorded to them.

Basis of competence of the Provisional Government

Before any one of the various Committees headed by General de Gaulle claimed the status of a French Government, there was no definite difference of opinion concerning the status of these bodies. Such difference arose, however, when, in June 1944, the C.F.L.N. proclaimed itself the Provisional Government of France.

As early as September 1943, the C.F.L.N. had submitted to Washington and London the draft of an agreement designed to regulate the co-operation between the C.F.L.N. and Allied troops in France upon the liberation.[5] This step, which implied that the C.F.L.N. claimed to become at least a Provisional French Government, had evoked no response from the Allies. In March 1944, the C.F.L.N. issued an ordinance regarding the re-establishment of public powers in France upon the liberation, a measure which was justifiably interpreted to constitute a claim to the status of a provisional government.[6] No Allied approval, however, was given to these plans. Nor was any recognition accorded when, on 3 June 1944—three days before the invasion began in Normandy—the C.F.L.N. formally proclaimed itself the Provisional Government of France. In the first months following the invasion, there was indeed no formal agreement among the Allies indicating any recognized French authorities in France, and confusion appears to have resulted from this circumstance, as well as from the absence of any organized liaison between the invading forces and General de Gaulle's organization in metropolitan France.[7]

---

[4] The existence of the Vichy Government, which claimed to represent France, and which enjoyed some support in the State, obviously constituted an important obstacle to the recognition of the authorities in exile as fully representative of France, especially in the early part of the war.

[5] De Gaulle, vol. II, p. 135.

[6] *Ibid.*, pp. 218, 620; see also Flory, pp. 234–236.

[7] De Gaulle, vol. II, pp. 186, 227; Flory, p. 234.

It cannot be doubted that the prevailing situation ought to have made the Anglo-Saxon powers inclined to recognize the governmental status that was claimed by the C.F.L.N. When they nevertheless reached a negative conclusion in this regard, it is curious to find that there was, in fact, no difference of opinion between them and the C.F.L.N. as to what elements they considered decisive for a body to attain governmental status. As will be seen, the difference arose rather from the varying amount of evidence which they required of these elements.

It is convenient first to examine the status which the Allied governments ascribed to the C.F.L.N. and the theory behind their position. The general policy championed by the United States, and adhered to by the United Kingdom, was to treat with and to recognize such French authorities as wielded actual effective power, wherever they existed, and regardless of their constitutional status. From the outset, this policy had permitted the United States to deal with General de Gaulle's organization as an *effective local authority*. A statement made by the American Vice-Consul at Nouméa to the High Commissioner of New Caledonia and made public by the latter on 28 February 1942, is illustrative:

"... In its relations with the local French authorities in French territories the United States has been and will continue to be governed by the manifest effectiveness with which those authorities endeavour to protect their territories from domination and control by the common enemy.

"With the French authorities in effective control of French territories in the Pacific this Government has treated and will continue to treat on the basis of their actual administration of the territories involved. This Government recognizes, in particular, that French island possessions in that area are under the effective control of the French National Committee established in London and the United States authorities are cooperating for the defense of these islands with the authorities established by the French National Committee and with no other French authority ..."[8]

From the view-point of the Fighting French, one disadvantage of the United States policy was that that policy also attributed competence to the Government of Vichy and to the authorities which took instruc-

---

[8] See *Department of State Bulletin*, vol. 6 (1942), p. 208. The declaration—in French—is quoted in de Gaulle, vol. I, p. 527.

A declaration similar to that quoted in the text was made public on 4 April 1942, in connexion with the stationing of a United States Consul at Brazzaville. See *Department of State Bulletin*, vol. 6 (1942), p. 273. The declaration—in French—is quoted in de Gaulle, vol. I, p. 533.

tions from that government.[9] As the Fighting French considered the Vichy Government devoid of all legal competence, domestic as well as international,[1] controversies were inevitable when, as actually happened, the Anglo-Saxon powers negotiated or took steps to negotiate with various authorities subordinated to Vichy.[2]

Another consequence of the theory of the competence of effective local authorities, perhaps even more injurious to the Fighting French, was that, while the theory readily took into account and recognized the power actually attained by the Fighting French authorities, it offered no ground for conferring upon that particular authority the power of administering territories liberated by the Anglo-Saxon powers. This circumstance was at the root of several of the grave controversies between these powers and the authorities of General de Gaulle. Although the latter did not care to claim the formal status of a Government of France until June 1944, they demanded nevertheless that the administration and control of French territories which fell into Allied hands should be immediately turned over to them. The Anglo-Saxon powers, however, not considering the Committees as competent to make demands on behalf of the State of France, felt no obligation to hand over liberated territory to them. When, as on occasion, they showed themselves inclined to exercise their discretion in this regard, sharp controversies followed with General de Gaulle.[3] Although the Chief of the Fighting French consistently emerged as the victor in these disputes, and consequently gradually increased and confirmed the authority of his movement, the reserve that the Anglo-Saxon powers—and in particular the President of the United States—held with regard to it persisted.

As the Anglo-Saxon powers continued to regard the C.F.L.N. as only an effective local authority even after that Committee had proclaimed

[9] This circumstance is referred to indirectly when the British and United States Governments, in their formulae of recognition of the C.F.L.N., stated that they did not pledge themselves to treat exclusively with the Committee in all questions concerning France until its liberation. See Flory, p. 69.

[1] See, in particular the declaration issued at Brazzaville on 27 October 1940, printed in de Gaulle, vol. I, pp. 313 ff.

[2] The most notable instance was undoubtedly that of the so-called Clark–Darlan agreement, signed on 13 November 1942. For facts and comments, see Churchill, *The Second World War*, vol. 4, p. 631 and de Gaulle, vol. II, p. 48. For another instance, see de Gaulle, vol. I, pp. 184 and 496.

[3] See, as regards the liberation of Madagascar, de Gaulle, vol. I, pp. 204 ff., and regarding French North Africa, *ibid.*, vol. II, pp. 5, 24.

itself the Provisional Government, they did not feel, of course, that the Committee could claim, as a matter of right, that metropolitan France, when liberated, should be handed over to it. The reason for their persistence was clearly that they continued to doubt that the actual popular support for General de Gaulle in metropolitan France was sufficient to sustain a democratic government headed by him.[4] Illustrative in this regard is the following passage from the war memoirs of Sir Winston Churchill:

"As our armies moved eastward and southward it became increasingly urgent to set up a unified and broadly representative Administration in France. We were anxious not to impose a ready-made Committee from abroad, and we tried first to gauge the feelings of the people themselves as the liberation progressed."[5]

Reserved though their attitude was, the Anglo-Saxon powers needed a basis for co-operation between their armed forces and the authorities which saw in the C.F.L.N. the Provisional Government of France. However, even the agreement signed on 25 August 1944 by the French, British and United States military commanders to satisfy this need attributed only the provisional civil administration of Liberated France to the authorities headed by General de Gaulle, and did not point to them as competent to engage the responsibility of the State of France in the international sphere. The United States Government was not even satisfied with these limitations but added as a further precaution:

"General Eisenhower is authorized to treat with the French authorities at Algiers considered as *de facto* powers of France, to the extent they receive the support of the majority of Frenchmen who fight for the defeat of Germany and the Liberation of France."[6]

A month later, on 28 September 1944, despite the fact that the underground movement and public opinion in France had given much evidence of its adherence to the Provisional Government headed by General de Gaulle, Mr. Churchill stated in the House of Commons that he was not yet satisfied that the Committee could speak in the name of the whole people of France, and suggested that, after the transformation of the Algiers Consultative Assembly into an elected body to which the C.F.L.N. would be responsible, and the apparent

---

[4] De Gaulle, vol. II, p. 218.

[5] Churchill, *The Second World War,* vol. 6, p. 244.

[6] See *U.N.T.S.,* vol. 138 (1952), p. 248; Flory, pp. 238 ff.; *cf.* de Gaulle, vol. II, p. 307.

approval of such an arrangement by the population, the committee would be recognized as a "Provisional Government".[7]

If the Anglo-Saxon powers thus clearly showed that to them the actual effectiveness, and, as a basis for such effectiveness, the popular approval of any French authority, was decisive for their attributing competence to it as a government or otherwise, the memoirs of General de Gaulle show him, on his part, to have been aware of and, indeed, subscribing to the very same rationale. From the very beginning of his struggle he realized that the existence and the use of military power was of importance to the status of the organization he was about to create. The following statement by him is believed characteristic in this regard: ". . . il n'y a pas de France sans épée. Constituer une force de combat, cela importait avant tout."[8] He further showed himself at all times eager to have French forces participate in the war effort, thus offering evidence of the power of Fighting France.[9] At an early stage, he began, furthermore, to build up and to keep under his control the resistance movement in metropolitan France, and he did not fail to impress upon the Allies the important support that that movement contributed to his organization.[1]

The Head of Fighting France was also aware of the necessity of making his organization as representative as possible of the French nation. In the early days in London, he sought to enlist the participation of representative French personalities who had escaped.[2] Later, he established the Consultative Assembly and included in his "cabinet" representatives of the French political parties, and of the resistance movement.[3] He, no less than the Allied governments, was mindful of the popular approval he gained, and considered this a decisive element. He quotes himself as having asked General Giraud if the latter thought himself able to gain from the French people "cette adhésion élémentaire sans laquelle un gouvernement ne peut être qu'une fiction, à moins qu'il ne devienne la cible d'une révolution." In another connexion he states that "la résolution nationale, plus puissante qu'aucun décret formel, me chargeait ouvertement d'incarner et de conduire l'État."[4]

---

[7] Churchill, *The Second World War*, vol. 6, pp. 245–246.

[8] De Gaulle, vol. I, p. 74.

[9] See de Gaulle, vol. I, pp. 69, 78, 90.

[1] *Ibid.*, vol. I, pp. 128, 233, vol. II, p. 38.

[2] *Ibid.*, vol. I, p. 83.

[3] *Ibid.*, vol. II, p. 150.

[4] For the two quotations, see *ibid.*, vol. II, pp. 81 and 123; see also p. 303.

No better understanding of the direct relation between the effectiveness and the international status of an exile organization can be found, indeed, than that reflected in the following statement in which General de Gaulle referred to the situation existing in the spring of 1944:

"La diplomatie, sous des conventions de forme, ne connaît que les réalités. Tant que nous étions dépourvus, nous pouvions émouvoir les hommes; nous touchions peu les services. Mais, aujourd'hui, l'unité française renaissante, cela pèse et cela compte. A mesure, la France réapparaît dans les perspectives du monde."[5]

This understanding also led General de Gaulle not to worry unduly about the circumstance that the Allied governments refrained from recognizing his Provisional Government. He felt that, if he only persevered, these formalities would take care of themselves.[6] The popular support for and the strength of his organization became increasingly evident and did not fail to impress the Allied governments as the liberation of France progressed.[7] The fact that these governments long delayed their recognition of the Provisional Government and their attributing to it the international competence to act on behalf of the State of France was not due, however, to their regarding anything but effectiveness as decisive for such competence. The time that was allowed to lapse between the moment when the claim for governmental status was put forward, and the day when recognition of such status was actually accorded, was caused by a difference as regards the amount of evidence that was required of the effectiveness, rather than any difference regarding the requirement of effectiveness itself. It may be noted in this connexion that most of the governments in exile resident in London were less rigid in this regard. Not unnaturally sympathetic to the claim of the C.F.L.N. to be the Provisional Government of France, they accorded their recognition almost immediately.[8]

It should be recorded, finally, that although elections in France had still proved impossible, the Governments of the three great Powers eventually, on 23 October 1944, recognized General de Gaulle's administration as the Provisional Government of France, despite its lack of any constitutional title. The ultimate conviction that the administration headed by General de Gaulle wielded, and would continue to wield, the necessary authority to be able to discharge the functions of a

[5] *Ibid.*, vol. II, p. 187.
[6] *Ibid.*, vol. II, p. 189.
[7] *Ibid.*, vol. II, p. 229; *cf.* Churchill, *The Second World War*, vol. 6, p. 245.
[8] De Gaulle, vol. II, p. 229.

government led to this step. The British Prime Minister stated in the House of Commons:

"I have been myself for some weeks past satisfied not only that the present French Government, under General de Gaulle, commands the full assent of the vast majority of the French people, but that it is the only Government which can possibly discharge the very heavy burdens which are being cast upon it, and the only Government which can enable France to gather its strength in the interval which must elapse before the constitutional and Parliamentary processes, which it has declared its purpose to reinstate, can again resume their normal functions."[9]

The above discussion suffices to show that the reason why the most powerful governments refrained for a long time from attributing to the C.F.L.N. the status and competence of a Provisional Government of France lay in their doubts as to its representativeness. On the other hand, there is no evidence that the lack of a constitutional title was of any importance. Nor is there anything to suggest that the Governments of the three great Powers would not have attributed to the C.F.L.N. the competence to represent the State of France before the liberation had begun, had they only been convinced of its actual popular support—its future effectiveness. As it was, although not yet a constitutional government, the C.F.L.N. was no longer an authority in exile, when it was eventually accepted as competent to enter into treaties on behalf of the State of France.

7. Criteria for Competence of Authorities and Governments in Exile

Questions concerning the basis of the treaty-making competence of governments in exile cannot be altogether separated from the broader issue of the sources of the general competence of both governments and authorities in exile.

The reason why the existence of authorities and governments in exile is at all possible lies in the circumstance that the international community is reluctant to concede title to a territory which has been subjected by means of belligerent occupation. The reluctance is caused in part, it may be assumed, by an unwillingness to sanction positions which have been attained by acts contrary to international law, and partly by the awareness that belligerent occupation is an insecure basis

---

[9] Churchill, *The Second World War*, vol. 6, p. 249; on the recognition, see also the pages preceding the one quoted.

for a territorial government. This view is in accord with the following opinion:

"... in upholding the continued legal existence of an occupied State whose premature annexation has been pronounced by the occupying power, international law does not act on a *certainty* of its restoration but on an *uncertainty* of its extinction."[1]

Further support for the view stated above may be derived from the following statement by Professor Kelsen:

"... as long as the status of the territory is that of belligerent occupation, and that means as long as there is a war between the occupied state and the occupying state, the control exercised by the latter cannot be considered as 'effective'. Apart from the fact that it is restricted by international law, it is not firmly established; for there is a war going on the purpose of which is to reestablish the effective control of the government now in exile."[2]

In the discussion that follows, an attempt will be made to draw some conclusions in the light of the three inquiries undertaken above. It will be convenient to discuss the case of authorities and that of governments separately.

Basis of the treaty-making competence of authorities in exile

The authority in exile, whose chief aim is to liberate the occupied territory from which it came, is generally dependent for its existence upon a permission to function in the territory of a friendly host state. This permission, alone, does not confer rights and duties under international law upon the authority, and does not, of course, make it a government of the occupied state in the eyes of international law. It would appear, however, that the moment the authority begins to display a minimum of effectiveness with a view to the liberation of the territory from which it came—such as the rallying of troops—it is likely to be considered competent under international law to assume *some* rights and duties, *inter alia* in the form of agreements made on behalf of the organization it heads.

Express recognition of some kind does not appear to be a requirement which must be fulfilled before an authority in exile is allowed to enter into agreements under international law. It has been emphasized above that Mr. Churchill made haste to transfer the agreements he had concluded with General de Gaulle to the C.F.L.N. before he was dis-

---

[1] Marek, p. 566.
[2] Kelsen, pp. 288–289.

posed to accord any kind of formal recognition to that body. While it seems that a degree of effectiveness is all that is required of an exile authority in order that some treaty-making competence may be attributed to it, it must be admitted that the attainment of that degree is for the most part signalized by some kind of recognition, before treaty relations are entered into.

What have here been termed authorities in exile—as distinguished from governments in exile—do not seem to need any standing whatever under the constitutions of the states they wish to liberate. As found in two of the cases examined above, they may be spontaneous revolutionary bodies with a general competence deriving exclusively from international law. These cases further point to the conclusion that the competence of authorities in exile to undertake obligations by way of agreement is limited to matters which fall within their apparent ability of fulfillment, and that the reason why these authorities are not, correspondingly, accorded competence to engage the responsibility of their home states lies in the circumstance that their future standing and ability to assert themselves in these states seem uncertain.

Basis of the treaty-making competence of governments in exile

Much more is needed than the limited effectiveness required to attribute some competence under international law to an authority in exile before an organ will be considered a government in exile, *i.e.,* an organ that may be competent under international law to engage the responsibility of a state, for example, in the form of treaties concerning post-war matters.

It should first be noted that although governments in exile, like authorities in exile, are generally dependent for their existence upon a permission to function upon the territory of a friendly host state, such permission in itself does not confer any governmental competence upon them.

Before discussing the elements which do seem to confer such competence, it may be convenient to consider certain features which appear *not* to be indispensable for such competence.

Constitutional functioning and origin

From the cases which have been examined above, it seems first of all that neither constitutional origin, nor functioning in conformity with a particular constitution, should be required in order that a body that claims to be a government in exile should be competent under international law to act on behalf of a state. The absence of a constitutional origin was conspicuous in the case of the Czechoslovak Government in exile, which was held competent to enter into treaties on behalf of the State of Czechoslovakia, although it was established altogether outside the framework of the Constitution of that State. It seemed, further, that the reason why the French authorities in exile were not considered to possess the competence of a government in exile lay in circumstances other than their lack of a constitutional origin. The conclusion that a constitutional origin is *altogether irrelevant* is drawn by Kelsen:

"Just as international law does not require constitutionality of a government established on the territory of its own state, it does not require constitutionality of a government in exile."[3]

There are other authorities, however, who hold that, to be attributed the competence of a government, it is necessary—and sufficient—that an exile body should be identical with the last government that was established in the state before the occupation. Generally, but not invariably, this will mean a government that has a regular constitutional origin. This, indeed, seems to be the view of Sir Hersch Lauterpacht, who ventures to suggest that even the case of the Czechoslovakian Government in exile might be explained in the light of this theory. To reach that conclusion, Sir Hersch is obliged to accept the construction that the presence in England of the "last freely elected Head of State" of Czechoslovakia "and the government formed under him constituted the requisite link in legal continuity".[4] Quite consistently, Sir Hersch also expresses the opinion that one of the reasons why the Algiers authorities were not recognized as a government lay in the circumstance that they were not "in a position to rely on legal continuity as being identical with or the constitutional successor of a previously recognized government."[5]

Although Sir Hersch cites no evidence to support this explanation of the French case, arguably it is sound. For reasons which have been advanced above,[6] the construction cannot be accepted, however, that the Czechoslovak Government in exile was identical with or a direct

[3] *Ibid.*, p. 290.

[4] Lauterpacht, *Recognition in International Law* (1947), p. 92, in note.

[5] *Ibid.*, p. 165, in note.

[6] Above, p. 163.

successor of the last Government in Czechoslovakia before that State was invaded. Had that construction not also been rejected by the governments of the Allied powers, it is difficult to see why they should have considered acts of recognition necessary.

Like Sir Hersch Lauterpacht, a German writer, Dr. Mattern, and Dr. Marek, have adhered to the view that the character of a state organ can only be attributed to governments in exile which have been—to quote the latter writer—"constituted in their own countries and simply transferred their activities abroad, following the total occupation of their territories, with no break in their legal and actual continuity."[7] While Dr. Mattern does not attempt to reconcile the case of the Czechoslovak Government in exile with this view, Dr. Marek, who ably discusses the matter, is driven to suggest effectiveness as an alternative source of governmental competence.[8]

The isolated case of Czechoslovakia does not, perhaps, suffice to justify the conclusion that it should be completely irrelevant to the competence of a body in exile whether or not it was the government of the state when the occupation took place. The conclusion may safely be drawn, on the other hand, that such identity and, consequently, a constitutional origin, have *not* been deemed *indispensable* for the existence of governmental competence and the power to make treaties on behalf of a state which is occupied. Below, the suggestion will be advanced that the importance of these elements possibly may lie in the circumstance that they may offer some evidence of the effectiveness— the representative quality and hypothetical future power—of an exile organ.

In view of the conclusion that the constitutional origin of a government in exile is not a prerequisite of its competence to make treaties on behalf of the state it purports to represent, it is not surprising that the international treaty-making competence of such governments should be unaffected by constitutional flaws in the functioning of such governments generally, and independent of any constitutional basis for or particular restriction upon that competence. Authority has been cited above to demonstrate that, in some way or other, all governments in exile infringed upon the constitutions of the states they represented, without this circumstance being considered to have the effect of depriving them of their general competence as state organs under international

---

[7] Marek, p. 97. *Cf.* Mattern, p. 15.
[8] Marek, p. 314.

law. Evidence bearing directly upon treaty-making competence was offered, furthermore, in the form of certain treaties made by the Polish
and Czechoslovak Governments in exile.

Recognition

There is nothing to suggest that the recognition of governments in
exile should be of more importance to the treaty-making competence of
such governments than to that of revolutionary governments or authorities in exile. It is concluded, therefore, that the act of recognition
merely signalizes the view of the recognizing party that the recognized
body has attained a certain degree of competence under international
law, normally—and here of particular interest—including the competence to engage the present and future responsibility of the state by
treaty.

Effectiveness

In view of the conclusions reached above, and in view of the results
of the three inquiries undertaken, it would seem that the only condition which must be fulfilled—and which need be fulfilled—in order
that an exile body may be attributed the general competence and the
treaty-making competence of the government of a state is its possession of
a certain amount of effectiveness. It must be admitted, of course, that
there is a limit to the effectiveness that is attainable by any government in exile, since its territory is occupied. Its competence can evidently arise at a degree of effectiveness that falls short of that which
is attainable by, and required of, a territorial government.[9] The following statement by Professor Kelsen is to the point:

"The requirement of exercising effective control of the territory is replaced
by the requirement of making efforts to regain effective control. This requirement, too, is an application of the principle of effectiveness. The efforts of the
government in exile to regain control of the territory under belligerent occupation must be 'effective'..." They are said to be effective, "... if they are made
by means of war, that is to say, by armed forces sufficient to prevent the control
of the occupying power from becoming firmly established."[1]

[9] One writer suggests that these governments must exercise power "sur le territoire
ou à l'égard du territoire:" Jumeau, *Le Refuge du Gouvernement National à
l'Étranger* (1941), p. 41.

[1] Kelsen, pp. 289–290; see also Raestad, "La cessation des états d'après le droit
des gens" in *Revue de droit international et de législation comparée*, 3 ser., vol. 20
(1939), p. 446.

There seem to be various ways in which an exile body may display an effectiveness considered sufficient to endow it with the character and competence of a government. It may do so, first, by rallying large numbers of its nationals to the cause of the liberation of their country, by the establishment of armed forces, the control of merchant ships carrying its flag, the maintenance of authority over overseas territories, etc. Furthermore, although it is crippled in its control of its own territory, it may display some effectiveness even in the home country by well-developed underground movements.

These types of physical effectiveness do not appear to suffice, however, to cause the central organ of an exile movement to be considered a government. It has been stressed several times above that a chief distinction between authorities in exile and governments in exile lies in the competence of the latter to commit the state for the future. This competence, in particular, appears to be attributed only on the basis of an assessment—of a prognosis—of the effectiveness that the government will display in its proper territory once that territory is liberated.

Several elements appear to be taken into account in the assessment of the apparent future power of an exiled government. Just as the authority of a revolutionary government is thought seriously affected, should it not be alone in claiming competence to represent the state, the hypothetical future effectiveness of a particular exile body claiming to be a government will be looked upon with scepticism if it has not succeeded in rallying round it all national resistance against the enemy. The apparent future power will be subjected to even more doubt if there should be two or more organizations constituting potential future authorities. The future effectiveness of an exile body seems further to be considered highly dependent upon the support it enjoys, and is expected to enjoy, from the population which it purports to represent.

The final point mentioned is perhaps where the constitutional origin of a government in exile, and its identity with the last, pre-occupation government of the state may be of importance. If the government has once been established in the state democratically, there is some likelihood that, at that time, the government enjoyed the confidence and support of a large part of the population, and that it may be able again to command the respect of the same population.[2] To judge by a case such as that of the Luxemburg Government in exile which, during the second world war, displayed little actual activity, but undoubtedly had

---

[2] But see Flory, p. 36.

a regular constitutional origin, and was allowed fully to represent the State, it would seem that such origin might even be considered to make up for deficiencies in effectiveness in other regards.[3]

Evidence of a representative quality and some assurance as regards future authority might well be seen also in an exile movement's being headed by a number of political leaders whose past or present following in the state is not subject to doubt. It seems probable that the unity of the Czechoslovak exile movement and the representativeness of its leaders were the elements which, in addition to actual physical effectiveness in the pursuit of the war, helped the Czechoslovak Government in exile to be regarded as competent to engage the responsibility of the State of Czechoslovakia. Correspondingly, it seems probable that the doubts felt concerning the presence of the same elements in the French movement headed by General de Gaulle prevented the C.F.L.N. from being regarded as competent to represent the State of France until it exerted actual physical control over large areas of metropolitan French territory, and was given obvious support by the French people.

There is no need here for an exact assessment of the minimum level of effectiveness required of an exile body to be considered a government competent to engage the future responsibility of the state by entering into treaties. Perhaps such an assessment is not even feasible. For the purpose of this study, the conclusion suffices that the existence and extent of competence of authorities in exile, not held to be governments, to conclude agreements under international law is dependent upon the extent of their actual effectiveness. Similarly, the competence of a government in exile to enter into treaties on behalf of a state which it purports to represent is dependent, not upon its functioning in conformity with constitutional requirements, but upon its being expected —because it was once a representative constitutional government or for other reasons—to wield the authority necessary to fulfil pledges, or to give assurances that pledges will be fulfilled in the future.

The suggestion of one writer has been noted to the effect that there may be certain "inherent" limitations upon the extent of the treaty-making competence of governments in exile.[4] Precisely what limitations

---

[3] Dr. Marek, who does not discuss a constitutional title as possible evidence of effectiveness, reaches the following conclusion:

"... the relation between effectiveness and title seems to be one of inverse proportion: while a strong title can survive a period of non-effectiveness, a weak title must rely heavily, if not exclusively, on full and complete effectiveness." *Op. cit.,* p. 102.

[4] Marek, quoted above, p. 158.

that writer had in mind is not easily perceived, if not merely such as may be connected with the—supposedly temporary—limitation in the actual power of the government in exile over the occupied territory. The wide range of subjects on which treaties have been made by governments in exile suggests that it would not be possible to deduce any other limitation upon the extent of the treaty-making power of a government in exile.

CHAPTER XII

THE TREATY-MAKING COMPETENCE IN STATES WHICH HAVE NO MUNICIPAL RULE ON THE MATTER

1. PRELIMINARY REMARKS

It has been shown above that, in states where revolutionary governments have assumed power, and with regard to states which possess governments in exile, the rule commonly asserted to the effect that the treaty-making power of a state is indicated by its constitutional provision or practice on the question fails to give sure guidance, and that, in these situations, another rule is, in fact, followed. In some other situations, too, it appears certain that the rule traditionally referred to simply does not work, for the reason that there exists no municipal regulation of the treaty-making power. This seems likely to be the case where a state has recently acquired independence and has not yet adopted a constitutional provision or developed a constitutional practice which may be said to hold out to other governments the authorities municipally competent to conclude treaties. It will now be seen whether the cases of Israel and Ceylon may have fallen into this category, and what organs, if any, were in fact deemed competent to assume treaty obligations on behalf of these states.

The reference of the question of treaty-making competence to municipal law seems likely sometimes to fail, further, in states which have re-emerged into a condition of independence after a belligerent occupation, and which have allowed the old constitutional order to lapse without introducing a new regulation which answers the question of which organ is municipally competent to assume treaty obligations on behalf of the state. In this category, which is not very different in principle from the cases where a constitution has been abolished by a revolutionary government, the case of France in the period immediately after the second world war will be examined, with a view to ascertaining which authorities were, in fact, deemed competent to act on behalf of that State.

2. The Case of Israel

On 14 May 1948, the mandate of the United Kingdom over Palestine expired, and a People's Council, consisting of 38 members representing large Jewish organizations, proclaimed the independence of the State of Israel, declared itself the Provisional State Council—the legislative organ of Israel—and distributed the portfolios of the Provisional Government to 13 of its members.[1] No constitution was proclaimed at this time. Did there exist, in the absence of any such formal instrument, any other fundamental internal act which indicated the municipally competent treaty-making organ?

Relevant stipulations

The relevant section of the declaration of independence read as follows:

"WE DECLARE that, with effect from the moment of the termination of the Mandate, being tonight, the eve of Sabbath, the 6th Iyar, 5708 (15 May, 1948), until the establishment of the elected, regular authorities of the State in accordance with the Constitution which shall be adopted by the Elected Constituent Assembly not later than the 1st October 1948, the People's Council shall act as a Provisional Council of State, and its executive organ, the People's Administration, shall be the Provisional Government of the Jewish State, to be called 'Israel'."[2]

Section 3 of a proclamation of the same day laid down:

"So long as no laws have been enacted by or on behalf of the Provisional Council of State, the law which existed in Palestine on the 5th Iyar, 5708 (14th May, 1948) shall continue in force in the State of Israel, in so far as such continuance in force is consistent with the contents of this Proclamation, with the future laws and with the changes arising from the establishment of the State and its authorities."[3]

Shortly after the declaration of independence, on 21 May 1948, there was further issued by the Provisional Council of State a "Law and Administration Ordinance",[4] declared to have retroactive effect from the date of independence. Some articles of this Ordinance are relevant

---

[1] For a detailed account, see Rackman, *Israel's Emerging Constitution* (1955).

[2] *Laws of the State of Israel* (authorized translation from the Hebrew), vol. 1, Ordinances, 5708–1948, p. 4 (published by the Israeli Government Printer).

[3] *Ibid.*, p. 6.

[4] *Ibid.*, pp. 7 ff.

to the following discussion of the treaty-making organ of the State. Thus, Article 2 (b) stipulated:

"The Provisional Government shall act in accordance with the policy laid down by the Provisional Council of State, shall carry out its decisions, shall report to it on its activities and shall be answerable to it for its activities."

Article 11 provided, not very differently from the proclamation of 14 May:

"The law which existed in Palestine on the 5th Iyar, 5708 (14th May, 1948) shall remain in force, insofar as there is nothing therein repugnant to this Ordinance or to the other laws which may be enacted by or on behalf of the Provisional Council of State, and subject to such modifications as may result from the establishment of the State and its authorities."

Article 14 (a), finally, is also of interest:

"Any power vested under the law in the King of England or in any of his Secretaries of State, and any power vested under the law in the High Commissioner, the High Commissioner in Council, or the Government in Palestine, shall henceforth vest in the Provisional Government, unless such power has been vested in the Provisional Council of State by any of its Ordinances."

Was the treaty-making structure prevailing under the mandate preserved?

In a memorandum of 11 March 1951 submitted to the United Nations by the Government of Israel,[5] it is asserted that Section 11 quoted above had the effect of maintaining in force the "law and practice regarding the negotiation and conclusion of treaties" which prevailed during the mandate, with modifications of such rules as were incompatible with the sovereignty of the new State. Although the law thus referred to is found neither in the Palestine Order-in-Council of 1922 which embodied the basic constitutional law for Palestine during the mandate, nor in the British Foreign Jurisdiction Act of 1890, which governed British jurisdiction in Palestine, the memorandum rightly assumes that the power of conclusion of treaties was implicit in the British jurisdiction as part of the Royal Prerogative, and vested exclusively in the British Sovereign or in the High Commissioner of Palestine, subject to the limitations imposed by the mandate.

The argument seems ingenious, but not altogether convincing, that, to the extent that this pattern was not inconsistent with the independence of the State, it subsisted by virtue of the declaration of

---

[5] U.N., *Compilation*, pp. 67 ff.

independence and, later, of Section 11 of the Ordinance of 21 May. Unless it is permissible to reduce the municipal principles governing the conclusion of treaties during the mandate to a generalization like "The executive branch of the government concludes treaties binding upon the state without any need for prior legislative approval", the finding would seem inevitable that the pattern followed during the mandate was totally inconsistent with the independence of the new State and, consequently, lapsed. The conclusion would follow that, for the period between 15 May and 21 May 1948, the laws of Israel contained no indication of where the treaty-making power of the State was vested. It may perhaps be suggested with reason, on the other hand, as is done in an official Israeli reply to a questionnaire issued by the United Nations International Law Commission, that some of the doctrines based upon the practice of the mandatory period had 'at least a considerable persuasive value', even if they were not binding in law.[6]

There might seem to be more force in another argument put forward in the Israeli memorandum of 11 March 1951.[7] It is there suggested that as under Article 14 (a) of the Ordinance of 21 May 1948, the powers vested in the King and various other British authorities, among them the High Commissioner for Palestine, were to devolve upon the Provisional Government of Israel, unless they were arrogated by the Provisional Council of State by means of an ordinance, and as such ordinance had not been issued, the plenary treaty-making power devolved upon the Provisional Government.

Even the above construction, however, cannot have been received with much confidence by foreign governments if they cared to examine the matter: the treaty-making power of the British Crown had been limited by the mandate.[8] None of these limitations could apply to the organs of the State of Israel. Consequently, if only the powers possessed by the authorities which functioned under the mandate were inherited by the Provisional Government, that treaty-making power which was not possessed by these authorities, but which must be attributed to the independent State, would appear not to have been touched by the Ordinance, and thus been left unregulated. Furthermore, Article 2 (b)

---

[6] U.N. *Doc.* A/CN.4/19, 23 March 1950, p. 29.

[7] U.N., *Compilation,* p. 70.

[8] Articles 10, 12, 18, 19, and 20 of the mandate "conferred some degree of treaty-making power upon the Mandatory acting for Palestine...", see the Israeli memorandum cited above, p. 68. The text of the mandate may be found in U.N. *Doc.* A/70, October 1946.

of the Ordinance of 21 May 1948 prescribed that the Executive Government should act in accordance with the policy laid down by the legislature, carry out the decisions of the latter and report and be answerable to it. This being so, it must have been subject to some doubt —before a settled practice had developed—whether the Executive Government had full authority to ratify—and perhaps even to sign—treaties without prior approval of the legislature.

The position under the Transition Law of 1949

The legal position described above remained unchanged until 16 February 1949, when a Constituent Assembly, chosen in general elections, met and approved the so-called Transition Law.[9] That instrument was not adopted as a constitution of the State, but nevertheless regulated a number of fundamental questions regarding the governmental structure of the State. In this connexion the question immediately arises whether this Law offered any clear indication of the municipally competent treaty-making organ of the State and of the conditions for the exercise of the treaty-making function.

It should be noted, first of all, that Section 12 of the Transition Law provided that the Government should have "all the powers vested by law in the Provisional Government." Thus, whatever treaty-making power that Government may have possessed by virtue of the Law and Administration Ordinance were confirmed and transferred by this provision. Section 6 of the Transition Law stipulated, further, that "the President of the State shall sign treaties with foreign states which have been ratified by the Knesset . . ." The provision is somewhat puzzling and its terminology unfortunate. It appears, indeed, that the purpose was simply to assure that, for treaties which were submitted to the approval of the legislature—in spite of the fact that no new provision expressly required the Executive Government ever to do so—the instruments of ratification were to be signed by the President.[1] Obviously, if the Executive Government were never required to submit a treaty for the approval of the Knesseth, and, in fact, never did that, the Article quoted would remain a dead letter.

It was suggested above that Section 2 (b) of the Law and Administration ordinance contained a wide and vague potential legislative control of the treaty-making power of the Provisional Government. By Section

[9] For the text of this law, see *Laws of the State of Israel,* vol. 3 (5709–1949), pp. 3 ff.

[1] See memorandum of 11 March 1951 in U.N., *Compilation,* p. 70.

14 of the Transition Law, this provision was repealed, and a new check upon the Executive Government was created in Section 11 (d), according to which a government which receives a vote of no confidence must resign. It would seem that, with this development, the executive branch of the Government consolidated its claim to the unconditional possession of the treaty-making power, for the new provision could not easily be used, as could the old, to make it a duty for the Executive Government to submit treaties for the approval of the legislature.

Treaty-making power in practice

It may be concluded, on the basis of the above account, that, before the Transition Law was adopted, at any rate, the treaty-making power of the State was only vaguely regulated by express domestic provisions. In that period, consequently, the definite treaty-making pattern, including the question whether legislative approval would be required before the ratification of certain types of treaties, was left largely to be developed by custom.

The development of a practice did not offer a picture of complete consistency. It is of interest to note that, although the Provisional Government proceeded on the theory that it was not required to submit treaties for the approval of the legislature, the declaration of 29 November 1948, by which Israel accepted the obligations of the United Nations, was worded as follows:

"On behalf of the State of Israel, I, Moshe Shertok, Minister for Foreign Affairs, being duly authorized by the State Council of Israel, declare that the State of Israel hereby unreservedly accepts the obligations of the United Nations Charter and undertakes to honour them from the day when it becomes a member of the United Nations."[2]

As may be seen, the above act, which there were special reasons to expect to be issued by the constitutionally competent treaty-making power, not only made reference to a legislative authorization, but, indeed, seemed to indicate by the expression "duly authorized" that such authorization was required by municipal law. This example goes to show, it is submitted, that the treaty-making pattern of the State was not yet clearly established.

The absence of a settled constitutional custom does not seem to have deterred foreign governments and international organizations from concluding treaties with the State of Israel as early as 1948. For whatever reasons there may be, however, these treaties have not been

---

[2] See *U.N.T.S.*, vol. 30 (1949), p. 54.

published in the treaty series of that State. Two acts in the nature of treaty-making—apart from the declaration quoted above—by Israel in 1948 are nevertheless recorded in the *United Nations Treaty Series*. Thus, it appears that, on 3 August 1948, an Israeli instrument of accession regarding the Convention of 27 July 1929 for the amelioration of the condition of the wounded and sick in armies in the field, and the Convention of the same date relating to the treatment of prisoners of war, was received by the Swiss Federal Council, as depositary, and subsequently registered by that Government with the United Nations.[3] The acceptance by the Swiss Government of the document,[4] the same Government's reporting the documents for registration—but not the act of registration by the Secretary-General[5]—is likely to have taken place on the assumption that they emanated from an authority competent under international law to bind the State of Israel.

That this view was shared by the governments of other states, parties to these Conventions, may perhaps also be inferred from the fact that none of them—whether or not they recognized the new State—seems to have voiced any objection to the accession of Israel.

An agreement of 20 September 1948 entered into by U.N.I.C.E.F. with the Provisional Government of Israel[6] points to the conclusion

---

[3] *U.N.T.S.*, vol. 31 (1949), pp. 495, 497.

[4] In this connexion, it may be noted that the Israeli memorandum submitted to the International Law Commission indicates that the Israeli Government experienced difficulties when, at the beginning of its existence, it sought to accede to multilateral conventions, the depositary governments of which had not recognized the State of Israel. It is reported that the accessions were then submitted to the depositaries through the intermediary of a third government which had recognized Israel, and which, at the same time, maintained diplomatic relations with the depositary government. It is not known whether this reference is to the Swiss Government. The stand taken by these depositaries is criticized in the memorandum, and it is pointed out that it might have serious consequences. A government involved in hostilities from its establishment might in this manner, it is said, be prevented from acceding to conventions which regulate hostilities. The function of depositaries, it is argued, is primarily "administrative and organizational" and such governments are asserted not to be "juridically entitled to refuse communications" regarding the treaty for which they act as depositary "merely because they emanate from a government which it does not recognize". (See U.N. *Doc.* A/CN.4/19, 23 March 1950, pp. 52–53.) On depositaries, see further below, pp. 265 ff.

[5] The acts of registration by the Secretary-General of the United Nations are expressly stated not to imply any judgment concerning the status of the parties to the treaties registered. See Note by the Secretariat inserted in *U.N.T.S.*, vol. 212 (1955) ff.

[6] *U.N.T.S.*, vol. 71 (1950), p. 17.

that that international organization (a unit of the United Nations), like the depositary and parties to the Convention cited above, considered the Provisional Government competent under international law to bind the State of Israel. In neither of the cases cited does it appear that the legislature of the new State was consulted.

Treaty-making practice under the Transition Law

The treaty-making activities of the State of Israel subsequently to the adoption of the Transition Law is of limited interest to this inquiry, as at that time the domestic law on the matter was better defined. It may be noted, nevertheless, that, as late as December 1949, when the Genocide Convention was to be ratified by Israel, one member of the Knesseth maintained that the practice of the Government not to submit treaties for the approval of the Knesseth amounted to a denial of the rights of that body.[7] Another member commented that, although there was not yet a law which obligated the Government to submit treaties to the Knesseth before ratifying them, he hoped that a constitution would soon establish this duty.[8]

In the same debate, the Minister of Justice, Mr. Pinchas Rosenne, declared that there was no uniform international custom to the effect that treaties ought to be submitted to parliaments for approval, and that the systems adopted varied from one state to another. At the time, he said, the system which prevailed in the State of Israel was one in which signature and ratification were acts belonging exclusively to the executive branch. A treaty would not, however, become internal law but for legislation passed by the Knesseth. It is interesting to note, further, that, in spite of the fact that the Minister urged the Knesseth merely to *recommend* ratification of the Convention before it, the Knesseth chose to *resolve* that the Convention should be ratified. As a result, the instrument of ratification deposited with the Secretary-General of the United Nations on 9 March 1950 read in part as follows:

"And whereas the Knesset of the State of Israel at its session on 28 December, 1949, decided that the said Convention should be ratified . . .

"Now, therefore, by these Presents it is declared that the Government of Israel confirms and ratifies . . ."[9]

[7] Statement on 26 December 1949 by Mr. Johanam Bader. See *Divrei Haknesseth,* vol. 3 at p. 318.

[8] *Ibid.,* p. 322. Statement by Mr. Jacob Klibanov.

[9] The instrument is not printed in the *United Nations Treaty Series.* The wording has been copied from the original document at the headquarters of the United Nations.

In view of what has been related above, the conclusion seems permissible that the constitutional theory that the treaty-making power belonged exclusively to the executive branch of the Government was strengthened by the adoption of the Transition Law, and that the Government apparently acted fairly regularly on this theory. At the same time, it seems justified to conclude that neither the legal construction behind this theory, nor the developing custom, were sufficiently convincing to pass unchallenged in the legislature, and, in part, by a majority of the legislature.

Conclusion

The examination of the case of Israel has shown that the constitutional regulation of the treaty-making power of the State was somewhat uncertain, especially during the first year of its existence as an independent state. This circumstance did not cause other organs representing international law subjects to refrain from concluding treaties with Israel. It may be taken for granted that these organs—governments and international bodies—would not have entered into the treaties with Israel had they not felt confident that, by international law, the treaties would be binding upon the State of Israel. Accordingly, they must also have judged that, in spite of the uncertain constitutional position, the Executive Government of Israel, which held itself out as competent to bind the State, and which undoubtedly appeared able to fulfil treaty obligations, was competent under international law to assume treaty obligations on behalf of the State.

3. THE CASE OF CEYLON

On 4 February 1948, Ceylon became an independent state, and a member of the British Commonwealth. This event was brought about by five different acts,[1] all approved by the British and Ceylonese Cabinets. They were as follows: an Order-in-Council in Great Britain; an Act of the Parliament of the United Kingdom; a Defense Agreement between the Governments of the United Kingdom and Ceylon, signed on 11 November 1947;[2] an External Affairs Agreement of the same date;[3] a Public Officers Agreement of the same date.[4]

[1] See Peaslee, *Modern Constitutions*, vol. I (1950), pp. 436 ff.
[2] *U.N.T.S.*, vol. 86 (1951), p. 19.
[3] *Ibid.*, p. 25.
[4] *Ibid.*, p. 31.

Relevant stipulations

The question of interest here is whether the treaty-making power of the new State was indicated and regulated in any of the fundamental documents enumerated above. The Constitution, which was contained in the Order-in-Council, had no provision which expressly regarded the treaty-making power. A few of its provisions are nevertheless of interest. Section 45 provided:

> "The executive power of the Island shall continue vested in Her Majesty and may be exercised, on behalf of Her Majesty, by the Governor-General in accordance with the provisions of this Order or any other law for the time being in force."

Section 4 (2), added to the provision just cited, made the constitutional conventions of the United Kingdom relevant as regards the exercise of the executive power in Ceylon:

> "All Powers, authorities and functions vested in Her Majesty or the Governor-General shall, subject to the provisions of this Order, and of any other law for the time being in force, be exercised as far as may be in accordance with the constitutional conventions applicable to the exercise of similar powers, authorities and functions in the United Kingdom by Her Majesty."[5]

A leading authority on British constitutional law has maintained that these provisions are decisive of the matter under consideration. According to him, "the theory in law is that executive power is vested in the Queen throughout the Commonwealth," and while he further holds defense and external affairs to be "branches of executive government", and consequently vested in the Queen by virtue of Section 45 cited above, he adds that the manner in which this power is exercised "depends upon law and practice for the time being."[6] He concludes that the Governor-General is empowered to enter into treaties on behalf of the state, provided that he has obtained—in accordance with Section 4 of the Constitution—the advice of the Ceylonese Government, or rather of the Prime Minister, as under Article 46 (4) the latter is in charge of defense and external affairs.

It must further be noted that, in the External Affairs Agreement referred to above, Ceylon declared its readiness to adopt and follow the resolutions of past Imperial Conferences.[7] Among these, Sir Ivor Jen-

---

[5] The two provisions are reprinted in U.N., *Compilation*, p. 34.

[6] Jennings, *The Constitution of Ceylon* (3rd. ed., 1953), pp. 137, 216.

[7] *Ibid.*, p. 254.

nings, discussing the case of Ceylon, cites the following rules laid down in 1923 as "not wholly applicable to the present conditions":

" '3. Ratification.
'The existing practice in connexion with the ratification of treaties should be maintained.' "

This practice, the same conference explained, included the two features quoted below:

" 'The ratification of treaties imposing obligations on one part of the Empire is effected at the instance of the Government of that part.' "

and:

" '... It is for each Government to decide whether Parliamentary approval or legislation is required before desire for, or concurrence in, ratification is intimated by that Government.' "

In addition to the solemn procedure of ratification, the Conference had noted a simplified procedure to which Sir Ivor also makes reference:

" 'Apart from treaties made between heads of States it is not unusual for agreements to be made between Governments. Such agreements, which are usually of a technical or administrative character, are made in the name of the signatory Government, and signed by representatives of those Governments, who do not act under full powers issued by the heads of the States: they are not ratified by the heads of the States though in some cases some form of acceptance or confirmation by the Governments concerned is employed. As regards agreements of this nature the existing practice should be continued...' "[8]

The various provisions cited above appear to point to the conclusion that the constitutional practice of the United Kingdom regarding the conclusion of treaties and international agreements was imported, with possible necessary modifications, and subject to changes effected through subsequent legislation and practice, to be valid in the State of Ceylon.

Were the stipulations conclusive?

It must be admitted that the very general scope and apparent elasticity of the rules cited above—in which the treaty-making function is not mentioned once—must have attached some doubt as to the correctness of the conclusion which seemed indicated. In this connexion, it is of particular interest to note an official memorandum which was submitted on 18 May 1951 by the Ministry of External Affairs of Ceylon

[8] *Ibid.*, pp. 258 ff.

to the United Nations. Although the memorandum, in its second point, makes reference to Sections 2 (2) and 45 of the Constitution of Ceylon, it draws no conclusions from them. It seems to diminish, indeed, if not completely to negate, their relevance by prefacing them as follows:

"1. There is no general legislation in Ceylon, and no provision in the Constitution, governing the negotiation and conclusion of treaties and other international agreements; nor are there any decrees, regulations or judicial decisions having a bearing on this subject."[9]

The impression that the constitutional provisions were not considered helpful as guidance is further strengthened by the third and last point of the memorandum which makes no reference to any constitutional or legislative provisions, but simply reports:

"3. In practice, international agreements are negotiated and concluded under the authority of the Minister of External Affairs acting with the approval of the Cabinet. The agreements, when concluded, are laid before Parliament for information or, when appropriate, for approval before ratification."[1]

No information is given as to when, under this practice, it is considered "appropriate" to obtain the approval of Parliament prior to ratification, nor whether the propriety is one of law or convenience.

Practice: Adoption of the Independence Constitution

Before any discussion is undertaken of the theory upon which foreign governments may have acted when concluding treaties with Ceylon, the development and establishment of the practice outlined in the memorandum will be traced.

It appears that the question concerning the need for parliamentary approval of international compacts arose at the very beginning of, indeed, before, the independence of Ceylon. In a debate in the House of Representatives of the Parliament of Ceylon—referred to below as "the House"—in February 1954, Mr. Senanayake stated that the opposition had demanded a discussion of the Independence Constitution before that instrument had been accepted by the Government. Mr. Bandaranaike, at that time a member of the Government, had also urged such a debate, but the Cabinet had decided otherwise. It had been objected on that occasion that were there to be a parliamentary discussion before the Government could affect ratification or acceptance,

---

[9] U.N., *Compilation*, p. 34.
[1] *Ibid.*

normal Cabinet government would become impossible. A great English constitutionalist had been cited, and it had been maintained that the Government would not in any way be acting unconstitutionally were it not to seek prior approval by the legislature.[2] Although, as will be shown, this position was subsequently repeatedly taken by the Government, and a constitutional practice to this effect thereby gradually established, support for it was never sought in the expressions of the Order-in-Council, nor in the External Affairs Agreement.

Practice: First parliamentary session, Agreement of 1948,
The tabling of agreements

It may first be noted that, on 10 December 1947, in the course of the first session of the Parliament of the independent State of Ceylon, the Prime Minister, having replied in the negative to the question whether any trade agreement had been signed on behalf of Ceylon, declined to promise to come before the House prior to the signing of future agreements of this kind.[3]

The first full debate on the constitutional question of the duty of the Government to obtain the approval of the legislature prior to binding the State occurred in July 1948. The background of the debate was that, on 30 April 1948, the Governments of Ceylon and the United Kingdom had signed an agreement regarding sterling assets. It had become binding by an exchange of cables effected on 12 and 14 May 1948.[4] On 18 May 1948, the Government had tabled this agreement in the Parliament and indicated its readiness to debate the issue.[5]

In the debate which took place on 9 July 1948, one member of the House moved that the House should decline to "endorse" ratification of the agreement.[6] It was objected on behalf of the Government that the agreement was not submitted for endorsement and that the Government did not admit that the agreement required the endorsement of the House. Upon a suggestion made by the Speaker of the House, the

---

[2] Although the Constitution was not in the form of an agreement, but an Order-in-Council, the questions were analogous, and the procedure adopted with regard to the Constitution was here, indeed, invoked as a precedent regarding the constitutional treaty-making procedure. See Ceylon, *Parliamentary Debates* (Hansard), *House of Representatives*—referred to below as "Ceylon, *Hansard*"—vol. 16, col. 2218.

[3] *Ibid.*, vols. 1–2, col. 1084.

[4] Ceylon, *Treaty Series*, No. 1 (1948).

[5] Ceylon, *Hansard*, vol. 3, col. 176.

[6] *Ibid.*, col. 931.

originator of the motion agreed to substitute the word "approve" for
the term "endorse". He mentioned that, although it had a comfortable
majority in the House of Commons, the Government of the United
Kingdom had submitted the agreement embodying the Marshall Aid
Plan to that body and obtained its approval. Such, he suggested, was
the correct attitude to adopt if the Government wanted to abide by
democratic principles. Dr. Perera, who had tabled the motion which
was before the House, ended the debate by urging that the agreement
regarding sterling assets should not be approved, and expressed the hope
that that position would affect any future agreement the State might
enter into. The defeat of the motion by a large majority[7] may be viewed
as a first important precedent in the constitutional practice of Ceylon
concerning the conclusion of treaties.

The beginning of a practice may also early be perceived to the
effect that the Government refused to discuss in Parliament, and refrained from tabling in Parliament, any agreements before they were
binding upon the State.[8]

Practice: Debate of March 1949, The tabling of agreements

A second parliamentary debate on the treaty-making procedure of
the State took place in March 1949.[9] Dr. Perera, who was again the
originator of the debate, moved as follows:

"That in the opinion of this House no tariff agreements or treaties should
be signed by any representative of this country without the prior approval of
Parliament."

Dr. Perera deplored that the Government had not chosen to set up
"healthy precedents" in the signing of treaties or conventions, and

---

[7] *Ibid.,* col. 1010.

[8] Some examples may be offered as an illustration. Thus, the "Heads of Revised
Copra Agreement" which was initialled in London by the United Kingdom and
Ceylon on 5 August 1948, was finally accepted by notification to the United Kingdom
Ministry of Food before the agreement was read to the Parliament of Ceylon, on
12 August 1948. (See Ceylon, *Hansard,* vol. 4, col. 1312.) An agreement with the
United States on the exchange of official publications entered into force by an
exchange of notes on 31 January 1949, but was presented to Parliament only on
1 March 1949. (See Ceylon, *Treaty Series,* No. 1 (1949) and Ceylon, *Hansard,* vol. 5,
col. 1417.) An agreement concerning air services was signed with the Indian Government on 21 December 1948. It was presented to the Parliament of Ceylon only on
15 March 1949. (See Ceylon, *Treaty Series,* No. 4 (1949) and Ceylon, *Hansard,* vol. 5,
col. 1776.)

[9] It is recorded in Ceylon, *Hansard,* vol. 5, col. 2097–2119, from which source all
facts and quotations in the text above are taken.

pointed to the fact that other Governments treated their democratic assemblies in a very different manner. What he resented in particular was to see the country irrevocably committed without the House being given an opportunity to express its point of view. *Faits accomplis* were placed before the members and, as they might feel that the House and the country had been committed, and that the good name of the country was involved, they might not like to repudiate an agreement that had been arrived at. The acceptance of the motion, he asserted, would mean that, whenever an important matter was due for consideration, the Prime Minister would discuss the matter in the House, express the Government's point of view and "give the House an opportunity to express its own point of view."

In the ensuing exchange of views, Mr. Suntharalingam, defending the Government, distinguished between the stage of negotiations and the position after negotiations, when an agreement had already been signed. He would not allow the negotiators to discuss the agreement in the House before signing. After signature, however, the agreement could be placed before the Assembly, and that body be given the choice of accepting the agreement or rejecting it, and, thereby, if the latter, bring the Government down.

Mr. Kumaraswamy, another member of the House, expressed the legal principle followed by the Government as follows:

"The Prime Minister, whoever it be, whether it be X or Y, enjoys the confidence of the House. Therefore, he has the inherent right to represent the country, whether in Ceylon or outside Ceylon. In pursuance of the powers vested in him by the Constitution, he has the right to conclude treaties. If we do not agree with the Prime Minister, then we must throw him out. That is the Constitutional method which should be followed."

The Prime Minister, Mr. Senanayake, expressed a similar view. He stressed that it was only when finality was reached that it was possible for the Government to submit a treaty to the House and say: "Well, this is the final agreement. We would like it to be ratified." If it were not then accepted, the consequence would be that the Government resigned.

The somewhat dogmatic view of the speakers for the Government, who all seemed to assume that an agreement was either under negotiation, and as such not suitable for parliamentary debate, or irrevocably concluded, in which case it must be adopted or the Government would resign, was not lost upon Dr. Perera. By the end of the debate, he explained that he had not, indeed, asked that the House should be consulted whilst negotiations were in progress, or that every step in the negotiations should be placed before the House. He seemed to go back somewhat on the demand contained in his motion, however, when, in his final statements in the debate, he merely put the purpose of the motion to be that of ensuring that, before the House was committed to anything, statements should be made by responsible ministers explaining their policy with regard to a particular problem. However that may be, the motion was put to the vote and defeated. Thus, a second important precedent was established in the State's constitutional practice regarding the conclusion of treaties.

Not surprisingly, the general practice continued of tabling agreements only after they were irrevocably binding upon the State.[1]

Practice: Treaties and enabling legislation

On occasion, bills ensuring performance under certain treaties were introduced in the House before the same treaties were ratified, and the legislature was thereby placed in a position to express its views before the State was committed.[2]

It was notable, however, that, whether or not implementing legisla-

---

[1] Thus, on 25 November 1949, the House was told by the Minister of Commerce and Trade that Ceylon's Ambassador to Washington had been instructed to sign the General Agreement on Tariffs and Trade before 30 November 1949, and that the terms of the agreement would be made available to the House thereafter (see Ceylon, *Hansard,* vol. 7, col. 859–860).

Extreme reluctance to give any information regarding an agreement yet under negotiation may be seen in the reply given by a Minister to a member of the House who expressed concern at the possible consequences of an agreement with India regarding tobacco, and who inquired whether the agreement had been ratified or was still under consideration. The Minister, appearing in the House on 7 August 1953, replied:

"According to international practice [sic!], proposals of that nature are carefully considered by the Government and the Government either ratifies or does not ratify those proposals. That is the position." (See Ceylon, *Hansard,* vol. 14, col. 2061.)

One further example may be cited. The Minister of Industries and Fisheries, who had been asked when a Ceylon–Czechoslovak agreement on mutual assistance would be tabled, replied on 21 August 1956 that "the normal procedure is that the agreement should be tabled after it is ratified." (See Ceylon, *Hansard,* vol. 26, col. 1319.)

[2] Thus, Ceylon's instrument of acceptance of the Bretton Woods Agreements of 27 December 1945 was deposited with the United States Government only on 29 August 1950 (see *U.N.T.S.,* vol. 2 (1947), p. 39 and *ibid.,* vol. 141 (1952), p. 355) and thus after a Bretton Woods Agreement Bill had been passed by the Parliament of Ceylon on 18 August 1950, and the texts of the agreements had been presented to the House, on 16 August 1950. (See Ceylon, *Hansard,* vol. 8, cols. 2930 and 2733.) It may

tion was required, the Government repeatedly acted on the theory that it was competent to commit the State by treaties without first submitting them to Parliament. Although this mode of proceeding frequently evoked the protests of members of the Parliament, it was always upheld, and may undoubtedly be considered a gradually settled constitutional convention. Some examples may be cited by way of illustration.

On 1 February 1950, one member moved that the House should express its lack of confidence in the Government and, in particular, condemn the Government's policy of subscribing aid to Burma. This action, he asserted, was a "major departure" in foreign policy and the Government should have consulted Parliament in advance. In his opinion, it was not "fair" for the Government first to commit the country to a subvention or a loan and then come to Parliament for a money vote.[3]

The Japanese Peace Treaty to which Ceylon was to become a party was ordered to lie on the table of the Parliament on 2 August 1951, at a date prior to its being signed. On the occasion of the tabling of the Treaty, the Prime Minister stated that the Government intended to sign the Treaty on 4 September 1951. Being asked whether he would allot a date for a debate on the draft Treaty before the State had committed itself by signature, the Prime Minister replied that he had no objection to dealing with questions regarding the Treaty. He made it clear, however, that he considered parliamentary discussion before the State was committed inconvenient. He stated in part as follows:

"...I do not think this Peace Treaty could be a subject of debate and discussion because it must be signed, and the sooner peace is established the

---

be noted, however, that in one of the final clauses these agreements provided as follows:

"Each government on whose behalf this Agreement is signed shall deposit with the Government of the United States of America an instrument setting forth that it has accepted this Agreement in accordance with its law and has taken all steps necessary to enable it to carry out all of its obligations under this Agreement." (Art. XX, Sec. 2(a) of the Articles of Agreement of the International Monetary Fund.)

On 19 July 1951, furthermore, a Minister stated in the House that certain I.L.O. conventions would be ratified as soon as the necessary legislation giving effect to their provisions had been introduced. (See Ceylon, *Hansard,* vol. 10, col. 1045.)

[3] See Ceylon, *Hansard,* vol. 7, col. 1376. The agreement in question was, in fact, signed by a number of Commonwealth countries on 28 June 1950 (Ceylon, *Treaty Series,* No. 8 (1950); or *U.N.T.S.,* vol. 87 (1951), p. 153). It was presented to the Parliament of Ceylon on 14 August 1950 (Ceylon, *Hansard,* vol. 8, col. 2401). No appropriation proved necessary, as the Government was able to use blocked sterling assets to fulfil obligations under the agreement.

better it is. My good friend . . . will . . . appreciate that anything that is likely to delay our participation in it would be regrettable."[4]

The leader of the Opposition, on the other hand, asked an early date for the debate, "because the country's views must be known before it is committed to this Treaty." A debate was, in fact, held on a motion of adjournment before the Treaty was signed.[5] While on that occasion the Parliament was thus not asked to give any expression of approval or disapproval of the State's adherence to the Treaty, a bill was introduced and passed on 20 February 1952—almost six months after signature— to enable the Government to carry out the terms of the Treaty.[6]

Practice: Debate of February 1954

One debate must finally be reported which had regard to the question whether the Government was ever under an obligation to consult Parliament before committing the State to a treaty. On 2 February 1954, Mr. Bandaranaike raised the question whether, before a final decision was taken on a proposed agreement with India, the House would be given an opportunity to discuss the matter. He conceded that, as regards ordinary agreements on trade and similar matters, the Government had no duty to consult Parliament in advance:

> "Governments have a right to enter into agreements of that nature, ratify them and bring them up before Parliament or table them in the House. Thereafter, if any questions are to be asked or any debate raised thereon, the Government gives an opportunity for that to be done."[7]

In the opinion of Mr. Bandaranaike, the particular agreement in question was of such great importance, however, that a debate prior to ratification ought to be held. Mr. Senanayake stated that he presumed the constitutional propriety of the conduct of the Cabinet was not questioned. As pointed out already,[8] he cited as a precedent the procedure used for the adoption of the instruments which conferred independence upon Ceylon. He stated further that it was a "recognized constitutional convention", and a "constitutional practice that has been established by the Parliament" that the Government should act as it did. In conclusion, he maintained that a debate could not be asked "as a

---

[4] Ceylon, *Hansard*, vol. 10, col. 1907 ff.
[5] *Ibid.*, cols. 3801–3849.
[6] *Ibid.*, vol. 11, col. 1897.
[7] *Ibid.*, vol. 16, col. 2220.
[8] Above, p. 206.

matter of right", and that the proper procedure was for the Government to ratify the convention and thereafter stand or fall by its act of ratification.[9]

In this debate, for the first time apparently, the constitutional theory underlying the Government's treaty-making practice was succinctly spelled out to the House. Mr. Nalliah, Parliamentary Secretary to the Minister of External Affairs, explained it as follows:

"The executive powers which are vested in the Crown are exercised in Ceylon by the Cabinet and, therefore, it is my contention that the right to enter into a treaty is exclusively that of the Government, and the Government cannot share that right with any other party. ... Under our system of Government sole executive and prerogative powers are exercised on behalf of the Crown by the Cabinet and as such the right to enter into treaties with foreign countries is that of the Government."[1]

Mr. Senanayake, who expressed no dissent from this declaration, ended the debate by promising that, when the agreement had been ratified, he would place it before Parliament, thus again asserting the constitutional competence which, as shown in the preceding analysis, the Government had frequently ascribed to itself in the past.[2]

Conclusion

The foregoing examination has shown, it is submitted, that although some kind of regulation of the treaty-making power of Ceylon may possibly be deduced from the fundamental instruments of the State, not even the Foreign Ministry of the State, when officially asked in 1951 about the constitutional provisions regarding the treaty-making function, ventured to seek the answer in these documents, but referred to constitutional practice. The consistency of that practice and its development into a firm constitutional convention has also been verified.

As foreign governments cannot be supposed to have been more diligent than the Foreign Ministry of Ceylon in discovering in the fundamental instruments of that State an indication of the competent treaty-making power of the State, the conclusion seems permissible that, before the constitutional practice was established, at any rate, these governments concluded agreements without any knowledge of the constitutional competence of the authority acting on behalf of Ceylon. It must

---

[9] Ceylon, *Hansard*, vol. 16, cols. 2220–2221.

[1] *Ibid.*, col. 2248.

[2] See *ibid.*, col. 2258. The agreement which was signed on 18 January 1954 and was ratified on 13 February 1954 is found in Ceylon, *Treaty Series*, No. 1 (1954).

be assumed, on the other hand, that they considered their opposite parties acting for Ceylon competent, under international law, to undertake treaty obligations on behalf of that State. Consequently, it would seem that the rule of competence upon which they relied was broad enough to include the case where an executive branch of a government holds itself out to be competent, and appears to possess the actual authority necessary to secure the performance of treaty obligations.

4. The Case of France, 2 November 1945 to 24 December 1946

The treaty-making activities of the Free French authorities functioning during the second world war have been discussed in a previous chapter. In this connexion, another relatively brief period of the constitutional history of the same State is of interest, namely, that between the promulgation of the law of 2 November 1945 regarding the provisional organization of the public authorities and the entry into force of the Constitution of 27 October 1946 on 24 December of the same year. That period will be discussed below on the basis, chiefly, of information found in an interesting article by Professor Charles Rousseau.[3]

It appears that no provision of the law of 2 November 1945 indicated which organ was competent to conclude treaties on behalf of the State of France. Foreign governments could not, consequently, have looked to that instrument for information before relying upon the pledges of any organ which held itself out to represent France. With which organs were they satisfied to treat, and on what conditions, if any?

The majority of the treaties concluded by the Provisional Government of the French Republic are reported to have been ratified by the President of that Government, acting alone.[4] It is nevertheless certain that a large number of treaties were made in the same period by the Provisional Government in its own name and without the use

---

[3] "Le régime actuel de conclusion des traités en France" in *La Technique et Les Principes du Droit Public, Études en l'honneur de Georges Scelle* (1950), vol. II, pp. 571–572.

[4] The Chicago Convention of 7 December 1944, regarding International Civil Aviation, although signed for France before the beginning of the relevant period, is thus stated to have been ratified for France on 25 March 1947 in conformity with a decision taken by the Provisional Government on 13 November 1946. For the treaty, see *U.N.T.S.*, vol. 15 (1948), p. 295, and see Rousseau (p. 571), who further mentions an agreement on reparations concluded on 14 January 1946 (Great Britain, *Treaty Series*, No. 56 (1947)) and a Franco-Siamese agreement of 17 November 1946 concerning the retrocession of territory.

of the procedure of ratification.[5] It is further known that a number of agreements entered into on behalf of France in this period were submitted to the approval of the Constituent Assembly before final expression of consent was given.[6]

What conclusions, if any, may conceivably be drawn from the treaty-making activities referred to above? Professor Rousseau has suggested that, in the absence of any constitutional regulation, the President of the Provisional Government was legally competent to "donner effet" to treaties on his own initiative. He might submit them to the Council of Ministers or to the Constituent Assembly, "pour des raisons d'opportunité", but, in the opinion of the same authority, no provision made this procedure a legal obligation.[7] Professor Rousseau remains faithful to this position when, referring to two agreements actually submitted to the Constituent Assembly, he explains that as their execution—if not their ratification—presupposed action by the Assembly, it was preferable "pour des raisons de commodité pratique" to ask the approval of the Assembly.[8]

These opinions, which seem based on the assumption that there exists a principle of customary international law to the effect that the head of a state is vested with plenary competence to conclude treaties on behalf of the state, unless that competence is somehow limited by

[5] See, for instance, an additional protocol to a declaration regarding scientific, literary and educational relations, signed, to be immediately binding, by France and Czechoslovakia on 8 December 1945. (Text in *U.N.T.S.*, vol. 46 (1950), p. 77.) Reference may also be given to an exchange of notes concerning the supply of aircraft and equipment to France, effected between the Governments of France and the United Kingdom on 24 November 1945 and 4 December 1945 (Text in *U.N.T.S.*, vol. 9 (1947), p. 121).

[6] The Bretton Woods Agreements were approved by a French law of 26 December 1945 and entered into on behalf of France by the deposit of an instrument of acceptance on 27 December 1945. (See *U.N.T.S.*, vol. 2 (1947), p. 39 and vol. 19 (1948), p. 280, and see Rousseau, p. 572.) The instrument of amendment of 7 November 1945 of the Constitution of the I.L.O. was approved by a French law of 9 May 1946 and a French instrument of ratification was deposited on 22 July 1946. (See *U.N.T.S.*, vols. 2 (1947), p. 17 and 15 (1948), p. 443, and see Rousseau, p. 572.) The Constitution of the U.N.E.S.C.O. of 16 November 1945 was approved by a French law of 17 May 1946 and an instrument of acceptance was deposited on behalf of France on 29 June 1946. (See *U.N.T.S.*, vol. 4 (1947), pp. 275, 300 and see Rousseau, p. 572.) A Franco-Canadian agreement of 9 April 1946 was approved by a French law of 9 May 1946 and instruments of ratification were exchanged on 2 May 1946. (See *U.N.T.S.*, vol. 43 (1949), p. 43 and see Rousseau, p. 572.)

[7] Rousseau, p. 571.

[8] Rousseau, p. 572.

a constitution, are not contradicted by the practices described above. In view of the fact, however, that at least one act of ratification appears to have been effected "in conformity with" a prior decision of the Council of Ministers, and in view of the fact that numerous agreements were entered into in the name of the Government, rather than the President, that organ must perhaps also have been considered to possess treaty-making competence.

From the view-point of this inquiry, it is of particular interest to note that the absence of a constitutional indication of competent treaty-making organs did not, apparently, in the least deter foreign governments from entering into treaties with France. When treating with that State, they seem to have accepted without questioning—so far as is reported—the competence of the provisional executive Government which functioned in the State, which held itself out as competent to bind the State, and which appeared to possess the actual authority necessary to execute its promises. Nothing suggests that any foreign government concerned itself with the question whether French legislative approval was ever needed.

5. CRITERIA FOR TREATY-MAKING COMPETENCE IN STATES WHICH HAVE NO MUNICIPAL RULE ON THE MATTER

Where a state assumes independence without any written constitutional provision governing the conclusion of treaties, foreign governments must necessarily look elsewhere for guidance as to the organ competent under international law to make treaties. For, although the new state may develop a constitutional practice supplying the municipal criteria of treaty-making competence, it cannot be expected to possess such practice from the outset. The purpose of the examination undertaken in this chapter was to ascertain in these situations with what organs, if any, foreign governments made treaties. As it must be assumed that foreign governments only chose to treat with organs which they considered competent under international law to assume treaty obligations on behalf of a state, the character of the organs with which they treated must have been such as to satisfy the criteria of treaty-making competence under international law.

The two cases of new states selected for analysis proved less than completely satisfactory, from the particular viewpoint pertinent to this inquiry, as there were found to exist in both of them at least broad constitutional concepts, which the governments of these states and foreign governments, with some ingenuity, might interpret to indicate municipally competent treaty-making organs. The cases examined are nevertheless believed to be instructive for, in practice, the broad constitutional concepts which existed in the States of Israel and Ceylon must have appeared most inadequate to foreign governments, had they actually looked to them for guidance as to competent treaty-making organs.

It would no doubt have been helpful to have found some explicit evidence of how foreign governments considered the question of competence in the cases examined. Despite the apparent absence of such evidence, some of the findings made above are believed to be significant. First, there is the fact that the absence of adequate constitutional guidance regarding municipally competent treaty-making organs did not deter foreign governments from concluding treaties with the new States. Second, there is the circumstance that foreign governments were apparently invariably satisfied to treat with the executive branch of government of these States, and, as far as can be seen, never considered that branch of government incompetent to bind the State, even when it acted without legislative authorization where the need for such authorization had been urged in the municipal sphere. Third, there is the consideration that the executive governments in question appeared to wield effective authority in their respective States, and actually were generally capable of securing the performance of treaty obligations.

The conclusion that, in cases of the kind examined, where no sufficient constitutional regulation exists, the executive branch of government may be considered competent under international law to bind the State derives further support, it is submitted, from the examination of the situation in France, a case which did not, evidently, fit into the category of new states, but was nevertheless of interest in this connexion, as France had adopted a constitutional instrument which failed to indicate competent treaty-making authority.

Chapter XIII

CONCLUSION

Against the background of the above examination of some different types of cases, it is now convenient to discuss whether there is any one formula which is capable of embracing the criteria of competence manifested in each particular type of case.

The theory that the constitution of every state indicates the internationally competent treaty-making organ is obviously unworkable in several situations, where such authorities are nevertheless deemed to exist. Furthermore, the traditional theory that the head of state is always the competent treaty-making organ frequently fails to prove illuminating. The suggestion that the executive government should always be competent to assume treaty obligations on behalf of a state also is not always very helpful. Admittedly, that proposition would have pointed satisfactorily to the treaty-making organs actually held competent in several of the cases examined. It would not, however, have given any guidance in the selection of competent treaty-making authorities among revolutionary and exile bodies purporting to represent states. However, with a definition of the term 'executive government' that would be consonant with the findings set forth above regarding competent revolutionary and exile bodies, the suggestion would admittedly become more practical. It would seem, indeed, that a formula indicating competent treaty-making state authorities might be framed as follows: Under international law, treaty obligations may be assumed on behalf of a state by authorities possessing apparent ability to secure the fulfilment of such obligations.

This formula, it is submitted, emerges from, and adequately explains, the positions taken by governments in all the various situations examined in this section of the present work. While it serves to identify a competent treaty-making organ, if there is one, it does not, on the other hand, point to any restrictions upon, or conditions attached to, the competence thus attributed. With one possible exception,[1] the

---

[1] See above, p. 193.

material examined has not offered evidence of any such restrictions or conditions.

One eminent authority, it is true, has cited the hesitation of a United States diplomat at the prospect of concluding a highly important treaty with a shaky Mexican government.[2] No case has been found, however, where a government or a court has deemed legally inappropriate the conclusion of treaties of far-reaching consequences with governments whose future has seemed somewhat uncertain. Quite to the contrary, revolutionary governments and exile governments are frequently found accepted as organs competent to enter into treaties of signal importance.

It may be noted, furthermore, that the formula proposed above does not confine the competent authority to assuming only obligations the fulfilment of which appears to be within the apparent ability currently possessed by that authority. Such a restriction would obviously be highly inconvenient and no evidence points to its existence. Were it to exist, indeed, it would reduce the authority from an organ competent to commit the state for the future to a body acting only for, and only committing, the organization currently under its control—somewhat like the "local revolutionary governments" and exile authorities not considered to be governments.

[2] See above, p. 109.

THE RULE WHERE TREATY-MAKING COMPETENCE IS REGULATED BY MUNICIPAL LAW

PRELIMINARY REMARKS

In the previous section of this part, the conclusion was reached that, in a number of situations, at least, the legal competence to enter into a treaty on behalf of a state flows from apparent ability generally to secure performance of treaty obligations. Does a different principle prevail in the determination of the authority competent under international law to conclude treaties on behalf of a state where the treaty-making competence is effectively regulated by municipal law? Or, perhaps, do constitutional provisions merely constitute evidence of an apparent ability, which, alone, is relevant under international law? No obvious and compelling analogy points to an affirmative answer to this question. Nor should the temptations of the possible practical advantages or the symmetry of a simple, uniform theory capable of general application lead to such answer. Only a detailed, empirical examination of all evidence relevant to the question can give a reliable answer.

As most treaties are made between subjects whose internal law regulates the competence of their treaty-making organs, the problem posed above is of considerable practical importance. This circumstance may explain why it has frequently been treated by writers.

It is inevitable that much of the relevant material should have been already examined and presented by earlier writers, or by some of them. A presentation, sometimes rather detailed, of the same material has nevertheless been deemed necessary in view of the circumstance, particularly, that the re-examination of the material has not infrequently led to evaluations and conclusions different from those reached by other writers. In some instances it has even been thought desirable, in order to rebut certain conclusions drawn by other writers, to present a re-examination of material merely to show that it cannot be attributed any evidentiary value at all.

The historical origin of the present problem will be discussed first. Then it will be examined whether, as has been contended, the attitudes underlying various constitutional provisions on treaty-making power offer any evidence of the relevant rule of international law. With the same purpose, a number of cases decided by national courts will be reviewed. The question whether governments allow each other to make inquiries concerning the municipally competent treaty-making organ will be considered, as well as the views which may be reflected in the positions taken by depositary organs. Certain express clauses inserted into full powers, treaties and instruments of ratification will further be discussed, as well as positions assumed in a number of diplomatic incidents, and, of course, the views expressed in some cases decided by international tribunals. Finally, before a conclusion is sought, various theories advanced by scholars will be critically examined against the background of the evidence presented.

CHAPTER XIV

HISTORICAL ORIGIN OF THE
MODERN PROBLEM

The modern controversy as to whether international law refers the
question of competent treaty-making authority to constitutional law,
and thus makes the observance of constitutional provisions relevant in
the international sphere, has already been mentioned.[1] It goes back to
the development of a democratic control over the making of treaties
which was started by the French Revolution, and by the adoption of the
Constitution of the United States. It may be useful to recall these
developments before the doctrinal controversy is discussed.

It may first be noted that even a pre-revolutionary advocate of the
supremacy of the popular will, like Rousseau, stopped short of demand-
ing that the treaty-making activity of the state should be placed under
the control of the people.[2] The men of the Revolution had a clearer
vision of the importance of treaties. Thus, Petion observed:

"Si le pouvoir exécutif n'a pas le droit de faire la loi la plus simple,
pourquoi lui donnerait-on celui de faire des traités dont les conséquences
sont si importantes?"[3]

Constitutions adopted in the course of the French Revolution accepted this argument, and introduced popular control over the making
of treaties.[4] It is from these Constitutions, and from that of the United

---

[1] Above, p. 102.

[2] The following statement by Rousseau may be quoted:
"L'exercice extérieur de la puissance ne convient point au peuple; ... Ce qui importe essentiellement à chaque citoyen, c'est l'observation des lois au dedans, la
propriété des biens, la sûreté des particuliers. Tant que tout ira bien sur ces trois
points, laissez les conseils négocier et traiter avec l'étranger."
Rousseau, Lettres écrites de la Montagne (ed. Paris, 1912), partie II, ch. VII, p. 147.
Quoted from Mirkine-Guetzévitch, p. 98. Cf. de Visscher, pp. 120–121.

[3] Statement in the Constituent Assembly, 17 May 1790. Quoted from Mirkine-
Guetzévitch, p. 100.

[4] See the provisions quoted by Mirkine-Guetzévitch, pp. 101–103.

States, that the modern precepts of legislative, democratic control over the treaty-making activities of states derive.[5]

A number of problems have arisen, and are perhaps inherent, in the adjustment between the spreading adherence to these precepts, on the one hand, and the need for secret negotiations, for ability to settle matters of international concern without delay, and for unequivocal and convenient forms of consent to treaties, on the other.[6]

One of the problems encountered, which will not be subjected to close examination, has regard to the difficulty of exerting popular control, not over the conclusion, but over the negotiation of treaties. This problem was, and still is, important, because once a treaty has been negotiated, the positions of the parties have become settled, and the popular assemblies have very poor means of bringing about desired modifications.[7] In the early practice of the United States, the problem was

---

[5] See Jones, pp. 12 ff.; de Visscher, pp. 120 ff.; and de Visscher, "Les tendances internationales des constitutions modernes" in *Recueil des Cours*, 1952, vol. I, at p. 538. It may also be noted that a Soviet writer has maintained that the turning point in the history of the institution of ratification is not the French Revolution, as contended by writers he terms "bourgeois", but the October Revolution in Russia, when, in his opinion, ratification became a truly "democratic progressive procedure." Polents, *Ratifikatsiia mezhdunarodnykh dogovorov* (Moscow, 1950), p. 11.

[6] That the difficulties encountered upon the road towards a democratization of the treaty-making of states has not been viewed only with complaint may be gleaned from the following statement, made in 1924 by Dupuis:

"La souveraineté a changé de mains. Elle est passée du monarque à la nation, du moins en théorie, et la théorie voudrait que le peuple souverain donne ses instructions, suive les négociations ou du moins s'en fasse rendre compte et se prononce sur leur résultat. L'infortuné peuple souverain est parfaitement incapable d'exercer ainsi sa souveraineté et tout essai de plier la pratique à la théorie pure se tournerait contre ses intérêts. C'est une faiblesse des principes démocratiques de se heurter sans cesse à la nature des choses—et des hommes,—de ne pouvoir être suivis en leurs exigences logiques, sans méconnaître les exigences impérieuses de la vie et du gouvernement de toute société humaine."

Dupuis, "Liberté des voies de communication relations internationales" in *Recueil des Cours*, 1924, vol. I, p. 323. See also Genet, who observes that the democratic form of government entails less perfection in the external representation of a state than the monarchic form. *Traité de Diplomatie et de Droit Diplomatique*, vol. 3 (1932), p. 360.

[7] The complaint voiced by a speaker in the French Chamber of Deputies in 1921, when the French Government was about to open certain international negotiations, may be noted:

"...et quand viendra l'heure d'approver, messieurs, nous aurons la main forcée parce que vous ne pourrez pas désavouer les accords qui auront été passés entre les Gouvernements..."

Quoted from Mirkine-Guetzévitch, p. 115. A similar statement, made in the Parliament of Ceylon, has been cited above, p. 209.

met by the negotiators being highly dependent upon the Senate: their instructions were submitted for its approval, and the course of the negotiations was reported to it, and subjected to its control. The system was found impractical, however, and was abandoned.[8] At the present time such measures as the inclusion of members of legislatures in negotiating missions, or the early consultation of such smaller groups as parliamentary commissions on foreign affairs in secret session,[9] or even more informal arrangements,[1] have proved more successful.

Generally, the control exercised by the legislature over the treaty-making activities of states has come to take the form of a power of withholding authorization required by the executive branch of government in order to ratify treaties, or categories of treaties.[2] This structure of the control[3] has led to certain difficulties, some of which have been solved.

Among the first difficulties to appear was the circumstance that, there being no certainty that a legislature would, in fact, authorize ratification, that measure could no longer, logically, be promised. From having

[8] See Moore's *Digest,* vol. 5, p. 197; Hackworth's *Digest,* vol. 5, pp. 58–59; and see Jones, p. 14.

[9] See Articles 12 and 54 of the Swedish Instrument of Government of 6 June 1809, as amended in 1921. For a doctrinal treatment of the function of the commission established under these articles, see Olsson, H. A., *Utrikesnämnden* 1937–1953 (Lund, 1957); *cf.* article 19, paragraph 3 of the Danish Constitution of 5 June 1953; and see Brusewitz, *Nordiska Utrikesnämnder i Komparativ Belysning* (Uppsala, 1933).

[1] See Mirkine-Guetzévitch, pp. 121 and 123, on such arrangements in the United States. See also the proposals *de lege ferenda* made in Peffer, *America's Place in the World* (1945), pp. 199–219.

[2] With regard to the United States, see Hackworth's *Digest,* vol. 5, p. 59.

[3] Mention should be made of the important mode of exercising democratic control of the conclusion of treaties which is found in many states in the circumstance that the government may be driven out of office by a vote of no confidence. Though this form of democratic control over the making of treaties does not raise difficult problems in the international sphere, and will not, therefore, be commented upon at length, it appears to be less than satisfactory from the municipal point of view. Once a treaty is irrevocably concluded by a government in a state practising this system, it is cold comfort to a majority in the legislature to which the treaty is repugnant that it is able to drive the government out of office. It is not surprising, therefore, that, in states where this is the only form of democratic control of the making of treaties, there are tendencies to require that the government should submit drafts of treaties for the approval of the legislature *prior* to committing the state. See, for instance, the data noted in the section on treaties in Mr. E. Lauterpacht's fourth survey and comment on "The Contemporary Practice of the United Kingdom in the Field of International Law", covering the period 1 January – 1 June 1957, *I.C.L.Q.,* vol. 6 (1957), pp. 528–529.

been viewed by the doctrine as a duty under international law, ratification came gradually to be an unquestionably discretionary act, however,
and the difficulty was in this sense obviated.[4]

Other difficulties have been felt much later. Due to the ever-growing
number of agreements made between states, extensive control exercised
by legislatures over the treaty-making activities of states has become
impracticable.

It is true, as asserted in 1931 by Dr. Mirkine-Guetzévitch, that at that
time there was still a general tendency to enlarge the power of legislatures over the treaty-making activities of the states.[5] That tendency was
all the more understandable in view of the ever-greater importance of
treaties in the life of states, and in view of the notion that democratic
control over the foreign relations of states offers guarantees for a
peaceful policy, while autocratic forms of government are inherently
more dangerous to the peace.[6] Parallel with these developments, however, another development has led, in most states, to the withholding
of large numbers of treaties from legislative control. This has been
brought about by the important practice of concluding treaties in so-
called "simplified forms", *i.e.* types of informal treaties, such as exchanges of notes, agreed minutes etc. In certain states such types of
treaties have been used extensively, because considered not to require
a legislative assent, otherwise constitutionally necessary.[7]

Another problem resulting from the manner in which democratic
control over the conclusion of treaties is predominantly exercised has
regard to the legal relevance in the international sphere of manifesta-

---

[4] See Jones, pp. 16 and 78.

[5] Mirkine-Guetzévitch, p. 138.

[6] For the view that treaties made with democratic sanction offer better guarantees
of fulfilment than do those made by heads of states, see Wohlmann, p. 101, and
quotation below, p. 371, note 4.

[7] On this development, see the very interesting lectures by Professor Paul de
Visscher on "Les tendances internationales des constitutions modernes" printed in
Recueil des Cours, 1952, vol. I, pp. 534 ff.

Professor Scelle is reported to have declared in the International Law Commission,
on 22 May 1951, that "there was a veritable spate of simplified treaties..." In his
opinion, "such a system was anarchical and anti-democratic. Someone might commit the State without having consulted the nation." See U.N. *Doc.* A/CN. 4/ SR 86
(27 June 1921), p. 10. Professor Siotto-Pintor states that "la pratique internationale
admet cette procédure simplifiée—par laquelle les prescriptions les plus solennelles
du droit interne sont souvent déjouées...:" "Traités internationaux et droit interne"
in *R.G.D.I.P.*, vol. 42 (1935), p. 529. See also Chayet, "Les accords en forme simplifiée"
in *Annuaire Français de Droit International*, vol. III (1957), pp. 3–13; and see
below, p. 291.

tions of popular approval, or the satisfaction of other requirements under constitutional law. This is a problem that is of special interest in this section of the present study.

Expressions of consent, such as signature, ratification, and accession have remained acts performed by the executive branch of government. The speakers of legislatures are never called upon to sign treaty documents in evidence of approval given by the bodies over which they preside, nor are certificates to the same effect ever issued.[8] Furthermore, though it may well have been expressly prescribed in full powers, in the texts of treaties, or in connexion with the signing of treaties that authorization by a legislature would be required before the state could be committed irrevocably, and though sometimes mention of the existence of such authorization may well be made in connexion with the final expression of consent, such as ratification, formal evidence of such authorization is never offered or requested in the practice of states. To the extent that authorizations occur, they remain municipal acts of which another party becomes cognizant, if at all, either by their being public knowledge,[9] or by contentions made by the executive branches of the other parties to the effect that they have received due authorization.

If the mechanism thus established has put effective constitutional checks upon the treaty-making executive organs without introducing any cumbersome procedures,[1] there nevertheless remains doctrinal controversy over the question whether such checks, and other requirements under municipal law, are allowed to operate in the realm of international law.

[8] Undoubtedly it is still a general rule that all communications and inquiries between state organs shall be made through the channels of the departments of external affairs. See, for instance, Hackworth's *Digest,* vol. 4, pp. 604 ff. And see below, p. 260. It is no doubt customary, too, that legislatures, as organs of states, do not address themselves to foreign governments, or to foreign legislatures. It may be noted, however, that, when the legislature of the Soviet Union, the Supreme Soviet, adopted, on 21 December 1957, a resolution setting out seven points for the preservation of peace, the speakers of the Swedish legislature were informed of the resolution through the channels of the executive branches of the two governments, such communication having been requested by the Supreme Soviet.

[9] See Bittner, pp. 81 and 95.

[1] The following statement by de Visscher (p. 278) may be noted:

"Les Etats démocratiques sont en réalité à la recherche du point idéal d'équilibre qui permettra un contrôle sérieux et efficace des relations extérieures par les assemblées, sans devoir pour cela livrer à l'étranger cette part de secret inséparable de toute politique extérieure. Ce point idéal est atteint, croyons-nous, dans le système du partage de la compétence internationale."

See also Masters, *International Law in National Courts* (1932), p. 198.

CHAPTER XV

THE CONSTITUTIONS OF STATES

1. PRELIMINARY REMARKS

Several writers have examined large numbers of municipal constitutions in order to throw light upon the question of the international validity of a treaty made by a constitutionally unauthorized organ,[1] and, indirectly, upon the rule of international law relating to the competence to conclude treaties on behalf of a constitutionally organized state. Are constitutions, in fact, apt to give an answer to the questions raised?

It is clear that a single constitution's provision to the effect that a treaty entered into by a constitutionally incompetent authority will have no validity in regard to the other party, is not, in itself, sufficient to bring about that result between the state and the other party. A treaty's validity between parties must depend upon the common solution given to that question by parties in treaty relations. Indeed, it has been well stressed by Professor Ross[2] that, as a promisor and as a promisee, one and the same state has an interest both in upholding constitutional provisions, and in the full reliability of the undertakings of which it is the beneficiary.

Constitutional regulations of competence may conceivably be made relevant generally between certain states, by means of a convention to that effect.[3] Alternatively, they may conceivably be made relevant

---

[1] See notably Chailley, pp. 170–180; that writer's discussion of the matter is examined in some detail below; see also Dehousse, pp. 124–138.

Most writers who discuss the conclusion of treaties in detail, and who treat the problem of competence under international law, consider the various types of constitutional provisions regulating the municipal competence. Not all writers, however, examine the text of constitutions with a view to finding evidence of the rule of international law on competence. See, for instance, Freymond, *La ratification des traités et le problème des rapports entre le droit international et le droit interne* (1947), p. 58; Georgopoulos, *La ratification des traités et la collaboration du Parlement* (1939), pp. 6 ff.; Vexler, *De l'obligation de ratifier les traités régulièrement conclus* (1921), pp. 62 ff.

[2] Ross, p. 207.

[3] See the Havana Convention, cited below, p. 353.

specifically between two parties with respect to a particular treaty, by means of a special provision inserted in the treaty.[4] In these cases, the basis for the relevance of the constitutional regulation would be the express agreement between the parties. On the other hand, the assertion made by de Visscher[5] that, where a state declares in its constitution that it will not be bound by a treaty but for consent given to the treaty by the state's representative organs, it becomes superfluous to examine if this requirement is also mentioned in the formulae of full powers and ratifications, is not necessarily correct.

In the case of such express provisions in full powers, treaty texts, or instruments of ratification, there is a presumption that the other party agrees to the provisions by accepting the instruments. No presumption exists generally, however, regarding the relevance of constitutional provisions.

It follows that even if a great number of constitutions were found to be concordant in the manner in which they determine the competence of treaty-making authorities, this circumstance in itself would not suffice to elevate that determination into a rule of international law.[6] The determination must also be mutually accepted. Thus, if many constitutions were found to direct their treaty-making authorities to negotiate and treat only with such authorities of other states as are indicated in the constitutions of these states, such provisions, if indeed followed in practice, would constitute evidence of acceptance of the constitutional determination made by the other states. Though no such provisions have been found, the actual practice of states might furnish evidence of such acceptance.

If every constitution simply were to provide that the head of state, alone, was competent to bind the state to any treaty, and this provision were effectively followed, it may be assumed that, in international practice, it would gradually become customary to rely completely upon the promise of the head of a state. Similarly, if for municipal validity legislative approval of *every* treaty were to be required everywhere, that requirement would presumably soon be present in the minds of negotiators and find its way into international law. Practice, however, presents no such simple picture. Existing constitutional provisions are of the most varied kind, and there can be no presumption, at any rate,

---

[4] See below, chapter XIX.
[5] De Visscher, p. 148; see also Wohlmann, p. 26.
[6] See Anzilotti, p. 363.

that, in their intercourse, states habitually rely only upon promises given in a manner according with, and by authorities indicated in, constitutional provisions.

2. VALUE OF CONSTITUTIONAL PROVISIONS AS EVIDENCE

While to-day's varied constitutional regulation of the treaty-making power of states does not suggest any particular solution of the question of competence under international law, it must be admitted, on the other hand, that a given constitutional provision may presuppose a particular evaluation of the tenor of the rule of international law. The views on the possible international relevance of the constitutional regulation of the competence to make treaties held by the framers and interpreters of constitutions must be entitled to some respect. They are part of a latent attitude that might achieve expression in the state's international relations: it might be asserted by the state, or recognized as legitimate when taken by another state. It does not seem justified, therefore, to brush these opinions aside as only "le fruit d'une surprenante inexactitude de pensée..."[7]

By contrast, some writers seem to exaggerate the importance of the views underlying constitutional provisions. Thus, Mervyn Jones maintains that "the constitutional texts prevailing in the vast majority of States are at least *cogent evidence* of the attitude of those States, if not a source of a new rule of international law."[8] The expression "cogent evidence" seems too strong in view of the circumstance that there is no certainty that, in a concrete situation, a state will actually assert the attitude reflected in its constitution, either with respect to obligations already undertaken by itself, or, indeed, pledges supposedly given by another state. Dr. Chailley expresses himself with somewhat greater caution. Referring to constitutions, he states:

"... on les envisage comme des faits, *propres autant que d'autres,* à manifester, sur un point donné, la conviction juridique des États."[9]

To estimate the potential "juridical conviction" of a state with regard to the international treaty-making competence of some organ, *i.e.* the legal stand it may reasonably be expected to take in a concrete situation, it is necessary, of course, to take into account not only the bare text of a constitutional provision, but also the *travaux prépara-*

---

[7] Vitta, p. 82; see also Siotto-Pintor, "Traités internationaux et droit interne" in *R.G.D.I.P.,* vol. 42 (1935), p. 522.

[8] Jones, p. 154. Emphasis supplied.

[9] Chailley, p. 170. Emphasis supplied.

toires, and the interpretation given to it by practice, jurisprudence and doctrine.

A comprehensive analysis of this kind of national attitudes would require extensive research into the constitutional law and practice of various states, and is, unfortunately, outside the scope of this inquiry. Moreover, a better picture of the "juridical conviction" of states probably may be gained from an examination of the stands actually taken by states in concrete international situations, to the extent that such situations may have prompted public pronouncements. Under such circumstances, it may perhaps be asked if any purpose is served by a necessarily superficial examination of the provisions of a number of constitutions. Some writers have thought it possible to draw support from such inquiries into constitutions for their views on the international rule of competence.[1] In order to verify their conclusions, if for no other reason, it is here proposed to undertake an inquiry of this kind.

The constitutional provisions and official memoranda collected in a volume entitled *"The Laws and Practices concerning the Conclusion of Treaties"* and issued in the United Nations Legislative Series,[2] being the latest collection of this kind,[3] have been used as the chief basis for the examination. A few of the provisions reproduced there may have later been superseded by others, but the collection no doubt still gives a fairly accurate total picture of the types of provisions encountered at the present time. What, then, emerges from an examination of this material?

3. MOST CONSTITUTIONS ARE SILENT ON THE RELEVANT POINT

The fundamental fact emerges from the examination of the whole material that of some eighty-five provisions reproduced and practices

---

[1] See Bittner, p. 16. The relevant statement is quoted below, p. 388; see also Dehousse, p. 138; Chailley, pp. 175. The latter writer sees support in constitutions for his view that there exists no rule of international law on the competence to conclude treaties.

[2] U.N. Publication, Sales No.: 1952. V. 4.

[3] Reference may be made to two older compilations of constitutional provisions regarding the conclusion of treaties: *The Treaty-Making Power in Various Countries. A collection of memoranda concerning the negotiation, conclusion, and ratification of treaties and conventions, with excerpts from the fundamental laws of various countries.* (Washington, Government Printing Office, 1919); and Arnold, *Treaty-making Procedure* (London, 1933). The two following collections of constitutions may also be cited: Dareste, Delpech and Laferrière, *Constitutions modernes* (6 vols., Paris, 1928–32); and Peaslee, *Constitutions of Nations* (3 vols., London, 1950).

described in the cited collection, the vast majority—some seventy—merely prescribe the procedure to be followed in the conclusion of treaties, and lay down the division of duties between the various organs of states, without expressly dealing with the situation which arises when the regulations are violated. It is not possible merely to write off this majority of constitutions without comment, and to take the evidence supplied by a minority of instruments as representative of a general attitude of states.

It must be kept in mind that although not made explicit in constitutional provisions on the conclusion of treaties, consequences may nevertheless be attached to violations of these provisions. First, of course, political sanctions are an effective deterrent against unconstitutional behaviour in most states.[4] Second, while express provisions on impeachment may not be found in articles on the conclusion of treaties, most constitutional systems possess that institution as an inducement, if need be, to government officers to respect all parts of a constitution, including, indeed, provisions on the conclusion of treaties.[5] Third, and more important in this connexion, constitutional precepts not made explicit in the texts of constitutions, or, at any rate, in the provisions on the conclusion of treaties, may nevertheless exist to the effect that an unconstitutional treaty shall be municipally void, or perhaps both municipally and internationally void.

Since it is the "juridical conviction" of the state that is of interest to the determination of the international rule, it cannot matter whether that "conviction" is spelled out in the constitution, or only figures behind it. The existence of such convictions is possible, of course, in the case of the vast majority of constitutions which have no express provisions on the point, and which cannot here conveniently be looked into. This being so, it goes without saying that the evidential value of the small minority of constitutions which do have express clauses on the effect of unconstitutionality upon the validity of treaties will be very limited. The risk is obvious that they might not be representative. Though in his inquiry into constitutions, Dr. Chailley cites as a first

---

[4] Votes of no confidence are such sanctions. See the memorandum of 11 March 1951 submitted by the Government of Israel to the United Nations in U.N., *Compilation*, p. 72; see also above, p. 227, note 3, and below, p. 235.

[5] See, for instance, Seidl-Hohenveldern, "Relation of International Law to Internal Law in Austria" in *A.J.I.L.*, vol. 49 (1955), p. 474; and see below, p. 235 on the provision in the new Danish Constitution. See also Chailley, p. 171.

group numerous provisions silent on the matter under discussion, he fails to mention this important point.[6]

To demonstrate that a "juridical conviction" in the question under discussion may underlie a constitutional provision on treaty-making, ostensibly silent on the point, and to illustrate the existence of a political sanction against violations of a constitution, and of rules on impeachment, the recent Danish Constitution offers an example in point. Article 19, paragraph 1, of the Danish Constitution of 5 June 1953 reads as follows:

"The King shall act on behalf of the Realm in international affairs. Provided that without the consent of the Folketing the King shall not undertake any act whereby the territory of the Realm will be increased or decreased, nor shall he enter into any obligation which for fulfilment requires the concurrence of the Folketing, or which otherwise is of major importance; nor shall the King, except with the consent of the Folketing, terminate any international treaty entered into with the consent of the Folketing."[7]

It may further be noted that Article 12 of the same Constitution provides that the King shall exercise his powers through his Ministers; Article 13, that responsibility for the acts of the Government rests upon the Ministers, and not upon the King personally; Article 14, that laws and decisions of the Government are rendered valid by their being signed by the King and countersigned by one or several Ministers, and that the Minister signing is responsible for the decision; Article 15, that no Minister can remain in office after the adoption in the Folketing of a motion of no confidence in him; Article 16, finally, provides that Ministers may be impeached by the King or by the Folketing for governmental acts for which they are responsible.

As may be clearly seen from the above, there exist in the Danish Constitution both political and legal checks upon a Minister who might be about to conclude an unconstitutional treaty,[8] even if these checks are not found in the very Article which deals with the conclusion of treaties. Furthermore, and of special importance here, in spite of the absence in that Article of any express mention of the status of treaties concluded in violation of the Constitution, it appears that the framers

[6] Chailley, p. 171.

[7] The provision is too new to have been included in the United Nations compilation cited above. The text above is the official Danish translation.

[8] It is interesting to note, on the other hand, that no such check exists as regards the King. This circumstance must no doubt make the international relevance of countersignature all the more desirable, at least from the national point of view.

of the Article had a very precise opinion on the matter. The report by the commission which framed the Constitution makes it clear that a memorandum prepared by Professor Max Sørensen served as a basis for the commission's deliberation of the new Article.[9]

A reading of the report of the commission reveals immediately, indeed, that the commission accepted without modifications the draft Article proposed by Professor Sørensen.[1] It may safely be assumed, then, that the commission also accepted the views advanced by the drafter in support of his formulation, and these acquire special significance for the understanding and interpretation of the provision. The following passage of the memorandum is relevant in this connexion:

> "... constitutional rules concerning the conclusion of treaties do not only have importance as such, fixing the duties of the government towards parliament ["rigsdagen"], but have importance under international law, too, so that their non-observance will have the result, in general, that the treaty is not binding upon the Danish state. It is generally said that these rules limit the competence of the government under international law. They have, consequently, a greater effect than common parliamentary practice. Thus, if a government were to enter into an obligation without the consent of parliament in a case where consent is not required by the constitution but by parliamentary practice, the minister concerned may possibly be made responsible, but the obligation entered into binds the Danish state. Only if the rules of the constitution are not observed, is it possible to contend that the obligation is invalid. It may consequently be of special importance carefully to weigh the formulation of these rules."[2]

This is not the place to go into a detailed discussion of the views expressed by the learned professor, and apparently shared by the framers of the new Danish Constitution. It may suffice to note that a distinction seems to be made between the rough lines staked out by the written Article, and practices arising under that Article, and that only the former are thought internationally relevant. To what extent, if any, parliamentary and governmental practice is thought internationally relevant as interpreting and defining, and perhaps modifying the written Constitution is not indicated.

What is believed clearly proved by the above, however, is the contention that behind a constitutional provision which is silent on the matter

---

[9] See *Betænkning afgivet af Forfatningskommissionen af 1946* (Copenhagen, 1953), p. 29. The memorandum by Professor Sørensen is found in an appendix to the report of the commission; see *ibid.*, pp. 113–127.

[1] See *ibid.*, p. 126.

[2] *Ibid.*, p. 114. Translation supplied by the present writer.

of the effect of an unconstitutional treaty, there may nevertheless be a "juridical conviction" as to the international validity or lack of validity of unconstitutional treaties.

4. Constitutions Containing Express but Allegedly Equivocal Provisions

As a second group of constitutions, we may examine those which Dr. Chailley has considered to deal expressly with the effect of unconstitutional treaties, but which, in his opinion, do not make it clear if the unconstitutionality entails only municipal, or perhaps also international invalidity of the treaties.

In this group, Dr. Chailley cites the Italian Constitution of 1848, the Belgian of 1831, the Luxemburg Constitution of 1919, and the Egyptian of 1930, all of which at the time of his writing prescribed that treaties of certain kinds which had not received parliamentary approval were to "have no effect".[3] Of these Constitutions, the Italian has been superseded by one whose provision on the conclusion of treaties is silent as to the effect of unconstitutionality.[4] The Egyptian Constitution has been suspended by President Nasser's revolutionary Government. In 1956, however, that Government introduced a new Constitution, which, on the relevant point, was similar to the previous one. The same is true of the corresponding provision of the Provisional Constitution of 1958 of the United Arab Republic.[5] The Belgian Constitution remains unmodified and the relevant part of its Article 68 reads as follows:

"Le Roi fait les traités de paix, d'alliance et de commerce. Il en donne connaissance aux Chambres aussitôt que l'intérêt et la sûreté de l'Etat le permettent, en y joignant les communications convenables.

"Les traités de commerce et ceux qui pourrait grever l'Etat ou lier individuellement des Belges, *n'ont d'effet* qu'après avoir reçu l'assentiment des Chambres."[6]

It is of interest to note that according to an official memorandum of 6 March 1951, submitted by the Belgian Government to the United

---

[3] Chailley, p. 172.

[4] See U.N., *Compilation*, p. 72.

[5] See article 143 of the Constitution of 1956, the text of which may be found in *Revue Egyptienne de Droit International*, vol. 12, tome I (1956), p. 165; article 56 of the Constitution of 1958, which may be found in *I.C.L.Q.*, vol. 8 (1959), p. 379.

[6] U.N., *Compilation*, p. 14. Emphasis added.

Nations, the expression "n'ont d'effet", has reference only to municipal effects:

"... le deuxième paragraphe de l'art. 68 stipule que pour sortir leurs effets — et, par comparaison avec le paragraphe premier, il ne peut s'agir que de leurs effets en droit interne belge — certaines catégories de conventions internationales ... doivent être sanctionnées par l'assentiment des Chambres."[7]

The Constitution of Luxemburg, cited by Chailley, likewise remains in force, and the relevant article still reads:

"Le Grand-Duc commande la force armée. Il fait les traités. Aucun traité *n'aura d'effet* avant d'avoir reçu l'assentiment de la Chambre ..."[8]

Here, too, the vagueness of the expression is conclusively dispelled by an official communication, namely, a memorandum of 20 February 1952 submitted by the Government of Luxemburg to the United Nations. It reads in part:

"Les règles juridiques internes, énoncées ci-dessus, déterminent exclusivement la compétence des organes ... pour autant qu'il s'agit d'actes de portée interne. Pour le reste, la matière des traités est régie par le droit international."

And further:

"... les pouvoirs reconnus dans les relations internationales au Chef d'Etat et au Ministre des Affaires Etrangères, pour représenter et pour engager l'Etat, sont bien plus étendus que ceux que le droit luxembourgeois reconnaît au Grand Duc et au Gouvernement ... les Etats étrangers et les organisations internationales attachent toujours foi à l'acte fait par le Chef d'Etat et le Ministre des Affaires Etrangères, sans contrôler si cet acte est régulier au regard du droit interne de l'Etat en cause."[9]

Thus, it appears that of four constitutional provisions cited by Chailley as equivocal, one has been substituted by a provision altogether silent on the point at issue, one has been replaced by a stipulation the tenor of which is similar to the previous one, but the construction of which is, so far, unknown, and two, although unmodified, have been authoritatively stated to aim only at the municipal effect of unconstitutional treaties.

---

[7] *Ibid.,* p. 16. For earlier Belgian doctrinal controversy over the right interpretation, see Dehousse, pp. 134–136; and Masters, *International Law in National Courts* (1932), pp. 199 ff.

[8] Article 37 of the Constitution. See U.N., *Compilation,* p. 76. Emphasis supplied.

[9] *Ibid.,* p. 78.

5. CONSTITUTIONS ALLEGED TO REFLECT THE VIEW
THAT UNCONSTITUTIONAL TREATIES ARE INTERNATIONALLY VOID

As a third group of instruments, we shall look into constitutional provisions which, in the opinion of Dr. Chailley, clearly demonstrate that their authors have thought non-observance of constitutional formalities to entail the lack of international validity of the treaties.[1] Of the constitutions cited by Chailley, those of Baden, Hessen and Mecklenburg-Schwerin have no longer any international interest, while those of Cuba, Albania, Rumania and Bulgaria have been superseded by new constitutions which lack express provisions on the question of the effect of unconstitutional treaties. Indeed, of all the constitutions cited by Chailley in this group, only those of Austria, Lichtenstein and Lebanon remain unchanged. However, one constitution cited by Chailley in this group has been replaced by an instrument very similar to its predecessor on the point under discussion. This new constitution and the three which have remained unchanged will now be examined.

The Venezuelan Constitution of 1925, cited by Chailley, appears to have prescribed that certain treaties were to have "neither validity nor effect", if they had not been approved by Parliament.[2] The Venezuelan Constitution of 1936 as amended in 1945 only provides that treaties not having been approved by the legislature "shall be invalid and shall not be ratified".[3] It must be noted that this provision does not aim at treaties which have been unconstitutionally ratified, but merely lays down that treaties requiring ratification and not being approved shall not be ratified, and thus *remain* non-obligatory. It might not, therefore, be relevant to the question of the effect of unconstitutional treaties.

The provision of the Austrian Constitution cited by Dr. Chailley[4] as clearly evidencing a conviction to the effect that constitutional flaws in the conclusion of treaties entail international invalidity, is still in effect. It reads as follows:

"Article 50. All international political treaties and all other treaties, in so far as they contain provisions modifying existing laws, require for their validity the approval of the National Council."[5]

[1] Chailley, p. 173.
[2] *Ibid.*, p. 174.
[3] U.N., *Compilation*, p. 135.
[4] Chailley, p. 174; *cf. ibid.*, pp. 176–177.
[5] U.N., *Compilation*, p. 7.

It is difficult to understand how the above formulation could be thought clearly to imply the view that international invalidity results from lack of approval of the Council. Indeed, it is now certain, as admittedly was perhaps not the case when Chailley stated his opinion, that, contrary to his contention, the Austrian provision only aims at depriving the treaty of municipal validity, and leaves the international validity unaffected. This interpretation has been sanctioned in the case of *Pokorny and Another* v. *Republic of Austria*,[6] in which, on 20 February 1952, the Austrian Supreme Court was careful to point out that it was the "municipal and constitutional validity" of an agreement that it negatived on the ground that the agreement had neither been submitted to Parliament for consent, nor been published. It appears, further, indeed, that the Court clearly implied that, in its opinion, the treaty remained internationally valid. The Court is reported to have said:

"Thus as the promise to pay embodied in the treaty concerned is ineffective and not binding under internal law, a special Federal Law (Art. 10(1) subpar. 15) will be required in order to regulate under internal law the compensation for war damages pursuant to the present treaty."[7]

The Lebanese Constitution of 1926 provided—with a formulation very similar to those employed in the French Constitutions of 1875 and 1946,[8] and in the Syrian Constitution of 1950[9]—that certain treaties "ne sont définitifs qu'après avoir été votés par la Chambre".[1] While in the French Constitution of 1958 it is merely provided that the treaties in question "ne peuvent être ratifiés ou approuvés qu'en vertu d'une loi", and "ne prennent effet qu'après avoir été ratifiés ou approuvés",[2] and the Constitution of 1958 of the United Arab Republic—comprising Egypt and Syria—similarly provides that the relevant treaties "will not become effective until after ratification by the National Assembly",[3] the Lebanese provision appears to remain unmodified.

---

[6] *I.L.R.*, 1952, p. 459. The case is also discussed below, p. 256.

[7] The passage quoted in the text is not included in the *International Law Reports*, but is found in an article published in 1955. See Seidl-Hohenveldern, "Relation of International Law to Internal Law in Austria", in *A.J.I.L.*, vol. 49 (1955), p. 473, note 158. The conclusion reached in the text has authoritative support in the cited article.

[8] U.N., *Compilation*, p. 46.

[9] *Ibid.*, p. 102.

[1] *Ibid.*, p. 74.

[2] See *Journal du Droit International*, vol. 86 (1959), pp. 530–532.

[3] See *I.C.L.Q.*, vol. 8 (1959), p. 379.

It seems somewhat rash to conclude, as does Chailley,[4] that formulations such as those employed in the present Lebanese, and earlier French and Syrian Constitutions, clearly imply the view that treaties lacking legislative approval are not internationally valid. It is not denied that a closer examination of the history of the provisions, and of the manner in which the provisions have been applied, might necessitate that conclusion. The assertion made by one writer may here be mentioned that there is "general agreement" in French doctrine "that the international competence of state authorities to conclude treaties is determined by internal law, and that the international validity of a treaty is, therefore, dependent upon its 'regularity' or constitutionality."[5] That the relevant provision of the French Constitution of 1875 has been understood to imply precisely this conviction is maintained by several modern writers.[6]

Although the present Lebanese Constitution is very similar to the older French Constitutions on the point under examination, it would have to be established specifically in the case of the Lebanese provision that its true meaning is identical with that which seems likely to have been implied in the earlier French provisions. Before that is done, not much evidential value can be attributed to the bare provision.

The criticism voiced above against Chailley's reliance upon the Constitution of Lebanon applies also to his views respecting the international validity of unconstitutional treaties in the formulation employed by the Constitution of Lichtenstein,[7] which declares that treaties of certain kinds "are not valid unless approved by the Diet",[8] and possibly by the 1927 Constitution of Greece, which provided that certain treaties were to have no obligatory force before they were approved by the Chambers.[9] It is submitted that only a closer examination of the background of these provisions, and of the manner in which they have been interpreted, can reveal if, as Chailley thinks, they are really expressions of the conviction that lack of constitutionally required legislative approval entails international invalidity. The present Greek Constitution, like that cited by Chailley, gives no obvious clue on the point in ques-

---

[4] Chailley, p. 173.

[5] Preuss, "The Relation of International Law to Internal Law in the French Constitutional System", in *A.J.I.L.*, vol. 44 (1950), p. 648, note 18.

[6] See Basdevant, p. 578; de Visscher, p. 56.

[7] Chailley, p. 174.

[8] U.N., *Compilation*, p. 75.

[9] Chailley, p. 173.

tion. It provides, in effect, that certain treaties "are not valid without the consent of the House of Representatives."[1]

If an illustration should be needed of the necessity to exercise the greatest care before the conclusion is drawn that a constitutional provision lends support to one view or another of the international validity of a constitutionally unauthorized treaty, attention may be called to the following example:

In 1956, the Committee on the Judiciary of the United States Senate issued a report on a proposed amendment to the United States constitutional provision concerning the treaty-making power. Part of the proposed amendment read as follows:

"Section 1. A provision of a treaty or other international agreement which conflicts with any provision of this Constitution shall not be of any force or effect."[2]

It would perhaps have been tempting to assume that the proposed amendment demonstrated that some Senators believed that treaties, the substance of which violates the United States Constitution lack international force. Such a conclusion, however, would be erroneous. The Committee, which, it may be noted, was in favour of the proposed amendment, commented in part as follows upon it:

"... The words 'shall not be of any force or effect' mean that the agreement will be void insofar as the municipal or domestic aspects of the agreement are concerned. The committee wishes to point out that the international obligations of the treaty are not affected by this language for the external force and effect of such agreements are governed by international law and usage rather than by constitutional provisions."[3]

From the above quotation it is clear that, contrary to what might have been inferred from a superficial interpretation of the proposed amendment, the Committee clearly distinguished between the domestic and the international validity of a treaty, and, indeed, was convinced that a treaty would not lose its international validity because in substance it violated the Constitution and thereby lacked domestic validity.[4]

[1] U.N., *Compilation*, p. 60. Georgopoulos asserts that the parliamentary and diplomatic practice of Greece is in favour of the international relevance of parliamentary approval. He admits, however, that this view is not unanimously taken in Greece. See *La ratification des traités et la collaboration du parlement* (1939), pp. 31–32.

[2] 84th Cong. 2nd Sess. Senate Report No. 1716. Calendar No. 1649, p. 1.

[3] *Ibid.*, p. 11.

[4] See also Oliver, "Historical Development of International Law—Contemporary Problems of Treaty Law" in *Recueil des Cours*, 1955, vol. II, p. 434. Admittedly the

6. CONSTITUTIONS FOUND TO REFLECT VIEWS ON THE INTERNATIONAL EFFECT OF CERTAIN UNCONSTITUTIONAL TREATIES

While none of the provisions cited above may safely be said to be an expression of the view of its authors that lack of legislative approval entails lack of international validity, it must be readily admitted that some other constitutional provisions, past and present, may be found which imply the conviction of their authors quite clearly.

Chailley cited a Costa Rican decree of 1888 by which certain treaties, if not made in accordance with a specified complicated procedure, would be "absolutely null".[5] While this particular decree might have lapsed and Costa Rica is endowed with a Constitution of 1949, a very similar rule seems to exist in that State. Article 7 of the new Constitution lays down that any person concluding a treaty conflicting with the sovereignty and independence of the Republic shall be tried for treason. The same Article prescribes very rigid conditions for the approval of treaties which affect the territorial integrity and political organization of the country.[6] While this Article itself does not contain anything that relates to consequences in the international sphere of its violation, it is asserted in an official Costa Rican memorandum of 29 November 1949 that such a treaty would be "invalid" as a result of Article 10 of the Constitution which is said to provide quite generally: "Enactments of the Legislative Power or of the Executive Power contrary to the Constitution shall be null and void."[7] It seems likely that these expressions have been thought to refer to the legal effect in the international as well as in the domestic sphere.

The Constitution of the Dominican Republic of 1947 provides that the President shall submit *all* treaties for the approval of Congress, "failing which they shall have no validity and shall not be binding on the Republic."[8] While there is no room for doubt as to the meaning of this provision, it is not known to what extent, if any, the provision is of any relevance under the dictatorship established at present in the State.

unconstitutionality to which the committee referred related to the substance of a treaty, rather than to the authority concluding the treaty. The example nevertheless well serves to show the need for cautious interpretation.

[5] Chailley, p. 173.

[6] U.N., *Compilation*, p. 38.

[7] See *Replies from Governments to Questionnaires of the International Law Commission*, U.N. *Doc.* A/CN.4/19, 23 March 1950, p. 25.

[8] U.N., *Compilation*, p. 41.

The Portuguese Constitution of 1933 provides that the President shall submit conventions to the National Assembly for approval, but does not combine this duty with any express provision on nullity of treaties in cases of violations. To the Article requiring the acts of the President to be countersigned by the President of the Council, or by the appropriate Minister (Article 82), on the other hand, is added the proviso that "otherwise they shall be null and void".[9] It is difficult to ascertain whether the provision would actually be of municipal importance in the dictatorship that has long prevailed in Portugal.

In distinction to what has been said about the three instruments cited above, the internal relevance of the provisions of two constitutions to be mentioned below, cannot be doubted. Article 5 (2) of the Irish Constitution of 1937 reads as follows:

> "The State shall not be bound by any international agreement involving a charge upon public funds unless the terms of the agreement shall have been approved by the Dàil Éirann."[1]

The Norwegian Constitution, enacted in 1814 and later amended, provides that certain treaties "shall not be binding until the Storting has given its consent thereunto."[2] A memorandum of 4 April 1951, submitted by the Norwegian Government to the United Nations, confirms the impression gained from the text of the article that in Norwegian official opinion, "the regulation ... limits not only the King's right but also his capacity to create binding obligations."[3]

Some comments are required, finally, on the Peruvian and Swedish provisions on the matter, the only articles which, in the opinion of Chailley, could conceivably be taken to imply that their authors thought constitutional irregularities in the conclusion of treaties without relevance internationally. The Peruvian provision cited by Chailley may now be overlooked, for it appears to have lapsed and to have been replaced by one which raises no implication of interest in this connexion.[4] The Swedish provision quoted by the same writer remains unchanged, however, and lays down, in effect, that any treaties which, under the Swedish Constitution, require the approval of the legislature, shall contain an express reservation which makes its validity dependent

---

[9] *Ibid.*, p. 95.
[1] U.N., *Compilation*, p. 67.
[2] *Ibid.*, p. 91. See Article 26 of the Constitution.
[3] *Ibid.*
[4] See *ibid.*, p. 93.

upon that approval.[5] It seems correct, as is maintained by several writers,[6] that the inference from this provision is that its authors acted upon the assumption that the absence of a constitutionally required legislative approval might not lead to lack of international validity unless such approval were made an express condition in the treaties.[7]

To the case of the Swedish Constitution, there may perhaps be added the new constitutional regulation of the treaty-making power of Ethiopia. Article 30 of the Constitution of 1955 requires that certain enumerated kinds of treaties "shall, before becoming binding upon the Empire and the inhabitants thereof, be laid before Parliament..."[8] The inference may well be that the State assumes internationally binding obligations by action on the international level, and that the effect of such action is independent of constitutionally required legislative assent.

7. CONCLUSIONS

The above examination of a large number of constitutional provisions regulating the treaty-making function of states has shown that the vast majority of such provisions is silent as to the possible municipal and international effect of irregularities. That in all these instances there may nevertheless exist less accessible constitutional precepts on the matter was demonstrated by an examination of the case of the Danish Constitution. An examination of some other case might likewise have yielded a positive result, although perhaps one evidencing another opinion than that held by the framers of Denmark's Constitution. It must be stressed that, in the absence of a penetrating inquiry into a very large number of constitutions, no safe assumption can be made concerning a general attitude, if there should be one, among the framers of constitutions as to the international relevance of violations of constitutional provisions relating to the conclusion of treaties.

An examination of the relatively small number of fundamental laws which do have some express paragraph on the matter under discussion

---

[5] *Ibid.*, pp. 96–97.

[6] Siotto-Pintor, "Traités internationaux et droit interne" in *R.G.D.I.P.*, vol. 42 (1935), pp. 525–526; Sundberg, *Lag och Traktat* (2nd ed., Stockholm, 1942), pp. 30–35, esp. p. 31. See also below, pp. 285 ff.

[7] But see Chailley (p. 179), who tries to explain this provision as evidence only of a spirit of political caution, rather than of juridical conviction.

[8] The text of the Ethiopian Constitution may be found in *Revue Egyptienne de Droit International*, vol. 12, tome II (1956), p. 151.

reveals no uniform tendency among the framers of constitutions. Some provisions were based upon the view that certain unconstitutional features entail both domestic and international invalidity. Among these were the Dominican and the Portuguese Constitutions. However, these instruments can hardly be accorded evidentiary value, since their practical importance as state instruments seems doubtful. It is submitted that, in the material examined above, the Irish and the Norwegian provisions, alone, clearly demonstrate their authors' view that certain unconstitutional features make treaties invalid internationally. The Danish Constitution, although on the face of it silent on this matter, has also been shown to have been written in the same conviction. In addition, it may be probable that the Costa Rican and Greek provisions were predicated upon the same view, and that there is some likelihood that the same is true for the Lebanese provision.

It must be noted that although the convictions underlying, or seeming to underlie, the provisions cited in the preceding paragraph would no doubt accord with a rule making constitutional irregularities generally, including violations of limitations of substance, relevant in international law, only one of the provisions—that of Costa Rica—actually necessitated such a rule for its functioning, while another—that of Portugal—merely required the international relevance of counter-signing, and the rest only could be taken to imply the belief that the constitutional requirement of legislative assent is relevant under international law. This position, it must be stressed, is much more moderate than the broad assertion that municipal irregularities of whatever kind entail the international invalidity of a treaty if they have the effect of domestically voiding the same treaty.

In contrast to the group of provisions cited above, the Belgian and Luxemburgian provisions, although explicit on the municipally invalidating effect upon treaties of certain unconstitutional features, have been shown to be officially and deliberately interpreted as not relating to the international effect of the same features. Indeed, the recent Luxemburgian attitude was to the effect that the international validity of a treaty would not be affected by its not being approved by the state legislature. The same has been shown to be the Austrian, and, possibly, Ethiopian constitutional convictions, and the drafters of the Swedish provision were shown to have acted upon the assumption that that position was possibly correct. In addition, it has been demonstrated that a United States Senate Judiciary Committee, although eager to void domestically treaties in any way unconstitutional in substance, did not consider affecting the international validity of the same treaties. It must finally be noted that it is not surprising that constitutions written or interpreted in the conviction that international invalidity of treaties does not necessarily follow with municipal invalidity do not make this position explicit: there is no reason why such a rule of international law—if actually it be a rule of international law—should be embodied in the constitution.

What has been said above ought to suffice to show that—with a reservation as to what might be disclosed by a fuller inquiry into the constitutional precepts of a large number of states whose provisions on the matter give no ready insight into their positions—it cannot possibly be maintained that the general 'juridical conviction' among those who have framed or interpreted constitutions is that unconstitutionality generally, or even certain unconstitutional features in treaties, make the latter invalid under international law, if invalid under municipal law.

Furthermore, it cannot be maintained that the circumstance that constitutional provisions on the conclusion of treaties universally indicate the division of duties and procedures to be followed must presuppose a rule of international law delegating to constitutional law the determination of the organ or person internationally competent to conclude a treaty on behalf of a state. It is true, of course, that the provisions of constitutions in no way exclude that possibility. It is equally possible, in theory, that such provisions are drawn up in the conviction that the rule of international law on the matter is sufficiently broad generally to *permit* the application of these provisions.

Chapter XVI

CASES OF NATIONAL COURTS

1. Preliminary Remarks

It is obvious that, in general, national courts will not have occasion to discuss the question whether a treaty which may be void under the domestic law of the state will also be void between the parties. In states where the courts are permitted to look into the constitutionality of treaties, they will pronounce themselves upon that matter alone, and their judgments cannot be expected often to be of direct interest to this discussion.[1] A systematic survey of cases confirms this expectation, but reveals also few instances where the courts have expressed opinions on the question of international law here at issue. To begin with, the first type of case will be illustrated.

In re Van Bellinghen, decided in 1950, the Court of Appeal of Paris refused to grant extradition which was requested on the basis of an exchange of notes between Belgium and France. The court found that the agreement had not been published and ratified, nor approved by a law, and could not, therefore, "override" Article 27 of the French Constitution which provided that treaties of certain kinds—and the exchange of notes in question was thought to be of such a kind—were not "définitifs" unless ratified on the basis of a law.[2] There was nothing in

---

[1] To the same effect, see *Harvard Research,* p. 1005. The opposite view is taken by de Naurois, but the evidence presented by that writer hardly supports the view taken by him. See de Naurois, *Les traités internationaux devant les juridictions nationales* (1934), pp. 169–172.

The following diplomatic exchange may also be noted. In 1899, it was suggested to the Chinese Minister to Washington that certain alleged treaty rights of Chinese citizens might be submitted for determination by the United States courts. In a reply of 25 January 1899, directed to the Secretary of State, the Chinese Minister stated *inter alia* that he could not, by any action on his part, "recognize the competency of a domestic tribunal of one of the parties to take such action as would irrevocably bind the other party to the convention." He concluded by saying: "... I apprehend you will not contend that adverse legislation or the judgment of a domestic tribunal can release a government from its solemn treaty obligations." Moore's *Digest,* vol. 5, p. 241.

[2] *I.L.R.,* 1950, pp. 276–278.

the language of the Court, as it appears in English translation in the *International Law Reports,* to suggest that the Court thought the exchange of notes invalid between the two States. Nor, indeed, was there any need for such a conclusion, since the Court was only asked to decide whether or not extradition should be granted.

In the above case, as in others, where an agreement has been refused application by a domestic court for the reason that it has been entered into in an unconstitutional manner, the question of the international validity is tacitly left for the executive branch of government to solve.[3] In the wake of such decisions there might consequently be expected diplomatic settlements bearing on the point of international law under discussion, unless, of course, the other party were always readily to accept the discontinued application of the treaty on the ground of its having been concluded unconstitutionally. In the apparent absence of published information as to diplomatic consequences, or lack of consequences, in this type of case, they must be deemed to be without any particular evidential interest.

There are nevertheless cases in which national courts have expressed their attitude to the problem under discussion. These opinions merit a certain consideration.

2. THE RELUCTANCE OF COURTS TO DECLARE TREATIES UNCONSTITUTIONAL

Before the cases of the last kind mentioned are considered, it may be noted that the United States Supreme Court, although it has had

---

[3] As additional examples, the following cases might be mentioned: *Four Packages of Cut Diamonds* v. *United States,* decided in 1919 by a United States Circuit Court of Appeals, see *Annual Digest,* 1919–1922, p. 314; *Lesec* v. *Luykfasseel,* decided in 1940 by the Court of Appeal of Brussels, see *Annual Digest,* 1919–1942, p. 10; *Benzoni* v. *Davidovici,* decided in 1950 by the Tribunal de Bonneville, see *I.L.R.,* 1951, p. 392; *Boileau* v. *Mélard,* decided by the Belgian Cour de Cassation in 1953, see *I.L.R.,* 1953, p. 409.

Examples of cases may here also be mentioned in which courts have barred application of a treaty, not because of unconstitutionality, but because of absence of enabling legislation. In these cases, too, the courts have not expressed any opinion regarding the international validity of the treaties, and the lack of correspondance between the treaty law and the domestic law is left a matter for diplomatic settlement: *Rhineland Ordinances Case,* decided by the German Reichsfinanzhof in 1926, see *Annual Digest,* 1925–1926, p. 9; *Public Prosecutor* v. *Managing Director of N.V. Zwitsersche Waschinrichting,* decided in 1934 by the Cantonal Court of the Hague, see *Annual Digest,* 1933–1934, p. 507; *Birma* v. *State,* decided in 1950 by the High Court of Rajasthan, see *I.L.R.,* 1950, p. 17.

many opportunities to declare various agreements void on the ground
of unconstitutionality, has always refrained from doing so.[4] It is possible,
of course, that the Court might have exercised this caution regardless
of any possible conviction that the international validity of an agreement would remain unaffected, even if the Court chose to void the
agreement municipally. The Court's caution must at least imply, however, that it is aware that grave complications on the international level
might follow a declaration making the treaty municipally void, for the
reason that the other party might reject the view that the agreement
should be internationally invalid because found entered into in violation of constitutional limitations upon competence or substance, or for
the reason that the executive branch of the United States Government
might not want to make such an assertion, on the one hand, and on the
other, might not be able to fulfil what it would consider to be an international obligation. The general tendency of courts to interpret provisions
of treaties as not violative of constitutional requirements, rather than
refusing to accord municipal effect to their provisions,[5] may perhaps be
given the same explanation.

Of greater interest than the circumstances referred to above are
certain cases in which domestic courts have used language possibly
reflecting their views upon the international law problem under discussion. These will now be examined.

3. Cases Possibly Reflecting the View that Constitutional Provisions are Internationally Relevant

In the case of *Co Chiong et al.* v. *The Mayor of Manila et al.*, the
Supreme Court of the Philippines held that treaties to which the

---

[4] See, for instance, *The United States* v. *Capps*, 348 U.S. 296 (1955), where the
Supreme Court affirmed the judgment of the appellate court, but expressly refrained
from ruling upon the holding below that an executive agreement was unconstitutional, 204 F.2d 655 (1953). These two decisions are noted in *A.J.I.L.*, vol. 49 (1955),
p. 407 and *ibid.*, vol. 48 (1954), p. 153, respectively. See also the case of *United
States* v. *Reid*, decided in 1934 by a Circuit Court of Appeals, *Annual Digest*, 1919–
1942, p. 6.

[5] See, for instance, *The Mazel Tow*, decided by the United States Supreme Court
in 1933, *Annual Digest*, 1931–1932, p. 3; *Steinberg* v. *Attorney-General*, decided in
1951 by the Supreme Court of Israel, *I.L.R.*, 1951, p. 10; *Sharma* v. *State of West
Bengal and Others*, decided in 1954 by the High Court of Calcutta, *I.L.R.*, 1954,
p. 272. See also *the Georges Pinson Case*, decided in 1928, in which an international
tribunal—a Franco-Mexican Mixed Claims Commission—referred to the "principle

Philippines was not a party could not invalidate a municipal ordinance, and added: "The Philippines is bound only by the treaties concluded and ratified in accordance with our Constitution."[6] The conclusion seems here inevitable that the Court had in mind obligations under international law.

The second Philippine pronouncement was made by the Court of First Instance of Manila, which, having discussed in some detail the constitutionality of an agreement entered into with the United States, and affirmed it, declared:

"As an international agreement concluded with prior authority from the Congress of the Philippines, it is binding upon the Philippine Government..."[7]

The conclusion, *e contrario,* might be argued to be that an agreement concluded without prior authority from the Congress would have been held not binding upon the Philippine Government.

In view of the circumstance that the international effect of unconstitutionality was probably not in the minds of the judges in either of the Philippine cases cited, it is perhaps not very significant, however, that the Courts chose the broad expressions used rather than narrowing their language to cover only the applicability of the agreements.

4. Cases from the British Commonwealth Pointing to the Executive Branch as Always Competent to Conclude Treaties

In a series of cases decided in states members of the British Commonwealth, various courts have held that the conclusion of treaties is a function attaching to the executive branch of government, and that, although parliamentary action may be needed for the implementation of treaties, such action is never required to give validity under international law to the same treaties.

In the case of *The King* v. *Burgess; Ex parte Henry,* decided in 1936,

---

of interpretation pursuant to which municipal law must, in doubtful cases, always be read in the sense that ensures its conformity with international law." *Annual Digest,* 1927–1928, p. 9.

[6] Judgment No. L–1891 of 31 March 1949. Quoted from *Replies from Governments to questionnaires of the International Law Commission,* U.N. Doc. A/CN.4/19 of 23 March 1950, p. 64. The quotation is also found in Briggs, *The Law of Nations* (2nd ed., London, 1953), p. 59.

[7] *USAFFE Veterans Ass. Inc.* v. *The Treasurer of the Philippines,* Judgment of 5 January 1956. Report in *A.J.I.L.,* vol. 50 (1956), p. 686.

the High Court of Australia stated that, although a law passed by the Parliament of the State in pursuance of a treaty might be invalid, the power with which the treaty had been made "would, if the treaty had been ratified, have cause for complaint." The Court continued to declare that relations between political communities are necessarily established by governments "which act for their people in relation to other peoples, rather than by legislatures which make laws for them." The court added:

"This fact of international intercourse is unaffected by the fact that a government may think it wise or (as in the United States of America) be bound, to obtain legislative approval of certain of its international acts . . ."[8]

The case of *Attorney-General for Canada* v. *Attorney-General for Ontario*, decided in 1937 by the Judicial Committee of the Privy Council, is well-known. In this case, the Court discussed the internationally binding effect and the applicability in Canada of certain I.L.O. conventions which had been ratified by the Federal Government of Canada. The Court said:

"Within the British Empire there is a well-established rule that the making of a treaty is an executive act, while the performance of its obligations, if they entail alteration of the existing domestic law, requires legislative action."

The Court continued:

". . . If the national executive, the government of the day, decide to incur the obligations of a treaty which involve alteration of law they have to run the risk of obtaining the assent of Parliament to the necessary statute or statutes . . ."

In the opinion of the Court, this risk could not be eliminated by the Government submitting the treaty to the approval of Parliament before binding the State by ratification. The Court said:

". . . It cannot be disputed that the creation of the obligations undertaken in treaties and the assent to their form and quality are the function of the executive alone. Once they are created, while they bind the State as against other contracting parties, Parliament may refuse to perform them and so leave the State in default . . ."[9]

An attempt to take a step back from the firm position assumed in the two preceding cases may perhaps be discerned in the case of *Bitter* v. *Secretary of State for Canada*, decided by the Exchequer Court of Canada in 1944. In this case, the Court cited a British constitutionalist

---

[8] *Annual Digest*, 1935–1937, p. 54, at pp. 63 and 64.
[9] *Ibid.*, p. 41 at p. 43.

to the effect that "where a treaty involves a charge upon the people, or a change in the general law of the land, it may be made, and be internationally valid, but it cannot be carried into effect without the consent of Parliament." The Court added, however:

"It has been the practice in such cases to give legislative approval to the Treaty. This view appears more consistent with the general concepts of English law than the statement under discussion."[1]

In *re Westerling,* decided in 1950 by the High Court of Singapore, one of the parties before the Court had discussed the treaty-making power of the King and had admitted that a treaty could not alter the law of the land, but urged that the government making it would probably be in a position to obtain any necessary change of the law from Parliament. The Court, discussing the issue with specific reference to a treaty of extradition, said:

"The powers to extradite all flow from the Act, and until the Act is applied the treaty remains in the clouds, or, at least, its existence and force are confined to the realms of international law."[2]

A case decided by the High Court of Calcutta in 1954 is also in line with the two first cases cited in this section. In the case of *Union of India* v. *Jain and Others,* the Indian Court stated firmly:

"Making a treaty is an executive act and not a legislative act. Legislation may be and is often required to give effect to the terms of a treaty . . .; but the treaty is complete without legislation."[3]

It can hardly be doubted that the two first and the two last of the Commonwealth cases cited above are expressive of a juridical opinion within the British Commonwealth to the effect that the executive branch of a government—at any rate one of a member of the Commonwealth[4]—is always competent under international law to bind the state by treaty, regardless of its possibilities of subsequently securing implementing legislation.

[1] *Ibid.,* 1943–1945, p. 264, at p. 265.
[2] *I.L.R.,* 1950, p. 82 at pp. 86 and 90.
[3] *Ibid.,* 1954, p. 256, at p. 257.
[4] In *Minister of the Interior* v. *Bechler and Others,* decided in 1948, a South African court used language which possibly implied that the position of executive governments of some states might differ from that of governments within the Commonwealth, *Annual Digest,* 1948, p. 237, at p. 244.

5. Re Vigoni

The Supreme Court of Chile had occasion, in 1950, to consider what organs may give binding promises on behalf of a state. In the case of *Re Vigoni,* the Court rejected a request by Argentine authorities for the extradition of an Italian citizen charged with smuggling. There existed no extradition treaty between the two States. Both had signed certain Conventions of 1928 and 1933, but, as Argentina had ratified neither of these, they were not decisive. In the absence of any conventional regulation of the matter, the Argentine authorities which had requested extradition had extended "an offer of reciprocity in like cases". This was not, however, satisfactory to the Chilean Court, which stated as follows:

"... as is well known, only the Head of the State may undertake commitments *vis-à-vis* other States. Matters of extradition are precisely the kind of question which must be determined by the interested Governments, whatever may be the part played in the matter by the courts in accordance with the laws of each country."[5]

6. Dyer v. Sims

An interesting discussion of the effect in international law of constitutional limitations upon the treaty-making power is found in two decisions examined below. The first of these is the case of *Dyer* v. *Sims,*[6] decided in 1951 by the Supreme Court of the United States. Admittedly this decision has regard only to relations between the States subject to the Federal Constitution of the United States, and is an expression of that law, but some of the problems which confronted the judges have parallels in the international sphere, and the answers are consequently of interest here. The circumstances were the following. With the authorization of the Congress of the United States, West Virginia and seven other States entered into a compact to control pollution in the Ohio River system. Subsequently, the West Virginia Supreme Court of Appeals found the act approving West Virginia's adherence invalid as violating the State's Constitution. On the question of whether West Virginia was nevertheless bound by the compact, the Supreme Court of the United States held:

"It requires no elaborate argument to reject the suggestion that an agreement solemnly entered into between States by those who alone have political

[5] *I.L.R.*, 1950, pp. 263 and 264.
[6] 341 U.S. 22 (1951).

authority to speak for a State can be unilaterally nullified, or given final meaning by an organ of one of the contracting States. A State cannot be its own ultimate judge in a controversy with a sister State."

The Court went on to say it would give weight to the interpretation that the highest court of a state gave to its constitution, but it would not be bound by it. After an examination of the West Virginian Constitution, and the relevant parts of the compact, the Supreme Court concluded that the compact did not conflict with the Constitution.

Two separate opinions written in the case are also of great interest. Mr. Justice Black stated that he did not think the Supreme Court of the United States had the power to interpret the Constitution of West Virginia. He thought it was obliged to accept the State Court's interpretation of the Constitution of that State, unless it was prepared to say that that interpretation was "a palpable evasion to avoid a federal rule". Mr. Justice Jackson, on the other hand, expressed himself as follows:

"West Virginia, for internal affairs, is free to interpret her own Constitution as she will. But if the compact system is to have vitality and integrity, she may not raise an issue *ultra vires,* decide it, and release herself from an interstate obligation ..."

He continued:

"West Virginia points to no provision of her Constitution which we may say was clear notice or fair warning to Congress or other States of any defect in her authority to enter into this Compact."

He concluded:

"Whatever she now says her Constitution means, she may not apply retroactively that interpretation to place an unforeseeable construction upon what the other States to this Compact were entitled to believe was a fully authorized act. Estoppel is not often to be invoked against a government. But West Virginia assumed a contractual obligation with equals ... After Congress and sister States had been induced to alter their positions and bind themselves to terms of a covenant, West Virgina should be estopped from repudiating her act."[7]

The following features of the decision are worth noting. All the judges thought the Constitution of the State relevant to the determination of the binding force of the compact. On the other hand, none of the judges was prepared to accept as conclusive in the interstate sphere,

[7] *Ibid.*

whatever interpretation the highest State Court of the State in question might choose to give to its Constitution. If that proposition was not thought acceptable in a federal system, where the states treat with each other on the basis of a very high degree of mutual confidence and communal solidarity, how much less acceptable would the proposition not have seemed to the judges if they had applied it to the international community? Justice Jackson's important consideration may also be stressed that a state should not be allowed to apply retroactively an unforeseeable construction of its constitution; finally, his adherence to the view that only notorious constitutional provisions are of any concern to other states, is noteworthy.[8]

7. Pokorny and Another v. Republic of Austria

The case of *Pokorny and Another* v. *Republic of Austria* has already been referred to in the discussion of the Austrian Constitution,[9] and it may be recalled here that the Austrian Supreme Court clearly demonstrated that, though it considered a particular agreement municipally void because made in an unconstitutional manner, it held the same agreement to be fully valid under international law. It should perhaps also be emphasized that the Austrian Court thought fit to advise the Government that a solution of the conflict that its judgment caused between the domestic law and the international law could be obtained by the adoption of a special federal law, modifying the municipal law to conform with the treaty.

8. Cases Upholding the Validity of Treaties Despite Violations of Limitations of Substance

In addition to the cases discussed above, three cases in which domestic courts had occasion to discuss the validity of treaties which were not contended to have been entered into in violation of constitutional limitations relating specifically to the competence of the treaty-making power, but the substance of which was contended to conflict with constitutional provisions, are in point. The first of these cases is one decided by the Colombian Supreme Court. It is of interest in this connexion especially because of the directness of the language used in it.

It appears that a provision of the Colombian Constitution as amended

---

[8] For a discussion of the doctrine of notoriety, see below, p. 382.

[9] Above, p. 240.

in 1910 fixed the boundaries of the State, and laid down that these could only be "altered" by treaties approved by the legislature. In a treaty of 24 March 1922, duly approved by the means of a law, large tracts of land were ceded by Colombia to Peru. It was contended before the Court that changes permitted by the Constitution were only small alterations and that the law was unconstitutional. In its judgment of 6 December 1930, the Court refused to decide the issue of constitutionality. One of the reasons advanced for this position merits quotation:

"... if the Treaty were held unconstitutional, there would be an insoluble conflict between the discharge of the international obligation assumed under it and obedience to the judgment of the Supreme Court. After the ratifications had been exchanged, the Treaty was an agreement between two States. One of them must not have the right to relieve itself of its obligations under that agreement, even by the action of its highest court."[1]

An attitude similar to that held by the Colombian Court may be discerned in the case of *United States* v. *Reid,* decided in 1934 by a United States Circuit Court of Appeal. It had been contended in this case that the substance of a certain treaty violated the Constitution of the United States. The Court, which cited the well-known case *Missouri* v. *Holland,* stated:

"It is doubtful if courts have power to declare the plain terms of a treaty void and unenforceable, thus compelling the nation to violate its pledged word, and thus furnishing a causus belli to the other contracting power."[2]

---

[1] *Annual Digest,* 1929–1930, p. 338. In 1914, the same Colombian Court had refused to examine the constitutionality of a law approving a treaty, but there is no report in the digest either of the grounds for that decision, or of the manner in which the Constitution was alleged to have been violated. It is stated, however, that two judges dissented strongly against the decision. *Ibid.* See also the case of *Colombian Mining and Exploration Co. Ltd,* decided in 1926, and digested in *Annual Digest* 1927–1928, p. 411; and see Gibson, "International law and Colombian Constitutionalism" in *A.J.I.L.,* vol. 36 (1942), pp. 614–620.

Fears that international complications might arise from the municipal voiding of a treaty may further be supposed to lie behind the refusal of the Court of Appeal of French West Africa to examine a contention to the effect that certain treaties invoked before it had not been ratified as required by the French constitution. The Court is reported to have decided that "les traités constituent des actes diplomatiques rentrant dans l'exercice du pouvoir souverain, dont le contrôle n'appartient pas aux tribunaux, que ceux-ci ne peuvent pas être appelés à en apprécier la validité;" Quoted from de Naurois, *Les traités internationaux devant les juridictions nationales* (1934), p. 169.

[2] See *Annual Digest,* 1919–1942, p. 6.

The Swiss case *Varini* v. *Paoletti* is finally of interest in this connexion. In this case, which concerned the enforcement in Switzerland of a judgment rendered by an Italian court, the Federal Tribunal of Switzerland ruled that the provisions of a treaty which was ratified by the Federal Assembly were binding upon the court. The Tribunal added: "They must accordingly be applied even when they are in conflict with Article 59 of the Federal Constitution",[3] an article which had been invoked in the case, and which provided that a debtor must be sued in the court of his domicile. As the court thus considered a treaty obligation, the substance of which violated the Constitution, valid in the domestic sphere, there is all the more reason to conclude that the court would have held the obligation valid in the international sphere.

9. Conclusions

On the basis of the limited material presented above, it is impossible to draw with confidence conclusions regarding the general attitude of national courts to the question of international law under discussion. The scarcity of relevant cases is not surprising. It is, indeed, remarkable that national courts have dealt with the question at all, and even more remarkable that, while no more than uncertain inferences of the international relevance of constitutional limitations upon competence could be drawn in two cases, the views of the Supreme Courts of the United States and Austria were clearly to the effect that treaties concluded in violation of such limitations might nevertheless be binding under international law upon the state.

A number of courts within the British Commonwealth further held that the executive government of a state—at any rate one which is a member of the British Commonwealth—is always competent under international law to assume treaty obligations on behalf of the state. Since the present constitutional patterns of such states appear to indicate that the executive branch of government possesses unlimited competence to assume treaty obligations on behalf of the state,[4] the views of the courts mean, in effect, that treaty obligations remain valid in international law even when their substance conflicts with existing domestic law.

The same position as that assumed by various Commonwealth courts is reflected in three different cases, in which courts of states not members

---

[3] *I.L.R.*, 1954, p. 264.
[4] Stewart, pp. 240–241.

of the Commonwealth were found to give effect to treaties the substance of which may have violated constitutional law. Thereby, it is submitted, they implicitly adhered to the view that the international validity of these treaties was unaffected by the possible infraction of constitutional law, and to the position that the domestic law must yield in order that a conflict with a foreign state might be avoided.

CHAPTER XVII

THE PERMISSIBILITY OF INQUIRING OF A GOVERMENT WHETHER IT IS MUNICI-PALLY AUTHORIZED TO CONCLUDE A PARTICULAR TREATY

The question is sometimes discussed whether it is permissible for a government to direct an inquiry to another government regarding that government's municipal authority to assume a particular treaty obligation. It is argued that if inquiries are, in fact, not tolerated, this circumstance, while in no way constituting conclusive evidence of the proposition that municipal laws regarding the conclusion of treaties are not accorded relevance internationally, would undoubtedly make that proposition a reasonable one.[1]

Some writers' treatment of the matter will first be taken up. Wohlmann maintains that an inquiry has never been regarded as forbidden intervention; not even an inquiry concerning the head of state.[2] Mervyn Jones admits that it is not a practice of states to make inquiries into constitutional requirements for the conclusion of treaties. The same commentator suggests—far too optimistically, it is submitted—that "the fact that no instances are recorded of inquiries to this effect merely shows that, in most cases, information is so readily available, and the laws so obvious, that no inquiries are necessary."[3] He ventures the opinion, finally, that "in cases of doubt a State is certainly entitled to rely on representations made by the State concerned . . .", although that proposition seems hard to reconcile with his conclusion that constitutional

---

[1] Kelsen seems isolated in taking the following extreme position:

" . . . when a state through its government concludes a treaty with another state, the government of the latter has no reason and is not entitled to question the constitutionality of the act of the former. But this does not prevent the government of a state after having concluded a treaty with another state, from declaring the treaty null and void because concluded in violation of its own constitution:" *Principles of International Law* (1952), p. 324.

[2] Wohlmann, p. 57, and references therein.

[3] Jones, pp. 153–155.

provisions on competence are decisive for the international validity of a treaty.

Professor Basdevant declares that inquiries would be undesirable. In the opinion of the learned French jurist, ratification by the head of state ought to be relied upon with confidence:

"L'autre État n'a pas à la contrôler, à vérifier son exactitude constitutionelle. Un État ne doit pas s'immiscer dans les questions douteuses sur les limites au pouvoir de traiter du chef d'un État étranger: ces questions douteuses doivent être traitées dans l'ordre interne . . ."[4]

Other authorities have maintained with even greater emphasis that inquiries would not be tolerated, and have adduced this circumstance as an argument against the international relevance of constitutional provisions on the conclusion of treaties. Thus, Sir Gerald Fitzmaurice whose view carries the greater weight because of his practical experience, states:

"An intolerable situation would, it seems, be created if states were forced to make minute and often invidious inquiries before they could feel certain of their position."[5]

What answer, if any, is actually provided by the practice of states? An incident from the 18th century may first be reviewed. In 1793, the French Minister to Washington requested an exequatur for a consul whose commission was addressed to the Congress of the United States. Mr. Jefferson, Secretary of State, declared that an exequatur would be issued by the President only for a commission correctly addressed. He is further reported to have stated:

". . . as the President was the only channel of communication between the United States and foreign nations, it was from him alone 'that foreign nations or their agents are to learn what is or has been the will of the nation;' that whatever he communicated as such, they had a right and were bound to consider 'as the expression of the nation;' and that no foreign agent could be 'allowed to question it', or 'to interpose between him and any other branch of government, under the pretext of either's transgressing their functions.' "[6]

It accordingly appears that the United States Government would not have tolerated any inquiries regarding the competence of the President. A similar attitude was assumed in a later incident. In 1817, the Rush–Bagot agreement concerning armaments on the Great Lakes had been

---

[4] Basdevant, p. 581.

[5] Fitzmaurice, p. 135. See also Vitta, pp. 69 and 79; Fairman, p. 444; and Hendry, *Treaties and Federal Constitutions* (1955), p. 155.

[6] Moore's *Digest*, vol. 4, p. 680; *cf. ibid.*, pp. 781–782.

concluded between the United States and Great Britain by means of an exchange of notes which had the formal approval of Congress, but was not formally ratified. On 23 November 1864, the United States Minister to London, acting upon instructions, gave the required six months' notice of the United States' wish to terminate the agreement. This action was subsequently "adopted and ratified" by Congress. In view of changed circumstances, however, Mr. Seward, Secretary of State, declared early in March, 1865, that the United States was willing to preserve the convention "practically in force". The British Government, thereupon, inquired whether this was intended as a formal withdrawal of the denunciation, and was apparently given an affirmative answer. In a report of 1892, however, Mr. Foster, Secretary of State, commenting upon the incident, declared that the British Government was "incompetent to inquire" into the authority of the Secretary of State, and "could only accept and respect the withdrawal as a fact." He stated further that the question of competence, "being a matter of domestic administration, affecting the internal relations of the executive and legislative powers" in no way concerned Great Britain.[7]

The evidence afforded by the incidents described above is not contradicted by the circumstance that, in 1907, the United States Secretary of State, Mr. Adee, is reported to have transmitted a memorandum concerning the authority of his government to conclude executive agreements, to the Swedish Chargé d'Affaires, *in reply to an inquiry of the latter*.[8] The Swedish inquiry was one, it appears, which had no reference to any contemplated agreement with the United States Government. Rather, it was part of a general survey of foreign constitutional provisions on the matter, undertaken because the question of an amendment of the relevant provision of the Swedish Constitution was expected to be raised in the legislature.[9]

A recent official United States pronouncement again supports the position that foreign states should not concern themselves with questions relating to the constitutional competence of the United States Government. With a letter of 14 December 1949 to the late Professor Clyde Eagleton, the Department of State enclosed a memorandum, containing some comments upon the formula "subject to approval", used in modern treaty practice. The following passage is taken from the memorandum:

[7] The quotations are from Moore's *Digest*, vol. 5, pp. 169–170; the case is cited by Fairman, p. 444 and by Hendry, p. 155.

[8] See Hackworth's *Digest*, vol. 5, p. 391.

[9] Swedish Foreign Office, File 6 C 1.

"In any event, the national action which a particular government considers necessary in order to reach the point where it may take the requisite international action to become a full-fledged party to an agreement *is not the concern of the other governments* eligible to become parties to the agreement. So long as the terms of the agreement with respect to the method by which governments may become parties thereto are couched in sufficiently precise language, the way should be left open as far as practicable for each of the governments to handle its national procedure as it sees fit. That would seem to be the primary, if not the whole, object of the flexible formula which has lately gained popularity among negotiators; . . .[1]

A case decided by a Philippine court, and quoted above,[2] is of interest in this connexion as well. The plaintiff in this case having raised the point that a relevant agreement had been signed on behalf of the United States by the Secretary of the Treasury rather than the Secretary of State, the court declared that anyone could be appointed to sign an agreement on behalf of a state. It added:

". . . as correctly pointed out by the defendants' counsel, 'it is not for the Philippine Government or any of its organs to determine whether or not the Agreement contravenes the laws of the United States. Only the United States Government may make that determination. For courtesy and respect on the part of the Philippines require that it should not impose its own interpretation on the laws of the United States . . .' "[3]

Though the court did not expressly contend that the United States would be irrevocably bound under international law by an interpretation given by the executive branch of its government to its constitution at the conclusion of a particular agreement, the logical implication of the statement is obviously that a foreign government, being, in the opinion of the court, forbidden to challenge the opposite government's interpretation of the constitution on the basis of which that government operates, must be entitled to rely upon that interpretation.

If the evidence adduced above permits doubt that there is a general legal rule—and not only one of comity[4]—forbidding inquiries, such must be rare, indeed.[5] In view of the extreme uncertainty attaching to

---

[1] United States, *Treaty Practice*, p. 53. Emphasis supplied.

[2] Above, p. 251 and p. 91, note 1.

[3] *USAFFE Veterans Ass. Inc.* v. *The Treasurer of the Philippines*. Judgment of 5 January 1956. Report in *A.J.I.L.*, vol. 50 (1956), p. 686.

[4] See Pallieri, p. 476.

[5] "Les gouvernements ont confiance les uns dans les autres; si un gouvernement se déclare prêt à ratifier et à faire exécuter la convention, l'autre ne recherche pas s'il en a le pouvoir, d'après sa constitution interne": Cottez, *De l'intervention du*

the precise meaning of many constitutional provisions on the conclusion
of treaties, the circumstance must be considered of some importance that
the point of constitutionality hardly ever seems to be raised, or to
prevent governments from confidently entering into agreements with
states, such as the United States, whose constitutional provision on the
making of treaties has a literal meaning that is plain and even
notorious, but a real meaning that can hardly be assessed.[6] It is believed
that this circumstance must make it probable that governments are
confident that the competence under international law to conclude a
treaty is, at any rate, not directly dependent upon the competence
existing under constitutional law, or the strict compliance with procedures established in municipal law.

pouvoir exécutif et du parlement dans la conclusion et la ratification des traités
(1920), p. 138. See also Anzilotti, p. 364. But Mr. Alfaro, speaking in the International
Law Commission in 1950 seems to have asserted that "states invariably asked for
information as to the capacity of the other party to make the treaty under negotiation": U.N. *Doc.* A/CN.4/SR.52, 22 June 1950, p. 23.

[6] See McDougal and Lans, "Treaties and Congressional-Executive or Presidential
Agreements: Interchangeable Instruments of National Policy" in *Yale Law Journal*,
vol. 54 (1945), pp. 181 ff.

CHAPTER XVIII

DEPOSITARIES' CONCERN FOR THE CONSTITUTIONALITY OF TREATIES

While the foregoing analysis has had primarily in view parties in bilateral relation, it is clear that the problem and the reasoning is the same in multilateral treaty relations.

When one government is made the depositary of instruments relating to a multilateral treaty, there has merely occurred a centralization of some tasks which would have otherwise belonged to each party to the multilateral treaty. The depositary, acting on behalf of all the parties, receives the various instruments by which final consent is expressed by states, and examines the regularity of these documents.

It has been suggested, probably with good reason, that the control and judgment exercised by the depositary is not customarily of a final nature.[1] According to this view, the contracting parties—however that concept is defined[2]—charge an organ, such as a government, with various tasks as a depositary, but retain final judgment. Appeals by entities that desire to adhere to a multilateral convention, as well as protests from states which are parties to the convention may, therefore, be lodged against the determination made by the depositary, and decided by the contracting parties.[3]

Whether a government or an international organ, the depositary

---

[1] Dehaussy, "Le dépositaire de traités" in *R.G.D.I.P.*, vol. 56 (1952), p. 506. See also the view expressed by the Government of Israel, reported above, p. 201, note 4.

[2] See Oppenheim, vol. 1, p. 904, note 1.

[3] Support for the view advanced is found in a communication of 26 August 1930 from the United States Secretary of State to the Danish Minister to Washington. The Danish Government, having offered to issue a Royal full power to its Minister to Washington to adhere on behalf of Iceland to a multilateral convention, for which the United States Government was the depositary, the Secretary of State replied:

"... the Department, which, after all, as the depository of the convention, is but the mouthpiece of all the contracting Governments, does not insist upon having such full power in the absence of any comment having been received from any Government as to the sufficiency of the notice of adherence." See Hackworth's *Digest*, vol. 5, p. 80.

will nevertheless normally render a preliminary judgment—which becomes final unless appealed from or protested against—upon the validity of instruments submitted to it for deposit. Its further duties as a depositary, such as the declaring of a treaty in force when a specified number of states have become parties, will frequently depend upon such judgments. It would be of interest to find out to what extent, if any, depositaries concern themselves with the question of the municipal regularity of instruments expressing final consent.

A member of the legal division of the Secretariat of the United Nations states in an article published in 1951 that, in exercising the functions of a depositary, the Secretariat examines whether instruments of ratification, acceptance, or adherence emanate from a "competent authority",[4] but the author of the article does not report what, in the opinion of the Secretariat, constitutes a "competent authority". Judging by another author's treatment of the same matter, however, the Secretariat does not inquire into the constitutionality of instruments which express final consent, but is satisfied that these are internationally valid if emanating from the head of state, the head of government, or the foreign minister of a state.[5] The same writer ventures to suggest that the depositary organ ought to undertake a more rigid control. He is content to propose, however, that the depositary should refuse to accept an instrument emanating from the head of state only when the instrument is given in manifest violation of the constitutional law of the state.[6]

There appears to be only scant material on the principles followed by governments acting as depositaries, and what has been found relates to the practice of the Government of the United States.

An incident connected with the Washington Conference of 1922 on

---

[4] Leriche, "L'évolution récente de la société internationale et les traités multilatéraux" in *Revue de droit international, de sciences diplomatiques et politiques*, vol. 29 (1951), p. 35. Similarly, in case of doubt, the Secretariat must examine the question of the statehood of a community which seeks to deposit an instrument of accession to a treaty open only to states. See Schachter, "The Development of International Law Through the Legal Opinions of the United Nations Secretariat" in *B.Y.I.L.*, vol. 25 (1948), p. 112, note 3.

[5] It was reported by a United States Consul at Geneva, however, that the League of Nations Secretariat considered a ratification to be a "solemn and formal declaration given by a person or persons who, by virtue of domestic constitutional law, are entitled to represent the country concerned in its relations with other States." Quoted from Hackworth's *Digest*, vol. 5, p. 50.

[6] Dehaussy, p. 506; *cf.* Basdevant, p. 582; and see below, p. 382.

the limitation of armaments is of some interest.[7] One resolution of the conference provided that the parties to the conference should supply each other with lists of all treaties and agreements they had made with or regarding China. Switzerland being invited to adhere to the resolution, the Swiss Foreign Minister notified the American Minister to Berne on 27 June 1922 that the Swiss Federal Council had decided to adhere, and a copy of the only Swiss treaty with China was appended to its note. Subsequently the Swiss Government discovered that its adherence was illegal, because not effected in conformity with the Swiss Constitution. A secretary of the Swiss Legation at Washington called on the Department of State on 23 February and 6 March 1923, explaining the above circumstances and "asked how Switzerland should proceed to withdraw its adherence." He was informally advised that the Swiss Government should notify the American Minister in Switzerland about the difficulty, and ask that the Swiss adherence be cancelled or withdrawn. He was further informed that "such a note would be communicated to the other powers notified of the Swiss adherence and that if they raised no objection the Swiss adherence would undoubtedly be regarded as annulled."

No note of the kind recommended was addressed to the United States Minister, and when, in April 1929, the latter inquired whether Switzerland considered itself a party to the resolution, or desired to withdraw its note of adherence, the Swiss Government replied that it had supplied a copy of the only treaty it had with China, that the other parties had not communicated their treaties with China to the Swiss Government, and that the Swiss Political Department felt, therefore, that it was not called upon "to withdraw at the present date the declaration, which has always remained a dead letter."

Undoubtedly the incident described above reflects the opinion of the State Department, acting as depositary, that a constitutional deficiency in the adherence did not affect the validity of the adherence under international law; release from the obligation under that law could only be obtained by agreement with the other states. Without a doubt, too, the Swiss Government shared this view in 1923. The meaning of the Swiss reply in 1929 is somewhat more difficult to ascertain. Presumably the Swiss Government considered its own declaration a "dead letter" for the very reason that it advanced, namely, non-fulfilment by the other

---

[7] See Hackworth's *Digest*, vol. 5, pp. 83–84. The quotations in the text are from that source. The incident is cited in Lauterpacht's *First Report*, p. 164.

parties. It is conceivable, however, that, without advancing any express grounds for such an opinion, the Government meant to say that the declaration of adherence was a dead letter because unconstitutional.[8]

A memorandum of 1930, addressed by the Secretary of State of the United States to the Danish Minister to Washington has been cited in an earlier part of this discussion. In this connexion it is of interest to note the following passage of the memorandum:

> "That there might well be some uncertainty as to the degree of adherence given by a mere notice of adherence may be illustrated by the case of a notification given to the Government of the United States by a depository Government of the adherence of a third Government to a multilateral treaty, where, when an occasion arose to apply the treaty, it was stated in effect that ratification with the approval of the national legislative body was required to make the adherence complete and definitive, although no mention had been made in the notice of adherence that the adherence was subject to ratification."[9]

The incident described in the memorandum seems to indicate that, in exercising depositary functions, the State Department does not closely examine the constitutionality of instruments of adherence.[1]

When applied to at least one treaty for which the United States Government acts as a depositary, namely, the Charter of the United Nations, the observation made in the preceding paragraph has strong support in a detailed discussion by Professor Kopelmanas.[2] Paragraph 1 of Article 110 of the Charter provides that the Charter shall be ratified by the signatory states "in accordance with their respective constitutional processes"; paragraph 2 of the same Article lays down that ratifications shall be deposited with the Government of the United States, which shall notify all the signatory states of each deposit; paragraph 3, finally, prescribes that the Charter shall come into force upon the deposit of ratifications by the five great powers, and by a majority of the other signatory states.

It has been suggested by Kelsen that the second paragraph cited might be interpreted to mean that the Government of the United States, as the depositary, was obligated to accept instruments of ratification only when

---

[8] This seems to be the interpretation given to the answer in Guggenheim, vol. I, p. 64, note 52.

[9] Hackworth's *Digest*, vol. 5, p. 80.

[1] The memorandum does not, unfortunately, reveal how the Government of the United States and other parties to the treaty reacted to the notice that the adherence had not been definitive under the internal law of the state concerned.

[2] Kopelmanas, *L'Organisation des Nations Unies* (1947), vol. 1, pp. 121 ff.

it thought they satisfied the requirement of constitutionality.[3] Kopelmanas, on the other hand, does not attribute to the United States Government the power of refusing municipally irregular ratifications.[4] He attempts to prove that several instruments submitted were, indeed, unconstitutional, and he notes that the question of their regularity was not even raised. He suggests further that the only way out would have been to give the United States an absolute right or the duty to decide on the regularity of ratifications,[5] a solution he finds inconceivable in the present state of international relations. It may be added that, although in this case the right or the duty of the depositary to reject unconstitutional ratifications may be subject to discussion, the right of the signatories, including, indeed, the United States Government in that capacity, to raise the question of the regularity of ratifications cannot be doubted, and whether or not Kopelmanas is correct in maintaining that some instruments were unconstitutional, it is believed significant, at least, that apparently attention was not officially called to the question of the regularity of these instruments.

It is submitted that the rather meager material described, bearing on the attitudes of depositaries and of signatories of the United Nations Charter, points in the same direction as the discussion on inquiries, namely, that states feel confident of the binding effect under international law of expressions of final consent, although these may not have been given in perfect conformity with the municipal law of the state concerned.

[3] Kelsen, *The Law of the United Nations* (1950), p. 58.

[4] Kopelmanas, p. 123; see also Parry, p. 167, note 52.

[5] "...un droit de regard absolu sur la façon dont ont été acquises les ratifications de la Charte par les autres Etats signataires..." *Op. cit.*, p. 123. As to the Polish ratification of the Charter, see Skubiszewski, "Poland's Constitution and the Conclusion of Treaties" in *Jahrbuch für internationales Recht*, 7 Band (1958), p. 221.

CHAPTER XIX

THE EVIDENCE OF FULL POWERS,
TREATIES AND RATIFICATIONS

1. PRELIMINARY REMARKS

In examining the question of the relevance in customary international law of constitutional requirements for the conclusion of treaties, writers have often looked to instruments of treaties, full powers and ratification for possible clues to the attitudes of governments.[1] What kind of evidence may these documents be expected to yield? It appears that what is specifically looked for are express clauses in full powers and treaties, requiring the fulfilment of procedures—chiefly that of parliamentary approval—which must be satisfied under the domestic law of the state or states in question. In instruments of ratification, similarly, express references to the prior satisfaction of domestic procedures are sought.

The idea underlying the approach is this: were it to be found that a great many treaties expressly require the satisfaction of domestic law procedures, the conclusion might be drawn that governments consider such procedures relevant internationally. Conversely, the argument runs, were it to appear that mention is hardly ever made of domestic law procedures in instruments of full power, treaties and ratifications, the inference would be that such procedures are of no concern between states.

According to another train of thought, however, the inclusion of express requirements of this kind in some treaties would be inexplicable, if, under customary international law, the same requirement existed anyway: the function of the clauses is then understood to be that of derogating from a subsidiary customary rule. Consonant with this approach is the view, according to which the absence of express clauses or references relating to domestic requirements points to the existence of a rule of international law which makes such requirements relevant between states; express clauses and references are redundant.

---

[1] De Visscher, p. 147; Chailley, p. 189; Bittner, p. 88.

The warning has frequently been sounded that clauses of treaties, full powers and ratifications, being influenced by traditions of the past, must not be interpreted too literally. It seems to have escaped attention, however, that, in strict logic, it is impossible to know whether the presence of an express clause or reference is expressive of a rule of customary international law, or is devised to derogate from one, and that the absence of such clause or reference similarly is logically compatible with either position in international law. In spite of this fundamental reservation, there may be some purpose in the approach described.

It is true that, were it to be found simply that express clauses regarding and references to constitutional requirements are hardly ever found, this circumstance would not allow any conclusion. A finding, on the other hand, to the effect that there is a wide use of such clauses and references might perhaps justify the deduction that governments are anxious that their own constitutional procedures should be relevant internationally, and conceivably, that such relevance is not objected to by other parties. This formulation of the possible results of an inquiry is deliberately guarded. It cannot be taken for granted, as is occasionally done,[2] that the clauses and references actually have the effect of making compliance with all or some constitutional requirements necessary to the international validity of treaties.[3] It is further possible, however, that the formulation of some clauses, or the background or application of certain clauses, as well as other facts, may reveal something about the attitudes of governments toward the legal problem under consideration. For these reasons, an examination of various treaty clauses and references of the relevant kinds, and their use, will now be undertaken.

It has been suggested by some writers[4] that a distinction should be made between such references to constitutional procedures as are made in full powers and instruments of ratification on the one hand, and, on the other, those that are made in the texts of treaties. While the former types of documents are issued unilaterally, the second type is the outcome of deliberations between subjects of international law and therefore, it is suggested, of greater importance as evidence. There is not much force in this argument, for while full powers and instruments of ratification are the result of unilateral drafting, they are nevertheless

[2] See Jones, p. 121.
[3] See the conclusion below, p. 120; *cf.* Kopelmanas, p. 123.
[4] De Visscher, pp. 132 and 138.

exposed to the approval or disapproval of another government. Although this step in the procedure may normally be carried out in a perfunctory manner, treaty texts and minutes of the exchange of ratifications frequently recite that the full powers and instruments of ratification, respectively, have been found in "good and due form". Indeed, if any distinction were called for, there would perhaps be some reason for attaching special weight to the insertion or omission in instruments of ratification of references to the satisfaction of constitutional procedures. If constitutional requirements, or some of them, should be relevant internationally, it might conceivably be expected that this circumstance need not be mentioned in treaty texts or full powers, since it ought to be invariably known anyway. On the other hand, a government would always then need to ascertain that the requisite constitutional procedures have actually been satisfied. Though in many cases such information may no doubt be gained by its diplomatic representatives in official records of the foreign state, it would not seem far-fetched to expect ready references in the instruments of ratification.

When, below, as in most inquiries into the matter, the texts of treaties form the main object of study, the reason is simply that they are abundantly available in published form, while instruments of full powers and ratification are difficult to find.

2. Full Powers

It is impossible to assess with any precision how frequently references are made in instruments of full power to a need for the satisfaction of procedures required under domestic law. There seems to be general agreement among writers, however, that these references are rare. An examination of some fifteen full powers which were issued by various governments in connexion with the conclusion of treaties with the Swedish Government in 1951 included only one instrument in which the requirement of parliamentary approval was stated.[5] On the basis of authorititative information, it may also safely be stated that Swedish full powers hardly ever reserve parliamentary action.

The assertion has been made that the full powers issued by the Soviet Union specify that the acts signed by the person who is designated in

---

[5] This was a full power issued on 29 August 1951 in the name of the King of Iraq for the conclusion of an agreement with Sweden on air transport. The agreement which was signed on 28 October 1951 is found in *S.Ö.F.*, 1952, No. 48.

the full powers should be ratified in the manner prescribed by the laws of the Soviet Union.[6] Although at least two different types of printed forms of full powers currently used by the Soviet Government omit this specification,[7] the correctness of the assertion is not doubted.

For the understanding of the clause thus used in one type of Soviet full powers, certain views expressed in a book published in 1950 by a Soviet lawyer are of interest. In a discussion of the effect of treaty clauses regarding domestic procedures—and it is not unreasonable to assume that similar references inserted in full powers are covered by the discussion—that writer suggests that an express clause requiring the ratification by a *particular* authority has the effect only of justifying the other party in rejecting an instrument which emanates from another authority than that which is indicated. Treaties which contain only references to the domestic law of a party concerned, do not, however, in the opinion of the same writer, justify another party in verifying that the constitutional procedures for ratification have actually been observed, provided that the instrument of ratification emanates from the highest organ of state power, to which the right of ratification is supposed to belong.[8] Whatever the merits of this theory generally,[9] it very likely conforms with the construction that the Soviet Government places upon its own practice. Against that background, it would not seem warranted to impute to the Government of the Soviet Union, on the basis of the form of some of their full powers, the attitude that procedures, the satisfaction of which is required under the domestic law of the Soviet Union, should be relevant internationally.

The observation may be correct that Argentine full powers generally contain a reservation making the act of the plenipotentiary *"ad referen-*

---

[6] De Visscher, p. 137.

[7] One printed form used in 1958 was found to provide that the Council of Ministers of the Soviet Union empowers the person designated to sign a treaty on a specified matter with a specified state, without providing for ratification in conformity with domestic law. In the particular case in which this form was found to have been used, the treaty provided expressly that it should be ratified in the manner prescribed in the respective municipal laws. Another printed form, used for a treaty which entered into force by signature and which made no reference to municipal law, was issued in the name of the *Ministry* of Foreign Affairs, empowered the designated person to sign a treaty on a specified matter with a specified state, contained no reference to municipal law and was signed by the Minister of Foreign Affairs and countersigned by the head of the treaty-law division.

[8] Polents, *Ratifikatsiia mezhdunarodnykh dogovorov*, pp. 31–32.

[9] See below, p. 290.

dum".[1] The relevance of the observation as evidence in the present context is doubtful, however, for this expression usually has regard to the procedure of international ratification or approval,[2] and no reason has been adduced why it should be attributed a different meaning in Argentine full powers.

Some comments are merited by a statement of Crandall, which has been cited by some writers.[3] This American authority has expressed the view that the requirement of the approval of the United States Senate, if not expressly stated, should be read into all treaties and full powers issued for the conclusion of treaties on behalf of the United States.[4] Is this contention still justified?

To the extent that the United States Government continues to insert this express proviso in full powers, the purpose is possibly that of seeking to make the approval of the Senate a condition under international law. Such a proviso may still conceivably with reason be read into full powers which are silent on the point, and which are issued for the conclusion of a "treaty" as that term is understood in the constitutional law of the United States.[5] In practice, this is likely to mean compacts labelled "treaties". It would be a serious mistake, however, to assume that a tacit reservation of Senate approval could be read into full powers issued for the conclusion of other international compacts to which the United States intend to become a party. Furthermore, as will be seen

[1] See de Visscher (p. 137), who refers to an Argentine model full power quoted in Genet, *Traité de diplomatie et de droit diplomatique*, vol. 2 (1931), p. 238. The only recent Argentine full power found in the Swedish Foreign Office did not confirm the observation. It was issued by President Peron on 23 January 1951 for the conclusion of a protocol supplementing an earlier agreement with Sweden on commerce and payments. The protocol, on the other hand, expressly reserved approval, in the Swedish text "by the appropriate [vederbörande] authorities", in the Spanish text by "las autoridades competentes de ambos países." (See *S.Ö.F.*, 1951, p. 13.)

[2] See *Notes on the practice of the United Nations Secretariat in relation to certain questions raised in connexion with the articles on the Law of Treaties*, submitted by the Secretariat to the International Law Commission, U.N. Doc. A/CN.4/121, 23 June 1959. See also *Report of the International Law Commission Covering the Work of its Eleventh Session, 20 April to 26 June 1959*, U.N. Doc. A/CN.4/122, 2 July 1959, p. 44; Wilcox, *The ratification of international conventions* (1935); and above, p. 72, note 6; *cf.*, however, Camara, *The ratification of international treaties* (1949), p. 110.

[3] De Visscher, p. 137; Chailley, p. 192.

[4] See Crandall, *Treaties, Their Making and Enforcement* (2nd ed., 1916), p. 94.

[5] For a compilation of various types of full powers in use by the United States, see *Enabling Instruments of Members of the United Nations. Part I: The United States of America* (Carnegie Endowment, 1951), p. 110 ff.

below, in spite of the express or tacit reservations as to Senate approval in the full powers issued for the conclusion of "treaties", the United States are by no means inclined to allow another party to determine for itself what steps are required under the domestic law of the United States.[6]

In conclusion, it may safely be said that full powers only rarely contain express references to procedures required under the domestic laws for the conclusion of treaties. Such references must sometimes be understood to mean that the principals desire to make the satisfaction of these requirements relevant to the international validity of the treaty. The conclusion is further possible, though not inevitable, that the acceptance of such full powers indicates that the receiving governments do not object to the domestic requirements occasionally being made relevant internationally.[7] The findings made above do not, on the other hand, permit any conclusions concerning the attitude of states toward the relevance of domestic requirements, when no express references to such requirements are made in full powers.

3. INSTRUMENTS OF RATIFICATION

Difficulties caused by a shortage of published material arise not only in an inquiry into the formulation of full powers, but are also encountered in an examination of instruments of ratification.[8] In spite of the limited amount of material, which offers no possibility of statistical data concerning the presence of express references to domestic procedures, it appears to be generally admitted that such references are as rare in instruments of ratification as they are in full powers.

It is worth noting that, according to reliable information, references are never included in Swedish instruments of ratification,[9] although, especially in the period between the two world wars, the treaties signed by the Swedish Government frequently made parliamentary approval an express condition, when such approval was called for under the domestic law of the State.

On the other hand, an examination of a number of instruments by which the United States have entered into treaty obligations shows that that State frequently—perhaps consistently—makes mention of the

---

[6] See above, p. 263.
[7] See below, p. 290.
[8] *Cf.* Bittner, p. 94, note 352.
[9] To the same effect, Sundberg, *Lag och Traktat* (2nd ed., Stockholm, 1942), p. 31.

approval of the Senate where such approval has been given.[1] A similar practice appears to have been followed by the United States in documents by which the President has signified the "acceptance" by the United States of an international compact. In such documents, the President may refer, not to Senate approval, but to his being authorized by means of a prior joint resolution of the House of Representatives and the Senate.[2]

Although no means have been found of verifying the contention[3] that other states of the American continent follow practices similar to those of the United States, it is possibly correct.

As will be noted,[4] treaties sometimes contain express clauses providing for entry into force upon notification by one of the parties, or of both, that constitutional requirements have been satisfied, or, that parliamentary approval has been obtained. In these cases, the notes are presumably of the contents thus required.

Neither the rarity in instruments of ratification or approval of references to procedures required under domestic laws for the conclusion of treaties, nor the common presence of such references in the instruments issued by a few states, give rise to an inference as to the attitude of states generally, or American states, in particular, to the question of the relevance in international law of procedures constitutionally required for the making of treaties.

In the cases where an express clause in a treaty seeks to make domestic procedures relevant internationally, evidence of the satisfaction of such procedures may have been considered desirable for the convenience of the other party. They permit no conclusions, however, as to the view taken by the government in question of the position under the customary rule of international law. In other cases, it may be tempting to see in these references evidence that the issuer considered the domestic procedures relevant for the other party by virtue of customary international law. The explanation is also possible, however, that the reference is merely given for information, without any inference that the other party should satisfy itself that the domestic procedures have actually been observed.

---

[1] See *Enabling Instruments of Members of the United Nations.* Part I: *The United States of America* (Carnegie Endowment, 1951), at pp. 1, 2, 28, 46, 57, 68.

[2] See *ibid.,* pp. 32, 48, 52, 56, 63, 67.

[3] See de Visscher, p. 138.

[4] Below, pp. 280 and 296.

4. TREATIES

While an examination of instruments of full powers and ratifications involves considerable difficulties, the examination of the texts of large numbers of treaties is easily undertaken, because of the many comprehensive treaty collections in existence. Accordingly, the disagreement among writers on the question whether or not treaties only rarely contain express clauses by which compliance with some domestic procedures is made a condition for the entry into force of the treaty would seem superfluous.[5] The simple reading of the preambles and final clauses of a large number of treaties gives a fairly clear picture of state practice in this matter.

In connexion with an examination of numerous treaties, made for the purpose of finding out, *inter alia,* how frequently treaties were made subject to ratification,[6] the present writer noted also the frequency with which the need for satisfaction of domestic procedures of some kind was expressed. The material examined consisted of some 1,760 treaties published in the *League of Nations Treaty Series*[7] and some 1,300 treaties printed in the *United Nations Treaty Series*.[8]

It appeared that, in different sections of this considerable body of material, the proportion of treaties which referred, in one way or another, to domestic law procedures authorizing the conclusion of treaties varied between 5 and 15 %.[9] While these figures justify the general conclusion that references to domestic law procedures authorizing the undertaking of international obligations are an infrequent feature in treaties, certain other conclusions emerging from the examination are also worth noting.

The relevant references in the League material were considerably more homogeneous in type than those in the *United Nations Treaty Series*. In treaties registered with the League, the references appeared almost exclusively in treaties which were subject to ratification. The majority of them prescribed that the treaty was to be ratified in accordance with the constitution—or laws—of the respective parties.[1]

---

[5] The rarity of such clauses is maintained by Bittner, pp. 89–93; for another opinion, see Wohlmann, p. 24; Polents, p. 31 and de Visscher, p. 149.

[6] See Blix, pp. 361 ff.   [7] Vols. 130–202.

[8] Vols. 1–81.   [9] *Cf.* Bittner, p. 91.

[1] Article II of a Supplementary Convention of 6 May 1936 to an extradition treaty between the United States and Denmark may be quoted as an example:

"The present Convention ... shall be ratified according to the respective laws of the two Contracting Parties ..." (*L.N.T.S.*, vol. 172 (1936), p. 203.)

It was conspicuous that the insertion of references of this type was more common in the practice of certain states—in particular the United States, Latin American states and the Baltic states—than of others.

A minority of the relevant references in the League material consisted of clauses which provided specifically that the treaties were to be ratified with the approval of the legislature of either party or both parties.[2]

It may be assumed that generally, if not perhaps consistently, this requirement was due to a need for parliamentary action under the domestic law in question. This was true, for instance, as regards the Swedish treaties which formed more than one half of all the treaties which made references specifically to parliamentary action. The reason for this peculiar preponderance lay in the circumstance that the Swedish Constitution, in contrast to practically all other constitutions, required and requires the Government expressly to indicate in the texts of treaties the need for the approval of the Swedish Parliament, when such approval is called for under the Constitution.[3]

In the United Nations material, the two types of references discussed above continued to occur, especially in treaties to which the United States, Latin American states, the Philippines or China were parties. In contrast, it is of interest to note that, despite the fact that there had been no modification in the Swedish constitutional provision on the conclusion of treaties, the treaties concluded by Sweden no longer constituted a conspicuous group as regards references to the need for parliamentary approval or constitutional action.[4] Some other features in the United Nations material may also be noted. Thus, a distinct

---

[2] In illustration, the following clause contained in an agreement of 22 December 1931 between Great Britain and Estonia, for the Disposal of Estates of Deceased Seamen, may be quoted:

"The present Convention shall come into force ten days after notification to the Government of the United Kingdom of Great Britain and Northern Ireland of the approval of the Estonian Parliament..." (*L.N.T.S.*, vol. 131 (1932–1933), p. 323.)

As an example of a clause requiring parliamentary approval on both sides, a clause may be quoted which is found in a convention of 24 December 1936 for the avoidance of double taxation between Sweden and France:

"The present Convention, ... shall be ratified, in the case of Sweden by His Majesty the King of Sweden with the assent of the Riksdag, and in the case of France by the President of the French Republic with the assent of Parliament. The ratifications shall be exchanged as soon as possible at Stockholm." (*L.N.T.S.*, vol. 184 (1938), p. 35 at p. 51.)

[3] See above, p. 246, and below, p. 285.

[4] See below, p. 287.

group of treaties, in addition to those discussed, was constituted by treaties which were made by the United States and in which reference was made to the circumstance that the executive authority purporting to bind the state acted on the basis of specific legislation authorizing the type of engagements in question. An example illustrative of this type of reference is an agreement made on 16 March 1950 by the United States and the Philippines relating to air services. Its preamble reads:

"Whereas, the Philippine Property Act of July 3, 1946 (60 Stat. 418) authorizes the President of the United States of America, in his discretion and under such terms and conditions as he may deem appropriate, to transfer to the Republic of the Philippines any or all of the right, title, and interest of the Government of the United States of America or its agencies or its instrumentalities to any or all real or personal property within the Philippines vested in such agencies or instrumentalities."[5]

The *United Nations Treaty Series* offered yet another group of treaties which was of interest in this connexion. It appeared that a comparatively large number of the treaties to which international organizations were parties specified either that the person who purported to bind the relevant organization acted on the authority of a prior resolution of the competent treaty-making organ of the organization, or that the person signing on behalf of such organization did so only subject to a subsequent approval of the competent treaty-making organ of the organization. An agreement between the F.A.O. and the U.N.E.S.C.O. signed on 1 and 9 February 1949 may serve as illustration. Article XI of this agreement provided:

"This Agreement shall come into force on its approval by the Food and Agriculture Conference and the Executive Board of the United Nations Educational, Scientific and Cultural Organization."

---

[5] For the complete text, see *U.N.T.S.*, vol. 89 (1951), p. 199. As a further example, an agreement of 2 February 1950 between the United States and India concerning the financing of certain educational exchange programs may be quoted. The preamble of this agreement stated in part that the Government of India and the Government of the United States . . .

"considering that Section 32 (b) of the United States Surplus Property Act of 1944, as amended by Public Law No. 584, 79th Congress, provides that the Secretary of State of the United States of America may enter into an agreement with any foreign government for the use of currencies or credits for currencies of such foreign government acquired as a result of surplus property disposals for certain educational activities; . . .

"Have agreed as follows . . ." (For the full text, see *U.N.T.S.*, vol. 89 (1951), p. 127.)

The agreement, which was signed by the Directors-General of the two organizations, was reported to have entered into force on the date on which the two collective bodies had signified their approval.[6]

It may be noted, further, that while most of the treaties which were found in the League material to refer to domestic law action were made to enter into force upon the exchange or deposit of instruments of ratification, a much greater variation prevailed in the corresponding United Nations material. Frequently, action in conformity with domestic law was only required expressly by one of two parties. In such cases, the relevant clause may read as it did in a convention of 15 July 1954, made between Denmark and Italy and concerning military service:

"The present Convention shall enter into force on the date on which the Government of the Italian Republic shall notify the Government of the Kingdom of Denmark that the required constitutional approval has been obtained."[7]

In numerous cases where the internal law requirements of both sides were referred to, the parties preferred to exchange notes of approval rather than instruments of ratification. Thus, an agreement for co-operation concerning civil uses of atomic energy, signed on 13 February 1956 on behalf of the United States and the Federal Republic of Germany provided as follows:

"This Agreement shall enter into force on the day on which each Government shall receive from the other Government written notification that it has complied with all statutory and constitutional requiremens for the entry into force of such Agreement ..."[8]

Mention should be made, finally, of the fact that the treaties— frequently taking the form of exchanges of notes—which were found to refer to prior acts under the internal laws of the parties authorizing the conclusion of the relevant kind of treaties,[9] normally entered into force immediately upon signature or by an exchange of notes embodying the agreement.[1]

---

[6] See *U.N.T.S.*, vol. 43 (1949), p. 315. For an agreement which is signed on behalf of two international organizations by their Secretary-General and Director-General respectively, and in which the prior authorizations of responsible bodies is expressly stated, see *U.N.T.S.*, vol. 46 (1950), p. 327.

[7] *U.N.T.S.*, vol. 250 (1956), p. 43.

[8] *U.N.T.S.*, vol. 253 (1956), p. 119 at p. 130; see also Blix, p. 363.

[9] This type of treaty is discussed above, p. 279.

[1] For an example, see the agreement of 23 September 1950 between the United States and Pakistan found in *U.N.T.S.*, vol. 82 (1951), p. 132.

5. REASONS UNDERLYING THE USE OF EXPRESS CLAUSES AND REFERENCES

Turning now from a description of clauses and references found to be used in the practice of states to the question of what motives underlie this practice, no obvious answer is perceived.

As already suggested,[2] the varying practice admits of several interpretations. First, it does not even rule out the possibility that there may be no uniform, underlying concept. The conclusion is also entirely compatible with such practice that governments consider domestic law requirements irrelevant under international law and insert express clauses and references on the relatively few occasions when they wish to derogate from the customary rule. On the other hand, were governments generally of the opinion that their domestic law requirements are relevant for the conclusion of a treaty valid under international law, it would seem that any express clause or reference would be redundant. On the basis of this hypothesis, the limited practice of inserting clauses and references must probably be understood to mean that many governments do not feel entirely certain as to the direction of the relevant rule of international law, and state expressly what they none the less believe valid between the parties.

Against the background of the possible and mutually exclusive interpretations suggested, direct evidence concerning the motives which lead governments to insert or omit express clauses or references to domestic law requirements would be highly desirable. Unfortunately, if such evidence exists, little of it has been brought to light. Two cases have nevertheless been cited by some writers as helpful in this connexion and should, accordingly, be analyzed.

The drafting of the Berne Convention of 1886

The first of the cases cited concerns the drafting of the convention for the creation of an international union for the protection of literary and artistic works, which was signed at Berne on 9 September 1886.[3] A draft convention which was submitted in 1884 by the Swiss Federal Council to the conference charged with the task of formulating a convention, contained an article which read as follows:

"L'exécution des engagements réciproques contenus dans la présente convention est subordonnée, en tant que de besoin, à l'accomplissement des formalités

---

[2] Above, p. 271.

[3] De Martens, *N.R.G.*, 2 ser., vol. 12 (1887), p. 173.

et règles établies par les lois constitutionelles de celles des Hautes Parties contractantes qui sont tenues d'en proposer l'application, ce qu'elles s'engagent à faire dans le plus bref délai possible."[4]

The minutes of the fifth meeting of the conference, held on 17 September 1884, reveal that the conference confirmed the view already reached by the same conference sitting as committee, to wit:

"La disposition ci-dessus paraissant superflue, la Commission s'est prononcée pour la supprimer."[5]

It is doubtful whether the ruling of the conference really reflected adherence to the view that constitutional requirements for the conclusion of treaties are relevant under international law. Without discussing the case thoroughly, that conclusion has been drawn by several writers.[6] It must be noted that, in addition to the article quoted above, the Swiss draft, as well as the final convention, contained a provision which laid down that the convention was to be executed three months after the exchange of ratifications, without any requirement to the effect that the ratifications were to be made in conformity with the various constitutional laws. Although the meaning of the eliminated article was not very clear, it would seem that the satisfaction of constitutional requirements was not made a condition for the *entry into force* of the treaty, which was to occur by ratification, but only for the execution of the treaty. The underlying thought might well have been that, while the parties were supposed to undertake obligations under international law by ratification, the need for the satisfaction of domestic formalities might make immediate application difficult. Probably, the Swiss drafters sought to solve this problem by the twofold provision of permitting the parties to hold out their domestic difficulties temporarily as an excuse for non-application, and of obligating them to propose the application of the convention within the shortest possible delay.

If the above interpretation is correct, the view that the article was redundant may not have meant that the parties thought constitutional requirements concerning the conclusion or affecting the application of treaties automatically effective in international law, but rather that non-fulfilment of a binding obligation was permissible for a short time, while the parties secured the satisfaction of their various constitutional

---

[4] Art. 16 in *ibid.*, p. 3.

[5] *Ibid.*, p. 58.

[6] Pallieri, p. 473; Chailley, p. 196; Vitta, p. 94, note 2; de Visscher, p. 144; Wohlmann, p. 19. *Contra:* Bittner, p. 93, note 351.

requirements. This interpretation is further entirely compatible with the circumstance that while the Swiss draft offered no specific date from which the convention was to be executed, the conference found it "utile de fixer un délai pour la mise à exécution de la convention, et a estimé que trois mois étaient pleinement suffisants à cet effet."[7] It is not unlikely that the conference thought this delay of three months a substitute preferable to the provision which it eliminated, because it left less uncertainty as to when full compliance with the convention could be expected.

The International Sanitary Conference of 1893

The second case which has been cited in the literature as evidence of the motives of governments for inserting or omitting express references in treaties to constitutional requirements concerns an exchange of views which took place at the International Sanitary Conference held at Dresden in 1893.[8] Representatives of some twenty governments formulated a convention, one article of which laid down that the convention was to be ratified.[9] At the final meeting of the Conference, which took place on 15 April 1893, an exchange occurred which was reflected in the minutes as follows:

"M. le Premier Délégué des Pays-Bas rappelle qu'il a constaté, dans la Séance confidentielle de la veille, l'obligation où se trouvait son Gouvernement de soumettre la Convention Sanitaire du 15 Avril à l'approbation du Parlement Néerlandais et qu'il a indiqué son intention de signer sous cette réserve.

"Sans vouloir s'opposer à la réserve que M. le Premier Délégué des Pays-Bas désire faire inscrire au Protocole, M. le Président est d'avis que la clause de la Convention, concernant la Ratification, contient déjà tacitement cette réserve pour celles des Puissances Signataires qui sont obligées de soumettre cette Convention à l'approbation préalable de leurs Parlements respectifs.

"La Conférence se rallie unanimement à cette opinion.

"En présence de la déclaration de M. le Président et de l'approbation générale qu'elle rencontre auprès de la Conférence, M. le Premier Délégué des Pays-Bas retire la réserve qu'il se proposait de renouveler puisqu'elle n'a plus maintenant d'objet."[1]

The above passage has generally been seen as evidence that the delegates to the conference considered a constitutionally required parliamentary approval necessary under international law, regardless of any

---

[7] De Martens, *loc. cit.*, p. 59.
[8] See de Martens, *N.R.G.*, 2 ser., vol. 19 (1895), pp. 3 ff.
[9] *Ibid.*, p. 243.
[1] *Ibid.*, p. 147.

express reference thereto in the treaty text.[2] The wording of the minutes quoted undoubtedly make that interpretation plausible.[3] It is also possible, however, that, while the delegates may have believed that parliamentary approval was required under international law for the states whose constitutional law so provided, they nevertheless considered the determination of what the relevant constitutional law provided as a matter with which they did not need to concern themselves.

The First Hague Conference

A reluctance to prescribe in an international compact what domestic procedures were to be observed, and a corresponding desire to refer that matter altogether to the domestic sphere, seems to have underlain the following position taken at the first Hague Conference:

> "Il n'a pas été besoin de réserver l'intervention des Parlements. C'est à chaque Souverain ou Chef d'État à apprécier dans quelle mesure il est libre de ratifier la Convention."[4]

[2] Chailley, p. 196; Vitta, p. 94, note 2; de Visscher, p. 145; Pallieri, p. 473; Wohlmann, p. 19. *Contra:* Bittner, p. 93, note 351.

[3] Some writers have suggested that, when the procedure of ratification is provided for in a treaty, a tacit reference to constitutional requirements should be read into the provision (de Visscher, p. 148; Wohlmann, p. 63). This view might seem to derive some support from a memorandum approved by the United States State Department, reporting that it is the "invariable practice" in that state to send an agreement to the Senate as a treaty in the constitutional sense if it contains a reservation referring specifically to ratification. (U.N., *Compilation,* p. 128.)

Regardless, however, of any practice existing in a particular state, it is not easy to understand why treaties which provide for ratification should be singled out in international law as subject to constitutional requirements. (On agreements in simplified form, see below, p. 291.) A memorandum written in 1923 by Judge Hackworth as Solicitor of the Department of State is also of interest in this connexion. Having noted that the United States Constitution does not contain one word about ratification, that eminent authority concluded:

"As there is no reference to such action in respect of agreements of any character, it cannot reasonably be inferred that if the President instructs a Plenipotentiary to insert a provision for ratification in an agreement, he thereby imposes upon himself a duty to ratify solely under the conditions which would constitutionally arise if the agreement were a treaty..." (Hackworth's *Digest,* vol. 5, p. 400.)

There is no more justification for the contrary position that the procedure of international ratification must be used when parliamentary approval is called for. See Oliver, "Historical Development of International Law—Contemporary Problems of Treaty Law" in *Recueil des Cours,* 1955, vol. II, p. 438; but see Lauterpacht's *Second Report,* p. 21.

[4] See *Rapports faits aux Conférences de La Haye de 1899 et 1907* (Publications de la Dotation Carnegie pour la Paix Internationale, Oxford 1920), p. 87, cited by Bittner, p. 93, note 351; Wohlmann, p. 19.

Reasons for the Swedish practice

Reference has been made already to the practice of the Swedish Government—conspicuous in the period between the two world wars—to make express reservations for the approval of the Swedish Parliament in treaties which required such approval under the Swedish Constitution.[5] In another section of this work,[6] the view has been accepted that the Swedish constitutional provision which brought about the practice must be understood to have been adopted on the assumption that, in the absence of such express provisions, a treaty concluded without a constitutionally required parliamentary consent might nevertheless be valid under international law. While there is no reason to modify that conclusion, it is appropriate in this connexion to examine in greater detail the considerations which guided the authors of this article of the Swedish Constitution.

It appears that, in recommending the adoption of the provision to Parliament, the Government merely repeated a cryptic statement of the drafting committee, to the effect that the duty of the Government to insert express reservations for the approval of Parliament was laid down "in order to avoid international complications, which may conceivably arise as a result of the adoption in the constitution in principle, but not on every point, of the requirement of participation of Parliament in the conclusion of treaties."[7]

The statement quoted raises the question whether its authors would have cared to require the insertion of express reservations into the treaties, had they proposed an amendment which consistently required the participation of Parliament. The further question may also arise whether the authors believed constitutional requirements of parliamentary approval relevant to the international validity of treaties, and were only anxious to avoid controversies on the international level regarding the correct interpretation of the Swedish Constitution.

In answering the questions just posed, a memorandum used by the committee and drawn up in 1916 by the parliamentary committee on constitutional matters is of interest. The memorandum noted the

[5] Above, p. 278.
[6] Above, p. 245.
[7] See "Förslag till Grundlagsändringar åsyftande ett närmare samarbete mellan regering och riksdag i utrikespolitiska angelägenheter, avgivet den 15 mars 1919 av därtill utsedda kommitterade", printed in *Bihang till Riksdagens Protokoll*, 1919, 2 saml. 2 avd. 1 vol. (Stockholm, 1919), p. 29. Translation supplied by the present writer.

opinion that all constitutional limitations on the treaty-making power are immediately effective in the international sphere, as well as the view—said to be more common—that, in a given case, a constitutional limitation upon the competence of the Government may be ineffective on the international level. The memorandum went on to stress the committee's understanding, however, that it would be possible to limit the treaty-making competence of the Government with effect in international law by including clear and express provisions to that effect in the Constitution of the State.[8] Although the committee added that the question whether such provisions would be respected in the case of a concrete conflict was a different matter, the insertion of such provision was presumably the approach which the committee considered commendable.

The interpretation offered above conforms with the conclusion of the eminent Swedish constitutionalist, Brusewitz, who was the secretary of the commission which drafted the amendment.[9] That authority further reports that the parliamentary committee had doubts as to the international relevance of the limitations which, until then, had existed in Swedish constitutional practice, but which were not reflected in the written Constitution. He states, finally, that the amendment requiring the Government expressly to reserve parliamentary approval when constitutionally called for was devised especially to satisfy the wish that the parliamentary participation, when constitutionally needed, should become an unquestionable condition for the international validity of the treaties.[1]

Against the background of the views of the parliamentary committee, the distinct solution offered by the authors of the amendment is remarkable. It seems probable that, although they may have inclined to the view held by the parliamentary committee that it might be possible to draft a constitutional limitation—at least one of general application—effective in international law, they did not consider this method sufficiently safe. Accordingly, it has seemed justified to conclude that, in choosing the method which was finally adopted, the authors of the amendment acted on the assumption that, in the absence of an express

---

[8] *Ibid.*, appendix I, p. 8; *cf.* Bloch, "Der Abschluss von Staatsverträgen nach schwedischem Recht" in *Zeitschrift für ausländisches öffentliches Recht und Völkerrecht,* vol. 4 (1934), p. 40.

[9] See Brusewitz, "Riksdagen och utrikespolitiken" in *Sveriges Riksdag,* vol. XV (Stockholm, 1938), p. 57.

[1] *Ibid.*, pp. 57 and 65.

reservation of parliamentary approval in a treaty, ratification without such approval, even though unconstitutional, might not cause the treaty to be invalid under international law. It would obviously not be warranted, on the other hand, to go further and to impute to the same authors the positive view that treaties concluded in violation of express constitutional provisions or even practice would be valid under international law.[2]

In conclusion, it may be said that the evidence which may be deduced in one direction or the other from the attitude of the authors of the Swedish Constitution is slight. Perhaps the most striking feature is the authors' awareness of the controversial position of the matter in international law.

It must finally be noted that, in spite of the formulation of the constitutional provision discussed above, Swedish practice after the second world war has tended increasingly to omit the express reservation of parliamentary approval. According to reliable information, the reason for this development springs from the attitudes of other contracting governments. Apparently, a practice tolerated when exercised by a great power, such as the United States, may meet with a degree of resistance when followed by a small state. Although the reason for some governments' reluctance may have been a desire not to evoke a discussion of the correct constitutional procedure in their own cases, rather than any objection to Swedish parliamentary approval being referred to on the international level, their attitude nevertheless seems to reflect the view that the correct domestic procedure for the conclusion of a treaty is a matter that each contracting government should handle as it deems fit.

6. The Practical Effect of Express Clauses and References

The discussion of the value of express clauses and references to domestic procedures as evidence in one direction or the other would not be complete without some observations concerning the manner in which these clauses and references have functioned in practice.

---

[2] In 1938, Brusewitz expressed the opinion that, were the government to omit the reservation of parliamentary assent and to ratify a treaty which constitutionally called for such assent, the better view was that, if the treaty concerned a matter which by the constitution is to be regulated by the parliament alone, or by the King and parliament jointly, the treaty was invalid both under constitutional and international law; if it required parliamentary approval under the constitution because "of great importance", however, it was to be valid internationally, even though unconstitutionally ratified without such approval. (*Ibid.*, pp. 65–66.)

Earlier in this work, three incidents have been discussed, in one of which the presence, and in two of which the absence, of express clauses relating to constitutional procedures was used as an argument.

It may be recalled that, in the controversy concerning the validity of a treaty of friendship, commerce and navigation, signed by the United States and the Peru–Bolivian confederation in 1836,[3] Peru argued that, to be valid, the treaty would have required legislative approval by the confederation. While, in countering this argument, the United States put main emphasis on the circumstance that Peru had applied the treaty for more than six years, it may be noted in this connexion that it also pointed out that the treaty had contained no express clause requiring legislative approval.[4]

One aspect of the border dispute between Persia and Iraq which was brought before the Council of the League of Nations in 1935 has been discussed above, and another aspect of the same dispute will be considered below.[5] In that controversy the validity of a protocol of 1913 was challenged by the Persian delegate on the ground that it had not obtained the legislative approval required under the Persian and Turkish constitutions. It may here suffice, in this connexion, to mention that the Iraqi delegate submitted that a failure to obtain legislative approval required under constitutional law did not affect the validity under international law of "a treaty or protocol regularly concluded, which does not in terms refer to these matters." The Persian delegate rejoined that this submission was contrary to the doctrine and practice of international law, and the Council took no position in the question.[6]

While in the two preceding cases the position taken by the United States and Iraq admitted the implication that the presence of a clause prescribing the observance of constitutional requirements would have been operative to make the satisfaction of these requirements a condition—not otherwise existent—for the validity under international law of the treaty, a third case, also related above, evokes some doubt that even express clauses would always have such effect.

Article 7 of a claims convention of 17 March 1841 between the United States and Peru prescribed ratification within two years after signature,

<hr />

[3] Above, p. 125.

[4] Miller, *Treaties and other International Acts of the United States of America,* vol. 4, pp. 102–106; *cf.* Jones, p. 139.

[5] Above, p. 76 and below, p. 343.

[6] For the full quotations, see below, p. 344.

and subsequent to approval by the United States Senate and the Peruvian Congress. When, in the early part of 1843, the United States desired to effect the exchange of ratifications, revolutions occurring in Peru had caused there to be no Peruvian Congress in session since 1840. As appears from the instruction sent to the United States Minister to Lima,[7] the Secretary of State of the United States was fully conscious of the clause requiring Peruvian legislative approval. He was nevertheless prepared to be satisfied with an instrument of ratification issued by a person exercising the functions of President of Peru and deeming himself authorized to ratify the convention without submitting it to the consideration of the Congress of Peru. Although, as has been shown, Peru later challenged the validity of the ratifications which actually took place on the ground that the approval of the Peruvian Congress had not been obtained, as was prescribed by Article 7 of the treaty, and although the United States agreed to effect a new exchange of ratifications, it is worth noting here that the United States never acquiesced in the contention that Peruvian legislative approval would have been required. In disregarding the first exchange of ratifications, it preferred to argue that that exchange had not been effected within the time-limit prescribed. In this incident, consequently, the United States Government appears to have taken the view that a *de facto* executive government, acting alone, is competent to bind the state which it purports to represent, even though an express clause might require parliamentary approval.

It seems likely that this view of the effect of an express clause, which, adopted as it was in the presence of such a clause, carries more weight than those expressed in the two preceding cases. However that may be, one circumstance affecting the force of all the three incidents must further be noted, namely, the absence in all the three cases at the time of ratification of a legislature.

It does not seem unreasonable to see in the positions taken by the United States and Iraq some support for the view that, where there exists no legislature, legislative approval is not required under international law, even if such approval should be expressly prescribed in a treaty. In situations of this kind, it would presumably in any case be open to the executive branch to renegotiate the treaty with a view to eliminating the clause expressly prescribing parliamentary approval. It must be noted, however, that none of the cases is relevant as an au-

---

[7] Quoted above, p. 122.

thority in the normal situation where the clause applies to constitutionally constituted authorities functioning undisturbed.

No controversy is known, indeed, in which the effect of an express clause of the type discussed was considered between fully constitutional and constituted governments. It is of interest to recall, nevertheless, that, although the Charter of the United Nations contained a clause prescribing ratification in conformity with constitutional requirements, neither the depositary government, nor any other of the signatories even raised the question of the constitutionality of several of the ratifications, the regularity of which, in this regard, may have been subject to doubt.[8] This circumstance, it is submitted, points to the conclusion that governments do not feel that even an express clause prescribing compliance with constitutional procedures makes it necessary for them to examine the procedures actually employed by other governments. They appear to act, consequently, on the assumption that, although compliance with constitutional procedures may have been made an express condition for the international validity of a treaty, determination of what these procedures are remains a matter which they may confidently leave to the governments concerned, even though they may not perhaps, on the other hand, be precluded from inquiring into it.

This conclusion, which is limited to the most common case, where it is laid down generally that a treaty shall be ratified or approved in conformity with the constitutional laws of the states concerned, is entirely in accord with the results reached earlier in this chapter. As will be shown, it derives some further support from certain modern tendencies in treaty-making procedure. Before these are examined, however, the further question must be raised whether governments consider the effect of clauses also to be limited which expressly require the approval of a legislature or the satisfaction of some other *specified* requirement. Conceivably governments might consider themselves safe in a conviction to the effect that declarations—whether in the form of ratification or otherwise—made by the other side are issued only when the prescribed condition has been satisfied. In the absence, however, of any material pointing in this direction, it would hardly be warranted to interpret these formulae in such a liberal manner. Accordingly, when the approval of a legislature is made an express condition, the satisfaction of that very condition will be a matter of concern to both, or all parties, unless, of course, a *de facto* government should have suspended the legislature.

[8] See above, p. 268.

The objection may be raised that the above distinction is the result of formalistic thinking. It may not seem entirely satisfactory that a clause prescribing ratification in conformity with constitutional requirements may not render invalid a treaty ratified without parliamentary approval, constitutionally required, while the non-observance of a clause specifically prescribing such approval would render the treaty invalid. Taken against the background of the strained manner in which most constitutional provisions concerning the conclusion of treaties have frequently been applied,[9] it should not cause surprise, however, that governments generally seek to avoid the onus of examining the constitutionality of the procedures followed by the contracting parties. In contrast, the task of verifying that an express, specific requirement—normally one regarding parliamentary approval—has been satisfied involves no complicated elements, and may, accordingly, be more readily accepted.

7. MODERN DEVELOPMENTS IN TREATY-MAKING PROCEDURE

A lack of concern for the manner in which other governments observe their constitutional requirements seems to be reflected in some modern treaty-making procedures, the purpose of which appears to be to leave it to each government to handle its domestic procedures in any manner fit to bring about an effective and speedy participation in the treaty regime in question.

Agreements in simplified form

One of the most conspicuous modern developments in treaty-making procedure is the rapid increase of the number of agreements made in simplified form. This feature has been discussed already,[1] and it may suffice, in this connexion, to emphasize that a principal reason underlying this development has been the desire to withdraw agreements from time-consuming parliamentary procedures, and that the development has frequently taken place in doubtful conformity with constitutional provisions.

Professor Paul de Visscher, who has devoted much research and consideration to this matter, and who holds that generally constitutional limitations upon the treaty-making power are effective in international law, maintains that the agreements concluded in simplified form con-

---

[9] See de Visscher, "Les tendances internationales des constitutions modernes" in *Recueil des Cours*, 1952, vol. I, pp. 539 ff.; Wohlmann, p. 72.

[1] See above, pp. 17 and 228.

stitute a necessary exception to this rule.[2] In view of the fact that this kind of agreements constitutes more than seventy five per cent of all modern agreements, the "exception" must obviously be considered of major importance in the theory advanced by Professor de Visscher.

It is believed that, to be valid in the domestic sphere, agreements made in simplified form, like any other governmental act, must generally be entered into in accordance with law and constitution. If parliamentary approval were not to be constitutionally required for this kind of agreements or the requirement should be somehow circumvented, there might nevertheless be other constitutional requirements relating to countersignature, publication, etc. It is hard to understand why such requirements should not be relevant internationally, were the satisfaction of constitutional requirements generally to be a condition under international law.

Whatever the merits of the view thus advanced by Professor de Visscher, it seems very likely, in view of the strained interpretations of, or outright departures from, constitutional requirements of parliamentary approval, that governments, parties to this kind of agreements, are reluctant to admit foreign inquiries into the constitutionality of the procedures employed. More direct evidence in the matter under discussion is offered, however, in explanations and comments given to the post-war device termed the "triple option clause", which provides, in effect, that states may become parties to a convention by:

"(i) signature without reservation as to approval;
(ii) signature subject to approval followed by acceptance; or
(iii) acceptance."[3]

As may immediately be seen, the purpose of the clause has been to offer a very flexible procedure. There can be no doubt that the object has been to secure, with as little delay as possible, the adherence of a maximum number of states, leaving it to each government to adopt, without other governments being concerned, the domestic procedure fit to bring about effective participation. Strong support for this view is

---

[2] De Visscher, p. 261; *cf.* Dehousse, p. 100.

[3] See the Constitution of 22 July 1946 of the World Health Organization (*U.N.T.S.*, vol. 14 (1948), p. 185 at p. 203). The same clause is found in the Constitution of 15 December 1946 of the International Refugee Organization (*U.N.T.S.*, vol. 18 (1948), p. 4 at p. 16). For two additional examples, see Protocol of 22 July 1946 concerning the Office International d'Hygiène Publique (*U.N.T.S.*, vol. 9 (1947), p. 3 at p. 67) and Protocol of 11 December 1946 amending certain agreements, conventions and protocols regarding narcotic drugs (*U.N.T.S.*, vol. 12 (1948), p. 180).

found in a memorandum prepared by the State Department of the United States and quoted in a previous chapter.[4]

Although the triple option clause seems to have lost some of its popularity, there is no reason to assume that the views quoted above should have lost their pertinence. Furthermore, a practice of exchanging notes of approval rather than formal instruments of ratification is still in use,[5] and seems to fulfil the same function as that shown to be served by the triple option clause.[6]

Treaty-making procedure in the World Health Organization

Another modern treaty-making procedure merits analysis, as it leaves complete freedom to the governments concerned in their choice of domestic procedure, and, at the same time, seems to deprive their choice of any international significance. Under Article 21 of the Constitution of the World Health Organization, the Assembly of that Organization has the authority to adopt certain regulations. Article 22 of the same Constitution provides:

"Regulations adopted pursuant to Article 21 shall come into force for all Members after due notice has been given of their adoption by the Health Assembly except for such Members as may notify the Director-General of rejection or reservations within the period stated in the notice."[7]

What, in effect, is devised is a procedure by which governments may contract out or make reservations within a specified time, or else be-

---

[4] Above, p. 263. See also on the triple option clause, Saba, "Certains aspects de l'évolution dans la technique des traités et conventions internationales" in *R.G.D.I.P.*, vol. 54 (1950), at pp. 427–428; Liang, "The use of the term 'acceptance' in United Nations treaty practice" in *A.J.I.L.*, vol. 44 (1950), pp. 342–349; U.N., *Compilation*, p. 128. See also the discussion in the International Law Commission at its 88th meeting, on 24 May 1951 (U.N. *Doc.* A/CN.4/SR. 88, 27 June 1951, pp. 11 ff.) and at its 99th meeting, on 8 June 1951 (U.N. *Doc.* A/CN.4/SR. 99, 18 July 1951, pp. 7 ff.); Lauterpacht's *First Report*, p. 53; and Parry, pp. 167 ff.

[5] See Blix, pp. 363–364.

[6] A memorandum approved by the Department of State of the United States indicates that "a reservation 'Subject to approval' or 'Subject to acceptance' avoids the necessity for the negotiators to decide what national procedure shall be followed; this is sometimes a matter that requires careful consideration after the close of a conference at which an agreement has been formulated." (U.N., *Compilation*, p. 128.)

[7] W.H.O., *Handbook of basic documents* (6th ed., 1953), pp. 9 and 10. For some comments on the procedure, see Goodman, *International health organizations and their work* (1952), p. 73 and Masters, *International organization in the field of public health* (mimeographed, Carnegie Endowment for International Peace, Washington, 1947), p. 28.

come bound by regulations drawn up by the Assembly.[8] While the purpose of the procedure is to provide "a flexible means of treaty-making particularly suited to a technical international agreement which has to keep pace with the changing epidemological situation...",[9] and while the new technique does not in any way prevent the member states from adopting whatever domestic procedures they find required to secure application, the internationally binding effect is attached only to the expiry of a given period, or to the acceptance of reservations which may have been advanced.[1] This conclusion, if not inescapable under the articles which endowed the W.H.O. with the new machinery, must be drawn in the light of the manner in which these articles have been applied.

The fourth World Health Assembly, which met in 1951, adopted a set of regulations under Article 22.[2] The period within which the member states were allowed to contract out or to make reservations was stipulated to be nine months from the date on which the Director-General notified the states of the adoption of the regulations. Rejections or reservations received by the Director-General after the expiry of that period were expressly stipulated to have no effect.[3] Reservations received within the prescribed period were to have the effect of suspending the binding force of the regulations vis-à-vis the reserving state until the reservations were accepted by the assembly, or withdrawn; if rejected by the assembly, the reservations would place the reserving state outside the regime of the regulations (Article 107).

[8] For the use of the same technique in some other connexions, see Article 5 of the Convention for the Regulation of Whaling, signed at Washington on 2 December 1946 (Hudson, *International Legislation,* vol. IX (1942–45), p. 117 at p. 119); Articles 37, 38, 54 and 90 of the Convention on International Civil Aviation, signed at Chicago on 7 December 1944 (*U.N.T.S.,* vol. 15 (1948), p. 295, at pp. 320–322, 334 and 356); Article 60 § 3 of the Convention on the Transport of Goods by Rail, opened for signature at Rome on 23 November 1933 (Hudson, *International Legislation,* vol. 6 (1932–34), p. 527 at p. 560); for yet other examples, see E. Lauterpacht, "The contemporary practice of the United Kingdom in the field of international law: survey and comment, VII" in *I.C.L.Q.,* vol. 8 (1959), pp. 187–188.

[9] Explanatory memorandum to the International Sanitary Regulations, formulated by the Director-General of the W.H.O. See W.H.O., *Official Records,* No. 37, p. 332.

[1] See Leriche, "Quelques réflexions sur l'adoption et la conclusion des accords multilatéraux deposés auprès du secrétaire général de l'organisation des Nations Unies" in *Revue de Droit International pour le Moyen-Orient,* 3me année, No. 2 (Nov. 1954), at pp. 264–265.

[2] See W.H.O., *Official Records,* No. 37 (April 1952); apparently the regulations were adopted by unanimity, see *ibid.,* p. 323.

[3] *Ibid.,* pp. 337, 351–352.

According to the Annual Report for 1952 of the Director-General of the W.H.O., twenty-five out of eighty-nine countries concerned submitted reservations. Early in 1952, an *ad hoc* committee of jurists and doctors examined, commented upon and made recommendations with regard to the reservations received.[4] With few modifications the report of this committee was adopted almost unanimously by the fifth World Health Assembly which met in 1952,[5] and whose decision in this regard constituted official action under Article 107 of the Sanitary Regulations. Although the decision of the assembly settled a number of interesting legal points, including the precise manner in which the period for reservations was to be calculated,[6] it must here suffice to note that the reservations of three governments were regarded as being without effect, because received after the deadline. The states represented by these governments were, accordingly, held bound by the regulations.

Among the three cases referred to above, that of Norway is of particular interest, as the reservation of that State was submitted—like those received within the prescribed time limit from the Governments of Denmark, Germany, Sweden and Switzerland—to avoid the State's becoming bound internationally before the requisite domestic action had been taken. The Norwegian reservation was contained in a letter sent by the Director-General of the Norwegian Health Service on 8 March 1952 and received at Geneva one day after the deadline. It read as follows:

"In reply to your letter of January 24th . . . I should like to inform you that, for constitutional reasons, Norway will not offhand be able to become a party to the International Sanitary Regulations.

"According to the Constitution of this country, regulations of this order cannot be enacted directly. The empowered authority will consequently have to bring the laws into keeping with the International Sanitary Regulations by passing new acts, and/or amendments and supplements in addition to the existing laws.

"In the first place the Regulations passed by the World Health Assembly on 25 May 1951, must be ratified by the King. Previous to the ratification, the Regulations must be brought before the Storting (National Assembly) for its approval, and the adjusting acts, amendments or supplements called for must be passed.

"We trust, however, that the preliminary proceedings will be terminated at the time when the Regulations are put into force, viz., 1 October 1952."[7]

---

[4] W.H.O., *Official Records,* No. 45 (March 1953) at p. 41, and *ibid.,* No. 42 (November 1952), p. 358.

[5] W.H.O., *Official Records,* No. 42 (1952), p. 126.

[6] *Ibid.,* p. 359.   [7] *Ibid.,* p. 390.

In view of the contents of the above letter and of Article 26 of the Norwegian Constitution which provides that "... such treaties as, according to the Constitution, necessitate a new law or a decision on the part of the Storting in order to be carried into effect shall not be binding until the Storting has given its consent thereunto",[8] it is worth noting that there is no evidence of any Norwegian protest against the decision of the Assembly to hold Norway bound.

It is possible that the importance of the position taken by the Assembly escaped the attention of its members and that, in view of the imminent domestic Norwegian action, little significance should be attached to the absence of any Norwegian protest. The existence of a conflict between the position under international law and under Norwegian law could hardly have gone unnoticed by the *ad hoc* committee, however. Its recommendation, which was decisive, must have been based upon the view that it was not in the least concerned with the requirements which might exist under domestic law, but solely with the absence or presence of a reservation within the period prescribed.

Certain other clauses

A modern type of treaty clause may be noted further which expressly provides for the observance of constitutional requirements, and yet appears to imply that these requirements are of no relevance internationally. As an example the following provision may be quoted:

"This Agreement shall enter into force on the day on which each Government shall receive from the other Government written notification that it has complied with all statutory and constitutional requiremens for the entry into force of such Agreement..."[9]

The formulation quoted above invites the interpretation that the choice of domestic procedure required for the observance of the internal law is a matter of no concern to the other contracting party, and that the latter need not examine the domestic regularity of the final approval, but may rely upon the declaration which asserts such regularity.[1]

---

[8] U.N., *Compilation,* p. 91.

[9] Agreement of 13 February 1956 between the United States and the Federal Republic of Germany concerning co-operation on civil uses of atomic energy (*U.N.T.S,* vol. 253 (1956), p. 119). For similar clauses, see agreements found in *U.N.T.S.,* vol. 250 (1956), p. 43; vol. 251 (1956), pp. 215 and 357; vol 255 (1956), pp. 99, 167 and 199; vol. 256 (1956), p. 149.

[1] See Pallieri, p. 511.

Entry into operation "provisionally"

The question may be raised whether the clauses which provide for application provisionally upon signature, and definite force upon approval in accordance with domestic law requirements, must not logically rest upon the concept that a treaty may have binding force under international law although it has no legal force in the domestic sphere.[2] At the present time, when speedy regulation of international matters is often needed and constitutional requirements stand in the way, such clauses have become a frequent feature. As an example, Article 5 of a commercial agreement of 21 February 1946 between Norway and the Belgium–Luxemburg Economic Union may be quoted:

"The present agreement shall enter into force on the day on which it is approved by the competent authorities of the two Contracting Parties. The two Contracting Parties agree, however, to apply it provisionally as from the date on which it is signed ..."[3]

It is true that generally these clauses provide for application rather than "entry into force" provisionally, and that they sometimes expressly spell out that such application can take place only "within the limits of their constitutional powers."[4] These facts only seem to indicate, however, that the governments conceive their mutual obligation under international law as subject rather to limitations which may result from general constitutional restraints upon the executive branch of government than to the specific prescriptions concerning its treaty-making competence. While a government may thus perhaps be unable even provisionally to undertake an obligation the performance of which would require appropriations from a legislature, it might provisionally assume duties which, under the constitution, should be submitted to a complex procedure, provided that the performance of these duties are within the actual ability of the government. In illustration, the following clause contained in an air-transport agreement of 14 November 1947 between Norway and Brazil may be quoted:

[2] See also Dehousse, p. 105; *Harvard Research,* p. 760 and Pallieri, p. 495.

[3] *U.N.T.S.,* vol. 31 (1949), p. 435. For similar clauses, see the agreements found in *U.N.T.S.,* vol. 42 (1949), p. 125; vol. 44 (1949), p. 3; vol. 46 (1950), p. 215; vol. 53 (1950), p. 59; vol. 74 (1950), p. 41; vol. 253 (1956), p. 12; vol. 254 (1956), pp. 305, 329 and vol. 255 (1956), p. 49.

[4] See Article 15 of the Air Transport Agreement of 23 March 1953 between Sweden and Lebanon (*U.N.T.S.,* vol. 255 (1956), p. 83). Similar clauses are found in agreements published in *U.N.T.S.,* vol. 250 (1956), p. 13 and vol. 44 (1949), p. 163.

"This Agreement shall be approved or ratified as the case may be, in accordance with the terms of the Constitution of each Contracting Party, and shall come into force on the date of the exchange of diplomatic notes to this effect, which shall take place as soon as possible.

"The Contracting Parties shall endeavour to put the provisions of this Agreement into effect, so far as lies within their administrative powers, thirty (30) days after the date of signature."[5]

It does not seem possible to deny that there exists in cases of this kind a treaty obligation under international law. On the other hand, it must be difficult in many of them to maintain that there is a treaty obligation valid under domestic law. They point to the conclusion, indeed, that governments have considered it possible to a certain extent, and have been satisfied, to create obligations valid under international law only, when their constitutional procedures sometimes are inadequate to enable them otherwise to protect the national interest.[6]

Clauses devised to ensure applicability

In addition to the different types of formulae and procedures discussed above, there exist various kinds of clauses, some of which may seem to reflect a concern for the observance of domestic law procedures, but all of which, upon analysis, prove to be designed rather to ensure that the participating governments, when they assume treaty obligations, will be in a position fully to apply these obligations.

For example, one article of the convention of 8 March 1948 between Denmark, Norway and Sweden concerning the recognition and enforcement of judgments in criminal matters provided as follows:

"The convention shall be ratified and the instruments of ratification shall be deposited in the archives of the Danish Ministry of Foreign Affairs.

"The convention shall come into force between the ratifying States as soon as they have fulfilled the requirements necessary for its mutual application."[7]

---

[5] *U.N.T.S.*, vol. 44 (1949), p. 163.

[6] The same conclusion must probably be drawn in the light of a procedure which seems to reflect a remarkable lack of concern for the domestic legal status of the relevant agreement. Section 2 of Article 36 of the International Agreement on Olive Oil, which was opened for signature at the headquarters of the United Nations from 15 November 1955 to 15 February 1956 provides that the agreement shall be submitted for ratification or acceptance in conformity with the respective constitutional procedures of the signatories. Section 5 of the same Article, however, lays down that, for the purpose of bringing the agreement into force, "an undertaking by a Government to seek to obtain as rapidly as possible under its constitutional procedure ratification or accession will be considered an equivalent to ratification or accession". For the text of the agreement, see U.N. *Doc.* ST/LEG/3, 30 June 1958.

[7] *U.N.T.S.*, vol. 27 (1949), p. 117.

While this clause does not spell out any particular concern for the constitutional treaty-making procedures, it obviously seeks to delay the binding force of the convention until the participating states declare, in one way or another, that they have done everything to assure its application. A similar purpose is presumably behind the not infrequent use of a clause an example of which is found in an agreement for the avoidance of double taxation, signed on 5 June 1946 by the United Kingdom and Canada. This clause reads:

"The present Agreement shall come into force on the date on which the last of all such things shall have been done in the United Kingdom and Canada as are necessary to give the Agreement the force of law in the United Kingdom and Canada respectively..."[8]

Section 34 of the General Convention on the Privileges and Immunities of the United Nations, adopted on 13 February 1946, is also of interest here. It reads:

"It is understood that, when an instrument of accession is deposited on behalf of any Member, the Member will be in a position under its own law to give effect to the terms of this convention."[9]

In commenting upon this clause, Professor Pallieri has expressed the view that a member state which adheres under the clause can no longer invoke the lack of competence of its organs. The state remains bound.[1] Were the position in customary international law to be that a treaty made by a constitutionally incompetent organ is void or voidable, there would not, however, seem to exist any logical way by which such an incompetent organ might, by simply adhering to a clause contained in a convention, make itself competent under international law, and thus derogate from the rule of international law. The very derogation would obviously be void, because made by an incompetent organ.

It is believed that the meaning of the article quoted is rather that a government's failure or neglect to secure the legislation necessary to ensure application is not an excuse under international law for non-application. Admittedly, the formulation of the clause is so broad that it includes the implication that the adhering government assures that

---

[8] *U.N.T.S.*, vol. 27 (1949), p. 207. For other examples of this type of clause, see *U.N.T.S.*, vol. 86 (1951), p. 77 and vol. 254 (1956), p. 228.

[9] *U.N.T.S.*, vol. 1 (1946–1947), p. 15. See also, for similar clauses, United Nations, *Handbook of Final Clauses* (U.N. *Doc.* ST/LEG/6, 5 August 1957), p. 3, and Parry, p. 168.

[1] Pallieri, p. 511.

the application of the convention will not be impeded because the government was incompetent to accede. The effect of the clause, however, is not to except constitutional competence as a ground for invalidation, should such ground exist otherwise, but rather to spell out what is believed to be an established rule of international law, namely, that a government which purports irrevocably to assume a treaty obligation on behalf of a state is under an obligation to assure that the treaty is applicable from the moment the state becomes bound, unless some other time should be expressly indicated in the convention. This broader aim, rather than one concerned only with the question of competence, seems to have prompted the insertion of the clause.

8. Conclusions

The various findings resulting from the preceding examination and analysis of treaty clauses may be summarized in the following manner.

Full powers, treaties or instruments of ratification containing clauses expressly requiring or mentioning the approval of legislative authorities, or the compliance with constitutional provisions, are relatively uncommon. The occurrence of these clauses and references does not logically allow any conclusions as to the views of governments on the need under the rules of customary international law for compliance with domestic treaty-making procedures.

Theoretically, it is conceivable that the clauses or references are inserted to derogate from a customary rule of international law, thought to deprive compliance with constitutional requirements of relevance in the international sphere; it is also conceivable, in theory, that governments believe compliance with domestic treaty-making procedures a condition for the international validity of treaties, but feel somewhat uncertain in this regard and insert the clauses and references as a measure of insurance. Finally, the varying practices do not even exclude the possibility that there may be no uniform rationale.

Furthermore, it cannot even be taken for granted that the acceptance of these clauses and references without objection actually means that constitutional requirements, or some of them, become relevant under international law. There are reasons to believe, first of all, that such clauses may be ineffective in treaties made by a *de facto* government which has suspended or abrogated the relevant constitution.

An examination of the manner in which the clauses are applied between constitutional governments, and an examination of various modern treaty-making procedures, point to the further conclusion that governments tend to consider the choice and the satisfaction of appropriate domestic treaty-making procedures a matter of exclusively domestic concern, and that this attitude prevails also when express treaty clauses require the observance of constitutional procedures. This attitude, which must obviously be linked to the view that customary international law does not invalidate a treaty concluded in disregard of domestic law procedures, seems to be due in part to the increasing difficulty of determining what are lawful domestic procedures, and to abide by them. A similar attitude and interpretation has not been found to undermine, to the point of its being meaningless, the effect of the treaty clauses which contain an express and specific requirement, such as the approval of a legislature.

The examination of modern treaty-procedures revealed, in addition to the general attitudes discussed above, a concern behind certain treaty clauses that governments, when they purport irrevocably to bind the states which they represent, should be able immediately to apply the obligations thus assumed.

Chapter XX

DIPLOMATIC INCIDENTS

A number of diplomatic incidents and cases not settled before international tribunals will be examined below with a view to deducing, if possible, the principle or principles which may have been followed with regard to the determination of the competence under international law of authorities purporting to represent constitutionally organized states.

1. Incident of 1832 between the United States and France

In 1831, a treaty between the United States and France was concluded and duly ratified.[1] It provided that France should pay a large sum to the United States as compensation to American subjects for damages inflicted by France in the course of the revolutionary wars. Under the French Constitution of 1830, the executive branch of the Government was competent to enter into the treaty without legislative approval. In order to perform the obligations undertaken, however, the French Government needed an appropriation by the legislature. The bill introduced for this purpose in the chamber having been rejected, the Government became unable to perform under the treaty and resigned.

While in the conflict that ensued, the French Government apparently never disputed the binding force of the treaty, it claimed that it could not be accused of a breach of faith if it refrained from performing in violation of its constitution. In plain words, this defense amounted to an assertion that the validity of an international obligation was dependent upon the fulfilment of other municipal requirements than those relating to the treaty-making competence of the head of state. The United States rejected this contention, and maintained that, being concluded and ratified in accordance with the Constitution, the treaty

[1] The facts related in the text are taken from Chailley, pp. 224–225; de Visscher, pp. 154–157; Mirkine-Guetzévitch, pp. 105–106; McNair, pp. 7–8; and Jones, pp. 144–145.

was binding on every department of the contracting government. After a protracted controversy, including the rupture of diplomatic relations, the French legislative assembly eventually voted the necessary funds, and performance was secured.

It does not seem justified to argue, as has been done,[2] that the incident supports the contention that constitutional limitations upon the competence of the head of state are decisive for his competence under international law, simply because the United States maintained that, having satisfied its constitutional provisions on the conclusion of treaties, France was bound to perform. The conclusion does not necessarily follow that the treaty would not have been thought binding had these provisions been deemed violated. That question was simply not at issue. The United States Government might, indeed, have considered the treaty valid regardless of the constitutionality of the ratification, but have found the argument even more impressive that, under the law of the very party that made difficulties, the treaty was validly concluded.

It is submitted that the incident only lends some authority to the view that internal provisions relating to the execution of treaties cannot be pleaded in excuse of a failure to perform.[3]

2. INCIDENT OF 1832 BETWEEN THE UNITED STATES AND MEXICO

A United States–Mexican exchange of views in 1832 is cited by Mervyn Jones[4] in support of the contention that, on the American continent, constitutional limitations are thought relevant internationally.[5] The Mexican Chargé d'Affaires at Washington having proposed that ratifications of certain treaties should be exchanged, the Secretary of State, Mr. Livingstone, declining the proposal, stated in part, with a somewhat peculiar formulation:

"... in order to proceed to the exchange of Treaties, the ratifications of both the high contracting parties by their constitutional organs must have preceded such exchange ..."[6]

Though it is no doubt permissible to draw a certain support from the above statement for the view that constitutional requirements are

---

[2] See Chailley, p. 225; and de Visscher, p. 156.

[3] For a comment on that principle, see below, p. 380.

[4] Jones, p. 137. The facts are found in Manning, *Diplomatic Correspondence of the United States, Inter-American Affairs* (1831–60), vol. 8 (1937), p. 22.

[5] Manning, *loc. cit.*

relevant internationally, its primary meaning must have been only that it was not enough that Mexico was ready to proceed to the exchange. The United States, too, was obliged to have satisfied its internal requirements, before the exchange could take place. The Secretary of State simply did not have in mind the situation that would arise were either party to exchange ratifications without legislative approval.

3. INCIDENT OF 1849 BETWEEN THE UNITED STATES AND MEXICO

Another United States–Mexican exchange, likewise cited by Mervyn Jones,[6] appears also to be of limited value as evidence in the question under discussion. When performing the exchange of ratifications of the treaty of peace signed in 1848 at Guadalupe Hidalgo, the two commissioners appointed by the President of the United States for this purpose signed a "protocol" with the Foreign Minister of Mexico. In that instrument they purported to explain the meaning of certain amendments made by the United States Senate to the treaty that had been signed. Subsequently, the validity and nature of the protocol became the subject of a controversy, at the height of which in 1849 the Mexican Minister to Washington maintained that the protocol was a "real diplomatic convention".[7] The United States Secretary of State emphatically rejected that view. He stated:

"... inasmuch as that instrument does not on its face purport to be a diplomatic Convention, as it was not concluded according to the forms usually observed in negotiating or by men having power to make such Conventions, as it has not been approved by the Senate of the United States and the Congress of Mexico, or ratified by the President of either Republic agreeably to the requirements of their respective Constitutions, it is not and will never be held to be binding in honor or in law upon the Congress or the Executive of the United States."[8]

Though some support for the theory of the relevance of constitutions may undoubtedly be gained from the above statement, it must be stressed that the primary purpose behind it was not to prove that a treaty was invalid because made in an unconstitutional manner, but

---

[6] Jones, p. 140. The material used is found in Manning, *op. cit.*, vol. 9, Mexico (1937), pp. 11–41 and 309–332.

[7] *Ibid.*, p. 331.

[8] *Ibid.*, pp. 26–27.

rather that the absence of constitutionally required domestic procedures, in addition to other circumstances, indicated that the intention of the authors had never been to conclude any treaty at all.

4. WESTERN GRIQUALAND DIAMOND DEPOSITS CASE OF 1871

With a view to the judicial settlement of a boundary controversy, two *compromis* were signed on 1 March 1871 by President Pretorius acting on behalf of the South African Republic (the Transvaal Republic), and the British Governor of the Cape Colony, on behalf of native chiefs of territory in Western Griqualand.[9] Subsequently to this, but before the award was given, President Pretorius reported to the Volksraad of the Republic that he had signed the deeds of arbitration and that he hoped to be able to announce the final decision during the same session of the Volksraad.[1] This statement appears not to have provoked any adverse reaction on the part of the Volksraad.

The award rendered by Sir Robert Keate on 17 October 1871 was very unfavourable to the Republic.[2] In a letter of 10 November 1871, to Sir Henry Barkly, the British Governor of the Cape Colony, President Pretorius stated that he had not yet received the award; on its receipt he would, he said, "gladly comply with it."[3] When the award was made known in the Republic, however, the Volksraad denounced the *compromis* as unauthorized acts, and declared that it would not acknowledge the result of the arbitration.

The President immediately informed the Governor of the Cape Colony that the Volksraad had disapproved of the letter which he, himself, had sent on 10 November "as being opposed to the fundamental law" of the State. Sir Henry Barkly replied that he did not consider he had "anything to do with differences between the Executive and the Legislature, but looked to His Honour alone to redeem the engagements into which he had formally entered." The reply was later

[9] For the text of the *compromis*, see Great Britain, *Accounts and Papers*, 1871, vol. 47 (Colonies and British Possessions), Correspondence respecting the Affairs of the Cape of Good Hope. Presented to both Houses of Parliament by Command of Her Majesty, 17 August, 1871, p. 553.

[1] His speech is quoted in *Accounts and Papers*, 1872, vol. 43 (Colonies and British Possessions), p. 240.

[2] A report is found in de Lapradelle et Politis, *Recueil des Arbitrages Internationaux*, vol. 2 (1856–1872), pp. 676–705.

[3] *Accounts and Papers*, 1872, vol. 43 (Colonies and British Possessions), p. 221.

expressly approved by the British Minister for the Colonies, the Earl of Kimberley, who had, indeed, instructed the Governor of the Cape Colony that "Her Majesty's Government cannot admit the right of the South African Republic to set aside this award."[4]

On 25 November 1871, following the resignation of President Pretorius, the new Government of Transvaal protested against the award, and contended that the *compromis* were invalid, because in signing them President Pretorius had exceeded his constitutional powers.[5] In rejecting this argument, Sir Henry Barkly outlined the proceedings which had led to the *compromis,* and concluded:

> "I have judged it to be expedient ... to show that, ... he [Pretorius] was acting throughout with the advice of his constituted advisers, and with the knowledge and concurrence of the Volksraad. Whether or not, on all occasions, he strictly adhered to mere matters of form, it is impossible for me to know; if he did not, that might give rise to questions between himself and other representatives of the people over whom he had been placed by election, but would not release the Republic from any agreement entered into by him as President, while holding that office."[6]

While the Earl of Kimberley expressly approved the above position, the Acting President of the Transvaal, D. J. Erasmus, replied:

> "The great question for consideration is this, whether the Republic is bound by an act of submission, signed by the State President only without the production of any power from the highest authority of the land ... In one word, can the said act of submission, signed as it is, be considered as a lawful doccument? According to the laws of this country it is not of the slightest value."

And further:

> "The President of a Republic is no autocrat, whose word and will are law, but merely the administrator of the laws and resolutions of the people: to take such extensive measures it was requisite that the State President should have produced special authority, which he could not do, because he had none."[7]

Sir Henry Barkly declined to continue a discussion which, in his opinion, at best affected "merely the relations which existed between the late President of the South African Republic and the people who elected him", and informed President Erasmus that the British Government was of the opinion that all parties to the arbitration were bound by the award, and that it would be his duty to act accordingly.[8]

---

[4] *Ibid.,* pp. 221, 218, 222, and 241.
[5] *Accounts and Papers,* 1873, vol. 49 (Colonies and British Possessions), p. 248.
[6] *Ibid.,* p. 252.   [7] *Ibid.,* pp. 276–277.   [8] *Ibid.,* pp. 277–278.

In view of the firm juridical position thus taken, it is perhaps of slight importance that the British Government is reported to have subsequently actually insisted on compliance with the award only to the extent that British interests were affected.[9]

The position taken by the British Government, and its Governor, undoubtedly lends some support to the view that non-compliance with a constitutional requirement may be irrelevant under international law. The background of the action taken by Transvaal, on the other hand, inspires the doubt that the legal argument was a mere subterfuge, behind which there was no genuine view of the law.

It is not believed that the significance of the stand taken by the Government and the Governor is weakened, as has been suggested,[1] by Westlake's *note doctrinale* on the report of the case, endorsing a principle contrary to that advanced by the British Governor.[2] The special importance of positions taken in diplomatic relations lies in their being concrete expressions of the practice of states, as that practice is moulded by various functional needs. Doctrinal notes by eminent authorities may diminish the apparent importance of an incident by demonstrating that special circumstances explained the position taken, or that a special interpretation should be given to it. It is submitted, however, that they cannot deprive positions taken of their value as evidence merely by opposing them. Only the circumstance that the authority taking the stand that the *compromis* were valid had, in this case, a direct interest of its own in doing so,[3] may reasonably be advanced as limiting somewhat the evidential value of the positions taken.

[9] See de Visscher, p. 176.

[1] See Jones, p. 146; and *Harvard Research,* p. 1003. The incident is also discussed in Chailley, pp. 220–221.

[2] Westlake expressed himself as follows:

"Si l'interprétation donnée par le président Erasmus à la Constitution transvaalienne était exacte, il en serait, croyons-nous, résulté que les compromis et, partant, la sentence étaient frappés de nullité. Le pouvoir d'un agent public, quel que soit son rang, d'engager le pays qu'il représente, dépend uniquement de la Constitution. Peu importe sa bonne foi. Peu importe aussi la croyance que les étrangers peuvent avoir de son autorité." See de Lapradelle et Politis, *op. cit.,* p. 703.

Westlake suggested, however, that there are exceptions to the relevance of constitutional provisions. Thus, in his opinion, the treaty-making organ may validly contract in excess of constitutional limitations, when justified by a *force majeure*. He did not find any such exception applicable to the present case, and concluded:

"En signant seul les compromis, le President Pretorius avait dépassé sa compétence. Il avait fait un acte nul. Dès lors, la sentence n'avait pas de force obligatoire pour son pays." *Ibid.,* p. 705.

[3] *Cf.* McNair, p. 11.

5. The Termination, in 1873, of the Anglo-Uruguayan Postal Convention of 1853

After having been applied for some twenty years by the authorities of Great Britain and Uruguay, a Postal Convention signed on behalf of the two states on 28 November 1853 was denounced by a Uruguayan Government as not binding, because not sanctioned by the legislature of the State.[4] The British Government, on the other hand, declining to accept the argument, maintained that the Convention was binding and could only be revised or terminated after a year's notice, as prescribed by Article 6 of the Convention. In view of the circumstance that the Government of Uruguay, in fact, no longer respected the Convention, the law officers of the British Crown advised the British Government in 1873, however, that it would be justified in summarily terminating the agreement.

The apparent absence of any published account of the British replies to the Government of Uruguay admittedly makes the incident somewhat inconclusive.[5] It is true, furthermore, as suggested by de Visscher,[6] that it may be seen as evidence of a South American practice making legislative assent internationally relevant. Whatever may have been the precise grounds of the British stand, however, it is evident that in its opinion lack of a required legislative assent was either wholly irrelevant internationally, or else rendered irrelevant internationally under certain circumstances, such as actual application continued over a period of time.

6. The Denunciation, in 1885, by Ecuador of the Industrial Property Convention of 1883

In 1883, the Ecuadorian Government had adhered without any reservation as to ratification to the Industrial Property Convention of 20 March 1883. It had neglected, however, to submit the Convention for the legislative approval that was required under the Constitution of Ecuador, and when it later did so, the legislature refused to give its consent.[7] Faced with this situation, the Ecuadorian Government did not

---

[4] Material from McNair, *The Law of Treaties* (1938), pp. 38 and 506. For the text of the Convention, see Hertslet's *Commercial Treaties*, vol. 12 (1905), p. 955.

[5] This is the view of de Visscher, p. 158.

[6] *Ibid.*

[7] The facts are taken from Basdevant, p. 582, note 1. For the text of the Convention, see de Martens, *N.R.G.*, 2 ser., vol. 10, p. 133.

contend that the State was not bound internationally for the reason that the Government had acted in excess of its constitutional powers, but gave notice of its denunciation of the Convention in the manner prescribed by Article 18 of the Convention. The Bureau of the Union, accordingly, listed Ecuador as a member until a full year had passed after the denunciation.[8] The procedure employed must reasonably be taken to imply that the Government of Ecuador considered the State bound under international law in spite of the possible lack of validity of the treaty under the law of Ecuador,[9] and that the Bureau of the Union concurred in this view.

The above conclusion is admitted by Basdevant and by Vitta, while Chailley tries to see in the action of the Ecuadorian Government only the expression of a wish to avoid difficulties which might have arisen, had a different course of action been taken.[1] It is, of course, frequently possible to argue that a subject refraining from a certain course of action does so to avoid an adverse reaction from its environment, rather than to avoid the infraction of a legal principle, and the argument is especially convenient in the international field where there may not be a great difference between "difficulties" and what may be termed "decentralized sanctions of law". The evidential value of this incident would undoubtedly be greater if it could be shown that there was a positive juridical conviction behind the course of action chosen by the Ecuadorian Government. By any ordinary methods of interpretation, however, the conclusion must be permissible that a government giving notice of the termination of a convention in conformity with a provision of the convention, implicitly admits that it is bound by that convention.

7. THE AFRICAN BOUNDARY AGREEMENT OF 1889 BETWEEN FRANCE AND GREAT BRITAIN

An occasion on which the French legislature refrained from internationally asserting its constitutional right to pass upon treaties before their ratification is cited by Cottez.[2]

---

[8] *La propriété industrielle*, 1886, p. 24. (Citation from de Visscher, p. 159.)

[9] It is not known whether any case of application of the Convention arose in Ecuador in the relevant period.

[1] See Basdevant, p. 582, note 1; Vitta, p. 92, note 2; and Chailley, p. 222.

[2] Cottez, *De l'intervention du pouvoir exécutif et du parlement dans la conclusion et la ratification des traités* (1920), pp. 138–139. Cottez cites the *Journal Officiel* of 5 November 1890.

On 10 August 1889, an arrangement between Great Britain and France was signed at Paris, delimiting British and French possessions on the coast of East Africa. The French Government promulgated the agreement by a decree, without obtaining legislative approval. On 4 November 1890, M. de la Ferronays, speaking in the Chamber of Deputies, characterized this procedure as a "violation flagrante, positive, indiscutable de la constitution". He did not, however, deny that the treaty was valid internationally, and it is significant that he considered that the faith of the state was involved. He declared:

> "Le prestige de la France, le souci de sa dignité et de son honneur ne nous permettent pas vis-à-vis de l'étranger de discuter la signature de M. le Président de la République, qu'il l'ait donnée à tort ou à raison, nous n'avons même pas à l'examiner; c'est un fait, le traité est acquis... Nous devons accepter, subir, respecter, au nom de l'honneur français, les conventions qui ont été conclues."[3]

The Foreign Minister, M. Ribot, was eager to conclude that the treaty had been ratified by the President, and that no one required that the signature of the President be put in question.

Thus, though the treaty was alleged to have been ratified in violation of the Constitution, it was admitted by the very member making that allegation that the treay was nevertheless an internationally valid instrument, and this opinion was apparently not contradicted.[4]

8. Incident of 1914 concerning the Rumanian–Austrian Alliance of 1883

Without relying upon it as a precedent, Mervyn Jones—citing Mirkine-Guetzévitch as authority—states that in 1914 Rumania repudiated a secret treaty, alleging that it was unconstitutional.[5] This statement appears to be due to a misunderstanding of the authority cited. Dr. Mirkine-Guetzévitch maintains that a secret treaty of 30 October

---

[3] *Ibid.*

[4] Mentioning the instance here referred to, one writer states that the French Chambers "are not inclined to take advantage of the constitutional defects of signed and ratified treaties as this would compromise France internationally." See Masters, *International Law in National Courts* (1932), p. 133, n. 19.

Reference may here also be made to an occasion in 1901, when the President of the French Chamber of Deputies declined to put to the vote of the Chamber a motion inviting the Government to submit a treaty already ratified by it for the approval of the Chamber, apparently in order to avoid any possible conflict between Parliament and the executive, and between France and the other party. See Cottez, pp. 139–140.

[5] Jones, p. 142.

1883, by which Rumania bound herself in relation to Austria to place herself on the side of the Central Powers in case of a war with Russia, was unconstitutional, because by the Rumanian Constitution, to be valid, all treaties required the assent of the Parliament. He further states that the Rumanian Council of the Crown, meeting on 3 August 1914, at the outbreak of the first world war, decided almost unanimously to remain neutral, and he adds that the Council, drawing support from the position taken by Italy, considered that the *casus foederis* of the treaty did not correspond to the situation in 1914.[6] Thus, it does not appear from the account given by Dr. Mirkine-Guetzévitch that the unconstitutionality of the treaty[7]—whether or not it was considered in the Council—was invoked in relation to the other party, nor does that conclusion arise from the sources cited by him.[8]

If, as alleged by Dr. Mirkine-Guetzévitch, the treaty was unconstitutional, the incident may acquire a significance totally different from that assumed by Mervyn Jones. Since it appears the Council refused performance under the treaty only on the ground that the *casus foederis* had not occurred, it must be concluded, indeed, that if the Council, in fact, considered the treaty unconstitutional—and perhaps even invalid—it nevertheless considered itself bound under international law.

9. The Treaties of 1915 between China and Japan

It has been asserted by several writers that the treaties based upon the so-called Twenty-one Demands made by Japan upon China in 1915 were invalid internationally because made in violation of the Chinese Constitution.[9] The following account, which is a summary of a detailed

---

[6] Mirkine-Guetzévitch, p. 165.

[7] The text of the treaty is found in Pribram, *Les traités politiques secrets de l'Autriche-Hongrie*, 1879–1914, vol. I (1923), pp. 41 ff.

[8] Bourgeois, *Manuel historique de politique étrangère*, vol. 4 (Paris, 1926), p. 642; Renouvin in Hauser, *Histoire Diplomatique de l'Europe* (1871–1914), vol. 2 (Paris, 1929), p. 363.

[9] See Shuhsi Hsü, "The Treaties and Notes of 1915" in *Chinese Social and Political Science Review*, vol. 16 (1932–1933), pp. 57 ff.; Ling, *La position et les droits du Japon en Mandchourie* (Paris, 1933), pp. 258 ff.; Wou, *Histoire diplomatique de la Chine depuis 1919* (Paris, 1932), pp. 254 ff. But the following writers assert, or admit the international legal validity of the treaties: Young, C. W., *The International Legal Status of the Kwantung Leased Territory*, vol. 2 (Baltimore, 1931), pp. 163 ff.; Michael, F., *Der Streit um die Mandschurei* (Leipzig, 1933), pp. 57 ff.; Willoughby, W. W., *The Sino-Japanese Controversy and the League of Nations* (Baltimore, 1935), p. 23; Tullié, A., *La Mandchourie et le conflit sino-japonais devant la Société des*

investigation of the matter, will show, however, that the fact is conspicuous that the Chinese Government never argued the invalidity of
the treaties on that ground.

The conclusion of the treaties

On 7 May 1915, after lengthy negotiations on twenty-four demands
that had been made by Japan upon China, the Japanese Government
presented an ultimatum to the Chinese Foreign Ministry, while Japanese men-of-war headed for China. The following day, the Chinese
President and Cabinet, the Council of State, and the military leaders
met and resolved to accept the ultimatum.[1] As a result, on 25 May
1915, two treaties, one concerning Shantung, the other regarding South
Manchuria and Eastern Inner Mongolia, and thirteen exchanges of
notes were signed on behalf of China by her President, Yuan Shih Kai.[2]
The two treaties laid down that they were to enter into force upon
signature, but provided for ratification as well. They were, in fact,
ratified by the Chinese President, and instruments of ratification were
exchanged on 8 June 1915.[3] No assent was given to the treaties or the
notes by any Chinese legislature. It is possible, though not altogether
certain, that such assent was constitutionally required. The question
calls for a short discussion.

Were the treaties made in disregard of the Chinese Constitution?

According to the Provisional Constitution adopted in 1912, legislative
assent would unquestionably have been required.[4] However, Yuan Shih
Kai, who had legally been elected President under that law had dissolved
the National Assembly elected under the same law, by a decree issued in
January 1914.[5] Moreover, a conference called by him had drafted a

Nations (Paris, 1935), pp. 179 ff.; Jones, F. C., *Manchuria since 1931* (London, 1949),
p. 84. While not committing himself on the issue of international law, Korovin states
that the treaties were invalid under Chinese law, see *Japonia i mezhdunarodnoe pravo*
(Moscow, 1936), p. 68.

[1] Godshall, *The International Aspects of the Shantung Question* (Philadelphia,
1923), p. 91.

[2] For the texts of these instruments, see MacMurray, I.V.A., *Treaties and Agreements with and concerning China*, vol. 2 (1912–1919), pp. 1216 ff.

[3] See *For. Rel. U.S.*, 1915, p. 159.

[4] Chapter IV, article 35 of that Constitution provided:

"The Provisional President shall have power, with the concurrence of the National
Assembly, to declare war and conclude treaties."

For the text of the constitution, see *For. Rel. U.S.*, 1914, pp. 38 ff.; or *China Yearbook*, 1914, pp. 460 ff.

"Constitutional Compact", which was promulgated on 1 May 1914. Article 25 of this instrument—which should perhaps be considered the domestic law governing the issue[6]—provided as follows:

"The President makes treaties; but, should articles therein provide for any change of territory, or increase the burdens of citizens, the concurrence of the Legislature shall be required."[7]

It may safely be assumed that had the above Article, alone, been controlling, the treaties entered into would have been unconstitutional. It is to be noted, however, that the "Legislature" referred to in the Article had not come into existence at the time of signature and ratification of the treaties,[8] and that, this being so, Article 67 of the same Constitutional Compact acquired relevance. It read:

"Before the Legislature shall have been convoked, its powers and functions shall be assumed and discharged by the Council of State."[9]

The Council of State, mentioned in the above article, existed at the relevant time, and as has already been pointed out, the Japanese ultimatum was, indeed, accepted only after consideration and decision by this Council. The treaties, which in substance did not differ from the demands contained in the ultimatum, do not, however, appear to have been submitted to the Council.[1] Whatever constitutional provision is thought applicable to the case, there may thus be doubts as to the formal constitutionality of the procedure employed by the Chinese President in concluding the treaties. However, these doubts did not find any expression at the time of the conclusion of the treaties, or immediately thereafter, nor were there, at that time, any doubts as regards Yuan's actual authority in the country. One writer describes the situation as follows:

[5] *For Rel. U.S.*, 1914, p. 42; Pan Wei-Tung, *The Chinese Constitution* (Washington, 1945), p. 24.

[6] Of this opinion are: Willoughby, *Constitutional Government in China* (Washington, 1922), p. 16; and Hai-Chao Chiang, *Die Wandlungen im Chinesischen Verfassungsrecht seit dem Zusammenbruch der Mandschu-Dynastie* (Berlin, 1937), p. 41. *Contra*, see: Wood, *The Chino–Japanese Treaties of May 25, 1915* (New York, 1921), p. 16, but *cf. ibid.*, p. 25; see also Yen Liu, quoted below, p. 318, note 6.

[7] *For. Rel. U.S.*, 1914, p. 57.

[8] See Hai-Chao Chiang, *op. cit.*, p. 50; Wood, *op. cit.*, p. 27.

[9] *For. Rel. U.S.*, 1914, p. 60. For a comment on the Article, see Chen Wan Li, *Les développements des institutions politiques de la Chine* (Paris, 1916), p. 98.

[1] Wood, *The Twenty-one Demands*, pp. 89–90; and Wood, *The Chino–Japanese Treaties of May 25, 1915*, p. 27.

"During March to May, when these agreements with Japan were being negotiated there was, in fact, no parliament in China properly so called. 'President' Yuan Shih-k'ai was practically a dictator, whose monarchical aspirations were supported by a strong faction of politicians in actual possession of authority. 'President' Yuan signed those agreements as the only Chinese commanding authority in and for China from the point of view of competence to deal with foreign states."[2]

The death of Yuan Shih Kai and the Paris Peace Conference

In June 1916, Yuan Shih Kai died, and to secure the co-operation of all factions in the country, his successor, Li Yuan-hung, the Vice-President, proclaimed the Provisional Constitution of 1912 again to be in force.[3] It may be of interest to note, also, that the new President appears to have proclaimed that all treaties which had been concluded "subsequent to dissolution of [the] Parliament in May, 1914" were to be recognized as valid.[4]

The National Assembly, which was convened by the new President, and which actually met at Peking in June 1916, does not appear to have passed upon the treaties before it was dissolved again.[5] On 24 September, 1918, moreover, notes were exchanged between the Chinese Minister to Tokyo and the Japanese Foreign Minister on questions concerning Shantung.[6] However corrupt the origin of these notes may have been, and whatever were the precise circumstances of their being exchanged, their contents were predicated upon the continued validity

---

[2] See Young, *op. cit.*, p. 170. See also the following statement by another writer:

"Yuan Shih-kai was virtually supreme in the Chinese Government and had exercised so much personal control and oversight that it was unnecessary to engage in indirect discourse through the Foreign Office:" Godshall, *Tsingtau under three Flags* (Shanghai, 1929), p. 207.

In the same vein, see Hai-Chao Chiang, *op. cit.*, p. 50; Chen Wan Li, *op. cit.*, pp. 94 and 97; and Ichihashi, *The Washington Conference and after* (1928), p. 303.

[3] *For. Rel. U.S.*, 1916, pp. 86 and 98; Reinsch, P. S., *An American Diplomat in China* (Garden City, N.Y., 1922), pp. 193, 199 and 201; and see Hai-Chao Chiang, *op. cit.*, p. 51.

[4] See dispatch from the United States Minister to Peking, *For. Rel. U.S.*, 1916, pp. 85–86. The expression "dissolution of Parliament" presumably refers to the abolition by Yuan Shih Kai, on 26 May 1914, of an extra-constitutional body of supporters called by himself in December 1913 to share the responsibility of dissolving the National Assembly and to amend the Provisional Constitution of 1912. See Pan Wei Tung, *op. cit.*, p. 24; and *For. Rel. U.S.*, 1914, p. 61.

[5] See Shuhsi Hsü, *op. cit.*, p. 50; but see Wood, *The Chino–Japanese Treaties of May 25, 1915*, p. 28.

[6] The text of the agreements embodied in the notes may be found in an appendix to Gallagher, P., *America's Aims and Asia's Aspirations* (New York, 1920), pp. 463–464.

of the treaties of 1915, and they must be taken to have implied the then Chinese Government's recognition of those treaties. As such, as well as in themselves, they turned out to be highly damaging to the Chinese claims advanced at the Paris Peace Conference.[7]

At the Paris Peace Conference, the Chinese delegation urged the "abrogation" of the treaties of 1915 on the grounds, among others, that they were concluded under duress, and "lacked in finality".[8] The latter expression had no reference, as might be supposed, to constitutional finality; behind it lay a claim to the effect that for their permanence, the treaties required the assent of the Great Powers.[9] Among the legal arguments presented by the Chinese at the Peace Conference, there is indeed no trace of a contention that the treaties of 1915 should have been invalid because unconstitutional.[1]

In spite of initial strong United States support for the Chinese position at Paris, the final result of the conference was a complete rejection of the Chinese claim. Article 157 of the Versailles Treaty provided that "The movable and immovable property owned by the German State in the territory of Kiaochow ... *are* and remain acquired by Japan ..." (emphasis supplied), a formulation which seems to be predicated upon the view that valid acquisition had occurred by the treaties of 1915.[2] The United States, which did not ratify the Versailles Treaty, cannot, perhaps, be regarded as having acquiesced in this position,[3] and the Chinese delegation, which refused even to sign the treaty, may certainly not be said to have done so. By submitting the treaties of 1915 for

[7] See Quigley, "Legal Phases of the Shantung Question" in *Minnesota Law Review*, vol. 6 (1922), p. 392; Dillon, E. J., *The Inside Story of the Peace Conference* (New York, 1920), pp. 337–338; Gallagher, *op. cit.*, pp. 247, 256, 272, 296–297, and 343; Reinsch, *op. cit.*, p. 340; Lansing, R., *The Peace Negotiations* (Boston, 1921), p. 251; MacMurray, *op. cit.*, p. 1445; Godshall, *The International Aspects of the Shantung Question*, p. 109; and Temperly, *A History of the Peace Conference at Paris*, vol. 6 (London, 1920–1924), pp. 375–376.

[8] See an official memorandum submitted by the Chinese delegation to the Council of Ten, reproduced in Miller, D. H., *My Diary at the Conference of Paris* (New York, 1924), vol. 6, pp. 246–247.

[9] *Ibid.*, p. 241.

[1] It might also be noted that a pamphlet entitled "China's Claims at the Peace Table", published in New York by the "Chinese Patriotic Committee" urged the Peace Conference to nullify the treaties of 1915, without, however, citing unconstitutionality as a ground.

[2] See Temperly, *op. cit.*, p. 386.

[3] See Baker, R. S., *Woodrow Wilson and World Settlement*, vol. 2 (Garden City, N.Y., 1922), p. 264.

abrogation—and citing as a precedent the Congress of Berlin, where the Great Powers took upon themselves to revise a treaty between Russia and Turkey[4]—the Chinese stand must nevertheless be taken to have been that the treaties were, at the most, voidable.[5]

Positions taken at the Washington Conference

At the Washington Conference in 1921–1922, the Chinese Government again submitted the treaties of 1915 for "cancellation".[6] The four grounds on which the abrogation of the treaties was urged did not include lack of constitutionality,[7] although that ground appears to have been advanced by private writers at this time.[8] The Japanese apparently felt that their legal position was secure. On 2 February 1922, their delegate, Baron Shidehara, stated in part as follows:

> "It is presumed that the Chinese delegation has no intention of calling in question the legal validity of the compacts of 1915, which were formally signed and sealed by the duly authorized representatives of the two Governments, and for which the exchange of ratifications was effected in conformity with established international usages..."[9]

The Chinese, on the other hand, appear to have felt that their position was weak on what they termed "the technical or juristic validity of the agreements of 1915, as having been actually signed in due form by the two Governments", for they were careful to point out that the conference had not been called for the purpose of maintaining the legal *status quo*.[1]

---

[4] Gallagher, *op. cit.*, p. 298.

[5] Young prefers the admittedly more logical conclusion that the plea for abrogation implied admission that the compacts were binding: *op. cit.*, pp. 156 and 165. It is submitted, however, that the conclusion drawn above is a truer interpretation of the Chinese position. See the following note.

[6] It must be noted in this connexion, however, that Mr. Wang, the Chinese delegate, declared that "the mere fact that the Chinese asked for an abrogation of the Treaties would [not] imply that they recognized their validity... The Chinese Government and people had always considered the state of things arising under these Treaties as a *de facto* situation, without any legal recognition on the part of China." See *Conference on the Limitation of Armament*, Washington, November 12, 1921–February 6, 1922 (Washington, Government Printing Office, 1922), p. 1512.

[7] *Ibid.*, p. 1560.

[8] Wood, *The Chino–Japanese Treaties of May 25, 1915*, pp. 102–105; Hoshien Tcheu, *Etude sur les relations diplomatiques entre la Chine et le Japon* (Paris, 1921), p. 273.

[9] See conference report cited above, at p. 1508.

[1] *Ibid.*, p. 1560.

The repudiation of the treaties by the Chinese Parliament

Even when, subsequently, the Chinese Parliament had declared the treaties null and void, the executive branch of the Chinese Government appears not to have abandoned the position that Japanese agreement would be required for the abrogation of the treaties. Furthermore, that branch does not appear to have attached much significance to the contention that lack of parliamentary consent deprived the treaties of 1915 of validity under international law.

In the autumn of 1922, at the ordinary session of the Chinese National Assembly, two motions introduced independently of each other in the House of Representatives, called upon the National Assembly to declare the treaties of 1915 null and void.[2] Following a debate in the House on 1 November 1922, the two draft resolutions were merged into one and passed unanimously.[3] Apprehension concerning the effect of the resolution appears to have been voiced in the Senate, and the resolution was temporarily held up. A new and similar resolution appears to have been passed by the House on 17 January 1923, however, and to have secured adoption in the Senate on 19 January.[4] No translation of the exact text of this resolution has been found. However, in a memorandum presented to the Lytton Commission, it is stated:

"In its session of January 19th, 1923, the Senate unanimously adopted a Resolution declaring that the Agreements of May 25th, 1915, should be considered null, considering:
  (a) that they were imposed by force and they were contrary to the spirit of International Law;
  (b) that they had not been sanctioned by the Parliament; and
  (c) that the Chinese Delegations at International Conferences had on many occasions declared them not binding for the two reasons cited above."[5]

The wording of the passage quoted above cannot but give the impression that the Assembly passed its resolution on the basis of the theory that a constitutional requirement for parliamentary approval is

[2] For the text of one of these resolutions, see Shuhsi Hsü, *op. cit.*, pp. 55–56. A French translation of the same resolution is found in Ling, *op. cit.*, pp. 253–254. For the original text of the resolution, Shuhsi Hsü refers to *The Journal of the Chamber of Deputies*, Third Session, No. 12, Documents, p. 1.

[3] See Shuhsi Hsü, *loc. cit.* Cf. Young, *op. cit.*, p. 159, n. 8; and see Document No. 4 of *Memoranda presented to the Lytton Commission* by V. K. Wellington Koo, Assessor: "Memorandum on the Twenty-One Demands and the agreements of May 25th, 1915", vol. I, p. 148.

[4] Young, *op. cit.*, p. 159, note 8.

[5] The quoted passage is found at p. 148 of the memorandum, cited above.

relevant under international law.[6] Under such circumstances, it is of interest to find that a note addressed by the Chinese Government on 10 March 1923 to the Japanese Government, in pursuance of the resolution quoted above, failed to advance constitutional invalidity as a ground for international nullity of the treaties. This note read in part as follows:

"The Treaties and Notes of 1915 have been consistently condemned by public opinion in China, and it was based on the wishes of the people that the Chinese Government brought forward at Paris and Washington proposals for the abrogation of the agreements in question. The Chinese Parliament in ordinary session, in January, 1923, passed a resolution declaring the Sino-Japanese Treaties and Notes of 1915 null and void, and the Senate called on the Government to act accordingly. The foregoing facts are enough to show that the opinion of the Chinese people on the question has been unanimous throughout. The expiration of the term of the lease of Port Arthur and Dairen is near at hand, and the Chinese Government consider that the time is now ripe for improving Sino-Japanese relations, and declare that the Sino-Japanese Treaties and Notes of May 25, 1915, should forthwith be abrogated, ... The Japanese Government is hereby requested to appoint a day on which to discuss questions incidental to the restoration of Port Arthur and Dairen or consequent upon the abrogation of the Treaties and Notes in question . . ."[7]

As can be seen from the note, the Chinese Government seems to have reduced the international significance of the resolution of the Assembly to an expression of the "opinion of the Chinese people". The Japanese Government flatly refused to go along with the proposal. It cited the position it had assumed at Washington, and stated:

[6] Yen Liu, one of the sponsors of the resolution, writes as follows:

"According to international law, in concluding a treaty, both parties have the obligation to recognize the constitutional requirements of the other party of the ratification of the treaty. The provisional constitution of the Republic of China stipulates that the President in concluding treaties shall obtain the consent and approval of Parliament. The Sino-Japanese treaty covering the twenty-one demands was concluded under duress from Japan and at a time when the Parliament was dissolved, and to this day it has not obtained the consent and approval of the Parliament. This means that it has not fulfilled the requirement of ratification of treaties in our country. Without such requirement being fulfilled, this treaty is not finally concluded, and therefore certainly cannot have any effect. It is therefore proposed that the Parliament shall resolve to request the Government to declare the treaty null and void."

The same writer goes on to state that the resolution having been passed unanimously by both the Senate and the House, the Assembly "requested the Government to act accordingly." See Yen Liu, *Thirty Years of Chinese Diplomatic History* (2nd ed., in Chinese, Shanghai, 1931), pp. 150–151. For the above translation, the present writer is indebted to Mr. James Wang, formerly of Columbia University.

[7] The text of the Chinese note and of the Japanese reply is found in an appendix to Young, *op. cit.*, pp. 228–233; *cf. ibid.*, pp. 158–159.

"The attempt on the part of your Government to abrogate, of its own accord, treaties and notes which are perfectly valid ... should be regarded as contrary to the accepted principles of international intercourse ..."

Positions taken before and by the Lytton Commission

The attitude of the two Governments did not change in the following years, nor did the treaties of 1915 cease to be a source of conflict. As has been pointed out above, the Chinese memorandum submitted to the Lytton Commission in 1932 cited the resolution of 1923 of the Senate of the Chinese National Assembly as declaring the treaties of 1915 null on the grounds of duress, violation of the "spirit of international law", and lack of parliamentary assent, and as recording—erroneously, it seems, as regards the lack of parliamentary assent—that these two grounds had been advanced at several international conferences. The ground of unconstitutionality was not, however, further elaborated in the memorandum, and there is no indication that the government had now come to consider the resolution as more than an expression of the opinion of the Chinese people. The Japanese memorandum submitted to the Lytton Commission is of greater interest, for the lack of Chinese parliamentary assent is discussed somewhat in this document. It is worth noting that the Japanese Government cited the Chinese Constitution of 1914 (not the Provisional Constitution of 1912). It asserted:

"Yuan Shih-kai ... ratified the treaties without the consent of the Legislature, because he considered, in the sovereign capacity of Head of the State of China, that the agreements ... did not come within the proviso of that article."[8]

There may perhaps be a question whether, by citing Chinese constitutional law, the Japanese Government implicitly admitted the relevance of that law to the international validity of the treaties.[9] However, an affirmative answer does not seem warranted by the statement quoted above, which does not refer to any independent Japanese consideration of the Chinese Constitution, but merely to the judgment of the Chinese Head of State. Citing, further, the Chinese constitutional developments from 1912 to 1916, and the lack of a legislature with competence as

[8] *The Present Condition of China.* Document prepared by the Japanese Government and communicated to the commission of enquiry appointed by the Council of the League of Nations in pursuance of its resolution of December 10, 1931, Document A, Appendix No. 4: "Present condition and validity of the so-called Twenty-One Demands" (1932), p. 6.

[9] See the argument cited in the incident of 1832 between the United States and France, above, p. 303.

regards the conclusion of treaties at the relevant time, the Japanese Government asserted that it was absurd "to call the Treaties unconstitutional in character and to try to have them abrogated after so many years of existence."[1]

The report of the Lytton Commission, signed at Peking on 4 September 1932, although referring to the treaties of 1915,[2] and to "Japanese rights",[3] can hardly be said, as was later contended by the Japanese Government,[4] to have recognized the validity of the treaties of 1915. In the absence of any specific discussion of the question in the report, it must be assumed that the Commission took no position in the matter.

The subsequent course of Sino-Japanese relations appears to throw no new light upon the question at issue.[5]

Conclusion

No simple and clear-cut conclusion emerges from the long controversy outlined above. Several considerations come to mind, however. In the first place, it may perhaps be asked whether unconstitutionality in the conclusion of treaties can ever be of relevance in cases where the treaties are entered into while duress is exerted upon the whole state. It may not be doubted that there exists some rule of international law laying down criteria for the competence to conclude treaties on behalf of a state subjected to duress; for it is inconceivable that such treaties may with binding effect be made by anyone who presents himself to the other party. It would seem highly improbable, on the other hand, that in these situations—which will frequently have the character of emergencies—constitutional criteria for domestic competence would be internationally relevant.[6]

It is of interest to note that in the present instance, the Japanese Government seems not to have been concerned about the Chinese constitutional position. In its memorandum to the Lytton Commission, it appears to have taken the view that the Head of State was competent

---

[1] See the memorandum cited, at p. 7.

[2] League of Nations, *Doc.* C. 663. M. 320 (VII. Political, 1932, VII, 12), pp. 37–38.

[3] *Ibid.*, p. 49.

[4] See League of Nations, *Official Journal, Spec. Suppl.* 1933, No. 111, p. 99.

[5] Willoughby, *The Sino–Japanese Controversy and the League of Nations* (Baltimore, 1935).

[6] The matter is discussed below, p. 386.

under international law to determine his own constitutional competence and to have held, furthermore, that where there is no legislature, legislative assent to treaties cannot be required for their validity, regardless of the formal requirements of a constitution.

It is further believed significant that the Chinese Government chose never officially to argue the lack of international validity of the treaty on the ground of lack of parliamentary assent, not even when that contention had been forcefully advanced by the Chinese National Assembly itself. It is difficult to avoid the conclusion that the reticence was due to lack of faith in the force of the argument.

10. Chinese–Russian Treaty of 1913 on Mongolia

Against the background of the Sino-Japanese controversy, it may be of interest to examine the circumstances surrounding a treaty concluded in 1913 by the Chinese Government and the Russian Government. This treaty was made not only without the parliamentary assent required under the Provisional Chinese Constitution of 1912,[7] but, indeed, subsequently to an express rejection of the treaty by the Parliament. The facts were the following: At the end of October 1911, the Chinese province of Mongolia declared itself independent. This event had been preceded by Russian aid to the independence movement, and was followed, in 1912, by a treaty in which Russia pledged herself to assist Mongolia to maintain her autonomy. As a result, relations between Russia and China were seriously strained at the end of 1912. Negotiations were opened with a view to a settlement, and by the end of May 1913 an agreement had been drafted.[8]

On 28 May, the Chinese Government submitted this draft to the National Assembly at the request of that body. Despite efforts by the Premier and the Foreign Minister, the House of Representatives appears to have resolved to give its assent to the agreement only on the condition that certain modifications were secured.[9] Similar resolutions appear

[7] See above, p. 312 note 4.

[8] See Shuhsi Hsü, *China and her Political Entity* (New York, 1926), pp. 353 ff; Vinacke, *A History of the Far East in Modern Times* (New York, 1942), p. 242; Weigh, *Russo–Chinese Diplomacy*, p. 166. For the Russo–Mongolian agreement, see MacMurray, *Treaties and Agreements with and concerning China*, vol. 2 (1912–1919), pp. 992 ff.

[9] Hsü, *China and her Political Entity*, p. 356; Shih-Min Kang, *The International Relations of the Republic of China subsequent to the Revolution of 1911* (L.L.M.

to have been passed on 13 and 18 June 1913, and on the latter occasion
the House, itself, offered a draft of an agreement to which it would
agree.[1]

In the beginning of July, the Government having renewed its efforts
to persuade the House to accept the agreement as it was originally
drafted, and having declared that there was no hope of achieving any
modifications, the House finally gave its consent. However, the agreement was rejected by the Kuomintang-dominated Senate.[2] Following this
event the Russian Government withdrew its previous consent to the
draft and presented new conditions. In this situation, the Chinese Foreign Minister resigned, and the negotiations were discontinued for two
months. In the course of this period, a revolution which broke out in
the Yangtse Valley was effectively suppressed by Yuan Shih Kai, the
Provisional President. In September 1913, Yuan selected a new Cabinet,
and negotiations with Russia were resumed and lasted until the end
of that month.[3] Yuan Shih Kai's successful handling of the revolution
strengthened his political power, and in the beginning of October, he
was elected regular President. Not fully a month later, on 4 November
1913, the new President issued three Mandates by which he dissolved
the Kuomintang party. Its three hundred Members of Parliament were
banished from the capital and deprived of their right of representation.
Though complicity of the Kuomintang in the suppressed revolution was
offered as chief justification for the action, it is of interest to note that,
among other reasons listed, was the refusal of the Kuomintang Members
of Parliament to assent to the Sino-Russian agreement on Mongolia.[4]

The day after the action against the Kuomintang, which had left
the National Assembly without a quorum, on 5 November, the Chinese
Foreign Minister and the Russian Minister to Peking signed a declara-

---

thesis at Columbia Univ., 1919), p. 86; *For. Rel. U.S.*, 1913, p. 120; and *North China
Herald*—hereinafter cited as *N.C.H.*—vol. 107 (1913), 7 June, p. 741 and *ibid.*, 14 June,
p. 819.

[1] *Ibid.*, 21 June, p. 902; Hsü, *China and her Political Entity*, p. 356; Shih Min
Kang, *op. cit.*, p. 86.

[2] Shih Min Kang, *op. cit.*, pp. 89–90; *N.C.H.*, vol. 108 (1913), pp. 135–136; Weigh,
op. cit., p. 178; and Hsü, *China and her Political Entity*, p. 357.

[3] Pavlovsky, M. N., *Chinese–Russian Relations* (New York, 1949), p. 56; Hsü,
China and her Political Entity, p. 358.

[4] See *N.C.H.*, vol. 109 (1913), p. 447; *For. Rel. U.S.*, 1913, p. 139. The Russian
Minister to Peking carefully reported these events to his Government, see *The
Chinese Social and Political Science Review*, vol. 16, p. 656.

tion and exchanged notes settling the Mongolian question. The terms of this new agreement, which was not submitted to the National Assembly or its remnants, appear not to have differed substantially from those rejected earlier by the Assembly.[5]

The validity of the new instruments appears never to have been challenged, and some writers have even asserted that parliamentary approval was not constitutionally required for this kind of agreement.[6] One writer has explained that the Chinese Government held the agreement not to be a treaty in the formal sense, but merely a declaration not requiring submission to the National Assembly.[7]

Given the background described above, it is hard, if not impossible to accept the explanation advanced in favour of the constitutionality of the agreement. It seems highly improbable, indeed, that the Government should have fought bitterly in the Assembly to induce it to give an expression of consent that was not constitutionally required. How little respect the executive branch of the Government had for the Constitution is best evidenced, of course, by its ousting the Kuomintang members of the Assembly. The violation of the constitutional provision on the conclusion of treaties was, indeed, but a feeble echo of the first blow.

It is worth noting that the Russian Government apparently did not hesitate for a moment to conclude the agreement although its opposite party was a government that was obviously exceeding its constitutional powers. The conclusion seems tempting that the Russian Government was satisfied that they were secure in obtaining the pledge of the only Chinese governmental organ that appeared to wield authority. Perhaps the Russian Government did not even ask itself if the position in international law made it advisable to postpone the conclusion of the treaty until Yuan Shih Kai implemented the democratic prescriptions that had been proclaimed in the Constitution of 1912. If the question was posed, it must have been answered in the negative.

---

[5] See Weigh, *op. cit.*, p. 179; *N.C.H.*, vol. 109 (1913), p. 445; Shih Min Kang, *op. cit.*, p. 91; for the texts of the instruments, see MacMurray, *op. cit.*, pp. 1066–1067.

[6] Hsü, *China and her Political Entity*, p. 358; Pinghou C. Liu, *Chinese Foreign Affairs—Organization and Control* (typewritten dissertation at New York University, 1936), p. 191.

[7] Chung-tsu Cheng, *Contemporary Outer Mongolia* (in Chinese, Shanghai, 1922), book 2, pp. 14–17. For translations the present writer is indebted to Mr. James Wang, formerly of Columbia University.

11. The Adherence of Luxemburg to the League
of Nations in 1920

The background

An incident connected with the admission of Luxemburg into the League of Nations is of interest. The matter appears to have arisen as a result of there being in the Covenant no clear provision regarding the entry into force of the Covenant with respect to states admitted to membership by decisions of the Assembly. Paragraph 2, Article 1 of the Covenant provided:

"Any fully self-governing State, Dominion or Colony not named in the Annex may become a Member of the League if its admission is agreed to by two-thirds of the Assembly, provided that it shall give effective guarantees of its sincere intention to observe its international obligations, and shall accept such regulations as may be prescribed by the League in regard to its military, naval and air forces and armaments."[8]

Luxemburg not being mentioned in the annex referred to, its admission could only be effected under the paragraph quoted. By a letter of 23 February 1920 to the President of the Council of the League of Nations, Mr. Emile Reuter, Minister of State of Luxemburg, officially communicated his Government's wish that Luxemburg be admitted to membership. He pointed out that the Parliament of Luxemburg had repeatedly expressed the same wish. He added that constitutional reform might be necessitated as a result of affiliation, for, by a treaty of 1867, the neutrality of Luxemburg had been guaranteed by various European powers,[9] and that status had been sanctioned in a provision of the constitution of the Grand Duchy. Apparently sensing that Luxemburg's proclaimed neutrality might be thought incompatible with membership in the League, Mr. Reuter underlined the reasons for that neutrality. His country was eager to be admitted to membership without sacrificing its neutrality, and difficulties would attach to a repeal of the principle of neutrality.[1]

---

[8] By way of comparison it may be mentioned that paragraph 1 of the same Article laid down that States which were mentioned in the Annex were to become members by the deposition with the Secretariat of declarations of accession. The text of the Covenant may be found in many publications, e.g. Goodrich and Hambro, *The Charter of the United Nations* (2nd ed., 1949), pp. 555 ff.

[9] *B.F.S.P.*, vol. 57, p. 32.

[1] The text of the letter is found in Wehrer, "Le Statut International du Luxembourg et la Société des Nations" in *R.G.D.I.P.*, vol. 31 (1924), pp. 169–202, at p. 179.

In two memoranda, approved on 15 May 1920 by the Council of the League, the Secretary-General, Sir Eric Drummond, stated that it was doubtful if the maintenance of the neutrality of Luxemburg was compatible with Article 16 of the Covenant, and that the question of the conditions upon which the Grand Duchy could be admitted must be left to the Assembly.[2]

The admission of Luxemburg

The question of the admission of Luxemburg was considered by the Fifth Committee of the Assembly. In reply to a questionnaire, and in oral hearings before a subcommittee of the Fifth Committee, the Government of Luxemburg, represented by Mr. Reuter and three other delegates, made it clear that to qualify for membership, it was willing to agree to certain modifications in its proclaimed status of neutrality.[3] The delegates pointed out, in addition, that "La Constitution du Luxembourg ne permet à aucun gouvernement d'engager définitivement le pays en cette matière sans l'assentiment de la Chambre des députiés."[4]

In view of the replies given by the delegates, the subcommittee examined various possibilities of reconciling the admission of Luxemburg with the provisions of the Covenant.[5] Apparently fearing a negative outcome of the deliberations, however, the Luxemburg delegation, on 28 November 1920, addressed a letter to the President of the subcommittee, declaring that "le Luxembourg ne fait aucune difficulté pour se soumettre aux obligations découlant du Pacte de la Société des Nations et spécialement de l'article 16 de ce Pacte." It added that the admission of Luxemburg would necessitate certain changes in the text of the Constitution of the Grand Duchy, and that "le gouvernement s'engage à proposer en ce cas les changements appropriés sans retard à l'Assemblée législative."[6]

When, on 16 December 1920, the question of the admission of Luxemburg eventually came before the Assembly, the rapporteur of the Fifth Committee stated that the Constitution of Luxemburg, which had not yet been modified, sanctioned the status of neutrality, and that this was why the Grand Duchy had requested to be admitted without any modification in this regard. Luxemburg had realized, however, that the

---

[2] *Ibid.*, pp. 181–184, in notes.
[3] *Ibid.*, pp. 187–190, in notes.
[4] *Ibid.*, p. 190, in note.
[5] *Ibid.*, p. 188.
[6] *Ibid.*, p. 191, in note.

status was not compatible with Article 16 of the Pact, and eventually it had, by a letter, expressed its acceptance of that provision without any reservation. The condition of neutrality, consequently, should be considered withdrawn. In another letter, continued the rapporteur, the Government of Luxemburg had promised to take appropriate measures to make the Constitution conform to the obligations flowing from the admission into the League. In making that declaration the Government had simply had regard to paragraph 2, Article 20 of the Covenant which provided:

"In case any Member of the League shall, before becoming a Member of the League, have undertaken any obligations inconsistent with the terms of this Convenant, it shall be the duty of such Member to take immediate steps to procure its release from such obligations."

The rapporteur stated that the second letter cited by him formally announced the intention of the representatives of Luxemburg to adapt their legislation to the obligations which would flow from the admission of the Grand Duchy into the League. In view of what was thus reported, the Committee recommended the admission of the Grand Duchy, and the Assembly acted accordingly.[7]

Did Luxemburg become a member?

The decision of the Assembly was reported by Mr. Reuter to the Luxemburg Parliament, which, however, took no immediate action, either with a view to giving its consent to the affiliation to the League,[8] or to a revision of the Constitution. The question then arose whether the Covenant was in force with regard to Luxemburg before such assent was given, and such modifications effected.

That question was the subject of a letter of 25 April 1921 from Mr. Reuter to the Secretary-General of the League. He further inquired whether Luxemburg would be called to take part in the next session of the Assembly, were the constitutional revision not yet to have materialized.[9] In a letter of 20 May, Mr. Reuter reverted to the matter, explaining that the accession of Luxemburg to the League had not yet

---

[7] *Ibid.,* p. 194.

[8] Article 37 of the Constitution of Luxemburg then, as now, provided that no treaty would have "any effect" until it had received the assent of the Chamber. See above, p. 238.

[9] For this letter, and those of 20 May and 2 June, see *ibid.,* p. 197, in note.

received parliamentary ratification, and that that ratification was needed to give the Government the necessary means to pay the contribution of Luxemburg to the League. In a letter of 2 June, finally, Mr. Reuter requested the Secretary-General to submit the question to the Council, and stated that "au point de vue du droit interne la ratification parlementaire de l'incorporation du Luxembourg dans la Société des Nations devant intervenir sous la forme d'une revision constitutionnelle", and that the procedure required for this was complicated. He added that until such procedure had been satisfied, the Government did not dispose of the legal means necessary to fulfil obligations under the Pact.

When transmitting the correspondence between himself and the Government of Luxemburg to the Council of the League, Sir Eric Drummond commented that the expression "parliamentary ratification", occurring in the letter of 20 May, was used ambiguously: the accession of Luxemburg had taken place without any reservation with regard to the consent of Parliament, or other ratification.[1] The Secretary-General's opinion in the matter, which may easily be deduced from that comment, alone, was to be made quite explicit in a letter which he submitted for the approval of the Council, and by which, he proposed, the Council should reply to Mr. Reuter. The letter is of particular interest since it was, in fact, adopted by the Council on 21 June 1921, and may thus be said to express the official position of that body.

The letter stated, first, that Luxemburg had been admitted in a final and unqualified manner on the basis of an application the only reservation of which had been withdrawn. Second, it held that the rights and obligations of Luxemburg as a member resulted directly from the act of admission and from that alone. Third, the Secretary-General submitted that even if the Government of Luxemburg was obliged to bring about a revision of the Constitution and legislation of the Duchy to avoid conflicts with its international obligations, the situation was not provisional from the point of view of the League. The rights and obligations of Luxemburg had been established once and for all by the accession to the League. Fourth, the Secretary-General consequently advised that Luxemburg had the right to take part in every session of the Assembly. With regard to the Luxemburg contribution, finally, the Council proposed its payment to be deferred for four months.[2]

In this connexion it may be noted that no constitutional revision was

[1] *Ibid.*
[2] *Ibid.*, p. 198.

effected later, nor was the formal assent of the Parliament ever given to the accession to the League.[3]

Conclusion

The position taken by the Council has been criticized by several writers.[4] This is not the place, however, to enter into a discussion of the wisdom of the stand taken by the Council. The controversy is here merely seen as a concrete case in which the question of the international relevance of a constitutionally needed parliamentary action was at issue. The conclusion is inevitable that, in spite of the notice given by the delegation of Luxemburg to the effect that parliamentary assent was required for undertaking the final obligation, and in spite of the notice given later by the Government of Luxemburg that the internal legal basis for the fulfilment of the obligations under the Covenant did not exist, the Council very firmly took the position that no formal reservation as to ratification having been advanced, the application and the vote of the Assembly sufficed to create an obligation under international law, and that the constitutional position, whatever its effect internally, was of no relevance for the binding character of the international obligation. The position of the Council may be summed up as follows: an international obligation undertaken in conflict with a constitutional limitation of substance imposes a duty upon the state to modify its constitution; an international obligation entered into by a government in excess of its constitutional competence is nevertheless binding.

---

[3] De Visscher, pp. 170–171.

[4] See Wehrer, *op. cit.*, p. 197; see also Fairman (p. 449), who stresses that the Luxemburg delegation had made it clear that its action needed parliamentary assent, and that such could not very well have been given in advance, since the delegation went to Geneva to bargain for a special status. He concludes, however, that the subsequent conduct of Luxemburg constituted a tacit ratification.

De Visscher (pp. 171–172) asserts that when, as in the present instance, a state organ points to a constitutional provision limiting its competence, that clause comes to constitute a suspensive condition for the binding effect of the obligation undertaken by that organ. He concludes, however, that Luxemburg became irrevocably bound by the vote of the Assembly because the Luxemburg Parliament had earlier expressed the desire that the Grand Duchy should become a member, and the League, thus being assured of the position of the Parliament, was not concerned with the form which the approval of the Parliament ought to take under the law of Luxemburg. The reference made by the Luxemburg delegation to the need for parliamentary action had had regard to approval of a modification of the status of neutrality, not to the act of accession.

12. Controversy of 1921 between Austria and Rumania

In 1921 Rumania appears to have asserted that an agreement made with Austria lacked validity under international law, because Rumanian parliamentary assent had not been secured. The primary material on this incident has not been available to the present writer, but the accounts given of it by various writers do not substantially differ.

On 14 August 1921, a provisional commercial agreement was concluded at Bucharest between Austria and Rumania. It was to enter into force when approved by the two parties,[5] to remain valid for a year, and to continue in force thereafter unless denounced with three months' notice. According to one version, at least, the agreement entered into force on 6 October by means of an exchange of notes between the two Governments.[6] The agreement was at any rate published by both sides.[7]

In the summer of 1921 the Austrian Government appears to have suggested to the Rumanian Government that a convention should be concluded on certain matters cognate to those treated in the provisional agreement. When, in reply to this proposal, the Rumanian Government intimated a willingness to conclude a regular commercial convention, the Austrian Government remarked that there already existed one which had not been denounced. To this remark the Rumanian Government objected that that convention was not binding: some provisions of the convention, it contended, were contrary to the treaty of St. Germain. Moreover, although the agreement had been published, Article 11 of it provided for entry into force not by its being published, but by its being adopted by the respective Parliaments.[8] Such, indeed, seems to have been the Rumanian text of the treaty, while the Austrian text seems to have referred to approval by the Governments.[9] The Rumanian Government argued further that the Constitution of Rumania provided that treaties concerning commerce, navigation and similar matters re-

[5] By the two Governments, according to the Austrians, and by the two Parliaments, according to the Rumanians. See Wohlmann, pp. 91 ff.

[6] *Ibid.*

[7] *Bundesgesetzblatt für die Republik Österreich*, No. 40 (1920) and *Monitorul Official* of 19 October 1920, No. 157. See Seidl-Hohenveldern, "Relation of International Law to Internal Law in Austria" in *A.J.I.L.*, vol. 49 (1955), p. 473, note 156.

[8] McNair states that the Rumanian Government argued that the agreement was not binding because not approved by the Rumanian Government. All other writers, however, cite the Rumanians as arguing the lack of validity as a consequence of absence of parliamentary approval. See McNair, p. 12; *cf.* Chailley, p. 223; de Visscher, p. 160; Seidl-Hohenveldern, *loc. cit.*, and Wohlmann, *loc. cit.*

[9] Wohlmann, *loc. cit.*

quired legislative approval, and that but for such approval, they did not have binding force.[1] The convention in question, not having been submitted to Parliament, could not be binding.

The Austrian Government refused to accept the reasoning advanced by Rumania. It appears to have argued that, the convention being published on both sides, and being proclaimed in Rumania by a decree, carrying the signature of the King,[2] could not be challenged internationally on the ground of Rumanian constitutional law.

The controversy was eventually eliminated by the negotiation and conclusion of a new convention, but neither party ever accepted the juridical arguments of the other. The incident is generally, and it seems with good reason, regarded as inconclusive.

13. POLITIS INCIDENT 1925

An incident concerning the validity of an international obligation which a diplomat purported to assume on behalf of Greece, without being competent under the Greek Constitution to do so, occurred in 1925 in the Council of the League of Nations.

Under the auspices of the League, negotiations had taken place in 1924 between Mr. Kalfoff, representing Bulgaria, and Mr. Politis on behalf of the Greek Government, and agreement had been reached on the question of how to settle a dispute concerning minorities. Rather than put this agreement in the form of a convention between the two States, the negotiators suggested that each State should undertake certain obligations—identical in substance—vis-à-vis the Council of the League. For that purpose each of the two representatives submitted to the Council a proposal embodying the obligations to be undertaken by his Government, and each proposal ended as follows:

"The stipulations of the present scheme will come into force as soon as they have been approved by the Council of the League."[3]

Upon the basis of an authorization given by the Council which, on 29 September 1924, accepted the proposals made by the two representatives, the President of the Council and the Secretary-General of the League signed with the two representatives protocols embodying two

---

[1] *Ibid.*; and de Visscher, p. 160.

[2] Wohlmann, *loc. cit.*; Seidl-Hohenveldern states that the convention was "duly ratified by the King of Rumania": *loc. cit.*

[3] League of Nations, *Official Journal*, 5th Year (1934), No. 10, pp. 1349 ff. and 1599 ff.

sets of proposals, and their acceptance by the Council. Subsequently it turned out, however, that in purporting to sign the protocol on behalf of Greece with immediate binding effect, Mr. Politis, although in good faith, had acted not only in excess of the authority conferred upon him by his Government, but also of the authority possessed by that Government under the Greek Constitution. Though the Greek Government submitted the protocol to the National Assembly, it appears to have been unable to recommend the instrument to the approval of that body, and, on 3 February 1925, the National Assembly unanimously resolved to reject the protocol.[4]

By a letter of 11 February 1925, the permanent Greek representative to the League of Nations communicated the resolution of the National Assembly to the Secretary-General, who circulated it for the consideration of the Council. On 14 March 1925, the latter body adopted a report submitted to it by its President, and covering the issue. The report read in part:

"On signing with the representative of Greece the Protocol of September 29th, 1924, the Council of the League of Nations was justified in thinking that it was signing a document absolutely legal in all its parts and provisions, including the clause in accordance with which the proposal made by Greece came into force as soon as its stipulations were approved by the Council of the League of Nations.

"It now appears, however, from the official statements made by the Greek delegate accredited to the Council of the League of Nations, that the representative of Greece who signed the Protocol was not authorized to append to that instrument the final clause, by the inclusion of which the Protocol in question was withdrawn from the Parliamentary sanction required in the case of any international instrument of this nature, in accordance with the fundamental law of the country and the invariable usage obtaining there.

"The Council of the League of Nations expresses its deep regret at having proceeded to sign, through its President, an instrument which it felt justified in regarding as a contract between itself and the Greek Government. Although this document at the moment of signature, so far as the Council is concerned, assumed the character of a complete legal agreement, the Council does not desire to impose on Greece any new obligations which are not provided for in the treaties and to which the National Assembly has already refused its consent."[5]

---

[4] The facts related in the text are based upon a speech by Mr. Venizelos in the Council, on 14 March 1925. See League of Nations, *Official Journal*, 6th Year (1925), pp. 480–482. De Visscher states (p. 172) that the Greek Government had strongly recommended that the National Assembly approve the protocol, but the authority for the statement does not appear from his account. References to the debates in the Assembly are given by Georgopoulos, *La ratification des traités et la collaboration du parlement* (1939), p. 32.

The studiously vague formulation of the report has not failed to evoke conflicting interpretations. Chailley stresses that the Council did not say the protocol was valid; only that it had *believed* it valid. In his opinion, this shows that the Council wished to demonstrate that it had acted in good faith. But, asks Chailley, if the international validity of the protocol were not thought dependent upon Greek law, why should the Council have feared the reproach of having ignored that law? Chailley finds confirmation of his own interpretation in the circumstance that Mr. Venizelos, Greek representative in the Council, underlined that neither the prestige of the League, nor the honour of the Greek Government was affected by the refusal to apply a protocol which, juridically, did not exist,[6] and that the meeting, ending as it did, on that note, must be considered to have accepted the view thus propounded. This extremely subtle, not to say far-fetched, interpretation is justly criticized by de Visscher who, with much better reason, it is submitted, concludes that in the opinion of the Council, Mr. Politis had validly bound his country, and that, although the Council gave way to Greece, it did so in terms which did not conceal that the Council left law aside for reasons of courtesy and convenience.[7]

Among other writers' treatment of the incident, Professor Fairman's view may be noted to the effect that the resolution inferentially upholds the Greek position.[8] Mervyn Jones finds the resolution inconclusive, but stresses that the Council did not, at any rate, reject the view that constitutional provisions are relevant in considering the creation of an international obligation.[9] Vitta, finally—like de Visscher criticizing Chailley's interpretation—cites the report in support of his view that constitutional limitations have no international relevance.[1]

This writer finds it difficult not to agree with the interpretation suggested by de Visscher. The phrase "... the Council does not desire to impose on Greece any new obligations ... to which the National Assembly has already refused its consent" seems to imply that the Council thought it could legally have imposed such obligations, if it had only desired to do so, and that it refrained from doing so for reasons of expediency.[2]

---

[5] League of Nations, *Official Journal,* 6th Year (1925), pp. 478–479.

[6] Paraphrase by Chailley (pp. 232 ff.). Original formulation found in League of Nations, *Official Journal,* 6th Year (1925), p. 482.

[7] De Visscher, p. 174.

[8] Fairman, p. 450.

[9] Jones, pp. 142–143.

[1] Vitta, p. 93 and note therein.

[2] *Cf.* Pallieri, p. 485.

14. ARGENTINA'S MEMBERSHIP IN THE LEAGUE OF NATIONS

The international relevance of a constitutional requirement for parliamentary assent to treaties was at issue also in connexion with the admission of Argentina into the League of Nations.

Under Article 1 of the Covenant, Argentina, among other states, had the opportunity to become an original member of the League by acceding without reservation to the Covenant, such accession to be effected by a declaration deposited with the Secretariat within two months of the coming into force of the Covenant; under the same Article, notice of each accession was to be sent by the Secretariat to all members of the League.[3]

The acts of adherence

The Versailles Treaty was signed on 28 June 1919, and the Covenant entered into force on 10 January 1920. At that time Article 86 (14) of the Constitution of Argentina invested the President of the State with the treaty-making power, while Article 67 (19) of the same instrument gave the legislature of the State the power of approving or rejecting treaties. Apparently, action by Congress was therefore required before the President could legally express the final consent of the State to a treaty.[4] On 12 July 1919, however, without awaiting such action, and without even awaiting the entry into force of the Covenant, the Foreign Minister of the Argentine Republic instructed the Minister to Paris as follows:

"In accordance with Article 1 of the Covenant of the League of Nations, the Executive Power has decided to adhere to it without any reservation. Publish this decision. Please deposit with the Secretariat the appropriate communication."[5]

As a result, on 18 July 1919, the Argentine Minister to Paris addressed Sir Eric Drummond, the Secretary-General designate of the League, a letter reading in part as follows:

"... I am instructed to adhere unreservedly to the League of Nations in the name of the Argentine Republic, and in accordance with the terms of Article 1 of the Covenant.

"I hasten, therefore, to do so in order that you may take such action as you consider necessary."[6]

[3] For the article, see Goodrich and Hambro, *The Charter of the United Nations* (2nd ed., 1949), p. 555.

[4] Hudson, "The Argentine Republic and the League of Nations" in *A.J.I.L.*, vol. 28 (1934), p. 131.

[5] *Ibid.*, p. 126.

[6] *Ibid.*; and League of Nations, *Official Journal*, No. 1 (1920), p. 13.

In reply, Sir Eric stated that the League was not yet legally constituted, and that he could not exercise any functions as Secretary-General. He concluded by inquiring if the letter of the Minister signified that Argentina "désire faire son adhésion à la Société aussitôt que la commission des ratifications nécessaires au Traité de Paix lui en fournira formellement le moyen."[7]

On 29 July 1919, the Argentine Minister answered in the affirmative:

"Such is, in fact, the interpretation that should be given to my note of the 18th July: the Government of the Argentine Republic adheres to the League of Nations, and it will ratify this adhesion as soon as the Chambers have given their approval. The Secretariat-General of the League of Nations will be officially advised of this in due course."[8]

When did the adherence take effect?

Professor Hudson has concluded that the exchange of letters described above had no binding effect, but constituted merely an indication of the attitude of the Argentine Government. He refers particularly to the circumstances that the Versailles Treaty was not yet in force, that the Argentine Republic had not yet been invited to accede, and that practice offered examples of accession conditioned upon subsequent parliamentary approval.[9] Dr. de Visscher has come to the same final conclusion, but sees the basis for it in the circumstance that after the above-mentioned exchange of letters had taken place, on 10 January 1920, the date of the entry into force of the Covenant, M. Clemenceau, President of the Peace Conference, addressed an invitation to Argentina to accede to the Pact.[1] If Argentina had already been a member, the invitation would have been redundant.

In spite of the considerations advanced by these authorities, it appears that the League of Nations, or at least its Secretary-General, and possibly also the Government of the Argentine Republic, regarded the premature exchange of letters as effective.[2] Professor Hudson reports himself, indeed, that on 10 January 1920, the very day the Covenant entered into force, and the day M. Clemenceau formally invited accessions, and thus at a time when no reply had been rendered to the invitation, at any

[7] Hudson, p. 126.

[8] Cit. from Hudson, pp. 126–127. Original in League of Nations, *Official Journal*, No. 1 (1920), p. 14.

[9] *Op. cit.*, p. 127.

[1] De Visscher, p. 162.

[2] That view has support also in Schücking and Wehberg, *Die Satzung des Völkerbundes*, I Band (3rd ed., 1931), p. 292.

rate from the Argentine Republic, the Secretary-General notified the Argentine Foreign Minister that notice of the Argentine Republic's accession to the Covenant had been sent to other governments, and, on 11 February 1920, that note was formally acknowledged.[3] Presumably the Secretary-General, not unreasonably, regarded the letter of 18 July 1919 as an accession subject only to the condition that the Covenant should enter into force. It seems likely, moreover, that this was precisely what was wanted by the Argentine Minister to Paris, to judge by his expression ". . . the Argentine Republic desires to adhere to the League of Nations, as soon as the necessary ratification of the Peace Treaty makes this possible."[4] That early date was, indeed, 10 January 1920.

The circumstance that an invitation to accede was issued that day in no way contradicts this interpretation, for it may well be that the advance accession was considered effective the moment the invitation was sent. Hudson's statement that practice offered examples of accessions conditioned on later parliamentary approval, and that such procedure was not excluded by the language of the Covenant[5] will not be challenged. Nor is it subject to doubt that the expression "unreserved" in the letter of accession of 18 July 1919 had reference to absence of reservations regarding substance, and not reservations regarding the mode of entry into force. However, instruments of accession, like instruments of ratification, are certainly not presumed to be made subject to subsequent parliamentary or other approval, and the letter of 29 July 1919 from the Argentine Minister can hardly be said to have expressly subjected the accession to parliamentary approval. It was not so interpreted by the Secretary-General, at any rate. The interpretation here given to the exchange of letters seems, further, not precluded by the reply given on 16 January 1920 by the President of the Argentine Republic to the invitation of 10 January. He stated as follows:

"I take pleasure in transmitting to Your Excellency the formal ratification of the Argentine Government under the conditions of adhesion expressed in the note of July 18, 1919, addressed to the Secretary-General of the League by our representative in France."[6]

Any interpretation of this communication is necessarily uncertain. However, the statement does not appear in any way to contradict the

[3] Hudson, p. 128.

[4] Cited from Hudson, p. 126. Original in League of Nations, *Official Journal*, No. 1 (1920), p. 14.

[5] Hudson, p. 127.

[6] *Ibid.*, p. 128.

construction that the note of 18 July 1919 was held effective as from 10 January 1920. Perhaps the intention of the new statement was merely to confirm that note. That 18 July 1919 continued to be considered the date of accession, and that that act was thought ratified by the letter of 16 January 1920, may be seen from a message of 6 June 1923 in which President Alvear of Argentina asked the legislature of the State for an appropriation to pay the country's contribution to the League. He is reported to have referred to the accession as follows:

> "La referida adhesión se operó con el depósito de la communicación correspondiente hecha en la Secretaría de la Liga ... el 18 de Julio de 1919 ...; y fué ratificada por el Senor Presidente de la Nación en 16 de enero de 1920 respondiento a la invitación a adherir al Pacto de la Liga que dirigió el Presidente del Consejo Supremo de las Potencias Aliadas y Asociadas."[7]

The subsequent conduct of the Argentine Republic was also such as to bear out the conclusion that in regard to the League, the Argentine Government considered itself as definitely bound. It is true that the delegation of that State withdrew from the Assembly of the League at the first session, but the reason for this action was that certain Argentine proposals for the revision of the Covenant had not been accepted. The Argentine Government participated in other League activities, however, and paid contributions to the League, frequently basing itself upon authorization of the Argentine Congress.[8]

The position under Argentine law

In spite of repeated attempts by the Argentine executive to induce Congress to approve the Covenant, as was required by the Constitution of the State, such action was not taken until over ten years after the accession had taken place. There is evidence showing that in this period the Argentine Government considered its accession valid under international law, but illegal under constitutional law. Thus, *Harvard Research* cites Kelchner as saying that in April 1926, when the Cabinet of the State was considering whether it should send a delegation to a conference held under the auspices of the League, the conclusion was reached that "Argentina was a member of the League of Nations from the international point of view, but not from an internal constitutional viewpoint."[9] It may be noted, furthermore, that when the Covenant

[7] *Ibid.*, p. 129.

[8] *Ibid.*, pp. 128–129.

[9] Kelchner, *Latin-American Relations with the League of Nations* (1930), pp. 47 ff. Cit. from *Harvard Research*, p. 1004.

was, at last, successfully submitted for the approval of the Argentine Chamber of Deputies in September 1932, it appears to have been "explained during the debate that Argentina already was a member of the League from an international viewpoint, but not from an internal constitutional viewpoint, the purpose of the bill being to clear up this ambiguous situation."[1]

In view of the Cabinet decision of 1926, cited above, it is not likely, as suggested by de Visscher[2] that the explanation given in the debate in 1932 was merely a tactical move to facilitate approval.

Against the background given above, a cable of 26 September 1933, sent by the Argentine Foreign Minister to the Secretary-General of the League, is remarkable, for it implied that until the parliamentary approval had been given, the Argentine Republic had not been validly bound by the Covenant. The cable read as follows:

"The Argentine Parliament has just sanctioned in both Houses, the Chamber of Deputies and the Senate, which yesterday unanimously approved it, our country's accession to the League of Nations, at the same time approving the Covenant in accordance with the constitutional powers of Congress, which gives legal validity to the international tie that will henceforth bind us together."[3]

The communication quoted did not provoke any action whatever on the part of the League, and nothing further seems to have happened in the matter.

Conclusion

On the basis of the above description and discussion of the relations between the League and the Argentine Republic, it may be concluded that from July 1919 and until the cable of 26 September 1933, the executive branch of the Argentine Government consistently considered the State bound under international law by the Covenant, although it recognized that the situation was irregular from a constitutional point of view.[4] It seems to have considered the letter of 18 July 1919 as a declaration of accession with effect from 10 January 1920,[5] and, in spite

---

[1] *The New York Times,* 29 September 1932, p. 1, as cited by Hudson, p. 129.

[2] De Visscher, p. 163.

[3] League of Nations, *Doc.* A. 30. 1933. Cit. from Hudson, p. 129.

[4] The same conclusion is drawn by Fairman (p. 447), who remarks, however, that the Covenant was not included among the *Tratados y Convenciones Vigentes en la Nación Argentina,* published by the Ministerio de Relaciones Exteriores y Culto in 1926.

[5] Both Hudson (pp. 127 and 131) and de Visscher (p. 164) deny the possibility of accession being effected by the letter of 18 July 1919, and consider the cable of 16

of the reference in the Argentine letter of 29 July 1919 to parliamentary action, this view was shared by the League authorities. Dr. de Visscher's conclusion to the effect that the League must have considered the constitutional provisions of purely internal relevance[6] may be accepted, therefore, though it must be noted that the question seems never to have come to a head in that organization.

In the opinion of de Visscher, the incident has special interest as contrasting a state of South America where allegedly the concept of the international relevance of constitutional limitations is accepted, with an organization originating in Europe where, supposedly, the opposite doctrine prevails. Though it is admitted that the Argentine cable of 26 September 1933 is difficult to understand if not seen as an expression of the theory that constitutional limitations upon the treaty-making power are effective in the international sphere, that cable, while not insignificant, cannot alone cancel out the fact that for thirteen years the opposite view was taken by the executive branch of the Argentine Government, apparently without protest from the legislature. This circumstance, and the League's adherence to the same principle are, in the opinion of the present writer, the most significant features of the case.

15. IRISH FREE STATE ANNUITIES DISPUTE 1932

Upon taking office in the Irish Free State, in 1932, Mr. de Valera challenged the validity of two agreements made by the Government of that State with the United Kingdom in 1923 and 1926, alleging that the agreements required parliamentary ratification.[7]

January as the effective instrument. The discussion in the text shows why the present writer has reached a different conclusion.

[6] De Visscher, p. 164.

[7] Having reached the conclusion that it did not appear that both parties to this controversy regarded principles of international law as applicable even by analogy, Mervyn Jones refrains from using the case as evidence. *Op. cit.,* p. 148, note 6. The case is cited, however, by McNair (p. 13), and in *Harvard Research,* p. 1004. Though Sir Ivor Jennings has discussed the agreements in question and their relation to the public law of the British Commonwealth and to international law, it is not entirely clear to what extent he considered rules of international law relevant. He states that with some modifications caused by the common allegiance to the Crown, the relations between the nations of the Empire "sont essentiellement ceux du droit international", adding: "c'est pourquoi le droit interne de l'Empire Britannique doit contenir les principes du droit international, à moins que les rapports spéciaux dont il vient d'être question ne s'y opposent." See article entitled "Le Traité Anglo-

Before details of this incident are given the following facts should be noted. Upon the signing, on 6 December 1921, of "Articles of Agreement for a Treaty between Great Britain and Ireland," the Irish Free State was accorded independence and dominion status.[8] Article 18 of that agreement provided that the approval of the legislatures of both states was required, and such approval was given.[9] The Constitution of the Irish Free State, adopted by the Irish and British Parliaments in 1922, contained no express provision regulating the procedure for the conclusion of treaties.[1]

On 12 February 1923 an instrument termed "Financial Agreements between the British Government and the Irish Free State Government" was signed.[2] It did not provide for ratification, nor was it, in fact, ratified or submitted for the formal approval of either the British or the Irish legislature. Another instrument, called "Heads of the Ultimate Financial Settlement between the British Government and the Government of the Irish Free State" was signed on behalf of the two Governments on 19 March 1926.[3] Like the agreement cited above, this instru-

Irlandais de 1921 et son interprétation" in *Revue de Droit International et de Législation Comparée*, vol. 13 (1932), pp. 473–523, at p. 495.

Sir Ivor Jennings maintains that the treaties here under discussion were binding upon the Irish Free State "non à raison de son propre droit public, mais à raison du droit public général de la Communauté britannique des Nations, droit qui est fondé sur les conventions constitutionnelles générales qui règlent les rapports entre les membres de cette communauté." *Ibid.*, p. 510. While it cannot be inferred from this statement that its author thought rules of international law relevant, other statements by the same writer seem to imply this. See *ibid.*, pp. 512, 514 and 517, and see the quotation below, p. 342, note 7. It may further be noted, in this connexion, that in a recent work Sir Ivor has stated explicitly that "agreements within the Commonwealth are governed by international law." See Jennings, *The Constitution of Ceylon* (3rd ed., 1953), p. 138.

In the opinion of the present writer, the statements of the parties to the dispute leave little doubt that their positions were taken on the basis of international law. The same conclusion is reached by Hollis, *The International Effect of "Unconstitutional Treaties"* (Special Report, Columbia University, School of Law, 1936), note 142.

[8] The discussion whether this agreement implied the recognition of an existing international personality, or that personality came into existence only through the adoption by the British Parliament of the "Irish Free State (Agreement) Act of 1922" is not of relevance in this connexion. See Jennings, pp. 482–484. For the agreement, see *L.N.T.S.*, vol. 17.

[9] Jennings, p. 481.

[1] For the text of the Constitution, see *B.F.S.P.*, vol. 116 (1922), pp. 260 ff.

[2] *Cmd.* 4061 (1932); Jennings, p. 506.

[3] *Cmd.* 2757 (1932); Jennings, pp. 507–508.

ment does not appear to have provided for either parliamentary or international ratification, or to have, in fact, been submitted for the formal consent of either Parliament.

Throughout the twenties, the two agreements seem to have been respected by the Government of the Free State. The agreement of 1923 is stated to have been discussed in the Dàil, and payments to have been effected under it and reported in the accounts of the Free State.[4] The agreement of 1926 is, likewise, reported to have been discussed in the Dàil, on 8 December 1926, and to have been published.[5]

Upon gaining office in March, 1932, Mr. de Valera appears to have stated his intention to stop payments which had, until then, been made under the agreements.[6] Referring to this statement, the British Secretary of State for Dominion Affairs, in a communication of 23 March 1932 to the Minister of External Affairs of the Irish Free State, expressed the opinion of the United Kingdom Government, as follows:

"... the Irish Free State Government are bound by the most formal and explicit undertaking to continue to pay the land annuities ... and the failure to do so would be a manifest violation of an engagement which is binding in law and in honour on the Irish Free State, whatever administration may be in power, in exactly the same way as the Treaty [of 1921] itself is binding on both countries."[7]

Mr. de Valera having replied on 5 April 1932 that his Government was not aware of the existence of any formal and explicit undertakings to the effect contended,[8] the Secretary of State for Dominion Affairs, on 9 April 1932, expressed the surprise of his Government, made express reference to the agreements of 1923 and 1926, and reiterated the view of his Government that these agreements were binding in law and honour upon whatever administration was in power.[9]

In a subsequent exchange of letters concerning the possible submission of the controversy to arbitration, Mr. de Valera insisted that the items submitted should include all annual payments made by the Irish Government to the British Government "except those made in pursuance of agreements formally ratified by the Parliaments of both States." He added that any agreement on arbitration must be submitted for the

---

[4] Jennings, p. 512.

[5] *Cmd.* 4056 (1932), p. 8; Jennings, p. 508.

[6] Jennings, p. 508.

[7] *Cmd.* 4056 (1932), p. 3.

[8] *Ibid.,* p. 5.

[9] *Ibid.,* pp. 7 and 8.

approval of the Irish Parliament.[1] The British Government, which declined to accept the condition suggested for an arbitration, stated in reply to the specific point quoted above that it was "unable to admit the distinction sought to be drawn between agreements formally ratified by the Parliaments of the United Kingdom and the Irish Free State and other agreements formally entered into between the two countries."[2]

Mr. de Valera's intimation that only agreements formally ratified were not thought open to objection was confirmed in a later memorandum in which the Government of the Irish Free State declined to recognize that the agreements of 1923 and 1926 were binding, for the reason, among others, that they had not been submitted to the Irish Parliament for ratification.[3] On this point the British Government replied:

"According to the recognized practice of nations, agreements concluded between representatives of Governments are binding upon the Governments concerned unless they are expressly stated to be subject to ratification."[4]

The British Government added that no such statement occurred in the agreements, and pointed out that, on the Irish side, the agreement of 1923 had been signed by the President of the Executive Council, and the 1926 agreement by the Minister of Finance. Moreover, the Irish Free State Parliament had passed legislation in order to give effect to that part of the 1923 agreement which provided for payment of the land annuities.[5]

The Government of the Irish Free State continued to maintain, however, that the agreements were not binding. In a further memorandum, it contended that the agreement of 1923 had been kept secret from the Parliaments of both States for nine years, and that the terms of the agreement of 1926 had not been disclosed until eight months after the act of signature. It called attention to the circumstance that there had been a stipulation for ratification in the treaty of 1921, and argued that "a similar condition must be implied in any instrument intended to amend, extend, or abridge its terms." The agreements of 1923 and 1926 were of this kind, and the British Government had not explained "why, if these instruments were intended by both Governments to

[1] Communication of 16 June 1932, *Cmd.* 4116 (1932), p. 2.

[2] Communication of 22 June 1932, *Cmd.* 4116 (1932), p. 3.

[3] Memorandum forwarded by Mr. de Valera under date of 12 October 1932. *Cmd.* 4184 (1932), p. 3.

[4] Memorandum forwarded to the Irish Free State representatives on 15 October 1932, *Cmd.* 4184 (1932), p. 7.

[5] *Ibid.*

operate and rank as binding international agreements, the same practice was not followed in relation to them as in the case of those agreements for the amendment or variation of the Treaty [of 1921] which both sides agree were intended to be definitely binding." The Irish Government added:

"The Irish Free State Representatives cannot admit that agreements between Governments on matters of major importance are binding until they have been ratified. Ratification has become requisite by usage and is recognized by leading authorities on international law to be part of the positive law of nations. In the case of agreements which impose a charge on the revenues of the State the necessity for Parliamentary approval is universally accepted, and such approval is required by the established practice of the Irish Free State."[6]

No further expressions of the legal positions of the parties have been found, and the incident, therefore, does not offer much guidance. Sir Ivor Jennings, who has discussed the agreements, and reached the conclusion that they were valid, seems to accept all through his discussion that the Irish constitutional customs with regard to the conclusion of treaties were internationally relevant,[7] but the British Government appears not to have taken that position.[8]

It is hardly subject to doubt that the conduct of the Parliament of the Irish Free State constituted tacit approval of the agreements, but

---

[6] Memorandum forwarded by Mr. de Valera under date of 26 October 1932; in *Cmd.* 4184 (1932), p. 16.

[7] Assuming apparently that constitutional conventions of the British Commonwealth were relevant to the Irish Free State, Sir Ivor Jennings finds the agreement valid because "les traités n'ont pas besoin d'être ratifiés par le Parlement ou par les Oireachtas [the Parliament of the Irish Free State], excepté lorsqu'ils affectent des droits particuliers", which was not here the case. *Op. cit.*, p. 507. Commenting upon a contention made by Mr. de Valera to the effect that the agreement of 1923 had been concluded behind the backs of the people and could, therefore, be repudiated by him, Sir Ivor Jennings states, however, that "c'était là une nouvelle doctrine *de droit international* (et peut-être une doctrine très désirable)..." *Ibid.*, p. 512 (emphasis supplied). Having examined, further, the manner in which the Government of the Irish Free State had accepted and effected the agreements, the same writer concluded:

"Au point de vue constitutionnel, toute cette manière de procéder était parfaitement régulière. Et puisqu'elle était constitutionnellement régulière, les règles du droit international ont été observées dans la mesure où elles étaient applicables. Une violation des accords par le Gouvernement de l'Etat Libre d'Irlande serait une violation des obligations qu'il a en tant que membre de la Communauté britannique des Nations. Et si le droit internationale était pleinement applicable entre deux membres de cette Communauté, l'attitude du Gouverment irlandais constituerait également une violation du droit international." *Ibid.*, pp. 514–515.

[8] See the statement quoted in the text, p. 341.

although this circumstance may provide a conclusive answer to the question of the validity of the agreements, it is not very helpful to this discussion. It is here of greater interest to note that while the British Government took the position that ratification, whether parliamentary or international, is never internationally required unless expressly reserved, the Irish Government appears to have inclined to the view that a constitutionally required parliamentary ratification was relevant internationally, even if not expressly reserved in an agreement. The observation may finally be made that it is hard to avoid the impression that the constitutional objections advanced in this incident served chiefly as a legalistic subterfuge for the discarding of politically unpalatable agreements which were made in good faith by a preceding administration.

16. Dispute between Persia and Iraq before the League of Nations in 1935

A dispute regarding the boundary line between Persia and Iraq was brought before the Council of the League of Nations in 1935. Though the Council never declared its views in the matter, and the dispute was eventually left to the parties to be solved by negotiation, it is of interest to note the parties' divergent opinions as to the validity of treaties concluded without constitutionally required parliamentary assent.

In its first communication to the Council,[9] the Government of Iraq, as successor of the Government of the Ottoman Empire, invoked, *inter alia,* the treaty of Erzerum of 1847, and a protocol of Constantinople of 4 November 1913. The Persian Government, in its reply, immediately denied the validity of the two treaties;[1] the treaty of Erzerum for the reason, as has been developed in the first part of this study,[2] that when ratifying it in 1848, the Persian envoy, without being so authorized, expressed consent to an explanatory note; the protocol of 1913, because it had not been approved by the Mejlis although the Persian Constitution required parliamentary assent for modifications of the frontiers.[3] The Persian Government stated:

---

[9] Letter of 29 November 1934. See League of Nations, *Official Journal,* 16th Year (1935), pp. 196–197.

[1] See letter of 8 January 1935, in *ibid.,* pp. 216 ff.

[2] Above, p. 76.

[3] The relevant articles invoked were the following:

Constitution of 5 August 1906:

"Article XXII. The sale or cession of any part of the revenue or property of the

"... the Constantinople Protocol was not approved by the Mejliss; hence the condition essential for its validity, not only under municipal law, but, on the basis of municipal law, under international law, is lacking."[4]

The Persian Government pointed out, in addition, that the protocol had also not been approved by the Turkish legislature, and alleged that this was required under the Turkish Constitution.[5] To these arguments, a representative of the Government of Iraq remarked, on 14 January 1935, in the Council of the League that the Persian Mejlis had been suspended from December 1911 to December 1914. The Persian thesis, therefore, amounted to saying that in that period Persia would not have been able to conclude any valid treaty regarding her frontiers, and this could hardly be correct. He added:

"Apart from this point, however, I submit with confidence that failure to comply with constitutional provisions as to parliamentary approval or ratification does not affect the validity, under international law, of a treaty or protocol regularly concluded, which does not in terms refer to these matters, or, as in this case, provide for ratification at all."[6]

A Persian representative, appearing before the Council of the League on the following day, dealt at length with the treaty of Erzerum, but his discussion of that treaty is not of interest here, since he argued that it lacked validity primarily because the Persian envoy had exceeded his competence.[7] He also made reference, however, to the contention made by the representative of Iraq that a constitutionally required parlia-mentary ratification was not relevant under international law unless expressly reserved in the treaty, and maintained that it was contrary to the doctrine and practice of contemporary law. With regard, finally,

---

State, and any alteration or rectification of the frontiers of the State, may only take place with the sanction of the Mejlis."

"Article XXIV. The conclusion of treaties and agreements and the grant of commercial, industrial, or agricultural concessions (monopolies)—whether the beneficiaries be Persians or foreigners—must be ratified by the Mejlis, except in the case of treaties which must remain secret in the interests of the State and Nation."

Addition to the Constitutional Laws (October 7, 1907):

"Article III. The frontiers of the State, provinces, and communes may only be modified in virtue of a law." *Ibid.*, p. 234.

[4] *Ibid.*, p. 220.

[5] Article 7 of the Ottoman Constitution of 22 December 1909, read in part as follows: "The sanction of Parliament is required for the conclusion of treaties relating to peace, commerce, or the cession or annexation of territory." *Ibid.*, p. 235.

[6] *Ibid.*, p. 116.

[7] *Ibid.*, p. 121. Mervyn Jones, nevertheless, cites the Persian representative *in extenso* on this point. See Jones, pp. 143–144.

to the Iraqi observation that the Persian Parliament, being dissolved from December 1911 until December 1914, could not have been consulted, the Persian representative in the Council objected:

"... But the Constitution remained intact, with this vital article, embodied in the amendment of 1907, that 'the fundamental bases of the Constitution cannot be suspended.' The Mejlis, which was dissolved in December 1911, met again in December 1914. Iraq replies that it was impossible to wait for three years. Why such haste, when, as I have shown, this period of waiting, dating from 1847, amounted to nearly seventy years? ..."[8]

He added that parliamentary approval would have been required under the Ottoman Constitution, and that the Ottoman Parliament had been in session.

Consideration of the controversy was adjourned by the Council and later, at the request of the parties, left to them for direct negotiation,[9] and the Council therefore never had an opportunity to express itself upon the issue that is of interest in this connexion. The incident, therefore, only reflects the positions taken by the parties.

17. DENUNCIATION OF THE FINNISH–GERMAN PACT OF 26 JUNE 1944

It is reported that, on 28 August 1944, the Finnish Minister accredited in Berlin informed the German Under-Secretary of State, Mr. Steengracht, that the Finnish Government did not consider itself bound by an undertaking entered into on 26 June 1944, by the then President of Finland, Risto Ryti, not to make or permit the conclusion of a separate peace with the Soviet Union without prior German approval, and that Mr. Steengracht had voiced a vigorous protest against the Finnish position.[1]

The following account of the affair will demonstrate why the Finnish position does not, as has been suggested by one authority,[2] constitute evidence of the view that constitutional limitations are effective internationally.

By Midsummer 1944, Russian troops having broken through the Finnish lines on the Carelian Isthmus, the situation was critical for

---

[8] League of Nations, *Official Journal,* 16th year (1935), pp. 121–122.

[9] *Ibid.,* p. 1204.

[1] See Tanner, *Vägen till fred, 1943–1944* (1952), p. 258.

[2] Ross, p. 206, note 1.

Finland. The alternatives appeared to be either to capitulate or to obtain German support in return for a pledge not to make peace separately. The views in the Cabinet were divided, and the Parliament was thought to be split on the issue into two groups of approximately the same size.[3]

In his memoirs, Marshal Mannerheim, the then Commander-in-Chief, states that he thought the agreement should be made, and that such a form should be used that the President committed himself only, and not the Government and the Parliament. Were the President later to resign, the State would again be free to act as the situation required.[4] Mr. Tanner, Minister of Finance at the time, reports, on the other hand, that Mannerheim had suggested that the pledge should be submitted to Parliament and receive such treatment, if possible, that it might later be claimed that the decision had not been a true expression of the will of Parliament, and that a new government would be free to disregard it.[5]

Whichever account of the Marshal's view is correct, it seems that on 25 June 1944, President Ryti declared in the Cabinet that he would not sign an agreement without the consent of Parliament, and that the Cabinet decided that the matter should be placed before Parliament by way of information. Parliament should be told that the Government wished to make the pledge. Were Parliament to take a different view, this would be interpreted as a sign of no confidence, and cause the Government to resign.[6]

The following day, however, on 26 June, the President is reported to have reached the conclusion that he should take the responsibility for making the declaration alone, "as it was uncertain whether parliament would approve it."[7] According to Mannerheim, the German Foreign Minister, Ribbentrop, who had come to Helsinki for the purpose of concluding the agreement, after long negotiations stated that Hitler would content himself with an undertaking in the form of a letter signed by the President personally, without any countersignature.[8]

If it was only with difficulty that the German side accepted an undertaking in this form, it seems that the Finnish Government, too, hesitated to make use of the procedure. It is reported that as it was uncertain

---

[3] Tanner, pp. 198 ff.
[4] Mannerheim, *Minnen,* part II: 1931–1946 (1952), p. 394.
[5] Tanner, p. 207.
[6] *Ibid.,* p. 203.
[7] *Ibid.,* p. 208.
[8] Mannerheim, p. 395.

whether, under the Constitution of Finland, an undertaking of this kind could be signed by the President alone,[9] the opinion of two legal experts, Dr. Erik Castrén and Professor Kaarlo Kaira, were sought. While these experts are said to have reached the conclusion that there was no legal obstacle to the use of the procedure, their opinions have not been available to the present writer.[1]

The material reported above does not allow any certain conclusion as to whether the purpose of the form chosen for the undertaking was—as stated by Mannerheim—to enable the successor of President Ryti to consider himself free from any obligation under it, or—as reported by Tanner—to avoid complications in Parliament, or perhaps both. In any case, the formulation of the undertaking which was signed on 26 June 1944 by the President alone, without any countersignature—but after a formal recommendation on the part of the Government[2]—strongly suggests the interpretation that the document was intended to constitute no more than a *traité personnel,* an undertaking devised to bind the issuer only, but not to be imputed to the State of Finland. It is reported to have read in part as follows:

"... I have taken note of the pledge, given in the name of your Government, that the German Reich in the future, as before, will give Finland ... aid ...

"I ... assure you that Finland has resolved to continue the war against Soviet Russia jointly with Germany until the threat is eliminated, to which Finland is exposed by the Soviet Union.

"Considering the aid which Germany extends to its ally Finland in the latter's difficult position, I declare, in my capacity of President of the Republic, that, without the prior agreement of the German Reich Government, I shall not make peace with the Soviet Union, nor shall I, without the prior approval of the German Reich Government, permit the Government of Finland which

---

[9] The relevant provision of the Finnish Constitution of 17 July 1919 reads in part as follows:

"Article 33. The President shall determine the relations of Finland to foreign Powers; yet the treaties concluded with foreign Powers must be approved by the Diet in so far as they contain stipulations falling within the domain of legislation or otherwise requiring, according to the Constitution, the consent of the Diet. Decisions of peace and war shall be taken by the President with the consent of the Diet ..." U.N., *Compilation,* p. 44.

[1] It may be noted that Professor Kaira is the author of a book dealing with the conclusion of treaties. The Finnish title of the book is *Valtiosopimusten tekemisestä ja voimaan saattamisesta Suomen oikeuden mukaan* (1932). [German title: "Über das Eingehen und Inkraftbringen von Staatsverträgen nach finnischem Recht"]. A detailed review of the book, in Swedish, by Björksten is to be found in *Tidskrift utgiven av Juridiska Föreningen i Finland,* 1933, pp. 115–128.

[2] Tanner, p. 209.

I have appointed, or any other person, to initiate negotiations concerning armistice or peace, or negotiations which serve these purposes."[3]

The subsequent events demonstrate clearly that the responsible authorities in Finland regarded the undertaking as a *traité personnel* and sought to take advantage of that construction.

On 1 August 1944, little more than a month after the undertaking had been made, President Ryti resigned. A few days later, Marshal Mannerheim was elected President, and a new government was appointed by him. It is expressly and convincingly explained by Tanner that the sole reason for the change was to make possible such separate negotiations for an armistice with the Soviet Union—now desired—as could not have been authorized by President Ryti due to his undertaking of 26 June.[4] The same explanation seems to have been offered, indeed, in terms couched somewhat more diplomatically, by President Mannerheim on 17 August to Field Marshal Keitel, with a view to putting the German authorities on notice that the new President did not feel obliged by the undertaking made by his predecessor.[5]

On 28 August 1944, furthermore, the Finnish Minister to Berlin officially informed the German Under-Secretary of State that his Government did not feel bound by the undertaking entered into by the former President, and received the Under-Secretary's protests.[6]

In a speech before the Finnish Parliament on 2 September 1944, and in another speech over the radio in the evening of the same day, the new Prime Minister, Mr. Hackzell, explained that the undertaking did not satisfy the requirements of the Constitution to qualify as a treaty. Accordingly, and as a change had occurred in the Presidency, the head of state was not bound by it. This position, the Prime Minister added, had been brought to the knowledge of the German Government.[7]

It must be noted finally that Ryti, Tanner and several others were sentenced to jail on 21 February 1945 by a special tribunal, on the grounds, *inter alia,* that they had entered into the agreement of 26 June

---

[3] Translation from the Swedish text, found in Tanner (p. 211), supplied by the present writer.

[4] Tanner, pp. 224–250, *passim.*

[5] Mannerheim, p. 410; Tanner, p. 252.

[6] Tanner, p. 258; the text of the protest has not been available.

[7] Tanner, p. 265; the speech held in Parliament is recorded—in Finnish and Swedish—in the published minutes of the Parliament, *Valtiopäivet,* 1944, *Pöytä-kirjat,* III (Helsinki, 1945), pp. 57 ff.; the speech given over the radio is reported in *N.T.I.R.,* vol. 15 (1944), p. D 25.

1944. Neither the Court, nor the prosecutor appear to have held, however, that the agreement was concluded in disregard of the Finnish Constitution.[8]

On the basis of the above account of the incident, it seems warranted to conclude that at no time did any Finnish authority claim that the undertaking had been made in disregard of Finnish law, and was lacking validity on that ground. The position was taken, however, that the undertaking constituted only a *traité personnel* and was not, therefore, binding upon the successor of President Ryti. There appear to have been good reasons for that position.

[8] See Procopé, *Fällande dom som friar* (1946), pp. 82, 287.

Chapter XXI

VARIOUS STATEMENTS

Certain statements unrelated to any particular diplomatic controversy should also be registered in this survey of evidence of international practice, reflecting as they do, or have been alleged to do, official opinion on the problem under discussion.

1. United States and Venezuela 1909

On 21 August 1909, a protocol between the United States and Venezuela was signed by which the latter State agreed to satisfy certain American claims. Somewhat later, the United States Minister at Caracas reported that, under the new Constitution of Venezuela, a new Government Council had come into existence on 4 August of the same year. Though the Government of Venezuela did not feel that the protocol required to be submitted to the Council, the Minister had suggested that this should be done in order to avoid any question of its validity. This proposal did not meet with the approval of the United States State Department, which instructed the Legation at Caracas as follows:

"... In signing the protocol as a finality and not ad referendum, the Venezuelan Foreign Office gave assurance that it either had or would obtain power to make its action good. Upon these assurances this Government is, internationally speaking, entitled to rely, and behind them it is not entitled to go. With the steps, if any, which the Venezuelan Government should take to regularize its action according to Venezuelan municipal law, this Department has no concern and can tender no advice."[1]

2. United States Memorandum of 1911

The same position as that reported above was expressed unequivocally in a memorandum of 1911 by the Solicitor of the Department of State. Referring to agreements not made under authorization of acts of the United States Congress, Mr. Clark wrote:

[1] Hackworth's *Digest*, vol. 5, pp. 156–157.

"... So far as the international aspect of the question is concerned, there is little doubt but that a nation entering into an arrangement by the exchange of diplomatic notes is, certainly as to the other negotiating power, estopped to say that the Foreign Office, in making such arrangement, had not power or authority in the premises. *This is the position which has been assumed not infrequently by this Government in dealing with other countries ...*

"Of course, the principles here stated must not be so extended or so announced as to interfere with our own doctrine—that the mere signature of a treaty by our representative does not bind us internationally until the treaty has been ratified by the Senate. This matter is, however, practically always met in our treaties by the provision which requires that the treaty shall not go into effect until it has been ratified, the ratifications exchanged, and the treaty proclaimed."[2]

3. CODIFICATION UNDER THE LEAGUE OF NATIONS 1927

At the end of the nineteen-twenties, it was proposed within the League of Nations that the procedures for the conclusion of treaties, among other matters, should be made the subject of codification. A sub-committee dealing with this matter pointed out that the democratisation of the national treaty-making process, on the one hand, and the respect for the traditional forms of international law, on the other, produced a conflict between international validity and domestic applicability of treaties. In order to shed more light upon the problem, this body suggested that members should undertake to communicate, reciprocally, the texts of their constitutions, as well as the authentic interpretations given to them. The proposal was included in a questionnaire, in which the member governments were asked if they considered it possible to formulate rules that might be recommended as guiding procedure for international conferences, as well as for the conclusion of treaties.[3] Among the many governments which answered the questionnaire only one objected to the proposal that constitutional texts should be exchanged. The Swiss Government answered on this point:

"Une semblable publication risquerait d'impliquer, qu'on le veuille ou non, que, dans certains cas tout au moins, un gouvernement pourrait, pour se délier d'un engagement international, exciper d'une inobservation de la Constitution. Il s'ensuivrait que, pour être certain de la parfaite régularité de l'engagement à intervenir, chacun des Etats contractants devrait vérifier si l'autre Etat ou les autres Etats ont correctement procédé selon leur propre droit constitutionnel et serait fondé, par conséquent, à présenter des objections, si

[2] *Ibid.*, p. 393. Emphasis supplied.
[3] See de Visscher, p. 211.

quelque formalité lui paraissait avoir été omise. La sécurité des relations internationales semble exiger que l'on s'en tienne au principe, généralement admis aujourd'hui, que les accords ratifiés par le pouvoir exécutif d'un Etat engagent définitivement celui-ci."[4]

The reply quoted does not leave any uncertainty as to the opinion of the Swiss Government upon the legal question discussed here. It is submitted, furthermore, that the mere circumstance that the other governments did not raise any objections to communicating their constitutional texts, leaves no inference that, unlike the Swiss Government, they did not object to the theory that the infraction of constitutional provisions on the conclusion of treaties renders treaties internationally void. That conclusion, indeed, is drawn by de Visscher,[5] who maintains that the reason why the subcommittee included the proposal on the exchange of constitutional texts must have been that the committee thought the respect for such texts an essential condition for the international validity of treaties.[6]

It is conceivable that the subcommittee held the opinion imputed to it by de Visscher. It seems somewhat rash, however, to draw that conclusion from merely the proposal cited. A compilation of constitutional texts and comments on current practice might facilitate the understanding of the internal procedures required, without necessarily implying their relevance under international law. It might be noted, in this connexion, that a compilation of constitutional provisions on the making of treaties edited by the United Nations in 1952[7] was the result of a recommendation made by the International Law Commission to the effect that the United Nations should publish:

"A collection of the constitutions of all States, with supplementary volumes to be issued from time to time for keeping it up to date. Precise knowledge of constitutional provisions of other countries is essential to those who in any country are engaged in negotiating treaties."[8]

If the conclusion drawn by de Visscher were correct that the League subcommittee's proposal for the exchange of constitutional texts implied adherence to the view that constitutionality of treaties was relevant

---

[4] *Ibid.*, p. 212.

[5] *Ibid.*, pp. 212, 215.

[6] *Ibid.*, p. 211.

[7] *Laws and Practices concerning the Conclusion of Treaties.* United Nations Legislative Series. U.N. *Doc.* ST/LEG/SER.B/3, December 1952.

[8] Report of the International Law Commission covering its second session, 5 June–29 July 1950. U.N. *Doc.* A/1316, p. 10.

under international law, the same conclusion ought to emerge from the statement by the International Law Commission. In view of the Commission's discussion of that question during the session covered in the report quoted, it is quite clear, however, that the Commission had taken no position on the issue. Indeed, there was wide disagreement in the Commission on the law governing the issue.[9]

4. HAVANA CONVENTION OF 1928

The Pan-American Convention on Treaties, adopted at Havana on 20 February 1928 by a large number of American republics, provided in its first Article as follows:

"Treaties will be concluded by the competent authorities of the States or by their representatives, according to their respective internal law."[1]

Writers have taken the Article to mean that a constitutionally invalid treaty is internationally null and void.[2] Such interpretation hardly seems warranted. It may be questioned, indeed, whether, by the provision, the parties to the convention undertook any obligation at all. To judge by the English formulation of the Article, it amounts merely to a non-binding prediction of policy. The Article does not prescribe that treaties "shall be" concluded by constitutionally competent authorities,[3] at the risk of otherwise being invalid. It does not seem certain, consequently, that the Article can be invoked with a view to the voiding of a treaty made by an unconstitutional authority.

The weak and ambiguous formulation of the article is all the more striking when seen in contrast to Article 5 of the same convention which lays down that "treaties are obligatory only after ratification ... even though this condition is not stipulated in the full powers of the negotiators or does not appear in the treaty itself."[4]

If, in spite of the considerations advanced above, the interpretation given here should not be found convincing, the Article would undoubtedly carry some weight in favour of the view that constitutional provisions on treaty-making competence are internationally relevant.[5]

[9] See Summary Record of the Fifty-Second Meeting of the Second Session, 22 June 1950, U.N. *Doc.* A/CN.4/SR. 52.

[1] Hudson, *International Legislation,* vol. 4 (1932), p. 2380.

[2] See Jones, p. 149; and de Visscher, p. 218.

[3] Mervyn Jones (p. 149) misquotes the Article to include a "shall" instead of the "will."

[4] Hudson, *loc. cit.*

[5] By 1951, seven states appear to have been bound by the convention. See Hudson, *Cases on International Law* (1951), p. 448; *cf.* Blix, p. 368.

5. Chaco Conflict 1935

One writer has cited the Government of Bolivia as maintaining in the discussion of the Chaco conflict that "approval by Congress is generally necessary in order that an international agreement may be valid."[6] It is believed that the statement referred to was the following:

"In the international practice of democracies, every international agreement means a limitation of national sovereignty, and, generally speaking, it cannot take effect without being approved by Congress."[7]

As it does not appear whether the statement quoted had reference to effect under domestic law or under international law, it is submitted that no significance can be attributed to it in this discussion.

[6] Jones, p. 141.

[7] League of Nations, *Official Journal*, Spec. Supp. No. 133 (1935), p. 43.

Chapter XXII

JUDGMENTS OF INTERNATIONAL TRIBUNALS

Had there existed a body of clear international judicial practice on the problem here at issue, the preceding inquiry would have been shorter. There have been few cases, however, in which international tribunals have had occasion to discuss the matter. For what they are worth, these cases must now be added to the evidence adduced above.

The oldest of the cases, and that which is cited as the strongest support of the theory of the international relevance of constitutional limitations, is an award rendered in 1888 by which President Cleveland, following a report submitted to him by the Assistant Secretary of State, Mr. Rives, sustained the validity of a treaty concluded in 1858 between Costa Rica and Nicaragua.[1]

1. Cleveland Award of 1888

The background of the case

The facts of the case were the following: From 1838 to 1858, the border between Costa Rica and Nicaragua had been in dispute. In 1857, the relations between the two States deteriorated to the extent that war was declared. In the course of the same year, it seems to have become generally recognized in Nicaragua that a reform of the Constitution of 1838 was called for, to end the three-year-old internal struggle, with two hostile governments claiming constitutional and supreme power in the country. A Constituent Assembly with ample powers was elected, and, meeting in November 1857, it immediately began drafting a new Constitution, as well as legislating generally.

On 18 January 1858, earlier negotiations for a settlement with Costa

---

[1] The award and the report may be found in several publications. The source consulted by this writer is *For. Rel. U.S.*, 1888, vol. 1, pp. 456 ff. Apparently, the award and the report are also included in Moore, *History and Digest of International Arbitrations*, vol. 2, pp. 1946 ff.; and in LaFontaine, *Pasicrisie internationale*, p. 298. All the facts related below are extracted from Rives' report, hereinafter cited as Rives.

Rica having failed, the Assembly ordered the appointment of new negotiators to draft a treaty of peace, limits, friendship and alliance between the two States. By a decree of 5 February, furthermore, the Assembly declared that "in the use of the legislative faculties with which it [was] vested", it authorized the executive branch of the Government to settle the boundary dispute with Costa Rica as it deemed best, and stated expressly that such a territorial treaty, if only concluded in conformity with instructions given separately, would be final and not require ratification by the legislative power. If the provisions of the treaty were to depart from the separate instructions, on the other hand, it would be subject to ratification by the Assembly.[2] What instructions were actually given does not appear to have been disclosed, and is irrelevant to the case, since in the dispute which arose later, it was not contended that legislative ratification would have been required on this ground.

On 15 April 1858, the boundary treaty was signed.[3] Article 12 of it provided that it should be ratified, and that the instruments of ratification should be exchanged within 40 days from the day of signing. Shortly thereafter, and without any prior approval by the Constituent Assembly, the President of Nicaragua issued a decree of ratification, in which he expressly stated that the treaty had been made in conformity with the instructions given separately.[4] The instruments of ratification were exchanged on 26 April 1858. Forty-two days after the day of signature, on 28 May 1858, the Constituent Assembly decreed that "in use of the legislative powers vested in it", it approved the boundary treaty concluded on 15 April.

The Constituent Assembly subsequently concluded its work on the new Constitution, and this instrument, adopted on 19 August 1858, expressly laid down that "the laws on special limits"—presumably the legislative approval of the treaty of 15 April 1858—formed part of the Constitution. No further act of Nicaraguan legislative or executive approval of the treaty has been reported, but it seems that the validity of the treaty continued to be recognized by Nicaragua until 1870, when that State first contended that the treaty was invalid. Nicaragua having thereafter persisted in denying the binding force of the treaty, it was agreed in 1886 that the question should be submitted for arbitration by the President of the United States.

[2] Rives, p. 463.
[3] For the treaty, see *B.F.S.P.*, vol. 48 (1857–58), pp. 1049–1052.
[4] Rives, p. 464.

The grounds on which the treaty was alleged to be invalid

Two of the grounds on which Nicaragua relied for the invalidity of the treaty are relevant in this connexion. The first of these was to the effect that the treaty had "not received that sanction which the constitution of the state of Nicaragua requires *to give effect to,* and validate, a treaty of its character."[5] In support of this contention, the Government of Nicaragua argued as follows: On 15 April 1858, when the treaty was signed, the Constitution of 1838 was in force. That Constitution fixed the boundaries of Nicaragua; it laid down, moreover, that to become valid, any amendment to the Constitution must be adopted by two consecutive sessions of the legislature. The boundary treaty allegedly curtailed the boundaries fixed by the Constitution. The conclusion was drawn that, to be valid, the treaty "must receive the same formal ratification that an amendment to the constitution itself demand[ed],"[6] and since it had, in fact, never been sanctioned by a second session of the legislature, it was not valid.

It should be noted in this connexion that what Nicaragua actually argued was that to give effect to the treaty of 1858, the approval of a modification of the Constitution of 1838 was required. From this circumstance the Government of Nicaragua inferred that the treaty itself required approval, as if it were, in itself, an amendment. The treaty was not an amendment, however, and in the arguments submitted to the arbitrator, the Government of Nicaragua did not even make clear what restrictions, if any, the Constitution of Nicaragua imposed upon the treaty-making power of the state. The submission in law, therefore, was to the effect that a treaty, the contents of which conflict with a constitutional provision, is invalid.[7]

The second ground on which the invalidity of the treaty was argued, and which is also relevant to this discussion, was to the effect that the instruments of ratification had been exchanged before the treaty was submitted to the Congress of Nicaragua, and that the treaty had not been "approved by the First Congress of Nicaragua until after the expiration of the forty days provided for the exchange of ratifications in Article XII" of the treaty.[8]

---

[5] *Ibid.* Emphasis supplied.

[6] *Ibid.*

[7] The same conclusion is drawn by Jones, p. 141.

[8] Rives, p. 464.

The award

The award rendered by President Cleveland in 1888 declared that the treaty was valid, but afforded no reasons for the judgment. The grounds on which the decision was based are found, however, in the report written to the President by the Assistant Secretary of State, Mr. G. L. Rives.

Mr. Rives found that the Nicaraguan contention that the treaty was invalid, because not approved by the legislature as an amendment to the Constitution, rested wholly upon the two assumptions that the Constitution of 1838 was in force, and that it actually fixed the boundaries. In an oft-quoted passage, Mr. Rives thereafter expressed himself as follows:

"The general doctrine that in determining the validity of a treaty made in the name of a state, the fundamental laws of such state must furnish the guide for determination, has been fully and ably discussed on the part of Nicaragua, and its correctness may certainly be admitted. But it is also certain that where a treaty has been approved by a government, and an effort is subsequently made to avoid it for the lack of some formality, the burden is upon the party who alleges invalidity to show clearly that the requirements of the fundamental law have not been complied with. In my judgment, Nicaragua has failed in establishing a case under this rule."[9]

In the first place, Mr. Rives thought it doubtful whether the Constitution of 1838 had been in full force when the treaty was concluded. Since the Constituent Assembly was created for the express purpose of amending the Constitution, it ought to have possessed the power to adopt a decree modifying the Constitution.[1] Second, and even more important in Mr. Rives' opinion, the Constitution of 1838 could not be said to fix definitely the boundaries of Nicaragua. It could not, therefore, be argued that the treaty of 1858 required an amendment to the Constitution. In further support of his views, Mr. Rives adduced the circumstance that for some ten years Nicaragua appeared to have acquiesced in the treaty. Mr. Rives added:

"I do not regard such acquiescence as a substitute for ratification by a second legislature, if such had been needed. But it is strong evidence of that contemporaneous exposition which has ever been thought valuable as a guide in determining doubtful questions of interpretation."[2]

[9] *Ibid.*, p. 465.
[1] *Ibid.*
[2] *Ibid.*

Mr. Rives, likewise, rejected the contention that the treaty was invalid because instruments of ratification had been exchanged by the executive branches of government prior to the legislative approval and that such approval was given only after the period prescribed for ratification. He stated:

"... Nicaragua can not now seek to invalidate the treaty on any mere ground of irregularity in the order of its own proceedings. If its legislature did in fact approve the treaty that is enough for the present purpose. Whether such approval was expressed before or after the exchange of ratifications is an immaterial matter now, certainly so far as Nicaragua is concerned."[3]

Mr. Rives continued, indeed, that he had not even been convinced that legislative approval had been at all required under the Nicaraguan Constitution, for that Constitution had not been submitted to the arbitrator and it had not been made clear what restrictions it imposed upon the treaty-making power. Mr. Rives added:

"Ratification by legislative authority is not always required, even in constitutional governments. The necessity for legislative ratification is not to be presumed, but must be established as a fact. Still less can there be any presumption as to the form and manner in which the legislative sanction is to be expressed ..."[4]

Value of the case

This case offers certain points of great interest to the problem under discussion. A preliminary observation of a non-legal nature may first be made: the impression is almost compelling that Nicaragua seized upon the argument of unconstitutionality as a subterfuge for denouncing a treaty that was thought politically objectionable. While this circumstance must have impressed the arbitrator and the rapporteur, and inclined them to hold the treaty valid, it does not, of course, deprive the legal reasoning of the report of interest or authority. It is important to note, further, that the validity of the treaty was not challenged on the ground that it was made in violation of constitutional limitations of competence, and that the rapporteur did not look into that particular problem. The questions he examined were whether the substance of the treaty conflicted with the Constitution of the State, and, if so, whether the Constitution prevailed over the treaty in the international sphere. To the extent, consequently, that expressions used by the rapporteur lend themselves as authority in the question of competence, they are, though not unimportant, *obiter dicta*.

[3] *Ibid.*, p. 467.
[4] *Ibid.*

This said, the first point that must be stressed is that the rapporteur did not, indeed, hold that compatibility with the Constitution was irrelevant to the international validity of the treaty, and refuse to discuss the provisions of the domestic law. Quite to the contrary, he thought that the fundamental laws of the State must "furnish the guide" in the determination of the validity of the treaty, and he had no hesitation at all in examining and interpreting the Constitution of Nicaragua with a view to discovering if a treaty of the kind concluded was compatible with it. Presumably, he would have proceeded in the same manner, had the validity of the treaty been challenged on the ground that it was concluded by a constitutionally incompetent authority. The rapporteur further held that the burden of proof lay upon the party that alleged the presence of a constitutional irregularity.[5] While Mr. Rives admitted that "the lack of some formality" might make a treaty internationally invalid, he was nevertheless not prepared to look upon the fundamental domestic law as more than a guide, for he refused to admit that "any mere ground of irregularity in ... proceedings" sufficed to void a treaty internationally. Where the border between the two cases should be drawn, Mr. Rives did not say. It is perfectly clear, however, that since, in his opinion, there existed irregularities that had no international relevance, and since such irregularities might, of course, entail lack of domestic validity of a treaty, Mr. Rives implicitly admitted that conflicts between the international and the domestic validity of a treaty might arise.

It is of interest, finally, to note that although Mr. Rives did not consider actual application of a treaty over a period of years a substitute for ratification, if such were constitutionally needed, he pointed, somewhat enigmatically, to such application as likely to constitute recognition of the domestic regularity of a treaty.

2. THE METZGER CASE 1900

This case, settled by arbitration between the United States and Haiti, offers some points of interest to this study, even though no direct reliance was placed upon the doctrine of constitutional limitations.[6]

---

[5] It does not seem justifiable to conclude, as does Chailley (pp. 227–228), merely from the broad terminology used on this point by Mr. Rives, that Costa Rica would have been entitled to challenge the validity of the treaty on the ground that it violated the Constitution of Nicaragua.

[6] The report of the case is found in *For. Rel. U.S.*, 1901, pp. 262 ff.

The American firm, Metzger & Co., which operated a mill at Port-au-Prince, had been unable to secure execution of a contract made with the local authorities. It applied to the United States Government for support, and the State Department took up the matter through the ordinary diplomatic channels. The official representatives of the two countries devised a mode by which the difficulty encountered by the firm might be settled. Although no instrument embodying this agreement was drawn up, the Government of Haiti appears to have stated that local authorities at Port-au-Prince were to take certain action envisaged by the Governments. Such action was not in fact taken, and before long the matter was submitted for arbitration to William R. Day, a former Secretary of State of the United States and a judge of the United States Circuit Court.

Perhaps the point of greatest legal interest in the decision was that, despite a Haitian assertion to the effect that the diplomatic exchanges had only amounted, on the part of Haiti, to a pledge to use its good offices with the commune of Port-au-Prince, the arbitrator held that they constituted a diplomatic agreement under which the Government of Haiti assumed full responsibility for a settlement. In this connexion, however, it is more important to note that although the Haitian Government had also objected that it had no authority over the commune of Port-au-Prince, and was obliged at all times to limit its interference to friendly advice and suggestions, the arbitrator refused to admit such limitations upon domestic competence as relevant under international law vis-à-vis a party having no notice of them. The arbitrator expressed himself as follows:

"I do not understand that the limitations upon official authority, undisclosed at the time to the other government, prevent the enforcement of diplomatic agreements."[7]

3. The Franco-Swiss Customs Convention Case 1912

The background of the case

Further material of great interest is to be found in the judgment rendered on 3 August 1912 in an arbitration between Switzerland and France.[8] The award has been interpreted in widely diverging ways. The

---

[7] *Ibid.*, p. 271. The case is cited also in Fairman, p. 458.

[8] For a report of the judgment, with a note by Anzilotti setting out the arguments of the parties and a comment on the case, see *Rivista di Diritto Internazionale*, vol. 7 (1913), pp. 518–523. The case is also reported in *A.J.I.L.*, vol. 6 (1912), pp. 995–1002.

facts and arguments of the case must, therefore, be set out in some detail in order to provide a satisfactory basis for a correct assessment of it.

On 20 October 1906, a commercial convention was signed between France and Switzerland.[9] After approval by the legislatures of the two States, the convention was ratified, and instruments of ratification were exchanged on 21 November 1906. On that occasion the plenipotentiaries signed a protocol, not previously submitted to the legislatures. In the latter instrument they stated that, during the period in which the convention was to be in force, the General Direction of French Customs would enforce regulations which were specified in certain annexes, and which had apparently already been applied by the French administration vis-à-vis goods entering France from Switzerland. Among these regulations was one reading: "N. 510. Rentrent dans ce numéro les turbines à vapeur."[1] No. 510 of the French tariff, it may be noted, prescribed the tariff imposed upon stationary steam engines.

In a French law of 29 March 1910, a new category of items entitled "machine à vapeur sans piston"—in practice applicable only to steam turbines—was created within No. 510 and subjected to a surtax of 50%. This measure adversely affected Swiss exports, and the matter was submitted to an arbitration tribunal with the distinguished membership of Eugene Borel, D. L. L. of the University of Geneva, M. Noël, Senator, and Lord Reay, former President of the Institute of International Law.

The submissions

The Swiss Government complained before the tribunal that the French law constituted a violation of the administrative regulation agreed upon in 1906. In reply, the French Government argued that by the acceptance of the protocol, which included steam turbines in No. 510 for the purpose of collecting customs duty, France had done no more than assume an obligation to preserve the article in the designated category.[2] Apart from this she had intended to reserve her entire freedom upon tariff decisions and upon revising and classifying the article.[3] The French Government thus admitted that steam turbines must remain included in No. 510, but maintained that not only was France free to change at will the rate of duty imposed upon articles

---

[9] See de Martens, *N.R.G.*, 3 ser., vol. 1, pp. 509–523.
[1] See *Rivista*, p. 520; the protocol is not reproduced in de Martens' collection.
[2] *Rivista*, p. 521.
[3] *A.J.I.L.*, vol. 6 (1912), p. 998.

under this item, but also to redefine at will articles under the item. The protocol, it was asserted, could not have had the effect of fixing the duty upon goods that were assimilated to steam engines.[4]

The French Government argued further that if, indeed, the protocol were interpreted to fix the tariff rate upon the article indicated, the conclusion would follow that a simple administrative measure, *not submitted to the parliamentary body,* would suffice to restrict the liberty of the state in tariff matters. To this position French legislation was formally opposed.

In brief, the French argument was that since French law did not authorize the conclusion of treaties affecting the tariff rates without parliamentary approval, and since such approval had not been obtained in 1906, it could not then have been the intention of the French Government to bind itself in such a matter. It was not denied that the protocol constituted a binding obligation, nor was the protocol asserted to be invalid under international law as concluded by an authority not constitutionally authorized thereto. It was merely submitted that the authority which had made the protocol must be presumed not to have intended to exceed its constitutional competence, and that the protocol must be interpreted accordingly.

The judgment

It is against the background of these arguments that the judgment of the tribunal must be read. The arbitrators referred to the protocol in which the plenipotentiaries had stated that the regulations specified in the annexes were to be applied through administrative channels, and held that the regulations constituted an integral part of the convention, and that the parties were bound to observe the tariff regime established in them. They further held as follows:

"Considering that the treaty of commerce and the regulations are international conventions governed by the sanction which the contracing parties, represented by their plenipotentiaries, have given thereto;

"The tribunal is not called upon to consider whether or not the regulations must be submitted to the sanction of the legislature: that is a matter pertaining to internal law;"[5]

They went on to refer to the principle of effective interpretation, and held that the regulation including steam turbines under No. 510 of the French tariff would have no meaning and practical importance

[4] *Rivista,* p. 522.

[5] *A.J.I.L.,* vol. 6 (1912), p. 1000.

if it signified only reference to a number of the tariff, for the numbering in itself was a matter of indifference. The tribunal admitted that France remained free to modify her customs duties upon item No. 510, but stated that she could make use of that freedom only within the limits of the undertaking made vis-à-vis Switzerland to treat turbines as machines under item No. 510. By imposing a surtax of 50% upon steam engines without piston, the new French tariff had, in fact, created a differential treatment prejudicial to steam turbines, and this was not compatible with the customs practice existing before the conclusion of the convention of 1906 and sanctioned by the protocol of 1906.

Evaluation of the case

On the basis of the above description of facts, arguments and judgment, the following summary of the relevant parts of the case seems justified:

The Swiss complaint was to the effect that a treaty obligation was being violated by a subsequent law.

The French defense aimed at showing that the particular obligation alleged had never been undertaken, on the ground that, since it would not have been permitted under French public law, it could not be assumed that the French negotiators could have intended to include it.

The Court, applying the principle of effective interpretation, found that the obligation had, indeed, been assumed. It expressly refused to interpret the intentions expressed in the international instruments in the light of national legislation, and held that the obligation was undertaken and binding internationally, whether or not submission to the sanction of the legislature was required internally.

Other writers' interpretations of the case

The above analysis of the case, which renders it of considerable importance to this study, has the support of a number of writers.[6] It must be noted, however, that some other writers have concluded—erroneously, it is submitted—that the case is irrelevant to the problem under examination.

Chailley correctly states that only points relating to the interpretation

---

[6] Anzilotti, in *Rivista*, p. 518; Verdross, *Völkerrecht* (2nd ed., 1950), p. 127; Guggenheim, vol. 1, p. 63; Siotto-Pintor, "Traités internationaux et droit interne" in *R.G.D.I.P.*, vol. 42 (1935), pp. 531–532; Vitta, p. 96, n. 1.

of the convention were discussed and that the question of the constitutionality of the treaty had not been raised.[7] For this reason he
denies that the case is authority for the view that constitutional rules
regarding the conclusion of treaties have no international significance.
It has been shown above, however, that the tribunal must have acted
upon this theory, since it proceeded to interpret the convention to
embrace an international obligation that was allegedly not assumed in
accordance with French constitutional law, and refused even to look
into the question of the constitutionality.

Wohlmann submits that the French Government demanded consideration of the question whether the validity of the protocol was not dependent upon parliamentary approval, and that the court did not look
into that question, because it had already affirmed the validity of the
protocol as an integral part of a valid convention.[8] To that interpretation it must be objected that since, contrary to Wohlmann's assertion,
the question of the validity of either the convention or the protocol
was simply not raised, it is not remarkable that the tribunal did not
answer it. What did take place was that the tribunal affirmed the
existence of an obligation within a treaty, the validity of which was
not challenged, and declared that it was irrelevant under international
law whether that particular obligation would have required parliamentary approval under constitutional law.

Finally, Mervyn Jones states that the "French Government objected
that the tariff could only be modified by legislation, thus adopting
exactly the same argument as she had put forward in 1832 against the
United States Government".[9] This interpretation, however, seems to be
based upon a misunderstanding of the judgment and of the arguments
put forward. In 1832, France had admitted that an obligation had
been assumed in conformity with her constitutional law, but pleaded
that the resistance of her legislature was an excuse for non-performance.
In the present case, however, France denied that a particular obligation
had ever been undertaken. She did not plead her internal law as an
excuse for non-performance. Rather she held it out to show that as the
executive branch of the government had had no constitutional authority
to undertake the obligation that was alleged to exist, it could not be
assumed to have intended to enter into such an undertaking. It was the
relevance of this consideration that the tribunal rejected by the state-

[7] Chailley, pp. 230–231.

[8] Wohlmann, pp. 89–90.

[9] Jones, p. 146. For a discussion of that case, see above, p. 302.

ment that has been quoted. Having thus found that there existed an international obligation, the tribunal had solved the problem before it. It is not surprising that it did not discuss any proposition to the effect that performance could not be demanded because not permitted under domestic law, since such a proposition had never been advanced.

4. THE RIO MARTIN CASE 1924

In 1923, Judge Huber, acting as rapporteur in certain claims between Great Britain and Spain had occasion to consider the relevance of constitutional provisions to the international validity of an agreement.[1]

By a treaty of 1783, the Maghzen of Morocco promised to provide a house for the English agent at Martin.[2] In 1896, an agreement was made by way of an exchange of notes between the Maghzen and the British diplomatic agent at Tangier, to the effect that the house should be made available at or near Tetuan, instead of Martin. In 1923 the British Government claimed performance from Spain under the agreement of 1896. The Spanish Government, which at that time exercised a protectorate over that part of Morocco, objected that the agreement had not been embodied in a Sherifian decree, and could not, therefore, be valid. Judge Huber's observations on this point are as follows:

"Il a été soutenu du côté espagnol que la proposition anglaise n'aurait pu être accepté que par un décret chérifien. Le Rapporteur ne croit pas avoir à élucider ce point de droit constitutionnel marocain. Il lui suffit de constater que l'échange de lettres mentionné ci-dessus et qui a eu lieu entre les agents autorisés des deux Gouvernements établit de façon manifeste l'accord de leurs volontés pour transférer sur une maison à Tetuan des droits que le Gouvernement britannique tenait sur la maison à Martin aux termes d'un traité encore en vigueur sur le point en question. Cet accord se trouve en outre confirmé par le fait que toute la correspondance ultérieure l'a explicitement ou implicitement pris pour base."[3]

The fact that the above statement occurred, not in a final award, but in a "report" to the parties hardly reduces its value as evidence of the law, for the circumstances in which it was rendered, and the purposes of it were practically the same as those of an award.

It is of considerable interest to find that so great an authority as

---

[1] The case is digested in *Annual Digest,* 1923–1924, p. 19.

[2] Hertslet's *Commercial Treaties,* vol. 1 (1840), pp. 110 ff.

[3] Quoted from the original report that was printed under the title *Reclamations Britanniques dans la Zone Espagnol du Maroc, Rapports* (The Hague, May 1925), p. 178.

Judge Huber flatly refused to enter into a discussion of the Constitution of Morocco, and contented himself with the observation that the agreement had been made by agents who were authorized by the two Governments. It should be noted, in addition, that he considered the agreement confirmed by the circumstance that subsequent correspondence was predicated upon it. The case undoubtedly constitutes important authority for the view that constitutional procedural provisions are not relevant to the international validity of treaties, and for the view that the behaviour of the parties may supply evidence of the validity of a treaty.

Judge Huber did not, in fact, spell out what he considered to be the relevant criteria of international competence. The expression "autorisés des deux Gouvernements" might imply, if the matter was at all present to his mind, that he did not question the view that the executive branch of a government is always competent to commit the state.[4]

5. The George Pinson Case 1928

The question of the relevance of constitutional law for the validity of treaties was the subject of some interesting comments in the *George Pinson case,* which was decided in 1928 by a Franco-Mexican Mixed Claims Commission, with Jan W. W. Verzijl as umpire.[5]

The Mexican agent had maintained before the tribunal that constitutional law should be given effect over treaties. The Presiding Commissioner, however, made the most express reservations with respect to this contention, which he considered to be in direct contradiction to the very axioms of international law. It could be explained, in his opinion, only as the result of a double confusion, namely, between the viewpoint of a municipal court and that of an international tribunal, and between the case of pre-existing constitutional provisions prohibiting a government to conclude—or a parliament to approve—treaties of a defined type, and the case of promulgation of a constitutional provision which conflicts with pre-existing customary or conventional international law.

National courts, it was explained in the judgment, might find them-

---

[4] It does not, however, seem warranted to impute to the judge the opinion that the head of state possesses a *jus repraesentationis omnimodae*. This is done by de Visscher, p. 177. Another comment upon the case is found in Jones, p. 146.

[5] The case is digested in *Annual Digest,* 1927–1928, p. 9; a report of the case is found in United Nations, *Reports of International Arbitral Awards,* vol. V, pp. 327 ff.

selves obligated by their municipal law to apply the constitution even when they found it to conflict with international law; to international tribunals, however, that approach was alien. With respect to the solution of the conflict between international law and constitutional law, the tribunal stated further:

"...il est extrêmement douteux qu'un... traité, conclu en dépit de la disposition prohibitive de la Constitution, puisse être considéré comme juridiquement valable, attendu que les organes constitutionnels auraient dépassé les limites que la Constitution trace à leur pouvoir de représenter l'Etat dans l'acte de contracter l'engagement international en question..."

It continued:

"...la situation est essentiellement différente... dans l'hypothèse de la préexistence de traités ou de règles de droit coutumier, [car] ce fait même empêcherait absolument l'Etat de promulguer valablement des dispositions constitutionnelles, contraires auxdits traités ou règles: l'existence de ces derniers comporte par elle-même une restriction correspondante de la souveraineté de l'Etat."[6]

The clear distinction which the Presiding Commissioner made between the position of a municipal court and that of an international tribunal is worth noting. Furthermore, although the first statement quoted above was *obiter dictum*, it is nevertheless of importance. While the umpire refrained from taking a definite position in the matter, his grave doubts as to the international validity of a treaty concluded in violation of constitutional provisions prohibiting the conclusions of treaties of the type in question are entitled to respect. It should be noted that he was referring to the somewhat unusual case of a constitutional provision which excludes from the competence of *all* state organs[7] the conclusion of treaties of certain types. The argument which he advanced —"attendu que les organes constitutionnels auraient dépassé les limites que la Constitution trace à leur pouvoir de représenter l'Etat..."—for his doubts seem nevertheless to apply equally in the case of constitutional limitations of competence.

6. The Eastern Greenland Case 1933

The dispute between Denmark and Norway about the sovereignty over Eastern Greenland has already been discussed in the first part of

---

[6] *Ibid.*, at p. 394.
[7] See above, p. 101.

this study.[8] In this connexion, it may merely be recalled that the conclusion was reached that the Court sustained the Danish argument to the effect that constitutional provisions relating to procedure are not relevant to another party, and that the Court did not take any position on the question of the international relevance of a constitutional requirement of parliamentary assent.

[8] See above, p. 34.

Chapter XXIII

THE OPINIONS OF WRITERS

The main theories which have been advanced to answer the question of what organs are competent under international law to conclude treaties on behalf of states have already been briefly outlined in the introduction to this part of the present study. These theories will now be analyzed in greater detail. The purpose of this examination is twofold: to ascertain to what extent various theories are supported by the evidence presented above, and to evaluate them from a functional point of view.

1. THE CONSTITUTIONAL THEORY

It has been noted that a majority of modern writers adhere to the view that a principle of international law refers the question of competent treaty-making authority to constitutional law.[1] A consequence of this principle, were it to be accepted, would be that a state organ concluding a treaty without being duly authorized under constitutional law to do so would be an organ that is incompetent under international law, and

---

[1] See, for instance, Basdevant, p. 577; Castberg, *Studier i folkeret* (1952), p. 25; Dehousse, p. 150; Fairman, p. 441; Fauchille, *Droit International Public*, vol. I, 3° partie (1926), p. 6; François, "Règles générales du droit de la paix" in *Recueil des Cours*, 1938, vol. IV, p. 158; Guggenheim, vol. 1, p. 61; Kelsen, *Principles of International Law* (1952), p. 323; Mirkine-Guetzévitch, p. 95; Ross, p. 203; Scelle, vol. 2, p. 439; Veicopoulos, "Accords internationaux conclus en forme simplifiée et gentlemen's agreements" in *Revue de droit international, de sciences diplomatiques et politiques*, vol. 27 (1949), p. 162; Verdross, *Völkerrecht* (2nd ed., 1950), pp. 123–124; de Visscher, "Les tendances internationales des constitutions modernes" in *Recueil des Cours*, 1952, vol. 1, p. 540; Lie, *Legitimation ved Traktat* (1912), p. 126; Schön, W., "Die völkerrechtliche Bedeutung Staatsrechtlicher Beschränkungen der Vertreterbefugnis der Staatsoberhäupter beim Abschlusse von Staatsverträgen" in *Zeitschrift für Völkerrecht und Bundesstaatsrecht*, vol. 5 (1911), p. 407.

It may also be noted that at its third session, in 1951, the International Law Commission tentatively adopted an article in which it adhered to the constitutional theory. See U.N. *Doc.* A/CN.4/L. 28, 19 July 1951. The Commission has not yet, however, presented a final formulation.

the treaty made by it, an act that is voidable or void.[2] The theory is succinctly stated by Schücking as follows:

"Un traité n'est obligatoire, pour les parties contractantes, que lorsqu'il a été conclu par les organes compétents et lorsque toutes les dispositions de droit constitutionnel régissant la conclusion des traités ont été observées."[3]

Possible advantages of the theory

There are some obvious advantages in this theory. First of all, it is capable of being applied to the most diverse systems of government, provided only that these possess some settled municipal law regulatory of the treaty-making power. Furthermore, regardless of what organs and what procedures the municipal order is found to embody, these are likely to secure reliable promises. To put it differently: if the municipal prescriptions on competence and procedure have been complied with, this circumstance is likely to diminish the risk that the treaties will subsequently be declared inoperative in the municipal sphere. There would be some justification, consequently, for maintaining that adherence to this theory would promote the effectiveness of conventional international law. This circumstance is perhaps the strongest point advanced in support of the contention that it is desirable that municipal provisions bearing on the conclusion of treaties should be relevant under international law.[4]

If constitutional limitations affecting the treaty-making power of state organs were acknowledged to be relevant under international law, the conclusion would follow that there existed in international law a

[2] See the description given of the theory in Lauterpacht's *First Report,* p. 160, and in Basdevant, p. 580.

[3] Schücking, "La portée des règles de droit constitutionnel pour la conclusion et la ratification des traités internationaux" in *Annuaire de l'Institut International de Droit Public,* 1930, p. 225.

[4] In this connexion, the following statements may be noted:

"International law might be regarded as stultifying itself if it insisted on the validity of treaties, which, being constitutionally void, would in most cases become admittedly ineffective and perhaps incapable of execution." Jones, p. 151.

"...die Rechtssicherheit, den Vertrag zu halten, viel grösser ist, wenn das Parlament oder das Volk ihm zugestimmt haben, als wenn das Staatsoberhaupt allein das Versprechen abgibt." Wohlmann, p. 101.

"Du point de vue pratique, la théorie de la validité, en assurant l'application des traités, permet une plus grande stabilité des relations internationales..." Georgopoulos, *La ratification des traités et la collaboration du parlement* (1939), p. 26.

The same point is made by Ross, p. 203; Dupuis, "Liberté des voies de communication relations internationales" in *Recueil des Cours,* 1924, vol. I, p. 326; Kopelmanas, *L'Organisation des Nations Unies* (1947), p. 111.

certain guarantee of part of the domestic order of many states.[5] Some who fear that the checks and sanctions commonly established under domestic law in order to enforce the regulation of the treaty-making power might sometimes prove an insufficient deterrent against abuses welcome such a guarantee in international law. Conversely, they feel that the constitutional regulation of the treaty-making power—often including certain means of democratic control of that power once attained and established only with great difficulty—would be undermined if some state organ were attributed unconditional authority irrevocably to pledge the faith of the state under international law.

Evidence supporting the theory

What evidence may be advanced in support of the contention that the constitutional theory is actually part of international law? As special care has been taken in this section of the present study to inquire into facts which have been alleged or might be expected to offer such evidence, these inquiries might well serve as a basis for an assessment of the support possessed by the constitutional theory in the practice of states and holdings of courts.

There is, of course, first of all the fact that governments normally conclude treaties with authorities and in accordance with procedures indicated by constitutional law, and that they feel confident that these authorities and procedures will bring into being commitments valid under international law. However, this fact, taken by itself, in no way necessitates the conclusion that governments consider competence in the international sphere directly dependent upon competence in the municipal sphere. It only shows that the relevant rule of international law must be broad enough to attribute competence in these circumstances. For the conclusion that limitations operative under municipal law are decisive for competence under international law, it must further be shown that in cases where such limitations are not observed, competence is, in fact, not generally deemed to exist under international law. This has in fact been understood by the writers who advance the constitutional theory to be the chief challenge.

The evidence examined in this work reveals that the notion that treaties made in violation of some constitutional rule are internationally void has not infrequently found official expression in and between

---

[5] See Anzilotti, p. 366; Sundberg, *Folkrätt* (2nd ed., 1950), p. 239; Ross, p. 207; Vitta, p. 69; de Naurois, *Les traités internationaux devant les juridictions nationales* (1934), p. 165.

states. It has been shown above, however, that the instances are far fewer than asserted by writers who maintain that constitutional provisions are directly relevant in international law. As may be understandable, these writers have sometimes seen evidence of their own view in instances or statements which, upon analysis, offer no such evidence, or offer insignificant or negligible evidence.[6] It has been pointed out, moreover, that, in several cases where the international relevance of constitutional provisions relating to the conclusion of treaties has been officially asserted, no serious juridical convictions seem to have underlain such contentions. The argument lends itself to, and has been used as, a subterfuge to justify the denunciation of politically undesirable treaties.[7]

There remains, nevertheless, some evidence that speaks more significantly in favour of the international relevance of constitutional provisions relating to and affecting the conclusion of treaties. Above all, there is the report upon which the Cleveland award was based.[8] There are, further, a number of constitutions, notably those of Denmark, Norway and Ireland, whose draftsmen must have assumed that the terms of their provisions would have some bearing on the international competence of the treaty-making authorities of the State.[9]

Evidence refuting the theory

It is submitted, on the basis of the foregoing examination of international practice, that the evidence of a practice treating constitutional provisions as not directly relevant in international law is both quantitatively and qualitatively more significant than that pointing to the direct relevance of municipal provisions.

The fact is conspicuous that no treaty has been found that has been admitted to be invalid or held by an international tribunal to be invalid, because concluded by a constitutionally incompetent authority or in an unconstitutional manner, either by an individual government in bilateral relations, or by an international organization, like the League of Nations. Furthermore, there is no lack of treaties made in violation of constitutions, or by constitutionally incompetent authorities,

---

[6] Chailley's interpretation of the Politis incident may be taken as an example. See above, p. 332.

[7] See the discussion of the *Western Griqualand Diamond Deposits case* of 1871, above, p. 307, the incident concerning the Irish Free State annuities, above, p. 343; and the incident settled by the Cleveland award, above, p. 359.

[8] Above, p. 355.

[9] Above, p. 246.

and yet admitted to be valid under international law. Some such cases have been recorded above.[1] Many more doubtless could be found which have never attracted international attention.[2]

It has been noted also that not only when states are treating with each other, but also when states and international organizations act as depositaries, they do not appear concerned about the constitutional competence of the authorities upon whose expression of consent they rely,[3] not even when express reference to constitutional requirements are made in full powers or treaty texts.[4] Inquiry between governments concerning their respective municipal treaty-making competence, if ever occurring, is a rarity.[5]

Numerous cases and incidents may be cited in support of this submission. There are, to begin with judicial cases, the *Customs Convention case* of 1912[6] and the *Metzger case* of 1925,[7] in which limitations upon the competence under domestic law of the authority making the treaty were declared internationally irrelevant. In addition, the judgments in the *Rio Martin case* of 1925[8] and the *Eastern Greenland case* of 1933[9] must be taken to indicate that certain municipal rules of procedure relating to the conclusion of treaties are internationally irrelevant.

Among diplomatic incidents, those in which organs of the League of Nations have expressed an opinion are of special interest and value.

---

[1] See the incident of 1875 concerning the denunciation by Ecuador of the Industrial Property Convention of 1883, above, p. 308; two treaties discussed in the French Chamber of Deputies, above, p. 309; the case of the Chinese–Russian treaty of 1913, above, p. 321; and the case relating to the admission of Argentina to the League of Nations, above, p. 333.

[2] At the present time, the ever-growing number of matters calling for treaty regulation has led, practically everywhere, to the conclusion of treaties by procedures which either patently violate constitutional provisions, or are at any rate in highly questionable conformity with constitutional law, without this circumstance leading to more than internal criticism. See, for instance, as regards France, Rousseau, "Le régime actuel de conclusion des traités en France" in *La Technique et les Principes du Droit Public, Études en l'honneur de Georges Scelle* (1950), vol. II, p. 582; as regards Sweden, Eek, "Makten över utrikes ärendena" in *Statsvetenskaplig Tidskrift*, vol. 57 (1954), pp. 380 ff.

[3] See above, pp. 264 ff. *Cf.* Oppenheim, vol. 1, p. 887, note 3.

[4] See above, p. 290.

[5] See above, p. 263.

[6] Above, p. 361.

[7] Above, p. 360.

[8] Above, p. 366.

[9] Above, p. 368.

The attitudes adopted by these authorities are not as open to the objection that they must be coloured by self-interest, as are attitudes taken by individual states in bilateral incidents. It is, therefore, significant that the Council of the League of Nations appears to have rejected the relevance of constitutional limitations upon treaty-making competence, both in the case of the admission of Luxemburg[1] and in the Politis incident of 1925.[2] The action of the League authorities in the case of the admission of the Argentine Republic is open to a similar interpretation.[3] Nor would it be right, in this connexion, to overlook the memorandum submitted by the Swiss Government to the League of Nations[4] and that submitted to the United Nations by the Government of Luxemburg.[5] Memoranda to the same effect have been employed by the United States Government.[6] There are, moreover, the remarkable cases in which certain national courts did not hesitate to adhere to the view that the violation of constitutional provisions relating to the conclusion of treaties does not affect the international validity of a treaty.[7]

The evidence cited above points to the conclusion that there is not sufficient ground for holding that, under international law, the authority competent to conclude treaties on behalf of a state and the procedures which should be employed for the conclusion of treaties are conclusively indicated by the municipal law of the state.

Functional analysis

From a functional view-point, several serious objections may be raised against the constitutional theory. Were it accepted, municipal provisions relating to competence and procedure would become a matter of primary importance to governments which are about to conclude treaties with each other. As a measure of protection against unwelcome surprises, they would be obliged to inquire carefully into the municipal law of the other party. The circumstance that governments do not, in fact, appear concerned about the relevant municipal law of their counterparties has already been adduced as evidence against the constitutional theory. In this connexion, attention should be called to the extreme

[1] Above, p. 328.
[2] Above, p. 332.
[3] Above, p. 338.
[4] Above, p. 351.
[5] Above, p. 238.
[6] Above, pp. 350 and 351.
[7] Above, p. 258.

difficulties which would face governments were they to concern themselves with the interpretation of constitutional provisions of other states.
An apt description of these difficulties is given by Pallieri:

> "Les constitutions internes sont devenues toujours plus compliquées, la
> détermination de l'organe compétent donne naissance à des questions toujours
> plus subtiles; à un certain moment, il n'y a presque plus de traité dont la
> validité ne soit douteuse à cause de l'incompétence de l'organe..."[8]

And further:

> "...un Etat peut croire avec la plus complète et la plus légitime bonne foi
> que le traité sera considéré valable par l'autre contractant, tandis que ce
> dernier peut trouver dans son droit interne le moyen de soulever des questions
> juridiques sur la compétence de l'organe..."[9]

It has been concluded above that governments rarely direct inquiries
to each other regarding their treaty-making competence under municipal
law, and this fact has been held to point to their lack of concern for the
municipal law of other parties.[1] A serious functional consideration that
should also be noted is that the inquiries in question could only be
directed to the executive branch of government of the state with which
a treaty is to be concluded, and, indeed, probably only to its Ministry
of Foreign Affairs.[2] Since that department of the government concerned must have already demonstrated its willingness to conclude the
treaty, and thereby presumably implied that it considered itself competent, most express inquiries would seem meaningless and redundant.
If one were made, and answered, as must be assumed, in most cases, in a
reassuring manner, the reply could only reflect the view of the very
organ whose constitutional competence is questioned. It would not be of

---

[8] *Op. cit.,* p. 475.

[9] *Ibid.,* p. 486. The following opinion expressed in a recent American monograph
may also be quoted:

"Constitutional requirements, no matter how clear and obvious on their face, are
invariably open to interpretation by the municipal judiciary, and are open to being
declared unconstitutional by that body. If a state were permitted to use such a
defense, in answer to the international validity of an agreement, the law of treaties
is on very uncertain ground. It might take years before the constitutionality of a
treaty is finally decided, and confusion would result from the lack of finality. Further,
non-compliance with constitutional limitations could conceivably become a device
for political manipulation, malfeasance, and bad faith in international affairs. Constitutional limitations are of no concern to other states..." Hendry, *Treaties and
Federal Constitutions* (1955), p. 154.

See also Lauterpacht's *First Report,* p. 159; Basdevant, p. 581; Ross, p. 207; Vitta,
p. 69; Scelle, vol. 2, p. 441; and Anzilotti, p. 365.

[1] Above, p. 264.

[2] See above, p. 229, note 8; above, p. 261; and see de Visscher, pp. 70 and 271.

much value if later denounced by a legislature or by a court as an illegal act, invalid because unauthorized by the constitution.[3]

Yet another practical disadvantage in the constitutional theory would appear to lie in the circumstance that it would require international tribunals to decide upon questions of constitutional law, and sometimes place them in the unenviable position where they would be obliged to reject an interpretation given to a constitution by the supreme court of the state governed by that constitution. It cannot, perhaps, be said that such obligation would impose an impossible burden upon these tribunals. However, these bodies, which consist of jurists who are trained in international law and who are likely to be familiar only with a constitutional system other than that relevant to the particular case before them, obviously are little fitted for that task.[4] While the existing practice of international tribunals in this regard is not completely consistent, a reluctance among them to undertake discussions concerning the constitutional law of states may sometimes be perceived.[5]

2. Variations of the Constitutional Theory

While the preceding discussion has had regard chiefly to the constitutional theory as that theory is usually presented, it must here be noted that there exist certain variations of the theory. Some writers have sought to temper the constitutional theory by bringing into play some additional principle; others have gone in the contrary direction and endeavoured to extend the application of the principle embodied in the constitutional theory. These variations will now be considered.

The international relevance of limitations of substance

Some authorities have maintained that not only the municipal provisions identifying the state organs whose assent is necessary for the conclusion of treaties of various kinds—here termed limitations of competence in the narrow sense[6]— and those relating to procedure, but also municipal limitations relating to the substance of treaties are relevant

---

[3] See Fitzmaurice, p. 134; and de Visscher, p. 245.

[4] Pallieri, p. 483.

[5] See the Franco-Swiss arbitration cited above, p. 361; the *Rio Martin case,* above, p. 366; but *cf.* Rives' report to President Cleveland, above, p. 360; the discussion in the case of *Dyer* v. *Sims* is illuminating, above, p. 254.

[6] For the definition, see above, p. 101.

in the international sphere. According to these theories, municipal provisions which expressly or implicitly forbid the conclusion of special kinds of treaties would be relevant in the international sphere.[7]

Although this extension of the constitutional theory has occasionally found official expression between states and even received some support in one international judicial case,[8] a convincing amount of evidence denies the international relevance of both express and implicit substantive limitations. With regard first to the implicit limitations of substance, it may suffice to refer, in addition to the evidence discussed earlier in this section,[9] to the following statement made by the Permanent Court of International Justice in its Advisory Opinion concerning the *Treatment of Polish Nationals and other persons of Polish origin or speech in the Danzig territory:*

"... a State cannot adduce as against another State its own Constitution with a view to evading obligations incumbent upon it under international law or treaties in force."[1]

While the court probably did not have in mind constitutional provisions relating specifically to the treaty-making power—including express limitations of substance—the statement is no doubt relevant as regards implicit substantive limitations upon the treaty-making power. Their irrelevance is also assumed by a majority of writers.[2]

There is less evidence refuting the view taken by some authorities who, while they reject the relevance of implicit substantive limitations, hold that express limitations of substance are effective in the international sphere.[3] The international practice on this particular matter seems too limited, indeed, to permit any safe conclusion merely on the basis of that material. It must be noted, however, that the conclusion that implicit substantive limitations have no relevance in international

---

[7] See McNair, p. 4; *Harvard Research,* pp. 992 ff.

[8] See the incident of 1832 between the United States and France, above, p. 302; and see the *George Pinson case* of 1928, above, p. 367.

[9] See the position taken by the United States Government vis-à-vis France in 1832, above, p. 302; the attitude taken by the Council of the League of Nations in the case of the admission of Luxemburg, above, p. 328; but see Rives' report to President Cleveland, above, p. 358.

[1] *P.C.I.J.,* Series A/B, No. 44, p. 24.

[2] Dehousse, pp. 143–144; Jones, p. 151; Pallieri, pp. 479–480; Scelle, vol. 2, p. 440; de Visscher, p. 268.

[3] See, however, the position taken by the Colombian Supreme Court in 1930, above, p. 257; and see a statement by Secretary of State Stimson, quoted in Hackworth's *Digest,* vol. 5, p. 155.

law appears to call for a similar conclusion as regards express substantive limitations. Otherwise, states might stipulate expressly in the constitutional provisions governing the treaty-making function that treaties, the substance of which violate the constitution, are forbidden, and, thereby, presumably make all implicit substantive limitations relevant internationally. It may be recalled that the United States Senators who proposed a constitutional provision (embodied in the so-called Bricker amendment) which expressly declared those treaties void, the substance of which violated the Constitution, explained that the provision was not thought to have effect in the international sphere.[4] If that position is taken as expressive of the legal situation, it would be somewhat peculiar were such provisions as forbid quite generally the conclusion of, say, treaties encroaching upon the constitutional rights of citizens, to be attributed international relevance.[5]

If it is necessary, as indeed seems to be the case, to conclude that implicit as well as express substantive limitations upon the treaty-making power have no relevance in international law, it remains to point out that this conclusion, when combined with the view that treaties are not valid if concluded in disregard of procedural limitations or limitations of competence in the narrow sense, introduces important differences in the international sphere on the basis of what is a purely formal distinction between different kinds of unconstitutional acts.

It is rightly claimed that a state cannot by its constitution limit its own capacity to undertake international obligations.[6] A state which has constitutional provisions expressly or implicitly forbidding altogether the conclusion of treaties of certain contents may modify or abrogate these provisions, and so rid itself of the limitations. Municipally, treaties of the prohibited class may thus only be entered into after a revision of the constitution. However, the writers who assert the international irrelevance of substantive limitations are content to suggest that, if such

---

[4] Above, p. 242.

[5] P. B. Potter and Mervyn Jones maintain that any substance limitations are ineffective under international law because a state cannot by its own constitution limit its capacity under international law to conclude treaties. This argument does not, however, seem convincing. The substance limitations do not, in fact, limit the state's capacity in this regard. They rather have the effect that no authority is indicated as competent to assume treaty obligations of the prohibited class. The views of the two authorities are found in Potter, "Inhibitions upon the Treaty-Making Power of the United States" in *A.J.I.L.*, vol. 28 (1934), p. 470; and Jones, p. 152.

[6] See the authorities cited in the preceding note.

a treaty were concluded by the procedure normally followed in the state, it would *ipso facto* be binding. On the other hand, if the constitution, instead of forbidding altogether the treaties in question, provided that, for the conclusion of these treaties, the government must have exactly the same kind of legislative approval as would be required for the modification of the constitution, or that ratification of these treaties must be effected only by virtue of a law revising the constitution, these writers would recognize the requirement as internationally effective. The least that can be said is that this position seems highly formalistic.

A similar anomaly is produced by the distinction made by adherents of the constitutional theory between municipal provisions requiring legislative assent for the conclusion of certain treaties and provisions which, although not expressly requiring such assent, nevertheless have the effect of requiring such assent in order that performance may be secured. Only the first kind of assent, it is asserted, is of any concern to other parties. The position in international law is thus made dependent upon whether the framers of the constitution have written the limitation upon the competence of the government into a special clause governing the conclusion of treaties, or have been content to establish such a general division of powers that the same actual limitation results. This distinction, too, seems to be the result of formalistic thinking.

The two distinctions criticized above are the less easy to justify in view of the argument, which is not contested, and which is commonly advanced by writers who make the distinctions, that the most important practical consideration in favour of the international relevance of limitations upon competence is the greater measure of reliability that that theory offers. If that argument is accepted in one situation, it would seem illogical not to apply it to the other. Conversely, if it is not allowed to be guiding in one situation, it is hard to see why it should be considered relevant in the other.[7]

Only effective constitutional rules are internationally relevant

A few writers have specified that their adherence to the constitutional theory has regard only to the international relevance of the municipal regulation of the treaty-making power that is actually followed in a state. If the written constitutional provisions of a state are, in fact,

[7] A clarifying discussion of the matter is found in Hendry, *Treaties and Federal Constitutions* (1955), pp. 145 ff.

disregarded, and a different practice followed than that which is prescribed, these writers attribute international relevance to the latter. Thus, Professor Verdross states:

"Steht... die geschriebene Verfassung nicht nur in einzelnen Bestimmungen, sondern grundsätzlich in Widerspruch zur tatsächlichen Staatsordnung, dann ist völkerrechtlich nicht die geschriebene Verfassung, sondern ausschliesslich die sich tatsächlich durchsetzende neue Ordnung massgeblich. Es ist somit auch in unserer Frage nach der *wirksamen* Verfassung zu beurteilen, welches Organ tatsächlich zum Abschluss von Staatsverträgen in Betracht kommt."[8]

Professor Verdross rightly refers to the judgment of the Permanent Court of International Justice in the *Serbian Loans case,* where the court declared:

"It is French legislation, as applied in France, which really constitutes French law..."[9]

This theory would appear to add to the constitutional theory a feature which, while it certainly does not facilitate the application of that theory, nevertheless is needed if that theory is not to lead to absurd consequences.[1]

Rules of procedure are not internationally relevant

In order to limit somewhat the scope of the theory that municipal provisions relating to the conclusion of treaties are directly relevant internationally, the view is not infrequently advanced that such relevance is not attributed to rules of procedure.[2] While some of the evidence examined offers particular support for this view,[3] it would seem that a necessity to uphold the distinction between procedural limitations and limitations of competence in the narrow sense would, in practice, make the constitutional theory even more complicated to apply than without the same distinction.

[8] Verdross, *Völkerrecht* (2nd ed., 1950), pp. 124–125; see also Guggenheim, vol. I, p. 61; and Kelsen, p. 324, note 26; but see the opinion of Professor Sørensen, quoted above, p. 236.

[9] *P.C.I.J.,* Ser. A, Nos. 20/21, Judgment No. 14, at pp. 46–47; the same view is expressed in the *Brazilian Loans Case, P.C.I.J.,* Series A, Nos. 20/21, Judgment No. 15, p. 124.

[1] For an excellent analysis of the theory, see Pallieri, pp. 480–481.

[2] See Jones, p. 154; *Harvard Research,* p. 995.

[3] See the *Rio Martin case,* above, p. 367; the *Eastern Greenland case,* above, p. 368; Rives' report in the *Cleveland award,* above, p. 360.

Only notorious constitutional provisions are internationally relevant

According to a theory advanced by Lord McNair, only such constitutional provisions as "are matters of common knowledge" would be relevant internationally, and constitutional defects of which the other party is "ignorant and reasonably ignorant" would not invalidate a treaty.[4] The same idea has been developed by Judge Basdevant in lectures at the Hague Academy. While maintaining that, in principle, there is no need to take account of the constitutionality of a ratification performed by the head of a state, Judge Basdevant makes an exception for constitutional provisions which are "notorious", for the reason that, in his view, "chaque État doit tenir compte des limites clairement apportées à ce pouvoir". If a treaty has been ratified in "manifest" violation of the constitution of a state, the other contracting party is under a duty, according to Judge Basdevant, not to invoke the treaty.[5] The same, or very similar opinions, are voiced by several other authorities.[6] The theory described has not, on the other hand, failed to draw criticism from several sources.[7]

It may here suffice to say that, were the constitutional theory to be accepted, some limitation would be needed to protect against possible abuses, and to afford a minimum measure of confidence and certainty in treaty relations. The great merit of the theory of notoriety lies, it is submitted, in the circumstance that it seeks to exclude as a source of conflict an element that might otherwise be likely to cause conflict, namely, obscure municipal rules, or subtle interpretations of the municipal regulation of the treaty-making competence. Its weakness, looked at from a functional viewpoint, lies in the difficulty of distinguishing between notorious and other constitutional provisions. A more decisive argument against the theory is, however, the lack of evidence in the practice of states and cases of courts of the relevance of even "notorious" provisions.[8]

---

[4] McNair, p. 6.

[5] Basdevant, p. 581.

[6] See de Visscher, pp. 270–272; Fairman, p. 453; Devaux, "La conclusion des traités internationaux en forme s'écartant des règles constitutionnelles, et dite 'conclusion en forme simplifiée'" in *Revue Internationale Française du Droit des Gens*, vol. 1 (1936), pp. 306–308; Ross, p. 208; and von Szaszy, "Die parlamentarische Mitwirkung beim Abschluss völkerrechtlicher Verträge" in *Zeitschrift für öffentliches Recht*, vol. 14 (1934), pp. 464–465.

[7] See Fitzmaurice, p. 131; Siotto-Pintor, pp. 533 ff.; Jones, pp. 154–155.

[8] Pallieri, p. 482.

Application of the principle of good faith

Professor Balladore Pallieri has recently advanced a theory in which he seeks to avoid some of the inconveniences connected with the international relevance of constitutional provisions by superimposing upon the constitutional theory the principle of good faith.[9]

In the opinion of the learned Italian scholar, an organ which is incompetent under municipal law as well as under international law may nevertheless conclude a treaty that becomes valid and binding, provided that the other party was in good faith with regard to the competence of the organ. It is not a subjective good faith that Professor Pallieri has in mind, but "une bonne foi objective, dans les sens qu'elle doit être fondée sur des circonstances objectives."[1] He concludes that the question before a court would not be one of law, but one of fact, namely, to determine whether the circumstances surrounding the conclusion of the treaty had been such as to make the other party believe, in good faith, that the treaty was valid. Among the circumstances to be considered, *nota bene,* would then be the application and interpretation given in each state to its municipal norms.[2]

While perhaps no serious objections can be raised against this theory from a functional point of view, some of the arguments advanced by Professor Balladore Pallieri in support of the contention that international law refers the determination of the competence to conclude treaties to municipal law cannot—with all respect—be accepted.

Professor Pallieri submits that it is a general principle of law that "tout corps moral décide quels sont ses organes, quels sont ceux compétents à traiter avec les tiers, et quelle est la compétence de chacun."[3] It is not denied that such a principle might exist in municipal law, nor is it disputed that states and international organizations may determine, each for itself, the competence of their organs,[4] and establish sanctions to uphold that determination. Furthermore, it is obvious that the determination of competence under international law must be expected to be such that its result approaches the result that is obtained by a similar determination under municipal law. All this does not prove,

---

[9] Pallieri, p. 483; for a similar view, see Wohlmann, p. 82; and see Sundberg who suggests such a theory as a possibility; *Lag och Traktat* (2nd ed., 1942), p. 33.

[1] Pallieri, p. 484.

[2] *Ibid.,* pp. 485–486.

[3] *Ibid.,* p. 472.

[4] See above, p. 117, note 5.

however, that international law refers the determination of the conditions of competence to constitutional law. For that conclusion, it must further be convincingly shown that such a reference finds full support in the practice of states. This, it is submitted, has not been done, and cannot be done.

Professor Pallieri seeks further support for the view that a municipal determination of competence may be accorded international relevance in the alleged circumstance that the competence under international law of plenipotentiaries exactly equates with that enjoyed by them under municipal law; and that the instruments of full powers offer an example of a domestic determination of competence which is accepted as internationally relevant.

To this argument it must be objected that, although the issuing of instruments of full powers is admittedly a municipal act, the determination of competence made in these instruments is of a uniform type which has emerged from centuries of adaptation among states. Furthermore, though nowadays mostly perfunctory, the examination and the acceptance of full powers may still be regarded as an agreement between the parties to the effect that the competence granted the agents offers a mutually satisfactory basis for negotiation.[5] No corresponding agreements are known to be made by which states accept as relevant between themselves precisely the highly varied regulation of the competence to conclude treaties that are made in their respective municipal laws. It does not seem, therefore, that the analogy to competence possessed under full powers in any way helps to show that the municipal regulation of the treaty-making competence should be accepted as decisive for the competence under international law.

The time-lapse theory

What may be termed the "time-lapse theory" is based on the notion that violation of a constitutional provision for the conclusion of treaties does not invalidate a treaty provided that, for some period of time, the state concerned has neglected to repudiate the treaty, despite its awareness of the violation. This principle is thought to apply with even greater force, of course, with regard to a state that for some period of

---

[5] It may be recalled that, in the past, negotiations were sometimes refused with agents whose full powers were not thought satisfactory. See Jones, pp. 7 ff.; see also above, p. 271.

time has allowed itself to benefit from a treaty of this kind, or carried out obligations supposedly flowing from the treaty.[6]

If the theory is looked at from another angle, it may be said that the treaty is suggested to be voidable only for a limited period of time. This theory has strong support among writers,[7] and it seems to have found support in some of the material examined.[8] There seems to be little, indeed, that can be advanced against the grounds on which it limits the constitutional theory, or the manner in which it does it. What may be objected is that the limitation is probably too modest to satisfy the need for finality and certainty in international relations.

It is true that the limitation which this theory does provide makes impossible denunciations where they would be the most obnoxious, e.g., in the case of treaties relied upon for perhaps some years without any previous suggestion having been made as to invalidity due to ir-regularities in their conclusion.[9] With respect to many treaties, however, measures of execution must be taken, and are taken, immediately upon their conclusion. It may be feared that such measures might not be taken with confidence, were there a risk that the treaty might later be repudiated on the basis of some obscure point of constitutional law. It is not surprising, therefore, that states have not, in practice, allowed their adherence to the time-lapse theory to induce them to admit the relevance of constitutional limitations.

[6] The notion is sometimes termed the principle of "estoppel", or presented as a special case of acquiescence. See Jones, pp. 112 and 155; and see Lauterpacht's *First Report,* p. 164.

It seems less fortunate to use the term "tacit ratification" in this connexion, as some writers do. See Halleck, *International Law* (3rd ed., 1893), vol. I, p. 277; Hall, *International Law* (8th ed., 1924), p. 385; and Fairman, p. 449. In modern international law, the term "ratification" does not usually convey the idea of an adoption of an unauthorized act, but suggests merely consent or confirmation.

[7] The following authorities adhere to the theory in some way or other: Lauterpacht in his *First Report,* p. 160, and in Oppenheim, p. 889; Halleck, *loc. cit.*; Hall, *loc. cit.*; Fenwick, "The Progress of International Law During the Past Forty Years" in *Recueil des Cours,* 1951, vol. II, p. 49; Vitta, p. 222; Ross, p. 216; Fitzmaurice, p. 137, note 1; and Fairman, pp. 447–448. See also MacGibbon, "Estoppel in International Law" in *I.C.L.Q.,* vol. 7 (1958), pp. 468–513, at p. 471.

[8] See, for instance, the report by Rives to President Cleveland, above, p. 358; the *Rio Martin case,* above, p. 367. And see, as regards the attitude of the Government of the United Kingdom, McNair, *The Law of Treaties* (1937), p. 44.

[9] That repudiations on the ground of unconstitutionality have been attempted even in such situations has been seen in several cases, e.g. the case of a Claims Convention of 1841 between Peru and the United States, above, p. 121; and in the case of the Anglo-Uruguayan Postal Convention of 1853, above, p. 308.

The effect of duress upon competence

The view has been expressed by some authorities that constitutional restrictions upon the treaty-making power must be deemed internationally irrelevant as regards treaties concluded under duress.[1] There would seem to be good reasons for accepting this position, which has not infrequently been acted upon in the practice of states.[2]

Performance of obligations embodied in treaties which are entered into under duress is generally secured by the pressure that is exerted. Accordingly, in these situations, the consent extracted is reduced to a formality. This being so, it is not surprising that states making treaties of this kind are often satisfied with an expression of consent that is given without any regard to constitutional requirements, provided only that it comes from an authority that wields some effective power in the state.

---

[1] See the position taken by Westlake, cited above, p. 307, note 2; *cf.* Hyde, vol. II, p. 1399; Wright, *The Control of American Foreign Relations* (1922), p. 57; the contrary position is, however, assumed by Lauterpacht in Oppenheim, vol. 2, p. 608; to the same effect, Castrén, *The Present Law of War and Neutrality* (1954), p. 135.

[2] Reference may be made to the peace treaties entered into after the second world war. These were to become binding upon their ratification by the major Allied powers and regardless of whether they were ratified by the respective ex-enemy states. The procedure must presumably constitute evidence that the victor states did not consider the satisfaction of constitutional requirements in the defeated states a matter of much importance. See, further, the discussion in Fitzmaurice, "The Juridical Clauses of the Peace Treaties" in *Recueil des Cours*, 1948, vol. II, pp. 351 ff.

The Soviet–Finnish peace treaty of 12 May 1940 provided for ratification but stipulated expressly that it was to enter into force upon signature. Doubts as to the constitutionality of the method were expressed in the Finnish Diet. See Tanner, *The Winter War* (1957), pp. 254 ff.; *Cf.* Castrén, *The Present Law of War and Neutrality* (1954), p. 135.

It may be noted, however, that the validity of the Munich agreement of 29 September 1938 and of the treaty entered into under duress by Czechoslovakia with Germany on 15 March 1939 has been challenged on the ground, *inter alia*, of unconstitutionality. The question is discussed in Markus, "Le traité Germano–Tchécoslovaque de 15 mars 1939 à la lumière du droit international" in *R.G.D.I.P.*, vol. 46 (1939), pp. 653–665; Táborský, *The Czechoslovak Cause* (1944), pp. 9 ff.; review of the same by Pergler in *A.J.I.L.*, vol. 36 (1942), pp. 737–738; Táborský in *Cz. Y.*, pp. 26 ff.; Mattern, pp. 48–51; Polents, *Ratifikatsiia mezhdunarodnykh dogovorov* (1950), p. 46; Jones, "International Agreements other than 'Inter-State Treaties'—Modern Developments" in *B.Y.I.L.*, vol. 21 (1944), at p. 121; Marek, pp. 282–283; Kunz, "Identity of States under International Law" in *A.J.I.L.*, vol. 49 (1955), at p. 75; Korkisch, "Zur Frage der Weitergeltung des Münchner Abkommens" in *Zeitschrift für ausländisches öffentliches Recht und Völkerrecht*, Band 12 (1944), pp. 83–105.

The damages theory

Yet another theory is that, although a treaty concluded by an organ in excess of its municipal competence will be invalid under international law, a contracting party having not unreasonably relied upon the competence of the agent will be entitled to compensation for damages resulting from the injury suffered by the cancellation of the treaty. Such a theory has found prominent support in the *Harvard Draft on the Law of Treaties*,[3] and in the first report on the law of treaties submitted by Sir Hersch Lauterpacht to the International Law Commission.[4]

It might seem, at first, that an obligation to pay damages must logically be predicated upon a breach of an obligation, and that this obligation cannot be other than a valid treaty. The fact that the proponents of this theory do not admit that the treaty is valid would accordingly seem illogical.[5] It appears, however, that the damages are supposed to arise from the responsibility of the state for the acts of its organs and agents, and are intended to cover direct injuries only— the so-called "negative Vertragsinteresse"—caused by the unauthorized acts of the organs.[6] If the treaty were thought valid, on the other hand, the responsibility of the state would have been to effect specific performance, or, in the last resort, perhaps to pay damages covering not

[3] Article 21 of this Draft reads:

"A State is not bound by a treaty made on its behalf by an organ or authority not competent under its law to conclude the treaty; however, a State may be responsible for an injury resulting to another State from reasonable reliance by the latter upon a representation that such organ or authority was competent to conclude the treaty." *A.J.I.L.*, vol. 29 (1935), *Supp.*, p. 992.

[4] Sir Hersch had suggested the following clause:

"In cases in which a treaty is held to be invalid on account of disregard of the constitutional limitations imposed by the law or practice of a contracting party that party is responsible for any resulting damage to the other contracting party which cannot properly be held to have been affected with knowledge of the constitutional limitations in question." *First Report*, p. 157; *cf.* Oppenheim, vol. 1, p. 890.

The following statement by Verdross may also be quoted:

"Hat... ein Staat *bona fide* einen Vertrag abgeschlossen, ohne die Beschränkung der Zuständigkeit der 'treaty-making power' des Partners zu kennen, dann ist dieser Staat schadenersatzpflichtig, wenn er die Verbindlichkeit des Vertrages nicht nachträglich anerkennt." *Völkerrecht* (2nd ed., 1950), p. 128.

See also Hall, *International law* (8th ed., 1924), p. 381; Freymond, *La ratification des traités et le problème des rapports entre le droit international et le droit interne* (1947), p. 105; Chailley, p. 169, note.

[5] Sir Gerald Fitzmaurice makes this point. See his article "Do Treaties Need Ratification?" in *B.Y.I.L.*, vol. 15 (1934), at p. 135.

[6] See Wohlmann, p. 82; Fairman, p. 462.

only injuries sustained by the breach, but also the loss of advantages to which it was anticipated the treaty would give rise.

Though an ingenious construction, the damages theory has obvious weaknesses, of which the most serious is the lack of support in the practice of states. Not even its distinguished formulators have attempted to adduce any other basis for it than its reasonableness. It may be doubted, however, that the award of damages actually offers a sound solution to the problem of treaties made by constitutionally incompetent authorities. Obligations undertaken in the form of treaties are most frequently of such a kind that the evaluation in terms of money of injuries resulting from non-fulfilment must offer extreme, if not insuperable, difficulties.[7] It may well be argued, therefore, that reasonableness is on the side of a solution that favours the adjudgment of either specific performance or absence of obligation, and introduces damages only as a remedy of the last resort.[8]

3. THE HEAD-OF-STATE THEORY

If the theory urging the relevance of all constitutional provisions is at the one extreme, the other extreme is found in the view that the head of state possesses plenary treaty-making power under international law.

Not even under this theory, however, is the relevance of constitutional law altogether eliminated by all writers, but its relevance is considered limited to its determination of the organ competent to *declare* the consent of the state to a treaty.[9] This is the position taken by Bittner:

"Als Vertreter der Staaten, als Organe der Vertragschliessung, werden diejenigen physischen Personen angesehen, denen diese Befugnis von der inneren staatlichen Rechtsordnung zugewiesen sind.

"Die Entwicklung der inneren staatlichen Rechtsordnung aller Staaten, die in den bestehenden Verfassungen jeweils ihren vorläufigen Endpunkt gefunden hat, weist nun die völkerrechtliche Vertretungsbefugnis den Staatshäuptern zu."[1]

The municipal procedures the fulfilment of which may be required to permit the head of state to declare the consent of the state are

---

[7] *Cf.* Scelle, vol. 2, p. 455.

[8] For criticism of the "damages theory", see further Fitzmaurice, p. 135; and Fairman, p. 462.

[9] This distinction is frequently made. See, for instance, Basdevant, p. 579; and recently, Holloway, *Les réserves dans les traités internationaux* (1958), p. 38.

[1] Bittner, p. 16.

regarded by this school as of no concern in the international sphere. It is thought to be a duty of these organs under municipal law to abide by the limitations and procedures established, and any tendencies to disregard these procedures and limitations are thought to be left to be checked by the municipal sanctions which might be inflicted upon those guilty of encroachments.[2]

Some modern authorities have adhered to this theory,[3] the practical advantage of which obviously lies in the measure of legal finality and certainty it seeks to offer. It has also occasionally been relied upon in the practice of states.[4] The most serious objection to the view that heads of states possess a *jus repraesentationis omnimodae* seems to be, as already suggested,[5] the thin basis of political reality which to-day underlies it. While in the era of absolute monarchies in which the theory has its origin, it had a solid foundation of political reality in the broad powers possessed by monarchs, modern heads of states are frequently deprived of all political power. If international law were found to attribute unconditional competence to the heads of states to promise specific conduct by the states, it would ascribe to them an authority which had no basis in the internal power wielded by many of them.[6]

4. THEORIES ATTRIBUTING COMPETENCE TO AUTHORITIES ACTUALLY WIELDING POWER

At this point, it is convenient to consider certain opinions the underlying ideas of which seem to be similar. It may first be noted that, in considering a residuary rule of competence, where constitutional provi-

---

[2] The well-known statement by Anzilotti in his dissenting opinion in the *Eastern Greenland case* may be noted in this connexion:

"As regards the question whether Norwegian constitutional law authorized the Minister for Foreign Affairs to make the declaration, that is a point which, in my opinion, does not concern the Danish Government; it was M. Ihlen's duty to refrain from giving his reply until he had obtained any assent that might be requisite under the Norwegian laws." *P.C.I.J.*, Ser. A/B, No. 53, pp. 91–92.

See also the view expressed in Anzilotti, p. 366. In the opinion of Bittner (p. 100), a person encroaching upon the municipal law in this regard at the same time commits an infraction of international law. *Cf.* Scelle, vol. 2, p. 439.

[3] Anzilotti, p. 366; Bittner, p. 16; Willoughby, *The fundamental concepts of public law* (1924), p. 315; and see Rousseau, cited above, p. 215.

[4] See the position taken by Japan in the dispute with China described above, at p. 319; see, further, the judgment of the Chilean court, cited above, p. 254.

[5] Above, p. 102.

[6] Jones, p. 150; de Visscher, p. 253.

sions did not exist to give guidance, Professor Scelle is reported to have relied upon the notion that, whether in regard to a state or an international organization, "competence belonged to the organ which actually wielded sovereignty. In certain cases, it might be the Head of the State; in others the Parliament."[7] A similar view has been expressed by Professor Pallieri in a different context.[8]

In contrast to the authorities cited above, a few other modern writers have relied upon the notion of actual power to formulate rules regarding the competence to conclude treaties on behalf of a state possessing an effective constitutional regulation of its treaty-making power. The first is Dr. Vitta, an Italian publicist whose conclusions are as follows:

"En somme, on s'en tient toujours à l'état de fait; la compétence de stipuler appartient à celui qui possède le pouvoir suprême, ou à celui qui se présente en son nom avec son assentiment."[9]

The following view recently expressed by Professor Morelli in lectures before the Hague Academy is further in point:

"Les normes de l'ordre interne du sujet (par example, les normes réglant, dans l'ordre étatique, la compétence à conclure des traités internationaux) sont, en soi, sans importance. Il faut, par contre, avoir égard à l'organisation effective du sujet."[1]

Even more explicit is Professor Siotto-Pintor. He writes:

"Le droit international ne reconnaît pas les Chefs d'Etat comme les organes compétents pour manifester la volonté étatique en cette matière, parce que la qualité d'organes leur est attribuée par le droit interne, mais parce qu'ils détiennent et tant qu'ils détiennent effectivement le pouvoir. Du moment qu'ils sont dépouillés de cette possession ils ne sont plus, d'après le droit des gens, compétents pour manifester la volonté en question ... Le droit des gens attribue directement la compétence dont il s'agit au détenteur efficace du pouvoir, quel qu'il soit. Rien de plus naturel que cette attribution coïncide la plupart du temps avec celle que le droit interne sanctionne, mais il n'y a là qu'une simple circonstance de fait, dont la doctrine juridique n'a pas à tenir compte."[2]

---

[7] U.N. *Doc.* A/CN.4/SR.52 (22 June 1950), p. 24.

[8] Pallieri, p. 490.

[9] Vitta, p. 79.

[1] Morelli, "Cours général de droit international public" in *Recueil des Cours*, 1956, vol. I, p. 594; *cf. ibid.*, p. 550. A similar opinion is found in Gihl, *Huvuddragen av den allmänna folkrätten* (Stockholm, 1956), p. 200.

[2] Siotto-Pintor, p. 540.

Some writers have further pointed to the executive branch of government as invariably competent to assume treaty obligations on behalf of
the states they represent.[3]

It is believed that the rationale underlying the opinions cited is one
and the same, namely, that treaty-making competence must—as suggested in the conclusion of the first section of this part—be attributed
to the authorities which possess apparent ability to secure the performance of such obligations without, at the same time, making constitutional law directly relevant in the international sphere. The
evidence examined in this section of the present work does not appear
to contradict such a conclusion. The question whether there is sufficient justification for reaching it also in regard to states which possess
effective constitutional regulation of their treaty-making power will be
discussed in the following chapter.

---

[3] This is the stand taken by Fitzmaurice, p. 135. It must also be noted here that
both Bittner and Anzilotti use the term "head of state" in a broad sense, comprising
both the formal head of state, and the executive government, which, in many states,
acts in the name of the head of state. See Bittner, pp. 68–69 and Anzilotti, pp.
366–367.

Chapter XXIV

CONCLUSIONS

In spite of the effort made to find and to analyze as much evidence as possible that might throw light upon the rule of international law which prescribes the criteria of competence to conclude treaties on behalf of a state whose treaty-making power is effectively organized by municipal law, it would be an exaggeration to maintain that any unmistakable conclusion has emerged. Some evidence has been found that supports the constitutional theory, other evidence speaks in favour of the head-of-state theory, yet other evidence points clearly to the conclusion that neither of these theories are born out by the practice of states.

It is obvious that the rule regulating the question is not a settled one. One may regret that, in contrast to the numerous writers who have inquired into the problem, courts and other authorities which have discussed the matter disinterestedly have been remarkably reluctant to pronounce themselves positively in one direction or the other. This circumstance should perhaps caution the present writer not to add to the confusion already existing on the problem by venturing a pronouncement of his own. However, although the emphasis of this work has been deliberately placed upon a presentation and an analysis of state practice, cases and doctrine, it does not seem unjustified to suggest, against the background of the preceding examination of evidence and doctrine, that the criterion of apparent ability which was found to be apposite in certain situations discussed in the first section of this part is also apposite as regards constitutionally organized states.

The authorities whose consent to treaties are sought and accepted as sufficient to bind a state are, in practice, invariably those that appear actually able to secure performance of treaty obligations without, at the same time, necessarily being those that are constitutionally authorized to act as they do. Thus, reliance seems normally to be placed on pledges given on the authority of a cabinet, by a president, a prime minister, or a foreign minister, and the cases and incidents and other evidence examined lend support to the position that such reliance is warranted under international law, even where constitutional precepts and provisions have been violated.[1] It is not surprising that, on the other hand, no treaties have been found declared or admitted to be void on the ground that they were concluded by authorities not possessing apparent ability to secure fulfilment of treaty obligations, for governments not unreasonably refrain from concluding treaties with such authorities. Thus, treaties are not made with courts,[2] legislatures,[3] or the executive branch of constitutional governments which no longer wield effective authority,[4] or are no longer expected, for special reasons, to regain such authority.[5]

As was concluded in the cases examined in the first section of this part, no evidence can be found of any limitations upon, or conditions attaching to, the treaty-making power of the authorities to which such power is attributed. The bodies having apparent ability, in general, to secure the performance of treaty obligations are attributed plenary competence under international law to pledge the state. There is no need to weigh in each case whether the authority in question is able to ensure performance of the obligations embodied in that particular compact.[6]

[1] See the *Franco-Swiss Customs Convention case* of 1912, above, p. 361; the *Rio Martin case* of 1924, above, p. 366; the position taken by the authorities of the League of Nations regarding the adherence of Luxemburg and Argentina, above, pp. 328 and 338, and in the Politis incident, above, p. 332. See, further, the practice of the Secretariat of the United Nations when acting as a depositary, above, p. 266; the Swiss reply to the League questionnaire, above, p. 351; the memorandum submitted by Luxemburg to the United Nations, above, p. 238, and the memoranda formulated by the United States in 1909 and 1911, above, pp. 350 and 351.

[2] See the Chilean case cited above, p. 254.

[3] See above, p. 227.

[4] It has been concluded above that where chaos or anarchy prevails, no organ—whether or not possessing a constitutional title—is deemed competent to assume treaty obligations, see p. 111.

[5] See the case of the Polish Government in exile, above, p. 161.

[6] In this connexion, a motion tabled in the British House of Commons on 5 December 1957 by eighteen opposition M.P.s (members of the Labour Party) may be noted. The background of the motion was that the Heads of Government of N.A.T.O. Powers were about to meet at Paris, and it appeared possible that important agreements might be entered into at the conference. The motion read in part as follows:

"This House ... solemnly declares that it will not indorse, ratify, or implement any agreement which has, in theory or practice, the result of divesting the House of Commons of its control of foreign or defence policies or its democratic right and duty to determine for this country the ultimate issues of war and peace."

The Times, 6 December 1957. On 11 December 1957, the matter was discussed in

The following considerations also seem relevant in this connexion, and, it is submitted, further support the view that the criterion of competence suggested above is applicable to constitutionally organized states: with the possible exception of emergencies and other situations where prompt action may be indispensable to protect the interests of a state, the maintenance of a particular constitutional regulation is an obvious municipal interest. It is not, however, an obvious interest of the international community. It is true that the importance of the world-wide maintenance of certain basic standards relating to human rights, labour conditions, etc., has become, or is becoming, generally recognized among states, and leads indirectly to a concern for constitutional rules on these subjects. The international community has not yet, however, developed to the point where its members recognize a mutual interest in the upholding of constitutional rules generally, or of constitutional rules relating to democratic control in particular. Indeed, the very reverse seems true, for it appears that only very specific mutual needs translate themselves into international custom and conventions.

The need for transacting business between states is obvious, and so is the need to treat with only those who appear able to fulfil promises. On the other hand, provided that that need is satisfied, there would seem to remain no practical need that could compel governments to deal only with authorities who satisfy all constitutional rules. Of course, to the extent that constitutional provisions indicate the authorities apparently able to ensure the fulfilment of promises, the provisions obviously become of interest in the international sphere as evidence of the only quality to which they attach importance.[7] If this is so, it may

the House. Mr. James Griffiths (Labour M.P.) urged the Prime Minister, Mr. Harold Macmillan, not to enter into highly important commitments without the prior approval of Parliament. The latter replied in part as follows:

"The making of agreements, or modifications to existing agreements, is historically and constitutionally a duty laid on the Executive. The Government's authority depends upon their ability to command the confidence of Parliament." (*House of Commons Debates,* vol. 579, col. 1262.)

The motion was not adopted, since the Government had the confidence of the House. It may be concluded that the Government was internationally—as well as municipally—competent to commit the State on issues that might come up for settlement at the conference. Had the motion been passed, the Government would, in this case, have resigned. However, even in a state where the adoption of a resolution of this kind might not cause the government to resign, its international legal competence to commit the state would probably not be affected by it.

[7] Similarly, Morelli, "Cours général de droit international public" in *Recueil des Cours,* 1956, vol. I, p. 550.

be asked why such limitations upon the power of treaty-making organs as are indicated in constitutional provisions, do not, at the present time, seem to be considered important evidence of the actual power of these organs. These provisions, too, it might be argued, are of importance to judge the ability of an authority to secure performance of treaty obligations. Such, of course, is the view of those who support the constitutional theory: they refer to the greater likelihood that performance will, in fact, be ensured if all municipal provisions are observed.[8]

Though there are no means of verification, it does not seem far-fetched to assume that, were all constitutions to require parliamentary approval of all treaties, or even of some well-defined category of treaties, such requirement would soon be taken into consideration on the international level, and the need for its observation gradually find its way into customary international law. It is even conceivable that, were a particular constitution to require legislative approval of all treaties—in the generic sense of the term—such requirement might come to be taken into account by foreign governments as evidence of an internationally relevant limitation upon the competence of the foreign treaty-making organ.[9] While these considerations are no more than speculations, there would seem to be good reasons to assume that it is the extremely uncertain position in practically all states of constitutional limitations affecting the treaty-making power that has led governments to disregard the various limitations upon actual ability of treaty-making organs, evidence of which may be found in constitutional provisions.

A similar reason may be assumed to underlie the position that such limitations upon actual ability to ensure performance as may result from vicissitudes in the political life of a state are not taken into account in the consideration of the international competence of an authority which purports to assume treaty obligations on behalf of the state, provided only that these political events are not of such magnitude that they actually deprive the organ in question of all but its nominal authority.[1]

---

[8] See above, p. 371.

[9] See above, p. 231, and see the view held by the drafters of the Swedish constitutional provision regulating the treaty-making power, above, p. 285.

[1] In this connexion, it may be noted that, on one occasion, Sir John Kotelawala stated in the Parliament of Ceylon that the Australian Prime Minister had thought it inappropriate for the Government to conclude an agreement—in the relevant case,

Applied to constitutional governments, the theory of apparent ability, if it may so be termed, avoids a number of inconveniences connected with the constitutional theory. There is no need under the present theory for the somewhat unsatisfactory distinctions by which several authorities have endeavoured to make the constitutional theory more attractive: between express and implicit substantive limitations, limitations of competence and procedural limitations, and between provisions which are notorious and those which are not.

The present theory further makes redundant a distinction—necessary if the competence of revolutionary governments were determined by the criterion of apparent ability and that of constitutional governments by the constitutional theory—between revolutionary governments and governments acting unconstitutionally. Such a distinction might prove of considerable difficulty,[2] as revolutionary acts or a *coup d'état* are hard to define except as violations of the fundamental order of the state,[3] and as it may perhaps not be unreasonable to suggest that even such deviations from constitutional provisions as may be modestly termed "new interpretations" are, in theory, revolutionary acts.

Under the theory of apparent ability, there is no need for governments to undertake minute evaluations of foreign municipal law, or to direct embarrassing inquiries to foreign governments. In view of some of the evidence examined,[4] it would also seem to be of some importance that the theory submitted does not enable unscrupulous governments to use alleged violations of subtle points of constitutional law as a subterfuge for what are really unilateral denunciations of treaty obligations. Furthermore, international tribunals will never be called upon to found their decisions upon fine points of constitutional law, but rather be

one on air transport—with another country on the eve of general elections in Australia. See Ceylon, *Hansard,* vol. 7, col. 2082, 4 April 1950. There can be little doubt that the self-restraint exercised in this case was due to political rather than legal considerations. Had important interests of the State demanded immediate treaty action, the outgoing Government would presumably have been ready to conclude a treaty and have been accepted as competent counterparty.

[2] See, for instance, the case of the Russo-Chinese convention described above, p. 321. Mervyn Jones seeks to argue that a revolutionary government cannot be unconstitutional because "the constitution is destroyed by revolution, and is no longer operative." *Op. cit.,* p. 155. However, if the argument were accepted, it might equally be used to prove that no successful violation of a constitution is really a violation, since, on the relevant point, the constitution is no longer operative.

[3] On this point, see Siotto-Pintor, p. 536; Marek, p. 25.

[4] See above, p. 373, note 7.

asked to make an evaluation of facts, for which they would seem eminently competent.

While the theory advanced eliminates a number of shortcomings connected with the constitutional theory, it does not in any way deny the validity of what has above been termed the time-lapse theory, and been found to be supported by some evidence.[5] Nor is the application of the principle of good faith[6] in any way excluded, a circumstance that might perhaps be of importance, not primarily, as in Pallieri's theory, to protect the party which concludes a treaty with an authority not constitutionally authorized so to act, but rather to the states whose authorities act in an irresponsible manner, of which action advantage is taken by a foreign government.[7]

It may be asked, finally, if the power here attributed to authorities possessing apparent ability to secure performance of treaty obligations amounts to anything but an attribution of plenary treaty-making competence to the executive branch of government. In practice, and apart from the situation where that body is deprived of actual authority, the answer to this question may well be in the negative at the present time. It seems preferable, nevertheless, that the basic rule on the subject should be so formulated that it will be possible to pay due regard to what is the predominant practice of states at any given moment: in the era of absolute monarchs, the authority possessing apparent ability to secure the performance of treaty obligations was no doubt the monarch, and to-day the practice of states normally points to the executive government. Were the municipal regulation of the matter to emerge from its present state of flux, where a continuous transfer of treaty-making power to the executive branch of government takes place everywhere, e.g., by the device of agreements in simplified form, and were reasonably simple and settled limitations upon the actual and constitutional power of the executive governments to develop in all or some states, it would not seem to be in any way inherently impossible that such limitations might gradually be looked upon as affecting the apparent ability of an authority to secure the performance of treaty obligations, and their observance become required under international law. That stage, however, does not seem to have been reached yet.

[5] See above, p. 384.
[6] See above, p. 383.
[7] *Cf.* Schwarzenberger, *International Law*, vol. 1 (3rd ed., 1957), p. 429.

SELECTED BIBLIOGRAPHY

The present bibliography contains only such items as have been cited. Furthermore, although cited, works which are of chiefly political or historical interest have generally been omitted below.

I. DOCUMENTARY MATERIAL

Annual Digest and Reports of Public International Law Cases. Year 1919– (London).

ARNOLD, R., *Treaty-Making Procedure* (London, 1933).

Ceylon, *Parliamentary Debates.*

— *Treaty Series.*

DARESTE, F. R., DARESTE, P., DELPECH, J. and LAFERRIÈRE, J., *Les constitutions modernes* (4th ed., Paris, 1928–1934).

DEGRAS, J. (ed.), *Soviet Documents on Foreign Policy* (London, 1951–53).

Denmark, *Betænkning afgivet af forfatningskommissionen af 1946* (Copenhagen, 1953).

— *Bilag til beretning til Folketinget afgivet af den af Tinget under 8. Januar 1948 nedsatte Kommission i Henhold til Grundlovens § 45; Part V: Udenrigsministeriet under Besættelsen,* Aktstykker Stenografiske Referater (Copenhagen, 1948).

— *Forhandlinger i Folketinget.*

— *Lovtidende for Kongeriget Danmark.* Afdeling C: *Danmarks Traktater.*

DESCAMPS, E. and RENAULT, L., *Recueil international des traités du XXe siècle* (Paris, 1901–1906).

Documents on International Affairs, 1939–1946, vol. II (ed. by M. Carlyle and issued under the auspices of the Royal Institute of International Affairs, London, 1954).

Finland, *Valtiopäivät, Pöytäkirjat.*

Fontes Juris Gentium (ed. by V. Bruns, Berlin, 1931–).

France, *Journal Officiel de la France Combattante.*

— *Journal Officiel de la France Libre.*

Great Britain, *Accounts and Papers.*

— *British and Foreign State Papers.*

— *Command Papers.*

— *Parliamentary Debates.*

— *Treaty Series.*

HACKWORTH, G. H., *Digest of International Law* (vols. I–VIII, Washington, 1940–1944).

HERTSLET, L., HERTSLET, E. a.o., *A Complete Collection of Treaties . . . so far as they relate to Commerce . . .* (London, 1840–1913).

HUDSON, M. O., *Cases on International Law* (3rd ed., St Paul, Minn., 1951).
— *International Legislation* (Washington, 1932–1945).
Hungary, Foreign Office, *Recueil des Actes et Documents relatifs à l'affaire de l'expropriation par le Royaume de Roumanie des biens immobiliers des Optants Hongrois* (Budapest, 1924).
International Civil Aviation Organization, *Documents*.
International Law Reports. Year 1950– (London).
Israel, *Divrei Haknesseth*.
— *Laws of the State of Israel* (authorized translation from the Hebrew, published by the Israeli Government Printer).
Japan, *The Present Condition of China*. Document communicated to the Commission of Enquiry appointed by the Council of the League of Nations in pursuance of its resolution of December 10, 1931.
KOO, WELLINGTON, *Memoranda Presented to the Lytton Commission:* "Memorandum on the Twenty-One Demands and the Agreements of May 25th, 1915."
DE LAPRADELLE, A., *Recueil de la Jurisprudence des Tribunaux Arbitraux Mixtes créés par les Traités de Paix* (Paris, 1927).
DE LAPRADELLE, A. and POLITIS, N., *Recueil des Arbitrages Internationaux* (Paris, 1932).
League of Nations, *Documents*.
— *Official Journal*.
— *Report of the Committee for the Progressive Codification of International Law to the Council of the League of Nations* (League of Nations Doc. C. 357. M. 130. 1927, V).
League of Nations Treaty Series.
MANNING, W. R., *Diplomatic Correspondence of the United States,* Inter-American Affairs (Washington, 1932–1938).
DE MARTENS, G. F., *Nouveau Recueil Général de Traités* (ser. 1–3).
MILLER, D. H., *Treaties and other International Acts of the United States of America* (Washington, 1931).
MOORE, J. B., *A Digest of International Law* (vols. I–VIII, Washington, 1906).
— *History and Digest of the International Arbitrations to which the United States has been a Party* (vols. I–VI, Washington, 1898).
PEASLEE, A. J., *Constitutions of Nations* (vols. 1–3, London, 1950).
Permanent Court of International Justice, *Publications*.
Poland in the British Parliament, 1939–1945 (ed. by W. Jędrzejewicz, New York, 1946).
PRIBRAM, A. F., *Les traités politiques secrets de l'Autriche-Hongrie* (Paris, 1923).
PROCOPÉ, HJ. J., *Fällande dom som friar. Dokument ur Finlands krigsansvarighetsprocess* (Stockholm, 1946).
Rapports faits aux Conférences de La Haye de 1899 et 1907 (Publications de la Dotation Carnegie pour la Paix Internationale, Oxford, 1920).
Réclamations Britanniques dans la Zone Espagnol du Maroc, Rapports (The Hague, May 1925).
SCOTT, J. B., *The Hague Court Reports* (2nd series, New York, 1932).
SONTAG and BEDDIE (ed.), *Nazi-Soviet Relations 1939–1941* (United States Department of State Publication 3023).

Sweden, Kungl. Utrikesdepartementets kalender för 1946.
— "Förslag till Grundlagsändringar åsyftande ett närmare samarbete mellan regering och riksdag i utrikespolitiska angelägenheter, avgivet den 15 mars 1919 av därtill utsedda kommitterade" (Stockholm, 1919), published separately as well as in *Bihang till Riksdagens Protokoll*, 1919, 2 saml. 2 avd. 1 vol.
— Aktstycken utgivna av kungl. utrikesdepartementet, *Handlingar rörande Sveriges Politik under andra världskriget: Frågor i samband med Norska regeringens vistelse utanför Norge 1940–1943* (Stockholm, 1948).
— Statens Offentliga Utredningar Nr 1950: 9: *Utredning angående de handelspolitiska arbetsformerna m. m.* (Stockholm, 1950).
— *Sveriges Överenskommelser med Främmande Makter.*
United Nations, *Documents.*
— *Handbook of Final Clauses* (U.N. Doc. ST/LEG/6, 5 August 1957).
— International Law Commission, *Law of Treaties, Text of Articles Tentatively Adopted by the Commission at its Third Session* (U.N. Doc. A/CN. 4/L. 28, 19 July 1951).
— International Law Commission, *Reports on the Law of Treaties.* See Brierly, Fitzmaurice and Lauterpacht.
— International Law Commission, *Reports* and *Summary Records* of Meetings.
— International Law Commission, *Replies from Governments to Questionnaires of the International Law Commission* (U.N. Doc. A/CN. 4/19, 23 March 1950).
— *Laws and Practices concerning the Conclusion of Treaties* (United Nations Legislative Series, New York, 1953).
— *Reports of International Arbitral Awards* (1948–).
United Nations Treaty Series.
United States, *Conference on the Limitation of Armaments,* Washington, November 12, 1921 — February 6, 1922 (Government Printing Office, Washington, 1922).
— Department of State, *Department Circular* No. 175 (13 December, 1955).
— *Executive Agreement Series.*
— *Federal Reporter* (F.).
— *The Law of Treaties as Applied by the Government of The United States of America* (mimeographed material ed. by the Department of State, Washington, D.C., March 31, 1950).
Papers Relating to the Foreign Relations of the United States.
— *Proceedings of the International Civil Aviation Conference,* Chicago, Ill., November 1 — December 7, 1944 (Government Printing Office, Publ. 2820, 1948).
United States Reports (U.S.).
United States, *The Treaty-Making Power in Various Countries.* A collection of memoranda concerning the negotiation, conclusion, and ratification of treaties and conventions, with excerpts from the fundamental laws of various countries. (Government Printing Office, Washington, D.C., 1919.)
United States Treaties and Other International Agreements Series.
World Health Organization, *Handbook of basic documents* (6th ed., 1953).
— *Official Records.*

ZEYDEL, W. H. and CHAMBERLIN, W. (ed.), *Enabling Instruments of Members of the United Nations.* Part I: *The United States of America* (Carnegie Endowment for International Peace, New York, 1951).

II. BOOKS AND ARTICLES

A. *Works having special regard to the law of treaties*

BASDEVANT, J., "La conclusion et la rédaction des traités et des instruments diplomatiques autres que les traités" in *Recueil des Cours,* 1926, vol. V.

BITTNER, L., *Die Lehre von den völkerrechtlichen Vertragsurkunden* (Berlin–Leipzig, 1924).

BLIX, H., "The requirement of Ratification" in *B.Y.I.L.,* vol. 30 (1953).

BLOCH, J. D., "Der Abschluss von Staatsverträgen nach schwedischem Recht" in *Zeitschrift für ausländisches öffentliches Recht und Völkerrecht,* vol. 4 (1934).

BLONDEAU, A., "La subordination des constitutions aux normes internationales" in *Revue de droit international,* 1932.

BRANDON, M., "Analysis of the Terms 'Treaty' and 'International Agreement' for Purposes of Registration under Article 102 of the United Nations Charter" in *A.J.I.L.,* vol. 47 (1953).

BRIERLY, J. L., *Third Report on the Law of Treaties.* Submitted to the International Law Commission (U.N. *Doc.* A/CN.4/54, 10 April 1952).

BRIGGS, H., "The Validity of the Greenland Agreement" in *A.J.I.L.,* vol. 35 (1941).

BRUSEWITZ, A., *Nordiska utrikesnämnder i komparativ belysning* (Uppsala, 1933).

— "Riksdagen och Utrikespolitiken" in *Sveriges Riksdag,* vol. XV (Stockholm, 1938).

CAMARA, J. S., *The Ratification of International Treaties* (Toronto, 1949).

CHAILLEY, P., *La nature juridique des traités internationaux selon le droit contemporain* (Paris, 1932).

CHAYET, C., "Les accords en forme simplifiée" in *Annuaire Français de Droit International,* vol. III (1957).

COTTEZ, A., *De l'intervention du pouvoir exécutif et du parlement dans la conclusion et la ratification des traités* (Paris, 1920).

CRANDALL, S. B., *Treaties, Their Making and Enforcement* (2nd ed., Washington, 1916).

DEHAUSSY, J., "Le dépositaire de traités" in *R.G.D.I.P.,* vol. 56 (1952).

DEHOUSSE, F., *La ratification des traités* (Paris, 1935).

DEVAUX, J., "La conclusion des traités internationaux en forme s'écartant des règles constitutionelles et dite 'conclusion en forme simplifiée'" in *Revue Internationale Française du Droit des Gens,* vol. 1, part 1 (1936).

EEK, H., "Makten över utrikes ärendena" in *Statsvetenskaplig Tidskrift,* vol. 57 (1954).

FAIRMAN, C., "Competence to Bind the State to an International Engagement" in *A.J.I.L.,* vol. 30 (1936).

FITZMAURICE, G. G., "Do Treaties Need Ratification?" in *B.Y.I.L.*, vol. 15 (1934).
— "The Juridical Clauses of the Peace Treaties" in *Recueil des Cours*, 1948, vol. II.
— *Report on the Law of Treaties.* Submitted to the International Law Commission (U.N. Doc. A/CN. 4/101, 14 March 1956).
FREYMOND, P., *La ratification des traités et le problème des rapports entre le droit international et le droit interne* (Paris–Lausanne, 1947).
GENET, R., "La clause tacite de ratification" in *R.G.D.I.P.*, vol. 38 (1931).
GEORGOPOULOS, C., *La ratification des traités et la colloboration du Parlement* (Paris, 1939).
GIBSON, W. M., "International Law and Colombian Constitutionalism" in *A.J.I.L.*, vol. 36 (1942).
GREWE, W. G., "Der Grönland-'Vertrag' von Washington" in *Monatshefte für auswärtige Politik*, vol. 8 (1941).
HAMBRO, E., "Gjensyn med Ihlen Erklæringen" in *Nordisk Tidskrift for International Ret*, vol. 26 (1956).
— "The Ihlen Declaration revisited" in *Fundamental Problems of International Law*. Festschrift für Jean Spiropoulos (ed. by Constantopoulos, Eustathiades and Fragistas, Bonn, 1957).
HARLEY, J. E., "The Obligation to Ratify Treaties" in *A.J.I.L.*, vol. 13 (1919).
Harvard Law School, Research in International Law, *Draft Convention on the Law of Treaties*, published in *A.J.I.L.*, vol. 29 (1935), Supp.
HENDRY, J. M., *Treaties and Federal Constitutions* (Washington, 1955).
HOLLIS, W., *The International Effect of "Unconstitutional Treaties"* (in microfilm, Special Report, Columbia University, School of Law, 1936).
HOLLOWAY, K., *Les réserves dans les traités internationaux* (Paris, 1958).
HSÜ, SHUHSI, "The Treaties and Notes of 1915" in *Chinese Social and Political Science Review*, vol. 16 (1932–1933).
HUDSON, M. O., "The Argentine Republic and the League of Nations" in *A.J.I.L.*, vol. 28 (1934).
JENNINGS, W. I., "Le traité anglo-irlandais de 1921 et son interprétation" in *Revue de Droit International et de Législation Comparée*, vol. 13 (1932).
JONES, J. M., *Full Powers and Ratification* (Cambridge, 1946).
— "International Agreements other than 'Inter-State Treaties'—Modern Developments" in *B.Y.I.L.*, vol. 21 (1944).
KAIRA, K., *Valtiosopimusten tekemisestä ja voimaansaattamisesta Suomen oikeuden mukaan* (Helsinki, 1932). German title: "Über das Eingehen und Inkraftbringen von Staatsverträgen nach finnischem Recht".
KORKISCH, F., "Zur Frage der Weitergeltung des Münchner Abkommens" in *Zeitschrift für ausländisches öffentliches Recht und Völkerrecht*, Band 12 (1944).
LAUTERPACHT, H., *Report on the Law of Treaties.* Submitted to the International Law Commission (U.N. Doc. A/CN. 4/63, 24 March 1953).
— *Second Report on the Law of Treaties.* Submitted to the International Law Commission (A/CN. 4/87, 8 July 1954).
LERICHE, A., "L'évolution récente de la société internationale et les traités

multilatéraux" in *Revue de droit international, de sciences diplomatiques et politiques,* vol. 29 (1951).

— "Quelques réflexions sur l'adoption et la conclusion des accords multilatéraux déposés auprès du Secrétaire général de l'Organisation des Nations Unies" in *Revue de Droit Internationale pour le Moyen Orient,* vol. 3 (1954).

LIANG, Y. L., "The Use of the Term 'Acceptance' in United Nations Treaty Practice" in *A.J.I.L.,* vol. 44 (1950).

LIE, M. H., *Legitimation ved Traktat* (Kristiania, 1912).

LIU, PINGHOU C., *Chinese Foreign Affairs—Organization and Control* (typewritten dissertation at New York University, 1936).

MARKUS, J., "Le traité Germano-Tchécoslovaque de 15 mars 1939 à la lumière du droit international" in *R.G.D.I.P.,* vol. 13 (1939).

MCDOUGAL, M. and LANS, A., "Treaties and Congressional-Executive or Presidential Agreements: Interchangeable Instruments of National Policy" in *Yale Law Journal,* vol. 54 (1945).

MCNAIR, A. D., "Constitutional Limitations upon the Treaty-Making Power" in Arnold R., *Treaty-Making Procedure* (London, 1933).

— *The Law of Treaties.* British Practice and Opinions (Oxford, 1938).

MEISSNER, H. O., *Vollmacht und Ratifikation bei völkerrechtlichen Verträgen nach deutschem Recht* (Göttingen, 1934).

DE NAUROIS, L., *Les traités internationaux devant les juridictions nationales* (Paris, 1934).

OLIVER, C. T., "Historical Development of International Law, Contemporary Problems of Treaty Law" in *Recueil des Cours,* 1955, vol. II.

OLSSON, H. A., *Utrikesnämnden 1937–1953. En studie i rätt och praxis* (Lund, 1957).

PALLIERI, B. G., "La formation des traités dans la pratique internationale contemporaine" in *Recueil des Cours,* 1949, vol. I.

PARRY, C., "Some Recent Developments in the Making of Multi-Partite Treaties" in The Grotius Society, *Transactions for the Year 1950* (vol. 36).

POLENTS, O. E., *Ratifikatsiia mezhdunarodnykh dogovorov* (Moscow, 1950).

POTTER, P. B., "Inhibitions upon the Treaty-Making Power of the United States" in *A.J.I.L.,* vol. 28 (1934).

PREUSS, L., "The Relation of International Law to Internal Law in the French Constitutional System" in *A.J.I.L.,* vol. 44 (1950).

"The Ratification of Treaties" in *The Law Times,* 24 April, 1953.

READ, J. E., "International Agreements" in *Canadian Bar Review,* vol. 26 (1948).

ROUSSEAU, C., "Le régime actuel de conclusion des traités en France" in *La Technique et les Principes du Droit Public,* études en l'honneur de Georges Scelle (Paris, 1950), vol. II.

SABA, H., "Certains aspects de l'évolution dans la technique des traités et conventions internationales" in *R.G.D.I.P.,* vol. 54 (1950).

SCHÖN, W., "Die völkerrechtliche Bedeutung staatsrechtlicher Beschränkungen der Vertreterbefugnis der Staatsoberhäupter beim Abschlusse von Staatsverträgen" in *Zeitschrift für Völkerrecht und Bundesstaatsrecht,* vol. 5 (1911).

SCHÜCKING, M. W., Report on "La portée des règles de droit constitutionnel pour la conclusion et la ratification des traités internationaux" in *Annuaire de l'Institut International de Droit Public,* 1930.

SEIDL-HOHENVELDERN, I., "Relation of International Law to Internal Law in Austria" in *A.J.I.L.,* vol. 49 (1935).

SIOTTO-PINTOR, M., "Traités internationaux et droit interne" in *R.G.D.I.P.,* vol. 42 (1955).

SKUBISZEWSKI, K., "Poland's Constitution and the Conclusion of Treaties" in *Jahrbuch für internationales Recht,* 7 Band (1958).

SØRENSEN, M., "Responsum vedrørende de problemer, der knytter sig til grundlovens § 18" in *Betænkning afgivet af Forfatningskommissionen af 1946* (Copenhagen, 1953).

STEWART, R. B., *Treaty Relations of the British Commonwealth of Nations* (New York, 1939).

SUNDBERG, H. G. F., *Lag och Traktat* (2nd ed., Stockholm, 1942).

VON SZASZY, S., "Die parlamentarische Mitwirkung beim Abschluss völkerrechtlicher Verträge" in *Zeitschrift für öffentliches Recht,* vol. 14 (1934).

TRISKA, J. F. and SLUSSER, R. M., "Ratification of Treaties in Soviet Theory, Practice and Policy" in *B.Y.I.L.,* vol. 34 (1958).

VEICOPOULOS, N., "Accords internationaux conclus en forme simplifiée et gentlemen's agreements" in *Revue de droit international, de sciences diplomatiques et politiques,* vol. 27 (1949).

VEXLER, P., *De l'obligation de ratifier les traités régulièrement conclus* (Paris, 1921).

DE VISSCHER, P., *De la conclusion des traités internationaux* (Brussels, 1943).

— "Les tendances internationales des constitutions modernes" in *Recueil des Cours,* 1952, vol. I.

VITTA, E., *La validité des traités internationaux* (Bibliotheca Visseriana, vol. 14, Leyden, 1940).

WEHRER, A., "Le statut international du Luxembourg et la Société des Nations" in *R.G.D.I.P.,* vol. 31 (1924).

WILCOX, F. O., *The Ratification of International Conventions* (London, 1935).

WOHLMANN, L., *Die Kompetenz zum Abschlusse von Staatsverträgen nach Völkerrecht* (Zürich, 1931).

WRIGHT, Q., *The Control of American Foreign Relations* (New York, 1922).

B. *Works not having special regard to the law of treaties*

ANZILOTTI, D., *Cours de droit international* (French transl. by G. Gidel, Paris, 1929).

BATY, T., "Can an Anarchy be a State?" in *A.J.I.L.,* vol. 28 (1934).

BENEŠ, E., *Memoirs of Dr Eduard Beneš* (London, 1954).

BENES, V., Review of Táborský, The Czechoslovak Cause and International Law in *Czechoslovak Yearbook of International Law* (London, 1942).

BRIGGS, H. W., *The Law of Nations* (2nd ed., London, 1953).

BYNKERSHOEK, C. VAN, *Quaestionum Juris Publici* (The Classics of International Law, Oxford, 1930).

CASTBERG, F., *Studier i Folkerett* (Oslo, 1952).

CASTRÉN, E., *The Present Law of War and Neutrality* (Helsinki, 1954).

CAVAGLIERI, A., "Règles générales du droit de la paix" in *Recueil des Cours,* 1929, vol. I.

CHEN, TI-CHIANG, *The International Law of Recognition* (London, 1951).

CHENG, B., *General Principles of Law* (London, 1953).

CHIANG, HAI-CHAO, *Die Wandlungen im Chinesischen Verfassungsrecht seit dem Zusammenbruch der Mandschu-Dynastie* (Berlin, 1937).

CHURCHILL, W., *The Second World War* (Boston, 1948–1953).

COHN, M. G., "La théorie de la responsabilité internationale" in *Recueil des Cours,* 1939, vol. II.

DÉAK, F., *The Hungarian-Rumanian Land Dispute* (New York, 1928).

DRUCKER, A., "The Legislation of the Allied Powers in the United Kingdom" in *Czechoslovak Yearbook of International Law* (London, 1942).

DUNN, F. S., *The Practice and Procedure of International Conferences* (Baltimore, 1929).

DUPUIS, C., "Liberté des voies de communication relations internationales" in *Recueil des Cours,* 1924, vol. I.

FAUCHILLE, P., *Droit International Public* (Paris, 1921–1926).

FENWICK, C. G., "The Progress of International Law in the Past Forty Years" in *Recueil des Cours,* 1951, vol. II.

FLORY, M., *Le statut international des gouvernements réfugiés et le cas de la France Libre* (Paris, 1952).

FRANÇOIS, J. P. A., "Règles générales du droit de la paix" in *Recueil des Cours,* 1938, vol. IV.

DE GAULLE, C., *Mémoires de Guerre* (Paris, 1954–1956).

GEMMA, S., "Les gouvernements de fait" in *Recueil des Cours,* 1924, vol. III.

GENET, R., *Traité de Diplomatie et de Droit Diplomatique* (Paris, 1931–1932).

GIHL, T., *Huvuddragen av den allmänna folkrätten* (Stockholm, 1956).

GOODMAN, N. M., *International Health Organizations and their Work* (London, 1952).

GOODRICH, L. and HAMBRO, E., *The Charter of the United Nations* (2nd ed., Boston, 1949).

GROTIUS, H., *De Jure Belli ac Pacis* (The Classics of International Law, Oxford, 1925).

GUGGENHEIM, P., *Lehrbuch des Völkerrechts* (Basel, 1948–1951).

HALL, W. E., *A Treatiese on International Law* (8th ed. by A. P. Higgins, Oxford, 1924).

HALLECK, H. W., *International Law* (3rd ed., London, 1893).

Harvard Law School, Research in International Law, *Draft Convention on the Law of Responsibility of States for Damage Done in Their Territory to the Person or Property of Foreigners,* published in *A.J.I.L.,* vol. 23 (1929), Supp.

HYDE, C. C., *International Law Chiefly as Interpreted and Applied by the United States* (2nd rev. ed., Boston, 1945).

JENNINGS, W. I., *The Constitution of Ceylon* (3rd ed., Oxford, 1953).

JUMEAU, A., *Le Refuge du Gouvernement National à l'Étranger* (Aix-en-Provence, 1941).

KELSEN, H., *Principles of International Law* (New York, 1952).

— *General Theory of Law and State* (Cambridge, Mass., 1949).

— *The Law of the United Nations* (London, 1950).

KOPELMANAS, L., *L'Organisation des Nations Unies* (Paris, 1947).

KUČERA, B., "La continuité de l'Etat Tchécoslovaque" in *Bulletin de Droit Tchécoslovaque*, Année V (1947).

KUNZ, J. L., "Identity of States under International Law" in *A.J.I.L.*, vol. 49 (1955).

LACHS, R., "Allied Governments in Exile" in *The Law Journal*, vol. 92 (1942).

LARNAUDE, F., "Les gouvernements de fait" in *R.G.D.I.P.*, vol. 28 (1921).

LAUTERPACHT, E., "The Contemporary Practice of the United Kingdom in the Field of International Law—Survey and Comment, IV" in *I.C.L.Q.*, vol. 6 (1957).

— "The Contemporary Practice of the United Kingdom in the Field of International Law—Survey and Comment, VI" in *I.C.L.Q.*, vol. 7 (1958).

— "The Contemporary Practice of the United Kingdom in the Field of International Law—Survey and Comment, VII" in *I.C.L.Q.*, vol. 8 (1959).

LAUTERPACHT, H., *Recognition in International Law* (Cambridge, 1947).

MacGIBBON, I. C., "Estoppel in International Law" in *I.C.L.Q.*, vol. 7 (1958).

MANNERHEIM, G., *Minnen*, part II: 1931–1946 (Helsinki, 1952).

MAREK, K., *Identity and Continuity of States in Public International Law* (Geneva, 1954).

DE MARTENS, F., *Traité de Droit International* (Paris, 1883–1887).

MASTERS, R. D., *International Law in National Courts* (New York, 1932).

— *International Organization in the Field of Public Health* (advance offprint of a chapter on Public Health in the forthcoming Manual of International Organization, Carnegie Endowment, Washington, 1947).

MATTERN, K.-H., *Die Exilregierung* (Tübingen, 1953).

McNAIR, A. D., *Legal Effects of War* (3rd ed., Cambridge, 1948).

MIRKINE-GUETZÉVITCH, B., *Droit constitutionnel international* (Paris, 1933).

MORELLI, G., "Cours général de droit international public" in *Recueil des Cours*, 1956, vol. I.

NUSSBAUM, A., *A Concise History of the Law of Nations* (2nd rev. ed., New York, 1954).

OPPENHEIM, L., *International Law*, vol. 1 (8th ed. by H. Lauterpacht, London, 1955).

— *International Law*, vol. 2 (7th ed. by H. Lauterpacht, London, 1952).

OPPENHEIMER, F. E., "Governments and Authorities in Exile" in *A.J.I.L.*, vol. 36 (1942).

PETRASCO, N. N., *La réforme agraire roumaine et les réclamations hongroises* (Paris, 1931).

PINTO, R., "The International Status of the German Democratic Republic" in *Journal du Droit International*, 86th year (1959).

PUFENDORFF, S., *De Jure Naturae et Gentium* (The Classics of International Law, Oxford, 1934).

QUIGLEY, H. S., "Legal Phases of the Shantung Question" in *Minnesota Law Review*, vol. 6 (1922).

RACKMAN, E., *Israel's Emerging Constitution* (New York, 1955).

RAESTAD, A., "La cessation des états d'après le droit des gens" in *Revue de droit international et de législation comparée*, 3rd ser. vol. 20 (1939).

Ross, A., *A Text-Book of International Law* (London, 1947).

Rousseau, C., *Principes Généraux du Droit International Public* (Paris, 1944).

La Ruche, F., *La neutralité de la Suède* (Paris, 1953).

Sander, F., "Das Faktum der Revolution und die Kontinuität der Rechtsordnung" in *Zeitschrift für öffentliches Recht,* vol. 1 (1919).

Satow, E., *A Guide to Diplomatic Practice* (2nd ed., London, 1922; 3rd ed., London, 1932; 4th ed. by N. Bland, London, 1957).

Scelle, G., *Précis de droit des gens* (Paris, 1932–1934).

Schachter, O., "The Development of International Law through the Legal Opinions of the United Nations Secretariat" in *B.Y.I.L.,* vol. 25 (1948).

Schücking, M. W. and Wehberg, H., *Die Satzung des Völkerbundes* (3rd ed., Berlin, 1931).

Schwarzenberger, G., *International Law* (3rd ed., London, 1957).

— *A Manual of International Law* (3rd ed., London, 1952).

Schwelb, E., "Legislation in Exile: Czechoslovakia" in *Journal of Comparative Legislation and International Law,* vol. 24, part II (1942).

Sibert, M., *Traité de droit international public* (Paris, 1951).

Smith, H. A., *Great Britain and the Law of Nations* (London, 1935).

Spiropoulos, J., *Die de facto-Regierung im Völkerrecht* (Beiträge zur Reform und Kodifikation des Völkerrechts, 2 Heft, Kiel, 1926).

Stone, J., *Legal Controls of International Conflict* (New York, 1954).

Táborský, E., *The Czechoslovak Cause* (London, 1944).

— "The Constitutionality of Official Acts of Allied Governments and International Law" in *Czechoslovak Yearbook of International Law* (London, 1942).

— *Czechoslovak Democracy at Work* (London, 1945).

Tanner, V., *Vägen till fred, 1943–1944* (Helsinki, 1952).

Taracouzio, T. A., *The Soviet Union and International Law* (New York, 1935).

Truman, H. S., *Memoirs by Harry S. Truman* (Garden City, N.Y., 1955–1956).

Tullié, A., *La Mandchourie et le conflit sino-japonais devant la Société des Nations* (Paris, 1935).

Vattel, E. de, *The Law of Nations* (The Classics of International Law, Oxford, 1916).

Verdross, A., *Völkerrecht* (2nd ed., Vienna, 1950).

De Visscher, C., *Théories et Réalités en Droit International Public* (2nd French ed., Paris, 1955).

Weigh, Ken Shen, *Russo-Chinese Diplomacy* (Shanghai, 1928).

Willoughby, W. W., *Constitutional Government in China* (Washington, 1922).

— *The Fundamental Concepts of Public Law* (New York, 1924).

— *The Sino-Japanese Controversy and the League of Nations* (Baltimore, 1935).

Wolff, E., "The International Position of Dispossessed Governments at present in England" in *Modern Law Review,* vol. 6 (1942–1943).

Wright, Q., "The Chinese Recognition Problem" in *A.J.I.L.,* vol. 49 (1955).

Wu, A. K., *China and the Soviet Union* (New York, 1950).

Young, C. W., *The International Legal Status of the Kwantung Leased Territory* (Baltimore, 1931).

INDEX